The Poetics of
JACOBEAN DRAMA

THE
POETICS OF
JACOBEAN
DRAMA

Coburn Freer

THE JOHNS HOPKINS UNIVERSITY PRESS
BALTIMORE AND LONDON

The Johns Hopkins University Press, Baltimore, Maryland 21218
The Johns Hopkins Press Ltd., London

Library of Congress Cataloging in Publication Data

Freer, Coburn.
   The poetics of Jacobean drama.

   Includes bibliographical references and index.
   1. English drama—17th century—History and
criticism.   2. Verse drama, English—History and
criticism.   I. Title.   II. Title: Jacobean drama.
PR658.V4F7   822'.3'09   81-47599
ISBN 0-8018-2545-8   AACR2

To Arnold Stein

CONTENTS

ACKNOWLEDGMENTS

An author's friends include those who supply assistance and those who enforce restraint. Decorum prevents any detailed elaboration of the latter process, but I would like here to thank all those who tried to cool the manuscript's raging motions and keep it from preposterous conclusions. In acknowledging direct assistance it is a pleasure to be more specific. Frank Warnke provided initial encouragement, as did Robert Heilman, who also made innumerable detailed suggestions: may every writer be blessed with such a reader. Walter King and Robert Johnstone shared their reading and asked the hard questions; the readers and editors of the Johns Hopkins University Press provided criticism that was both generous and close. My wife Mona was unfailingly helpful, assisting most at those times when the whole enterprise looked as if it would be news from an ever writer to a never reader.

I am especially grateful to the National Endowment for the Humanities, for a fellowship that allowed me a year's time in London to study and write.

INTRODUCTION

In his memoir of "Savonarola" Brown, Max Beerbohm offered the wise observation that it would be well for the writer of poetic drama to be a dramatist as well as a poet. While it may seem obvious to say that the poetic dramatist has two jobs, the point of Beerbohm's parody rests upon his knowledge—and our agreement—that the success of the final product is not to be measured by two different standards: some kind of artistic unity should issue from the dramatist's collaboration with himself. The two jobs may be one in that certain modes of characterization, for example, or forms of dramatic structure, may lend themselves more naturally to development in poetry than prose. Although the age in which the dramatist lives may supply him with poetic forms for the speeches he wants to write, the pressure of the dramatic experience within his characters will at once define and free those forms. It is also one aspect of Brown's dubious saga that those forms may have originated in conventions that, though once accepted by an entire culture, may not be fully comprehended in the present.

To understand better the growth of this relation between poetry and dramatic experience, the present study describes a tradition in English dramatic literature and shows its presence in five plays. Chapter 1 discusses problems in modern criticism of dramatic poetry, and suggests that a rethinking of several recent theories may be in order. The present thesis is that we have descended from a highway that was well marked in the past, and accordingly chapter 2 is a detailed study of English attitudes toward the poetry of drama from about 1580 to the Restoration. Here the main concern is the way that writers regarded the poetry of their plays, the way that actors performed it, and the way that audiences and critics heard it; this chapter concludes by proposing some of the reasons why poetic drama changed so radically after 1660. The rest of the book consists of separate studies of *The Revenger's Tragedy, Cymbeline, The White Devil* and *The Duchess of Malfi,* and *The Broken Heart.* The

Epilogue turns the focus back out again, by remarking the similarities and differences between the ways the four dramatists employ their verse, and by offering some speculative remarks on the achievement of poetic drama in the period as a whole. For convenience the title of the book uses the term *Jacobean,* although the context of the study takes in a considerably wider period of time.

The reader interested in this book for its comments on particular plays will want to know that those chapters do not treat simply the poetic techniques of the plays; in each case the argument is that our understanding of the play will be enlarged by listening to the poetry, hearing the way it first emphasizes certain actions, scenes, or themes, and finally takes on the force of metaphor itself. At the same time these particular plays are also of interest because of the functional differences between them as poetic structures; that is, the essays on the plays are offered, not as an historical account of the development of verse in drama, but rather as studies in types of sensibility and form. Thus each is planned as a specimen reading, or more literally an *essai.* Each essay deals with a play that is a masterpiece in itself, but each also should serve as a model for reading other plays that employ poetry to similar ends. *The Revenger's Tragedy* has puzzles in the text that are connected with the play's extraordinary verse, and the essay illustrates some of the ways one might study other verse plays with problematic texts, such as *Doctor Faustus,* for example, or *Hamlet.* Naturally, essays on these two plays would come to their own conclusions, because the verse in each case bears a unique relation to the other elements of dramatic meaning. But as in *The Revenger's Tragedy,* the textual problems of these plays should not so much inhibit study of their poetry as provide occasions for comparison and closer analysis. In this respect *The Revenger's Tragedy* is an especially important play—and it is important that it should come first in the study—because it consistently challenges the notion that dramatic blank verse was tied to a line of ten syllables and five beats. The easy movement toward and away from prose confers a special immediacy upon the verse, which demonstrates how the central character's irregular concentration is won only by great effort.

Cymbeline has a music that readers have praised for generations but have not related to the plan of the play or to the growth of its central characters. The play also provides an example of the stylistic données that ruled the later Jacobean and Caroline stage, principally under the aegis of John Fletcher. While *Cymbeline* is apparently one of Shakespeare's first efforts at tragicomedy, it outdoes anything Fletcher and his followers produced in that it employs every form of rhetorical pattern and posture, incorporates widely varying poetic styles, explores the technique of shifting one voice among several characters, and does all this with a high degree of self-consciousness, resisting none of the pathos (and bathos) that can result from these kaleidoscopic juxtapositions. *Cymbeline* subsists heavily on talk: most of the significant action occurs in the dialogue itself and in its tensions between contrasting rhetorical and poetic styles, and the play provides a catalog of the prismatic and stylized poetic structures that came to dominate the later Stuart stage. In this respect the play illustrates a not uncommon phenomenon, that of the genius who anticipates near the founding of a literary mode nearly all the variety the mode can contain.

The problem of understanding depth in dramatic characterization, and the connections between character and dramatic poetry, stands behind the selection of *The White Devil* and *The Duchess of Malfi*. As readers we recognize that not all characters in a play possess equal depth; we also recognize that some characters are present simply because they allow for the exposition of material necessary for the structure or tone of the work. Of the dramatists of his time, Webster was perhaps as ready as any to exploit his characters for the sake of moving "sentences" or set speeches, yet at the same time perhaps no other dramatist except Shakespeare was so able to endow characters with authentic and evocative poetry when the dramatic situation required it. At its thinnest, characterization in verse can become merely another species of occasional poetry; many Elizabethan revengers, for example, have speeches that are as set and self-contained as nineteenth-century effusions on minor colonial skirmishes or modern odes to the astronauts. One of Webster's achievements was that he broke down the enclosure of the set speech and made its very presence the subject of the drama. When the dramatic necessity of verse is intermittently removed, that absence can itself become one element in the dramatic character's constitution. Study of Webster's shifting poetic engagement can give us many insights into his characters and themes; it can also give us a model for dealing with other plays that have characters with fluctuating depths, such as those in many plays by Middleton, Chapman, and Ford.

The Broken Heart provides an opportunity to study the celebrated composure of Ford's verse and show its relation to his psychological insight. From a distance Ford's art seems a contradiction: How can severe limitation in poetic technique produce an increase in dramatic intensity? Experiments in this vein were attempted from well before 1600 up to the closing of the theaters, and seemed especially attractive to dramatists with strong classical training or sympathies; examples could include the closet drama of the 1590s and the tragedies of Jonson. In the high Jacobean mode, poetic economy and compression—the ascetic ideal, in terms of technique—could be employed in actions that would imitate great extremes of tension, and in these circumstances, controlled verse might not be a mode of distancing: The discipline of technique could heighten the expression of strong feeling as the old Tudor rant never could. The generally acknowledged master of the style was John Ford, and *The Broken*

Heart is perhaps our finest example of the way that technical limitation in poetry can raise dramatic tension and remain fully appropriate to theme and character.

Despite their differences, these five plays are alike in that they have significant patterns in their verse, to which members of an audience would have responded more or less consciously depending upon their education and their familiarity with drama in general. Their response to dramatic poetry would have been inevitable, since events in these plays occur in a manner naturally related to things that happen in the verse. The poetic structures are not just pretty but also have intrinsic meanings: the verse is, in short, a means of direct exposition. To varying degrees all of the plays possess this essential integrity, which is by no means the rule in the drama of the earlier seventeenth century. Many other plays from this time may have intricate and highly organized patterns in verse texture, but only two-dimensional characters and contrived plots, as if the dramatist were trying to achieve on one level what he could not make plausible on another. We know too that a large number of these plays, probably the greater number, were like the woods in *Titus Andronicus,* "ruthless, dreadful, deaf, and dull." The choice of plays for study, then, was determined by the presence of a deep bond in sound, characterization, and dramatic structure. All in all it seemed better to offer exhibitions on plays in which the poetry is the main impetus rather than to spend time on plays in which the poetry is interesting but merely decorative. One hopes to celebrate great achievements rather than to explicate near misses.

Each essay bears down on the play at hand, rather than moving out to general observations best saved for the end. It should be stressed again, however, that each play engages poetry in its own way; we could never abstract a single general formula to account for all different forms of the interconnection between poetry, action, character, and structure in all the plays of the period. Some dramatists are obviously more interested in broad patterns that appear in sequences of human action; some are more interested in the ideas they give their characters to expound; and others are more interested in striking off a series of breathtaking confrontations. Yet in work by sensibilities as different as these three types just described —and of course many others could be added—we still can find, if the dramatist was skilled or lucky, plays in which the poetry takes on a functional rather than an ornamental role. Such is the case with the plays studied here. In each play, the dramatic poetry is not an overlay or a matrix imposed upon the characters or the action or the structure of the play; it is the entire context of that character, action, and structure. Despite the great differences between these particular dramatists, despite the varying influences of convention, performance, and literary sources outside the drama, these plays still have in common an underlying web of connections that has poetry at its center.

That network is nearly limitless and may touch every aspect of the drama, including, for example, the relation between poetry and the illusion of time as it passes onstage. Where the movement of speech—and thus thought—becomes alternately laborious or easy, clotted or graceful, depending upon the syntax, rhythms, and sound patterns of the poetry, the passage of time in the play will seem correspondingly slow, swift, or uneven. The apparent flux of time in the verse will be related in turn to the action as it moves across the stage, pauses, and moves again; it is no accident that the Hamlets and Vindices of Renaissance drama, with their irregular and dilatory progress toward action, break into prose and fall into verse just as their minds move from one mode of organizing experience to another. And on the highest level, their own personal consciousness of their ability to move in time will be related to their poetry.

Or we might consider the bonding powers of verse in its relation to physical movement. When a rhythmic pattern that controls the verse in one kind of scene suddenly announces its presence in another kind of scene, the audience will sense some link between the two. If a dialogue of lovers sitting in an inner space begins to move to the same poetic rhythms as the pacing of a villain in a distant room, the verse will have taken on some of the chores that nonpoetic drama would have to handle through exposition. Much the same thing can happen if the dramatist repeats a certain poetic structure at various points throughout the play. A line of verse occurring late in a play can carry the weight of all similar preceding lines, and thus work like metaphor, or a metaphysical conceit; the particular instance can sum up the general case, and the last line give meaning back to all those that came before it. The process is not simply accretion, or the growth of a poetic stalagmite, because the line coming late can give the preceding similar lines a new and larger meaning: "O soul, be changed into small water drops." The power of verse to act in these ways as direct exposition is only one of many things in dramatic literature that changed after 1642; but this is to anticipate portions of chapters 2 and 7.

This outline is not intended to deprive the reader of his constitutional right to begin in the middle; its purpose instead is to note that the analyses of the plays have assumed their present form because of the material elaborated in the earlier pages. The connection is direct and is based on the assumption that the more we learn about the poetic circumstance of Renaissance drama, the more we will understand about the relation between character and dramatic conflict. In any approach to poetic style, however, it is true that some readers will prefer their own voice, all others being tyrannical. Fortunately there are several guides we can turn to, confident that they need not become commanders. Two are more or less familiar: one is provided by traditional accounts of the prosody of Shakespeare and his contemporaries, and the other by more recent statistically computed analyses of meter and syntax. A third guide is offered in this book: the collective judgment of numerous poems, letters, prefaces, notes, ballads, satires, squibs, and ripostes can give us some sense of the poetic ground of Renaissance drama. Often the play text can give us (as the author himself may point out) the play as it might have been offered under better circumstances, with more competent actors, a more intelligent audience, or dry weather. Considering the number and extent of these remarks, we will find that our critical necessities have been well provided for.

We may want to be wary of some would-be guides, though, as leading away from the historical realities of performer and audience, and two might be mentioned briefly as examples. We sometimes hear it said that we need a single authority in the analysis of dramatic verse texture, and thus should turn to a phonograph recording by a professional, whose job it is to "get the poetry across." Yet in doing this we would only be interpreting an actor's interpretation; we would still have to judge his handling of the poetry against our own reading of the text. We may be even more reluctant to generate these multiple echoes if we recall that many Elizabethan dramatists were quite frank in expressing their disgust for the ways that actors could mangle poetry.

A second guide that might appear on the surface more reliable would be the construction of a prosody relating verse patterns to the dramatic contexts in which they occur. Thus we might collect and classify rhythmic patterns that seem to be associated with particular emotions, and thereby understand the emotional content of any single prosodic pattern. The scheme has an initial plausibility that soon opens into an almost Swiftian logic: interpretation of the dramatic context of any given line would depend upon one's reading of the whole play, just as interpretation of the rhythm of a single line would depend upon hearing the rhythms present in similar lines, some of which will have the misfortune to occur in very different dramatic contexts. In the absence of agreed-upon meanings for complete texts, each assessment of an individual line could conceivably imply a new meaning for the complete play. The *Oxford English Dictionary* seems by contrast an elementary undertaking; James Murray and his co-workers did not have to settle, for cataloging purposes, such mysteries as the dramatic function of Hamlet's reference to *eale*. Our hypothetical master catalog of verse instances for any single dramatist would also be quite as long as the *OED,* for while the basic rhythmic unit in dramatic verse is the line, each line takes its value from those around it; at the least, *q.v.* would prove our handiest bibliographic ally.

These two proposals are not set up here as straw men, but they can indicate some of our reluctance to turn to the most obvious authority for studies in the poetics of drama, and that is the text itself. Chapter 2 will argue that in the earlier seventeenth century dramatists began to develop a conception of the audience as a species of reader sans book. During this period dramatists increasingly came to realize that even as actors assumed the roles from a text and gave them expression in action, such expression could also be imagined from the printed page, thanks in great measure to the movement of the verse.

Such a view of the dramatic text would seem at first to have some connection with recent studies in the presence of an implied reader, but the differences are important and worth comment here, since they do not directly enter the pages to come. The most basic contrast is apparent if we see what the dramatists themselves claim a play text is supposed to represent. As we shall see, the modern critic's idea that a Jacobean play could be literature in the same sense as the *Iliad* or a prose treatise on the soul may not have been shared by Jacobeans; more often the printed text of a play seems to have been regarded as a fortuitously preserved record of a performance, or more interestingly, a performance as it might have been. All the dramatists here studied are writing for what John Webster called "an understanding auditory," and except for the neoclassical closet drama of the 1590s, most English plays were written with the audience—literally, listeners—in mind. Even when social and economic pressures regularly urged plays into print, the reader was still regarded as a type of listener.

One related difference between the assumptions of the present study and those of most reader-response critics will be clear if we note that affective criticism has had its greatest successes with prose (chiefly fiction) and nondramatic verse. This may not be due to a simple coincidence of interests in the critics. Writers as diverse as Bacon, Milton, and Fielding all presuppose a reader alone with the text, but the Jacobean dramatist turning his play into print more typically conceives of his reader as being alone with the characters. The reader's process of balancing himself against the author, which many critics have described in close detail, may by the mimetic nature of drama become a function of the characters themselves: the central character of drama may be the prototype of the unaided critic sorting out his own experience to events. The situation is not the same in prose or nondramatic verse, for while a protagonist such as Adam in *Paradise Lost* is indeed struggling to comprehend an unraveling sequence of events, our response to him is very different in its form from our response to a character like Othello, because of Milton's presence in the poem and the way that presence conditions our response to every event the poem contains. Printed works in prose and nondramatic poetry may inevitably suggest, by their lack of a directly mimetic representation, the simultaneous presence of a separate ordering intelligence. If we wished, we could even call that intelligence the reflected image of an implied reader, whom we might also choose to endow with the personal history of having read other works like the one now in his hands. Renaissance drama, however, can create the illusion that the playgoer or reader is directly confronting the characters, without the mediation of another perception or mind. In fact, some of the Puritan attacks upon the theater are based upon what they regarded as the psychological surrender that one automatically makes in joining the audience of drama.

If the Renaissance audience then "participates" in poetic drama, it is with some fairly specific notions and expectations. This is not to say that those expectations have to be gratified; all but the least imaginative dramatists learn early on that because the audience is comfortable with the contours of blank verse, the roughening of that form may have some useful shock value. When everyone in the audience understands thoroughly the conventions of the spoken stage language, the result is liberation rather than confinement, as a play can both embrace a convention and resist it. The presence of the convention may end by making us uneasy with the modern dictum that beauty is in the eye of the decoder, but that presence also need not bind us to rigid applications, which might assume that the dramatists lacked any self-consciousness about their trade. In this way we come back around to the problem of representation, for the creation of dramatic illusion on the English stage involves this easy play with the freedom and restraint of poetic conventions well understood on both sides.

From one point of view the Renaissance drama's mimetic basis lies in a series of negatives—no narrative voice outside events, no confinement to one mind locked into its own experience, and no dependence upon a discrete time or narrative sequence (two consecutive scenes may be assumed to occur at the same time, and be followed by a third taking place a month later). But it also resides in several positives, the most significant here being the presence of dramatic poetry. The resources of blank verse could supply a dramatic character with an intensity of expression that may not have been realistic in the sense that it resembled ordinary discourse, but that was so impressive to the ear it could suspend disbelief and draw attention from otherwise apparent lapses in consistency or verisimilitude. Of course Renaissance comedies in prose took a different tack, making every kind of attempt to stress the arbitrariness of the play-world and to remind the audience of *its* special identity, there, that very afternoon. In the same way, modern authors and critics often seek to draw the audience into the creative act, stimulating a kind of self-consciousness that the Jacobean poetic dramatist tried to extinguish: he wanted the audience to become the person they saw. One of the remarkable things about Renaissance dramatic poetry was that even after drama went on to have the artistic authority of a medium existing in print, dramatic poetry was still held to be the force that could draw the reader back into the world of the playgoer, and ultimately into the character who had once been feigned on the stage.

In the investigation of these matters the reader should be warned—or reassured, as the case may be—that this study discovers no new plays, documents, or records; that would be a large order for those coming after Chambers, Greg, Wilson, Bentley, and others of the giant race, before the Flood. Instead it examines material we already have, some of it familiar and some perhaps less so, to define an important part of the dramatic sensibility of the Renaissance. Many readers will be able to think of allusions not mentioned here, and it may be an ambiguous assurance to know that behind this study are several folders of additional references and documentation. The examples given here should make the point, but surely in the luxuriant undergrowth of English dramatic history a healthy wild specimen of evidence will turn up just after this type has been set. The problem now, however, is deciding exactly which side of that jungle we should enter, and to do this we need to know the direction we have been traveling. That is the subject of chapter 1.

A NOTE ON TEXTS

In quotations from older texts, modern orthography has been employed in the use of *i* and *j*, *u* and *v*, and long *s*; typographical contractions such as *ñ* have been expanded. References to periodicals employ the standard title abbreviations, and unless otherwise noted, all quotations from Shakespeare come from *The Riverside Shakespeare,* ed. G. Blakemore Evans et al. (Boston: Houghton Mifflin, 1974).

The Poetics of
JACOBEAN DRAMA

1

POETRY IN THE MODE OF ACTION

LIMITS AND DEFINITIONS

Modern readers have countless ways of entering English Renaissance drama. Whether we are studying the plays of Marlowe, Shakespeare, Jonson, Chapman, Webster, Tourneur, Middleton, or Ford, we can approach them by analyzing theme, plot, structure, imagery, or problems in staging; then we can investigate their theological contexts, philosophical backgrounds, political and ethical commentary; and next we can turn on them all the heavier hardware, from Freud and Jung to Marx and Weber, from Vico and Sartre to Malinowski and Lévi-Strauss. Any casual reader can manage to work with at least one of these, and readers with better coordination can play off three or four at once. There is no denying that this sophisticated machinery has produced many insights into the drama of this period. But it also seems to have pressed the plays more and more into becoming intellectual structures of meaning, prismatic fictions, or self-contained and self-consuming visions. Given the history of dramatic criticism, this development may be salutary, but from another point of view it still seems to ignore an important way in which these plays work.

As far as the bulk of published criticism on English Renaissance drama is concerned, including criticism of Shakespeare, the plays might as well have been written in prose—highly figurative prose, but prose nevertheless. Indeed, the more strenuously ahistorical readings of the verse plays, which take them as metadramatic fictions or ritual ceremonies or psychological case histories, usually transform the works into novels in dialogue and costume and preclude any sustained examination of their verse. The transformation almost seems inevitable; perhaps critical tools devised for novels cannot avoid trimming plays into novels. Such readings that take the plays as visions or fictions or statements seem to assume that the drama's primary business is the creation of an order that is discursively accessible, available (to use the old heresy) even in prose paraphrase. Most studies of psychological exploration, political thought, or imagery in these

1

plays (to name only three honored approaches) seldom observe that the plays given the highest marks in their time and ours were written largely in blank verse. Indeed, as far as most modern criticism is concerned, the English propensity for a ten-syllable, five-stress line was only a kind of tic that affected writers and printers, an accident of convention and little more. For the greater number of studies that appear in literary journals and quarterlies, or that come from trade and scholarly presses, it would matter little if the plays were immediately edited into prose. When the verse is noted at all, it is made to sound like background Muzak, or something that provides a distracting experience at best. One model description of this kind is C. S. Lewis's remark that "in poetical drama poetry is the medium, not part of the delineated characters. While the actors speak poetry written for them by the poet, the dramatic personages are supposed merely to be talking."[1] By this reasoning it should be possible to wave off all sorts of elements of the drama: the setting is merely where the action takes place and does not affect it, just as time is only what a character swims in and has no relation to his actions.

Reductive as this attitude may be, it still has a distinguished genealogy, chiefly out of prose logicians and such; in *The Advancement of Learning,* for example, Francis Bacon states that poetic style "belongeth to the Artes of speech," while with respect to matter, poetry "is nothing else but FAINED HISTORY, which may be stiled as well in Prose as in Verse."[2] To the nonpoet, the verse of drama is an excrescence, as John Selden says: "There is no reason why plays should be in verse, either in blank or rhyme; only the poet has to say for himself, that he makes something like that which somebody made before him. The old poets had no other reason but this, their verse was sung to music, otherwise it had been a senseless thing to have fettered up themselves."[3] This rationalist bias is still alive and well, as I note from a brochure that has arrived in the mail as I am writing now. The author, who will remain anonymous, promises to use all the latest techniques in studying a classic English poet, and to ask only the most significant questions; of these, "One of the most interesting is why a man with a mind as highly controlled, secretive, and original as ——'s would choose the medium of poetry in the first place." The writer has assumed that the poetry is detachable from the ideas, that it is a medium separable from content, although this is like saying that a Rembrandt self-portrait has little to do with oil and pigment. Our rationalists forget too that often it is the poetry that chooses the poet, instead of the other way around. What is a writer to do if he starts hearing voices charged with rhythms of their own? At that moment, how much does he think consciously about choosing a medium, or following the something that a somebody made before him?

Bacon's attitude will not seem strange to anyone who has read his poetry, but the modern paring away of dramatic poetry is a curious business, for while we tend to approach this drama from the standpoint of prose readers, we agree nonetheless that these plays constitute a high-water mark for English poetry in general and blank verse in particular. We can point to achievements in blank verse after 1642, ranging from the magnificent to the merely brilliant—*Paradise Lost, The Prelude,* or Browning's monologues—but we can find no sustained example of strong or even important blank verse written by a relatively large number of writers for a space of over two generations. What happened in English dramatic poetry between the 1580s and the closing of the theaters was both peculiar and peculiarly great, but after acknowledging its uniqueness, we still have trouble accommodating it to our usual habits of reading.

On the surface, one might think that as readers we would be more responsive than ever to poetry in drama. According to trade statistics, more poetry is being produced now than ever, and presumably it is reaching larger and larger audiences.[4] In the American university, creative writing is often the healthiest part of the curriculum in English, at least as far as enrollments are concerned, and not a few creative writing students devise and perform in plays. But the modern enthusiasm for poetry has several inner controls, among them an unwillingness to annex the formal verse drama of the past. Even professors of literature, whose territory this is, must find that the facts of publishing can shape their responses: reference to verse drama is difficult in some journals and presses, which quote the poetry as if it were prose, running on the lines one after another without even slashes to indicate line breaks, and with only a vestigial capital letter now and then to mark the start of a poetic line. Certainly this practice saves paper and typesetting costs, and certainly it focuses our attention more on the "content" of the poetry, which is supposed to be what the author was interested in anyway.

Gerald Eades Bentley complained a few years ago that the professional aspects of Elizabethan drama had not been studied because the plays had been too much regarded *sub specie* poetic composition;[5] yet if we look at our most common ways of reading drama as poetic form, we may find that further study is still needed, and particularly study that has some basis in the facts of dramatic professionalism. Most readers now who approach the blank verse of Renaissance drama employ one of three methods, although they are not mutually incompatible; the first might be called the poem-in-itself approach. In this the critic assembles snips and extracts in the manner of Victorian album-verse anthologists, and although titles like *The Book of Gems* are no longer in vogue, the intention remains the same: the criticism purports to catch the poets at the peak of their form, riding the crests. Ted Hughes's anthology of Shakespeare's verse provides a good illustration of the method; lifting all the juiciest speeches out of context, Hughes discovers a predictably morbid pattern, which he is pleased to regard as consistent within its own terms.[6] Basically the same impulse (but without Hughes's pathological obsessions) stands behind the Intro. to Lit. textbooks that encapsulate soliloquies and highly charged exchanges. On the surface the practice seems harmless enough, but it could hardly lead the student to form an idea of rhythms that can shape the structure of an entire play. As in the anthology of gems, selection here becomes a form of criticism that invites the reader to fragment the work for himself.

The second method comes with better if dustier scholarly credentials, and that is statistical analysis. I do not refer here to the mathematical study of texts, in the manner of Greg's monumental *Calculus of Variants,* but rather to those comfortable and arithmetic studies that accepted a stable text as a given. In the past these typically involved the counting of Middleton's syllables or Massinger's feminine endings, but that kind of enterprise has slowed since stylistic "tests" of authorship developed a shady name, and today such study is usually relegated to a safer or less controversial service, giving second-rank support to the dating of individual plays.[7] In the last decade the use of literary statistics (as distinguished from textual analysis) has been put on higher ground. Particularly important in this respect is Dorothy L. Sipe's study, *Shakespeare's Metrics* (1968), which settles once and for all the question of whether Shakespeare was using an iambic pentameter line (he was), and in the process provides material for the resolution of several cruces.[8] However, Sipe's study does not set out to treat the broader connections between poetry and characterization, much less between poetry and the structure of a play as a whole, nor is it easy to imagine how statistical analysis by itself might be brought to bear upon these. The obstacle here seems to be that our criticism of the peculiar music of poetry in drama has evolved in such a way as to exclude any but the grossest use of statistics that cover whole plays; we are only beginning to assemble a critical vocabulary that will allow us to include large-scale numerical analysis in the estimation of literary value.

Although extractive and statistical readings of poetry in drama have had somewhat uneven fortunes, there has always been a steady trade in the third sort of reading, which we could describe as the impressionistic. Immensely adaptable, this sort of reading can go to any critical school yet still provide an artistic outlet for the critic. Usually the method involves either a sprinkling of moralistic code-words, which imply that one kind of poetry is more healthful and hygienic than another, or a straightforward paragraph or two of creative writing. The two approaches are not incompatible, although for the sake of internal consistency most studies in moralistic impressionism avoid whole paragraphs of inspired metaphor; instead there is a persistent reliance on such adjectives as *crisp, sharp, hard, firm,* and *taut*: a vocabulary of edges. Code-word impressionism implies that the reader should admire only one sort of poetry, and always reminds him that there can be no backsliding. In this scheme too there is no room for the idea that different sorts of verse might be appropriate to different characters, emotions, plots, or themes; instead, if the poetry does not meet the minimum standard of concentration and compression, it is degenerate, hollow, decadent, or (worst of all) sentimental. Thus one critic says of lines in *The Revenger's Tragedy* that "they have a rhythmic movement which is precise and clear, but which is also alive and urgent. It is an activating as well as a controlling force. . . ." The "sharply etched vivacity" and "crispness" of Tourneur's verse are opposed to "the soft-ened texture in the writing of plays like Ford's and Webster's," and thus Ford and Webster are decadent and inferior. Looking up *texture* in a dic-tionary of critical terms is not of much help here, for next we learn that "softness" is not the real problem anyway, since "the cloying texture of [Ford's] verse comes from the fact that such patterns in Ford are almost always allowed to exist uncriticized and unfocused."[9] "Facts" of that kind are usually the sort we are offered in this kind of reading, as when an-other critic discovers that "well-packed" verse is superior to the "smooth" variety, or when yet another finds a dramatist's poetry "easy, supple, and compact," or more precisely, "flexible, forceful, and concise."[10]

Code-word reading has a curious ancestry, growing out of T. S. Eliot's perceptive but fragmentary remarks on Renaissance drama.[11] It is as if Eliot, writing what was essentially journalism produced for a deadline, had been bestowing a critical method rather than casting off as many insights as possible in a short space. His ideas thus became not just starting points but exemplifications of a method that proved all too easy to imitate, particularly since his critical style lent itself readily to use by readers with prescriptive moral programs. It is evident too that Eliot's predecessors exerted a parallel modern influence of their own; chief among these would be Coleridge, whose fugitive notes and marginalia seem to have been im-portant as much for their critical method as for their content. Building toward a tight judgment in a single phrase or sentence loaded with impli-cation, this sort of criticism advertises itself as the unviolated expression of an intense sensibility: the critical style itself tries to approach the literary style of the work being endorsed. When the reader is blessed with the protean moral awareness of a Coleridge, such criticism can be a heady experience; but when that range is lacking, the results seem more the ex-pression of the social needs of the critic's world, and less the expression of the work's own inner order.

In contrast, the creative writing form of impressionism begins from the premise that each play can call forth its own kind of verse—but from that point distinctions begin to blur in an opposite direction. It is as if the ab-sence of moral qualifiers allowed the existence of all poetic effects at once. Thus one writer says of the verse in a late Shakespeare play that "the words are packed densely; instead of flowing out in sentences, they seem to break off individually, like chips of quartz under the hammer; they reach the ear in a rhythm that is abrupt yet elegiac, angular yet gentle." Gentle hammering is not easy to hear, but when in an effort to clarify matters one turns to another creative critic on the same play, the confusion only mounts; the next writer says of the same poetry that "sometimes with a sudden snake-like contraction, convulsion almost, it closes on itself, shedding all ornament and leaving little but the essential sinews of its structure."[12] Yet this is a reading of the same text that the creative Henry James said, "plays, at its better times, with an indifferent shake of its golden locks, in the high, sunny air of delightful poetry."[13]

The problem with this kind of reading is that it seldom allows for the development of characters *within* the poetry; we are told instead that the play has a certain normative style, which rests presumably upon a few well-known speeches by an assortment of characters. Seldom are judgments of the poetry tied to readings of themes, except when the critic launches a paragraph of dense metaphor. Since this criticism does not show how poetic forms may have specific significance in themselves, it often as not serves the purpose it sets out to defeat: far from being part of an integral whole, the poetry becomes quite easily separated from concerns for theme and structure. The difficulty of integrating a reading of the music of the verse with the overt concerns of the themes and plot probably explains why there are so many comments on the late Shakespeare like those quoted above, and still no comprehensive study of his final mastery in dramatic blank verse.

If part of the difficulty of writing intelligently on the poetry of this drama originates in the convenience of one-or two-paragraph impressions, another and perhaps larger part originates in the fuzziness of the term *poetry* itself. Some readers would go so far as to let the term *dramatic poetry* include the actors' physical gestures;[14] yet if we allow this, we may as well go all the way and include scenery too. Clearly this would not do, but where can lines be drawn? Perhaps the best approach would be to begin with a sample definition, qualifying and adjusting with the Elizabethan and Jacobean canon in mind. Ronald Peacock has distinguished three uses of the term *poetic* in relation to drama: the first is quite simply a text in formally identifiable verse; the second involves a set of Romantic themes and attitudes, often described as "poetic"; and the third would be a lyrical and musical style, which may or may not be in verse. "Differences in poetic forms," Peacock concludes, "should be viewed not in a simplified linguistic contrast of 'verse' against 'prose,' but as variations in *style,* style in this case being the character of all the dramatic imagery [that is, representation], and not a practical feature of language alone."[15] An expansive definition like this works quite well for Peacock's purposes, because he wants to read Chekhov, Eliot, Yeats, Lorca, and Cocteau with a commendable desire for as few labels as possible. But in the study of Renaissance drama such a definition would cause more problems than it would solve. The same may be said for similar definitions devised particularly for the study of modern poetic drama. Denis Donoghue, for example, echoes Peacock in saying that "The 'poetry' of poetic drama is not necessarily or solely a *verbal* construct; it inheres in the structure of the play as a whole."[16] The second clause is completely applicable to Renaissance drama, as my later chapters on specific plays will attempt to show. But the first clause is another matter. A Renaissance dramatist would—and in so many words, usually did—say that the poetry of poetic drama *is* necessarily a verbal construct, particularly to the extent that it uses a set poetic form like blank verse. We know that the dramatists themselves distinguished between plays written in formally identifiable verse and plays written in prose; and as we shall see in the next chapter, there is abundant evidence that Renaissance audiences could hear (as we often do not hear) verse lines emerging from and receding into prose. Why then adopt a definition of Renaissance dramatic poetry that is looser and less precise than one that contemporary audiences and dramatists used?

This question might also be asked regarding other recent definitions that locate the "poetry" of poetic drama in more specifically theatrical elements. William V. Spanos has suggested, for example, that pattern and variation in action can take on poetic stature,[17] but a definition of this sort works first by isolating one element of poetry (its use of pattern and variation), then by saying that artifacts that possess such an element are poetic; by this logic even a woven tapestry, for example, might be held to be poetic. There would be a problem in applying this kind of definition to Renaissance poetic drama, because the terms are difficult to anchor in the verse; like much other poetry, dramatic poetry often has few elements of verbal repetition except for repeated and varied rhythmic units. The idea that action can approach the state of poetry leads Spanos to some interesting conclusions, his definition of poetic drama being much fuller than this note from it might imply. But if we wish to understand the role of poetry in Renaissance drama, we cannot simply appropriate definitions evolved for treating looser and in some ways more sophisticated plays. To do so would blur the peculiar strengths of Renaissance drama, and would also misrepresent its cultural context.[18]

Perhaps the most flexible yet precise definition of *poetry* in the drama of this period would center on its prosodic component, in most cases the ten-syllable five-stress line in all its variations. Rhymed pentameter lines, tetrameter lines, interpolated prose and songs all can give variety to and highlight the distinctive achievement of a play's blank verse; but after about 1590, these forms alone are seldom employed for the full length of a play dealing with a serious theme, and that would include the genre that has come to be called tragic satire. As a medium for tragedy, tragicomedy, romance, and tragic satire, blank verse rules the roost until the close of the theaters, and as a poetic form it controls the dramatic poet's imagination. While it is true that metaphor is at the heart of all literary composition—including poetic technique itself, I shall argue in the next chapter—it does not work well on its own as a means of defining and sorting verse plays. Dramatic prose may be and often is radically metaphorical, as when Falstaff is speaking, yet one cannot imagine an Elizabethan audience that would say that Falstaff was speaking poetry. Plays in verse do not differ from plays in prose solely by their use of imagery, for example, or by the devices of formal rhetoric. One play in verse may differ from another in prose with respect to its use of metaphor or rhetoric (although sometimes these differences may not be so much in kind as in degree), just as one may differ from another with respect to theme; but these are all differences that can and do exist between two plays written wholly in verse or wholly in prose. Thus the presence of rhetoric or imagery does not by itself mean that we have poetic drama. What one hopes to find is a least common multiple (not that there can ever be a *single* multiple—no play is a prime number), by which we can tell a play in verse from a play in prose. The conventions of the verse would seem to provide that irreducible factor.

It might be well to underscore the turn our definition is starting to take, by noting that while it does not exclude the rhetoric of poetry—meaning by that its whole figurative level of meaning—it also does not use rhetoric as a starting point. Figures or word schemes or the self-describing logic of a dramatic language are not the intrinsically poetic element of Renaissance poetic drama. A few hours in a library will show, however, that most modern studies of the poetry of Shakespeare's plays or the poetry of Elizabethan drama are in fact studies of figurative language alone; in a full review of criticism one could cite, for example, studies in the poetic style of one play or another that make virtually no reference to the fact that the play in question was written in blank verse. Many of these studies are undeniably valuable; one recent example of a critical argument that locates the poetry of poetic drama almost entirely in rhetoric also happens to be one of the best, and that is Madeline Doran's *Shakespeare's Dramatic Language*. Even here, though, where the reading is full of the most spacious insights, there is only passing acknowledgement of the fact that dramatic poetry begins in a sensuous apprehension through the ear—which the dramatists and audiences of the time never forgot.[19]

While definition of dramatic poetry as a fundamentally rhythmic form would be unacceptable for all types of "poetic" drama, it does help straighten out one rather puzzling problem, and that is deciding how we are to handle the role of secondary sound patterns in blank verse drama. Rhyme and assonance may and sometimes do occur in passages of prose; but without a coincident and recurrent metrical pattern, such passages (at least in plays of this period) might be called poetic but not poetry. Conversely, a given passage in a play may consist of verse with no imagery, no metaphor, no rhyme, and only the most subtle secondary patterns in sound, yet still be unmistakable as poetry and quite moving as well; John Ford is perhaps the supreme master of this kind of verse, the power of which lies in the complete transparency between what is being said and the drama of acting out the content directly in the verse.

Another puzzle in the modern study of secondary sound patterns in Renaissance blank verse is strictly linguistic. Although in time such disciplines as generative phonology may be able to tell us how a given line sounded to an Elizabethan, our knowledge of Elizabethan pronounciation, pitch, and juncture still is not definitive. However, even if linguists could succeed in fully describing the sound values of a London dialect circa 1600, the existence of such a description would still not imply that any given actor would have been bound to them in a given play. From our own playgoing we know how important such elements as pitch, juncture, and volume or amplitude can be in establishing the tone of a dramatic speech or character; but we also know how much they can change from one performance to another, and in the process completely alter our understanding of the characters and the action as a whole. For us the risk is that by dwelling only on these secondary sound patterns we could soon start reconstructing performances that would be hopelessly hypothetical; we could design a reading of a play that might involve, for example, several crucial pauses, shouts, or nearly inaudible phrases, and end with a brand new play on our hands. Criticism of this sort can be unlimited in its ingenuity because there is ultimately no rigor in the method, given our present historical knowledge. Who could gainsay the claim that in the play at hand there is a sudden jump in the pitch contour of line 108 of act 3, scene 2, which casts a new light on act 5? The wonderful variety here—and it should not be disparaged, for these forms of surprise can be a main source of our delight in a stage production—is properly a part of performance and not of literary analysis. But there is no question that Elizabethan and Jacobean literary criticism gives us much more detail on the rhythmic basis of the verse than it does on secondary sound patterns.

It may seem belaboring the obvious to remark that if we use the pentameter line as a working definition, we need not imply as a result that every line must be regular. Some dramatic poets like Tourneur are very free with the line as a metrical base, dropping at times into meters that are nearly accentual, while others like Ford monitor every variation. Further, although the ten-syllable, five-stress line may be the norm, not every line as a consequence will have *either* ten syllables *or* five stresses. This ideal proved quite unworkable, luckily for us; in practice it could yield only the perfection of total monotony, and readers familiar with the backwaters of English verse drama know that there are some demonstrated achievements in that line. Despite these self-evident truths, since the eighteenth century countless editors of Elizabethan plays, especially those of Shakespeare, have been led by a pious zeal to "save" the meters of their subjects, as by elision, the removal of offending particles, and other more drastic measures. The officiousness of these efforts suggests something like the enterprise of Crashaw's angels, soaring through the heavens to catch a saint's tears on (of all things) a pillow. Actually there is little evidence that the major Elizabethan and Jacobean dramatists took the salvation of their irregular meters very seriously, and it is not until the successors of Fletcher that regular "numbers" become a virtue in themselves. In other words, if we use the line as a definition for poetic drama in this period, neither logic nor literary history should compel us to become metrical absolutists. (The foundation for these comments will be elaborated in more detail in the next chapter.)

There is no way or need to divorce the rhythms of dramatic poetry from other elements of meaning, including metaphor, plot, staging, and so forth. The rhythmic base of dramatic poetry will have a local significance, it cannot avoid that; it may have a broader metaphoric significance as well; and in the hands of a true craftsman it will always be related to the other elements of the drama, although the exact nature of that relation may be uneven or groping. The sometimes-encountered notion of "reading for the poetry alone" is a flat impossibility, at least if one is doing anything more than statistical programming, which would not seem to come under the heading of reading anyway.

By the same token, one should not be able to "read for theme alone" without some equally serious distortion. Reading a play without attending to its verse would be like listening to a Brahms symphony performed by an orchestra without a string section. Poetry is a vital part of the whole, even in works that are written with only intermittent poetic attention; the plays of Chapman, for example, may sound at times like essays, but one should never disregard their studied moments of excitement in the verse. Ideally, one would read on several levels at once, or on several coincident planes, realizing that if the author had wanted to write sermons or treatises or prose romances he could have found both printers and an audience. However, if he wanted to write poetry that would reveal and illuminate an event, his choice was clear. The drama is, as Suzanne Langer has reminded us, "poetry in the mode of action,"[20] a phrase that suggests concisely the relation between what is seen *on* the stage and what is heard *from* it.

MOTION AS MEANING

If one asks why so much modern criticism ignores the poetry of the drama, two problems immediately come to mind. The first is familiar to anyone who has tried the job: How does one actually *write* about the poetry? Does the poetry come into the argument as a salesman for the ideas? Or as a friendly caller? (An instance of the latter: the late James Smith's perceptive studies.[21]) Many scholars and critics have been able to light up passages and whole scenes by their patient and loving attention to the verse; John Russell Brown can always be informative in this way, or Nevill Coghill, or (to take a critic perhaps less well known) Richard Flatter.[22] But in studies by all these, the focus is still tight, confined to single speeches or scenes, and the question remains: How can poetry assume the center of an extended argument? Can every line of a play be analyzed and coordinated with every other line, as if the whole were a mammoth lyric, some sort of poetic dinosaur? How can even the most tireless reader respond to every line in a play? The challenge seems impossible, but Paul Alpers has assured us that each of the 4,000 stanzas of *The Faerie Queene* is addressed directly to us as readers;[23] if we can rise to that occasion, then we ought to be able to stand up and walk through plays like a man.

Assuming we could meet that challenge, we would still have to face the objection from some readers that any poetic study of plays is impossible, because the texts are all corrupt and besides, plays exist only in live performance. It is common knowledge, so the argument runs, that our copies of the plays are all defective, originally typeset by venal and illiterate printers; the censor, no Freudian bugbear but a real live Master of Revels, got the poet to delete oaths, lines, and sometimes whole scenes that constituted a threat to the state; the actors adapted and rewrote the plays for the stage; and the poet himself probably had at least one collaborator on the job, and evidence suggests that he was deaf. All this may be granted. Yet if these objections vitiate study of the poetry in Renaissance drama, they also invalidate every other kind of criticism, except the study of the text and the facts connected with its generation and transmission.

There is no need here to discourse on the place and possibility of criticism; there have been many spirited defenses of literary study in Renaissance drama,[24] and it will be the business of the next chapter to show that the most convincing defense can come from the dramatists and playgoers themselves. The objections to reading the received text can be greatly magnified; one could postpone indefinitely the tasks and joys of reading because we do not have books as tidy as we would like. And of course the textual problem is hardly unique to the Renaissance, touching as it does even Joyce, for example, and Faulkner. Whatever the dates of the author, one attempts to read with the fullest knowledge possible, realizing at the same time the provisional quality of any reading.

Rather than pursue textual problems now (time enough for that later, on specific works) we might go directly to our general reluctance—one hesitates to say inability—to hear the verse of this drama and to deal with it as an element that changes over the course of a play, developing as other elements of meaning also evolve and take shape. The comments of most modern critics are so brief, so limited to generalizing upon isolated lines or two or three speeches, that it seems as if the sound of a play were something that only flared and vanished. The philosophical bases of the change from Renaissance habits of listening are quite outside the limits of the present study; the historical changes in the ontology of sound in a text are a deep matter, best left to French theoreticians, and a more immediate source of our own modern attitude might be the strong visual bias of our time. It is not an original observation that as a culture we take in a proportionately greater share of our experience by eye than by ear, as compared with the generations before us. One may question this as a general hypothesis, but there is little doubt it is true with respect to modern views of Renaissance drama. As visual display the drama was highly dependent upon suggestion; countless plays have prologues or parenthetical comments that say the spectacle presented by the actors is only a feeble representation, and that tell the audience it must use its imagination if it is to enter the world of the play. Often it seems that as modern readers we take this injunction on only one simple level, when we might be applying it to others as well. Accepting readily the premise that poetic drama asks us to create a world, we have produced studies of imagery that are subtle and definitive, and we need to explore the verbal music of this drama with as deep a concern for pattern and development. The modern proliferation of imagery studies—even though there is little in Elizabethan dramatic poetics that alludes to this sort of reading[25] —may indeed have its source in our inability to *hear* relationships between the characters; on this subject Elizabethan criticism is, by contrast, quite specific and illuminating. We tend, in short, to view these plays as masterpieces of figurative language in which structure and *vision* are the dominant components. While the language of a play is always display, it is never an assemblage of pictures alone, even if they are pictures in motion.[26]

The relentlessly visual impulse of our attitude toward drama may be seen in the way many modern directors tend to rely heavily upon blocking, and seldom seem to let the actors work outward from the text. A good illustration here would be the *King Lear* that Jonathan Miller produced in 1975 for BBC television. In this production Miller attempted to arrange the actors visually, presenting numerous scenes of static tableaux after Mannerist painters, chiefly Georges de la Tour. Nothing wrong here and nothing new. From the present standpoint what was most interesting about the production was that the visual tableaux were accompanied by innumerable arbitrary changes in the verse, which suggested that Miller had set out deliberately to keep it from coming through and blunting the impact of the visual arrangements. The changes included expanded contractions and added auxiliaries, as well as elisions and the deletion of articles and metrically necessary exclamations ("O!" for example). Although neither thorough nor systematic, the editing was pervasive enough to have originated in a conscious decision on the director's part, and not in improvisation by the actors, since along with it went some revision of the play's diction, apparently in the interests of the audience's presumed illiteracy. The visual imagery of the language, fused with the dramatic imagery of the staging, finally took all precedence over the words in which the play was articulated. Miller's low regard for the verbal capacity of his audience was unfortunately all too justified by the critical reception of the play: one reviewer disparaged the "name-the-picture" staging but added that it was after all a real treat to hear Shakespeare's great verse again.[27] No reviewer seemed to notice that the rhythmic basis of the verse had been consistently nibbled away, or that the metaphor at the heart of the staging would have been incomprehensible to an Elizabethan audience: The public art gallery was unknown in Shakespeare's time.

There is no question that under the best of circumstances the study of the visual arts should enlarge our understanding of poetry rather than constrict it. The concept of rhythm in composition, for example, could offer useful models for describing the relation between the major themes of a work and the details of its execution. Three examples come to hand, from different media and periods. In his study of the Parthenon frieze, Martin Robertson has noted how "an easily apprehended rhythm can appear," as in the pattern of men's and horses' legs, or in "a bent head [that] picks up a recurrent accent among the riders."[28] The sense of motion in the frieze is one immediate result of this visual rhythm; another, less obvious but ultimately more significant, is the way in which the rhythm emphasizes some figures over others, affecting our understanding of the "meaning" of the frieze. A second example could take us into painting, where artists, particularly since the Impressionists, have been obsessed by the way in which tensions in the subject or composition may be resolved in the technique with which the paint is applied. The problem is vital to an understanding of artists as different as Cézanne and Francis Bacon, and the critical approach is by no means novel; Erwin Panofsky suggested many years ago that technique and subject are ultimately related.[29] This insight could be especially useful in the study of poetic drama, in which the movement of the poetry, as it develops in and through the action, may both contrast with and complement the development of character and theme.

One last example begins from just this pattern, with an artistic medium even closer to home. The Russian director Grigori Kozintsev kept a diary while directing his film of *Hamlet*, and one short note in particular bears directly upon the problem at hand: "The flow of verse must become a swarm of visual images of the same poetic quality."[30] A form of consciously controlled synesthesia, this absorption of verse texture into picture is very different from the process used in Miller's *Lear*, and has not been much discussed even by writers on "media," although one may suspect that it happens often in stage productions. Kozinstsev's recognition of what he had to do with the verse, when he would inevitably lose it in translation, has a certain ironic edge to it. As a non-English speaker Kozintsev *heard* the poetry; he found in it a freshness that demanded expression, while as native speakers we have forgotten the great emphasis that our own writers and actors once put upon it.

Some of the changes that have taken place in our understanding of rhythm and vision undoubtedly have their source in the evolution of modern education. In many if not most modern primary and secondary schools, oral recitation has come to be viewed as an instrument of psychological repression, and as a consequence children not only have less opportunity to organize their own speech but also have to do less listening that would require spontaneous yet specifically directed responses. In some progressive schools an increasing proportion of a child's talk goes into, and comes back from, a tape machine that the child controls—hardly an experience even remotely related to the give and take of stage and audience three and a half centuries ago. Even without the rise of electronic technology (and here is the place for the obligatory attack on television), one could account for significant changes in verbal awareness since the turn of the century. We insist, for instance, that every student be provided with a text, while students in many if not most Renaissance grammar schools had to copy out exemplary sentences, after *listening* to the schoolmaster read them aloud. After that they might construe the meters of lines and poems, and these not simply in their own language but also in the presumed classical ancestors of their own language. And so the lessons would proceed through the day, with great masses of information coming in through the ear, then being assimilated, parodied, or rejected outright by an intelligence with a strong aural bias.[31]

Modern literary education for the young sees things rather differently. In our multitude of Introduction to Poetry texts, for example, sound patterns of all sorts are usually herded together with a discussion of rhythm and are then sentenced to execution in a "unit" of their own, with exemplary poems for analysis. The beginning student does meters and then does allegory or symbols; the study of rhythm in language is merely an approach and not a condition of the whole act of reading. In reading Shakespeare the orientation is often the same: most Introductions and Companions and Guides, when they note the poetry at all, give it a potted treatment in a few pages that attempt to cover the entire canon.[32] Worse yet, on more elementary levels (as in the American secondary school), the subject is likely to be treated in a movie or filmstrip, by which the student could hardly fail to draw the conclusion that the sound of poetry is a kind of distraction from the visual display.

The English seem more sensitive to the loss than do Americans; it is a commonplace that English actors are better able to register the contours of blank verse.[33] English critics and teachers still complain, though, of a gathering dullness in their students' abilities to hear verbal rhythms. Denis Donoghue has written of the problem from a professorial point of view:

> I promise myself, one of these years, to find among my colleagues in the English Department an impassioned prosodist and let him loose upon our first-year classes in the first fortnight of Michael-mas term. Let him discourse of nothing but prosody. Those who stay the course will be deemed eminently qualified to read English. I want students who find it exhilarating to scan the line: "All whom flood did, and fire shall, o'erthrow." I want students who can read a poem aloud and know what they are saying.[34]

Conservative advice. Study of metrics may not be the only method of setting entrance requirements or building character, but it is without question the oldest critical tool that literary archaeologists have un-earthed; in the earliest extant Greek grammar, the second-century B.C. *Technē Grammatikē* of Dionysius Thrax, we are told that literary criticism begins in expert reading aloud according to the rules of prosody.[35]

One can acknowledge the noble antiquity of the method and still have reservations about its modern usefulness, as long as it is installed upon the scaffolding of much modern education. Reinstituting an ancient course of study, even an impassioned one, may not be much of a solution if it is running against other large-scale changes; and recent shifts in the curriculum, which have involved redefinitions of other academic subjects, make any return to simple prosodic drill unlikely and of doubtful value. Most significant has been the way that study of the history of the English language has become annexed to structural and generative linguistics, allowing it to participate less in literary analysis or appraisal. In a parallel development, the modern teaching emphasis upon practical criticism, and more recently structural criticism, has isolated texts in an empirical manner, not simply from literary history but also from the history of the language.[36] Raymond Williams has argued that one consequence of these changes, particularly with regard to the history of the language, has been "a loss of general capacity to handle problems of verbal rhythms, and especially the relations between spoken and written English formations which were crucial in several major literary forms, most notably written drama."[37] Freed from its place in the history of the language, a poem or a play becomes for the student a free object, whose kinship with other subjects may be seen best by narrowing the study to investigation of inherent intellectual form or structure. Soon the student forgets that the *sounds* that make up the work have a history of their own. Discussion of these changes, particularly as they involve the evolution of modern linguistics and its relation to the traditional curriculum, could easily take—and would deserve—a book in itself. The subject is brought up here in order to avoid any simple conclusion that our present uncertainty of response to verbal rhythms is due to a mere failure in higher education. The roots of the problem are in fact broader and deeper than these old remedies would allow, much as we might endorse them in principle.

Rhythm remains an appropriate place to begin the study of poetic form because that is where the act of creation so often begins. Modern literature supplies some fine illustrations: Frost chopping wood, Valéry climbing his hill, Yeats riding the train. Perhaps even more significant is the way that poets will work out of purely imagined rhythms that do not start from physical activity. What Northrop Frye has called a "rhythmic initiative" often appears to start the poet in cadences of words that superimpose themselves one upon the other, creating and resolving tensions that call in turn for more words.[38] There is little reason to suppose that the working habits of Renaissance poets differed greatly from those of their twentieth-century counterparts (except for that matter about the train), and it would be possible to go on at length about the way that modern poems get written. Fascinating as such study would be, it would not necessarily illuminate the composition of plays in the Renaissance, nor should we expect much help from modern writers of verse drama, for they are engaged in a task that carries an enormous burden of the past. The self-consciousness of the modern verse dramatist is entirely different in kind and degree from that of his predecessors, and because of this we may learn more about the role of rhythm in the writing of plays by listening to a modern dramatist who works in prose. Harold Pinter, when asked about the verbal form and rhythm of his plays, replied by saying: "I don't conceptualize in any way. . . . I think that what happens is that I write in a very high state of excitement and frustration. I follow what I see on the paper in front of me—one sentence after another."[39] Maybe it would be best to say simply that a dramatist is someone who hears voices; if he lived between 1590 and 1642, those voices would often as not speak in blank verse; and if he were lucky, they would take over his play. The conscious effort he might expend upon bringing them to life could be minimal or—as in the case of John Webster—enormous.[40] But at the source of the play, the rhythmic initiative must have been as natural and exciting as the presence that Pinter describes.

This miraculous birth can remind us of questions that we often ignore in studies of image and meaning in drama. To begin, are play characters approximations of people or are they mere occasions for the poetry that is clamoring to be written? The problem fans out quickly; if we come to find that the ground of a play character's existence lies in his poetry rather than in some psychological nexus or Bradleyan finite center (or any of its modern descendants), then to some extent we shall see the whole play as functioning more within a presentational mode, and less within a representational or realistic mode. The two modes are not mutually exclusive, for only rarely does a central character in Renaissance drama lack altogether a psychological center of some kind; even the characters of John Marston, whose human intuition and narrow technical brilliance often seem at odds, usually possess a recognizable psychological composition. (What makes them so interesting is that their vitality is sometimes at odds with the explicit moral content of their speeches.) In general, a closer interest in dramatic poetry will necessarily make us ask where a character's psychological center has been blurred or shifted for the sake of a rousing speech.

It will also raise questions about the difference between a play's major and minor characters. A major character will often move between depiction in psychologically realistic terms and deployment as a vehicle for the poetry (ideally, of course, the two coincide), while a minor character will have a uniform poetic flatness that is related to the thinness of his characterization. Occasionally it happens that in the work of Tourneur, Webster, or Middleton, a character who is fully developed will be surrounded by characters who are pure cardboard, and who are given verse that is mainly expository and involves little engagement on the author's part. This sort of characterization occurs less often in Shakespeare; from the major plays down to the more determinedly minor plays, he usually writes up the lesser characters, giving them poetry commensurate with their role in the central character's mental progress. Along with this, there can still occur numerous passages that are necessary for the play but do not do much poetically; perhaps it is the dramatist's pulling at this narrative thread that sometimes makes us experience the strong speeches as poetry looking for a place to happen.

Once we can discriminate between those characters who are largely pretexts for verse and those who become instead approximations of ourselves, making fully human claims, we will have moved deep into the dramatist's conception of form and, ultimately, into his conception of the significance of human action. For some readers, the critic who implies that discriminations of this kind can be made will seem to have moved into the ranks of the dreaded disintegrators. It may not be necessary or possible to be reassuring on this score within the subsequent chapters; instead, one has to ask whether shifts between modes of characterization were not accepted as a given fact of Renaissance drama. Recently J. L. Styan has argued, with examples up and down, that "the notion of Elizabethan characterization as a presentation of varied *personae* all having the same face is yet to be grasped by modern actors." In Styan's view, shifts in the mode of presentation within the same play pose no problem to an audience, which is following the movement of the voices it hears; and "as such speech, familiar or remote, personal or impersonal, penetrates the less conscious mind of an audience, it is guided to a range of responses which have little to do with the demands of realism."[41]

Our own expectations of stylistic unity in Renaissance drama may not, in fact, be proposed by the works themselves. Often we may look for levels of consistency that are the result of certain post-Romantic or modern attitudes toward unified effects, while the Elizabethan theater may have been, in Peter Brook's phrase, a "rough theater" capable of accommodating both realistic and symbolic modes of presentation without upsetting an audience.[42] Scholars might dismiss this hypothesis as only the self-justification of a freewheeling modern director, yet it is surprising how it can mesh with the best of modern criticism. One important example comes to mind. In *"King Lear" in Our Time,* Maynard Mack has shown how the separate elements of realism, fable, and dramatic shorthand have imposed limits upon the characters of the play and the actions they are permitted to take.[43] While Mack's argument does not carry him into consideration of the shaping power of the play's verse, his study demonstrates concisely the way in which simultaneous and shifting modes of dramatic presentation can enlarge and enrich a work rather than diminish or destroy it.

From a purely practical standpoint, however, the recognition of shifted modes will seem to some readers the opening of the floodgates. To present the problem in caricature: if your critical study lets you see plays as exercises of technique in which no fundamental unity need exist, you will finally be free to see every third-rate play as a spasmodic masterpiece. And this temptation to carry the recognition of mixed modes ad absurdum is faced not only by a covert disintegrator; when the conscientious scholar begins to sort the seeds from which any complex work grows, as Mack does with *King Lear,* he risks not meeting the central goal of criticism, which we may take to be the enlargement of delight through understanding. That Mack does this brilliantly is one reason his study illustrates the point. For many readers, however, those eating cares remain: once one admits that a masterpiece can be a botch, every botch would seem to qualify as a masterpiece. The problem admits of some circularity.

One scholar who met the impasse head on (which is not necessarily to resolve it) was F. L. Lucas, who stated quite bluntly that Jacobean plays should be read by scenes.[44] Now this is a clear program, and from one point of view it is undoubtedly correct, especially in the case of works that are the product of collaboration. Yet in its straightforward exaggeration Lucas's statement clarifies the task at hand: the argument is really one between necessity and preference. Some plays may possess underlying and coherent patterns in their verse, while their plots may be arbitrary and their characters waver in depth; Massinger and Middleton often work in this way, or so it seems to this writer. Of course one may prefer to read plays in which there is a complete meshing, so to speak, in which the characterization deepens with a consistent progression, the action has no arbitrary collisions, and the verse shows a full-time engagement on the part of the poet. The reader's preference for this kind of play may be urged upon the highest principles, but that is not to deny that works assembled in other ways may have a power of their own, which would have been fully affecting to an Elizabethan audience. We accept this idea in our experience of other arts; a taste for Mozart need not preclude a taste for Bartok. There do seem to be many Jacobean plays that hang together chiefly in their verse, and understanding how these plays work could let us appreciate all the more the wholly integrated play—if such a miracle there be.

There are already a few signs that modern criticism of Renaissance drama may be coming to terms with works that are disjunctive in their characterization, language, or action. We have already noted the work of Mack and Styan, readers who stress the need for historical and critical awareness in an audience, yet who still remain dubious about the search for "meanings" in Renaissance plays, as if the dramatists were actually tract-writers manqué. Hamlet's critique of Christian orthodoxy, Lear's analysis of Nature, or Antony's exploration of the heroic consciousness: the topics by which we kidnap the characters for the themes are all familiar, and most tend to turn the dramatist into a person who would have been much happier writing critical essays, if only he had the gift. Recently several critics have also pointed out that this approach to themes may involve some misconceptions of the nature of drama itself. Both the dramatist's perception of his task and the forms he creates from it may not be linear or ordered in any systematic fashion, much as we may succeed in abstracting discursively organized patterns out of the swirling motion of a play. Norman Rabkin in particular has written cogently about the modes of vision that the artist employs, and the themes as we perceive them; remarking the differences between the two, Rabkin has suggested that we try to accommodate the simultaneous insights and contradictions that lie at the heart of the drama written in Shakespeare's time.[45] Such is the construction of Rabkin's argument that our possible reservations about it can only become support for his thesis. We would strengthen his case by saying that it does not consider, as part of the simultaneously apprehended experience of drama, our hearing the verse line, the medium through which those unexpected harmonies and discords are all expressed.

Using Rabkin's valuable work as an example, we might ask how much the metaphor of vision can in itself become part of the reductive search for "meanings"; our concept of drama as an art best described in metaphors of sight may have slowed our understanding of Renaissance plays as poetic forms. Because medieval writers used the concept of vision quite self-consciously, the term is indispensable to the study of their work; and Renaissance dramatists were just as self-conscious in their use of metaphors of sound to describe the business they had in hand. But if we try to find in recent criticism a replacement term for *vision*, by which we could allow for hearing as a means of simultaneously apprehending systems of patterns, we have to acknowledge the poverty of our critical vocabulary. What is the aural equivalent of a vision? The only modern critical term that comes to mind here is *voice*, the very fuzziness of which has made it an invaluable aid to reviewers.

PROBLEMS OF FORM

Modern criticism of verse in Renaissance drama may also be uncertain in its conception of whole plays because so much of it has grown out of criticism of the lyric. We could return at this point to Eliot's essays, which helped so much to stimulate interest in this drama. It is obvious that Eliot's own needs as a poet guided his preoccupations as an essayist and reviewer, and that these needs provided, at least for a time, a foundation for our reading of dramatic poetry. When Eliot's attitudes toward blank verse underwent changes, his concerns as a critic naturally widened beyond Renaissance drama into studies of dramatic form and style in general. In one crucial respect, though, subsequent criticism of English verse drama in the Renaissance has remained peculiarly indebted to Eliot's early reviews and essays, and that is in the assumption that verse in drama has a generic relationship to the short poem. The passages Eliot offered for inspection imply that the poetry of this drama is to be found in shorter patches; his criticism suggests that the best guides to reading dramatic verse are the Poe-Baudelaire-Gautier dicta on short forms. The example of Eliot's own poetry, especially that which was written at the time of the influential essays on early drama, shows a similar concern for intense yet fragmented forms; in his prose there is also the reiterated conviction that the long form is as impossible for us as it was for the Jacobeans, because of the assumed social and intellectual disintegration that has attacked both cultures. Despite his stance, there is no question that Eliot was one of the most sensitive readers of blank verse we have ever had; the difficulty for us lies in the way his method as a critic of Renaissance drama was inseparable from the rest of his aesthetic program. Focusing on soliloquies and passages of charged dialogue, an Eliot essay on a Jacobean dramatist *looked* on paper like an Eliot essay on a seventeenth-century poet. Both set the same kind of limits on the material brought up for inspection, and gravitated toward material with a fairly narrow range of tones. By these means, the poetry of the period became the adopted kin of the drama, notwithstanding the historical inaccuracies of that link, and has remained so to this day; some recent surveys of literary history still announce that the closest equivalent to the verse of Jacobean drama is the poetry of John Donne.[46]

It is true that this dogma does have a tidy bit of sanction in Sir Richard Baker's well-known description of Donne as "a great frequenter of plays."[47] But in the context of Donne's poetry this biographical note turns out to be alarmingly unrevealing. It would be nice to know that Donne had seen something besides the first part of *Tamburlaine,* yet this is the only explicit dramatic reference that we get in the corpus of his poetry; his verse letters, a form poets have long used to describe life in the city, also appear to have only one vague reference to the theater.[48] Even his prose spoof of 1604, the *Catalogus Librorum Aulicorum,* contains (as Evelyn Simpson has noted) not a single reference to a playwright, although it pillories most of the important literary figures of the time.[49] Either Donne did not regard drama as a form of writing, or it made little impression on him altogether; certainly the experience of the drama mattered so little that it did not get into the poetry, unlike cartography or anatomy or alchemy. One explanation for the inconsistency between Baker's remark and the body of Donne's work may be that the note is actually something of a commonplace, echoed by many other writers talking about fashionable men-about-town; Nashe, for example, says "my vagrant Reveller haunts Plaies, and sharpens his wits with frequenting the company of Poets."[50] Baker's anecdote may be no more revealing or personal than would our noting of a modern novelist that he liked to go to the movies.

Of course even Donne's verified attendance at plays would not establish a connection between his poetry and contemporary drama, and other more serious objections may be raised to the idea that the two are naturally linked. For example, Donne's lyrics were hardly the first to place speakers in situations with a presumed listener or conversant; many of Sidney's lyrics are no less "dramatic"; and there is also that model for nearly everything, *The Shepheardes Calendar.* Dramatic monologues on love in particular are not one of Donne's unique inventions. The Elizabethans knew that Ovid's elegies, for example, are also plausible relatives for many speeches in plays that deal with the trials of a lover; Kempe is made to say to Burbage in Part 2 of *The Return from Parnassus* that "Few of the university pen plaies well, they smell too much of that writer Ovid."[51] The bookish antecedents of so much in Elizabethan drama make it hard to draw a simple parallel to the work of John Donne; instead we have, in this case, a tangent point at Ovid, who sent Donne off to his elegies and the university men off to drama.

In any case, the whole issue of literary pedigrees may be beside the point if we stop to consider the fundamental differences between poetry and drama, differences that we are often inclined to overlook but that ought to direct our understanding of the way poetry works in drama. The difference in audience is most immediate if not absolutely crucial. Poems are written for readers, but plays are written for audiences— literally, listeners. Here we must anticipate some of the argument of the next chapter, and note that in time those audiences also became readers, increasingly voracious ones at that, and they tended to listen to plays in the same way they read poetry on the page. Along with their reading came a growing power to elicit certain kinds of dramatic writing. The Elizabethan and Jacobean audience formed what Stanley Fish has called an "interpretive community," which could, by its special expectations and abilities, promote the development of dramatic blank verse. As Fish proposes, "it is interpretive communities, rather than either the text or the reader, that produce meanings and are responsible for the emergence of formal features. Interpretive communities are made up of those who share interpretive strategies not for reading but for writing texts, for constituting their properties."[52] Thus we shall see the apparent anomalies of an audience that can listen to a performance as though it were a text, and a playwright who can produce a text more notable for its verbal properties than its existence in print.

It is of course true that the dramatist may have been utterly indifferent to the reception of his work in print; Gerald Eades Bentley has pointed out that while many dramatists wrote for both playgoers and readers, many others—including Shakespeare—showed no interest in them whatever.[53] Bentley's argument is concise and strong, his examples persuasive albeit circumstantial; and still one has reservations. While a dramatist may show no concern for setting up and supervising the printing of his plays, that hardly means he despises readers; he may simply be busy writing, producing, and rehearsing his next play. (We could remember here that for somewhat similar reasons, William Faulkner often could not be bothered to correct and return his galleys.) Shakespeare's alleged indifference cannot logically be taken to mean that the text is not a literary document faute de mieux, in addition to being a recipe for a performance. Shakespeare's failure to address dedications or prefaces to the reader does not prove that his plays went unread: there is no reason to regard the work of any Elizabethan or Jacobean dramatist as a form of literature that predates writing, like the *Iliad* or the New Testament. Armed with study of Elizabethan acting styles, prosodic theory, and critical attitudes toward dramatic poetry, we may be in a position to recover from the text much useful information about its poetry and about the structure of the whole play—whether or not the dramatist pondered much on us or corrected his proof.

It is important also to remember, however, Bentley's stricture that "we ought to question the relevance of Shakespeare criticism which ignores the theaters and insists on the importance of recondite patterns of word play inaudible to the ear of any audience."[54] Study of a play's blank verse will take us back to the theater because the text conveys, through its poetic rhythms, a kind of information that the Renaissance audience could hear. Francis Berry has put the matter nicely in his fascinating book *Poetry and the Physical Voice,* where he says of Shakespeare (and this could apply to other dramatists too) that he seemed able to imagine "a vocal identity outside himself," and could "catch the voice ... sufficiently for later players to reproduce [it] from the printed signs."[55] In more up-to-the-minute terms, the verse of a Renaissance play is nothing less than a "sub-text,"[56] the significance of which would have been apparent to a contemporary audience but which has since been obscured. Use of that fashionable term should not block the main point, however, which is that the verse is *the* text, not a buried or latent set of meanings. Neither *sub* nor *infra*, it is our only means of getting to *any* meanings, apart from those in gesture and costume.

Returning to the basic distinction between the audience of lyric and the audience of drama, we can understand why study of the rhythms of lyric poetry has been far more systematic and detailed than that of dramatic blank verse, although drama is equally dependent upon verbal rhythms to convey its meanings. Because the Elizabethan reader of lyric poetry could retrace his steps at every point, juxtaposing and combining in "recondite patterns," he need not have been so thoroughly dependent on taking in meanings through the ear. If he chose, he could ignore the rhythms altogether. One can also think of many poems in the Renaissance that achieved great fame or notoriety when they had been read only in manuscript and presumably in private; but there is no instance of this occurring with the text of a play. Whatever a reader's own predispositions, in other words, when he went to a play he would have to deal in one way or another with the movement of the blank verse, and the actors would not have let him forget it.

On the immediate level of craft, there is also a kind of economy in a poem—however long or verbose it may be—that does not and cannot work in poetic drama. The poem creates its own time scheme, most conspicuously by virtue of its length. In the case of a lyric that can be seen as a whole on the page, we have inevitable expectations of an ending, with an intensification or reversal.[57] In the matter of a speaker too there is a certain economy that a poem observes. A verse letter or a satire usually contains only one speaker, a lyric two at most (one of whom may be dignified as an echo), and the poem is a document of the time passing in the mind of the speaker or speakers. That time need not be a continuous flow on the clock; in "A Lecture upon the Shadow" no more time elapses for the speaker than for the readers; "The Good-Morrow" moves back and forth in time, but the movement is still presumed to occur in a present reflection, just as it does in "They flee from me," which also moves out from a mind thinking continuously and discretely in a present.

In a play the control of time is far different, because any given speech exists within a time scheme established by the play as a whole. A poetic speech in drama has a pressure impinging upon it from the action, which generates the speech and contains it. Consider Richard II's last soliloquy, the one beginning "I have been studying how I may compare / This prison where I live unto the world." Standing between the flow of time in the play that precedes it and the flow of time that follows it, this meditation has been generated by events that cannot be present in the speech itself and to which it does not allude. The meaning of even so isolated a speech as this soliloquy must encompass those events around it, and this dependence of the individual speech, its great vulnerability, stands in contrast to the enclosure of the lyric. No matter how much the lyrist may assure us that there are events that preceded or will follow the poem ("Let's act the rest"), they are not events that we have seen or heard, and they exist as possibilities only as long as the lyrist goes on talking about them. A dramatic speech, on the other hand, lives among many speeches, presupposes and requires those other speeches. This assumption or presupposition would appear to be fundamental to drama, and it is not until the work of Samuel Beckett that we encounter a radical attempt to forestall or destroy it. In the case of Richard's soliloquy, the ironies are especially full because Richard's speech also happens to be *about* time; Richard sees his own isolation as parallel to the isolation of any moment in time. One imagines that for a self-conscious dramatist, the way in which all the poetry of a play can impinge upon a single speech must produce a confining hubbub, a great reckoning in a little room; so it must be for Beckett, who had been unsparing in his raids upon the articulate. To the lyric poet the metaphysical tidiness of a poem's self-enclosure can prove equally stifling; or so we may read several of Shakespeare's sonnets. Just as modern dramatists have tried to free themselves from the idea of sequential speeches, so poets since Mallarmé have tried by a variety of means to escape from the confines of lyric time, most often by such arbitrary means as separating chunks of the poem with asterisks or white space, or scrambling sentences or words.

Because our understanding of one speech in drama is conditioned by our understanding of the speeches around it, we can often hear the rhythms and accents of one speech within another. The rhythm of Hamlet's "To be, or not to be, that is the question" contains in itself the hesitant moves and final plunge that typify his speeches and actions throughout the whole play, and the third soliloquy in particular gains from these rhythmic associations. These patterns are also inseparable from the ideas that Hamlet thinks about. The process might be described as a sort of intellectual and audible version of the Doppler effect, in which one idea resonates with another. It is the sort of effect that was impossible to achieve with the lyric or narrative forms available in the seventeenth century, in which no different voices intrude upon the single speaker, who proceeds straight through the poem or alternates consistently with another speaker; there is no long hiatus, no interrupting voice, that can come between what is said at one point and what is said at another. (An exception might be claimed for the sonnet cycle as a lyric form that can generate resonances; but there the formal constraints necessarily make the effect of brief duration.) Reverberation of the sort described here can also occur between the speeches of different characters. The effect may be simply reinforcing, as in the intense and measured dialogues in *The Broken Heart*, or it may be ironic, as in the distorted echoes between the speeches of the Greeks and the Trojans in *Troilus and Cressida*. Again, this sort of echoing need not be simply lexical (a repeated word or phrase), or imagistic (a common metaphor), or discursive (the repetition of similar ideas); instead it may also involve, in addition to these, repeated and varied patterns in rhythm, secondary sounds (alliteration, assonance, or consonance), or syntax. Often the echoes will involve one or more of these elements.[58] Although not all such resonances may be discursive, they may still be linked with discursive meanings, and here perhaps the best analogy might be the leitmotif in music. Although variously employed before, this term has seldom been used to refer to the recurrence of patterns in verse rhythm that may extend over a whole play. When the last movemement of a symphony ends with an inversion of a theme that began the first movement, the precise musical relationship between the two themes may be understood only by the performers and such musicians as may be in the audience; but the audience will still be affected by this sort of resonance, even if they are not able to articulate much about the resemblance-within-contrast they have heard. In the case of poetic drama, we are all musicians.

These matters lead to more specific problems of form, and here too the differences between dramatic speeches and separate poems are substantial enough to preclude any simple equation between the two. The very limits of the two forms are evident: unlike a poem, a dramatic speech need not resolve all or any of its problems—logical, linguistic, or prosodic—before it comes to an end. This structural open-endedness of dramatic verse has some local consequences. In seventeenth-century poetry, form is usually an extension of content; each poem is the expression of a unique emotion or idea, the elaboration of which requires a unique form—and thus the enormous range of lines and stanzas in the poetry of Donne, Herbert, Vaughan, and others. However, high Renaissance drama generally eschews the resources of stanzaic form (except in the occasional song), and movement within the single line and through a speech becomes the dramatist's chief way of relating form to content. In the absence of enforced termination, or the formally required closure of a group of lines, dramatic blank verse has to live along the line, generating its own momentum and applying its own brakes. This may provide another reason why modern criticism of the lyric is relatively sophisticated, while criticism of blank verse has remained somewhat primitive; formal variation in a seventeenth-century poem is more easily seen on the page and more accessible to the modern reader.[59]

One last difference between lyric poetry and blank verse drama is so broad that one almost hesitates to call it a term of comparison: the way that poetry "means" in drama is as variable as all the other elements of dramatic meaning. One dramatist will think in terms of the single character, another in groups of characters; one will think in terms of visual images, associating them with particular metrical patterns, while another will be more interested in plot, the pattern and repetition of event as reflected in the currents of the verse; and yet another will think of poetry as a function of physical movement, in the combining and recombining of people on the stage. One dramatist may use poetry to supply a human dimension that the characterization or action may lack;[60] another may attempt instinctively to resolve problems in plot or structure by a deep investment in the poetry. Depending upon his friends, the crowds (or lack of them) at the gate, or the state of his acting company, the dramatic poet may attempt any or all of these strategies, successively or coincidentally. Generalizations finally become impossible because in each play, the poetry creates something like the law of gravity in a unique universe.

Dramatists who work in the medium know the power of poetry, and know a fact that criticism has a hard time coping with: poetry can easily take over a play. In several essays Eliot has remarked this problem, noting the effort that the modern poet must make in "disciplining his poetry, and putting it, so to speak, on a very thin diet in order to adapt it to the needs of the stage."[61] Good illustrations of this could also come from the work of two other modern dramatists. The history of the performance and publication of Archibald MacLeish's *J.B.* shows how the poetic dramatist can have a tiger (or at least a large tabby) by the tail. The first version of *J.B.*, as performed by the Yale School of Drama in April 1958, differs greatly from the Broadway version performed in December of that year; in the intervening months, revisions in the poetry, especially a general toning down, occupied both MacLeish and the director, Elia Kazan.[62] Arthur Miller's solution to the dominance of poetry was even more radical: after writing *The Crucible* entirely in verse, he leveled it all into prose.[63] Because poetry still has enormous powers of suggestion, even in a prosy age, it has to be curbed so we do not miss, for example, the philosophical ponderables of *J.B.;* in both cases the writers were reluctant to turn the poetry loose. One shudders to think what Robert Graves and his Goddess would say.

Whether the dramatist freely commits his play to poetry or not, it still can remain a source of enchantment, sometimes despite his best didactic concern. As just one example, there is Malheureux's speech on love and nature in *The Dutch Courtesan*, in which Marston's poetic sympathies are clearly on the side of the central character in all his anguish, even while the design of the play is didactically framed to show his pride and vicious folly. For some writers there is an inevitable tension between what has to be said, and the system of sound that the play wants to become. It would be a mistake to assume that the audience is the only subject of the poetic enchantment, although the poet's own engagement would be hard to track and is probably irrelevant in the end.

What is most important is understanding the centripetal force of the poetry itself, and the way it carries us all—including dramatists—past the stage action deep into states of mind that we could hardly approach in any other way. As Eliot has said:

> beyond the namable, classifiable emotions and motives of our conscious life when directed toward action—the part of life which prose drama is wholly adequate to express—there is a fringe of indefinite extent, of feeling which we can only detect, so to speak, out of the corner of the eye and can never completely focus; of feeling of which we are only aware in a kind of temporary detachment from action. . . . This peculiar range of sensibility can be expressed by dramatic poetry, at its moments of greatest intensity. At such moments, we touch the border of those feelings which only music can express.[64]

The formulation is admirable, but one might wonder if the poetry is so inaccessibly numinous that we have to stop here. Renaissance dramatists and audiences agreed in specific terms about that corner of the eye—a telling and modern metaphor—and now we should turn our attention to the bounds of their agreement.

CONTEXTS OF
BLANK VERSE DRAMA

AN UNDERSTANDING AUDITORY

The first point to stress about the poetry of Tudor and Stuart drama is that the audience could hear it, and a definition of *audience* could begin at the bottom, in the pit of the theater. Even the most unsophisticated listeners could respond to the movements of the blank verse, and were doing so well before 1600. Joseph Hall, describing a performance of *Tamburlaine,* says that if the author

> can with words Italianate,
> Big-sounding sentences, and words of state,
> Faire patch me up his pure *Iambick* verse,
> He ravishes the gazing scaffolders.[1]

In his emphasis upon "pure *Iambick* verse," Hall implies that the rhetoric is present to satisfy the demands of the poetry; modern readers, encountering Renaissance drama via modern critical concerns, usually have tended to see rhetoric as the sponsor of the verse. But for Hall the effect of the combination is plain enough: as long as the ten-syllable, five-stress line keeps coming, the groundlings will be in ecstasy.

This view of the affective power of verse was widely held, and much of the hostility toward the theater at this time was based upon it. Poetry in drama broke down the playgoer's moral resistance, making him likely to commit the indecent acts counterfeited upon the stage. The opponents of the theater also held the traditional antipathy toward any merely human language that would aspire to this power of moving; in Northrop Frye's terms, the conflict was that between true and false rhetoric, Word and oracle, and the false words always lead to false visual images.[2] Elizabethan moralists would have understood this perfectly; Hall's description suggests that there was some truth to the Puritans' claims that once he heard the measures of the poetry, the playgoer was somehow reduced to complete pliability and helplessness. As Stephen Gosson said eighteen years before

Hall, "cookes did never shewe more crafte in their junckets to vanquish the taste, nor Painters in their shadowes to allure the eye, then Poets in Theaters to wounde the conscience. There set they abroche straunge consortes of melody, to tickle the eare."[3] The costumes and gestures of the actors, all the visual spectacle of the drama, are immediately impressive but not as poisonous as the words of the poet: "these by the privie entries of the eare, slip downe into the hart, and with the gunshotte of affection gaule the minde, where reason and vertue should rule the roste."[4] Vice begins with verse, and there is no telling where it will stop:

> I should tel tales out of the Schoole, and bee Ferruled for my faulte, or hyssed at for a blab, yf I layde al the orders open before your eyes. You are no sooner entred [the theater], but libertie looseth the reynes, and geves you head, placing you with Poetrie in the lowest forme: when his skill is showne too make Scholer as good as ever twangde, he preferres you too Pyping, from Pyping to playing, from play to pleasure, from pleasure to slouth, from slouth too sleepe, from sleepe to sinne, from sinne to death, from death to the devill, if you take your learning apace, and passe through every forme without revolting.[5]

One need not get into Gosson's moral roller coaster to accept his idea of the power of poetry, and to be sure, the best poetic drama that he could have heard in 1579 would have been hardly musical compared to what lay ahead. But battle lines had been long in the drawing, for since the later Middle Ages poetry had come to be increasingly central in the dramatic effect,[6] and by the 1590s, the ability of the audience to discriminate among types of dramatic poetry was developing more rapidly than Gosson could have feared. Marlowe, for example, reminds his awestruck listeners that the poetry of *Tamburlaine* is a corrective to the earlier "jigging vaines of riming mother wits."[7] (*Rhyming* has of course the same general meaning as *versifying*.) The growth in poetic sensitivity and understanding on the part of the audience after the late 1590s must have been rapid, and it was apparently not the result of great changes in schooling or some startling new comprehension of critical dogma. From the standpoint of verse technique, the plays offered to audiences became more sophisticated with each passing year, but the sources of that new awareness were much deeper than technique alone. As Moody Prior has said, "The increase in metrical variety and flexibility was not only the result of defter handling of metrics, or even of closer approximation to ordinary speech; it was a function also of a change from rhetorical, patterned ordering of the diction to what might be called, in contrast, a poetic ordering."[8]

While tastes became more discriminating, the deep affective power of poetry still remained, perhaps because, as Prior suggests, it had adopted more flexible forms of ordering. Fifteen years after Hall's note on

Tamburlaine, at the height of Jacobean stage writing, Thomas Dekker describes this power in the Prologue to *If This Be Not a Good Play, the Devil Is in It* (1612). According to Dekker, even the coarsest and most illiterate laborer will be attracted to the drama as if by a supernatural force, and will respond to the music of its poetry. The verse, Dekker says,

> Can call the *Banished* Auditor home, And tye
> His Eare (with golden chaines) to his Melody:
> Can draw with *Adamantine Pen,* (even creatures
> Forg'de out of th'*Hammer,*) on tiptoe, to *Reach*-up,
> And (from *Rare silence*) clap their *Brawny hands,*
> T'*Applaud,* what their *charmd* soule scarce understands.[9]
>
> [31–36]

Dekker's idea has a long history—the music of poetry is supposed to reach the soul directly, without the necessary control of the understanding—and his implied distinction between faculties and understanding appears often in contemporary dramatic criticism. In *Plays Confuted in five Actions* (1582), Gosson says that plays have great power

> by the manner of penning in these dayes, because the Poets send their verses to the Stage upon such feete as continually are rowled up in rime at the fingers endes, which is plaucible to the barbarous, and carrieth a stinge into the eares of the common people. By the object, because Tragedies and Commedies stirre up affections, and affections are naturally planted in that part of the minde that is common to us with brute beasts.[10]

The same assumption stands behind John Webster's statement "To the Reader" that he is publishing *The White Devil* because the performance of the play "wanted (that which is the only grace and setting out of a tragedy) a full and understanding auditory."[11] Or as Ben Jonson points out in the Prologue to *The Staple of News* (1626), he is offering the play

> To *Schollers,* that can judge, and faire report
> The sense they heare, above the vulgar sort
> Of Nut-crackers, that onely come for sight.[12]
>
> [6–8]

It must not have been uncommon to see poets and scholars in the audience, listening critically to the meter of every line. In the Praeludium for Thomas Goffe's *The Careless Shepherdess* (c. 1620?), a group gathers to "passe our sentences upon this Play" and "censure [its] Poetry," while citizen Thrift exclaims, "O that I had my Gown!"[13] Everyone knew a play was, in Thomas Heywood's words, "an elaborate and ingenious poem."[14]

However, the opinions of poets were not always as judicious as Jonson implies in his prologue. Henry Fitzgeffrey describes (in a satire from 1618, upon the way that poets turn everything into meter) the behavior of jealous writers and critics at a play:

> See then how (*Envy*) gin's her eyes to fat
> On dainties plenty, and repines thereat!
> How mutteringly *Momus* (that knows not to bite)
> Grumbles and mumbles mouthfuls of spite.
> How currish (*Critticks*) most severely harke:
> Ready at each round of applause to barke.[15]

And a similar scene is described in the Induction to *The Poetaster* (1601), where Envy asks the audience to fill itself with venom and

> Helpe me to damne the Authour. Spit it forth
> Upon his lines, and shew your rustie teeth
> At everie word, or accent.
>
> [46-48]

Special pleading on behalf of weaker poets was common, and prologues often made touching disclaimers that praised the taste of the audience; as Dekker says in the Prologue to *Old Fortunatus* (1600), his "timorous Muse" is seized by

> a benumming feare,
> (That your nice soules, cloyd with dilicious sounds,
> Will loath her lowly notes).
>
> [4-6]

Given the critical members of the audience, it should not be surprising that many dramatists assure us that they have no intention of gratifying our taste for verse. In the Preface "To the World" of *Satiromastix* (1602), Dekker cheerfully admits that "the limmes of my naked lines may bee and I know have bin, tortur'd on the racke" (ll.43-44); John Marston, writing with his usual abrasiveness "To the Generall Reader" of *Sophonisba* (1606), says that "To transcribe Authors, quote Authorities, & translate *Latin* prose orations into English blank-verse, hath in this subject beene the least aime of my studies."[16]

The widespread demand for dramatic blank verse also must have ensured from the beginning that the ranks of dramatic poets would include a fair number of quacks. Nashe ridicules the pretensions of these fakes, whose wretched verse is a projection of their general inadequacy as human beings: they are

> ideot Art-masters, that intrude themselves to our eares as the Alcumists of eloquence, who (mounted on the stage of arrogance) thinke to out-brave better pennes with the swelling bumbast of

bragging blanke verse. Indeede it may bee the ingrafted overflow of some kil-cow conceit, that overcloyeth their imagination with a more then drunken resolution, being not extemporall in the invention of any other meanes to vent their manhoode, [and] commits the disgestion of their cholericke incumbrances to the spacious volubilitie of a drumming decasillabon.[17]

This is the level to which Greene tries to reduce Shakespeare, by saying that he "supposes he is as well able to bumbast out a blanke verse as the best of you."[18] The whole business of verse drama is so repellent to Hall, so full of intellectual fraud, that eventually he rejects it altogether, emphasizing in particular the link between its emptiness of content and its sloppiness of technique:

> Too popular is *Tragick Poesie,*
> Strayning his tip-toes for a farthing fee,
> And does besides on *Rimeless* numbers tread [:]
> Unbid *Iambicks* flow from carelesse head.[19]

Hall's conclusion: Better to stay home and read *The Faerie Queene.*

The better poets all proclaimed their alarm at the shameless ineptitude of the hacks with their unbid iambics. In the Prologue to his *The Northern Lasse* (1632), Richard Brome announces that he has a "Modestie/Unus'd'mong Poets,"[20] and Ben Jonson's poem prefatory to the play also takes the now familiar line of attack:

> Now each Court-Hobby-Horse will wince in rime;
>   Both learned, and unlearned, all write *Playes.*
> It was not so of old: Men took up their trades
>   That knew the Crafts they had been bred in, right:
> An honest *Bilbo*-Smith would make good blades,
>   And the *Physician* teach men spue, or shite;
>   The Cobler kept him to his nail; but, now
>   Hee'll be a *Pilot,* scarce can guide a Plough.[21]

The writings of verse drama seemed a mania of epidemic proportions; in the Praeludium to *The Careless Shepherdess* Brome has his character Thrift say that

> I do fear that writing Playes, will make
> Our Inns of Court-men Truants in the Law.
> Shortly they will be *Ovid*-like, who could
> Not chuse but put Indentures into Verse.
> E're I am Sheriff, I warrant we shall have
> Master-Recorder rhime upon the Bench.[22]

As Jonson says to the reader of *The Alchemist* (1610), "thou wert never more fair in the way to be cos'ned (then in this Age) in *Poetry,* especially in Playes" (ll. 4-5). In his self-appointed capacity as arbiter elegantiarum of the English stage, Jonson led a tireless and often tiresome battle against hack dramatic poets, prosecuted most directly in 1601 with *The Poetaster.* At the climax of this play set in Rome, a pretentious poet is sentenced to take some emetic pills compounded by Horace, whereupon he vomits up a whole basin full of inflated language and bad lines; as one of Caesar's court asks, "Who would have thought there should ha'beene such a deale of filth in a *poet*?" (5.3.490-91). The prescription for good poetic health is to read the best classical authors, and then to quit torturing the pentameter line in order to make it contain outlandish words and phrases.[23] Fortunately, few took the recommended medicine, and Jacobean stage writing went on to gain as much variety in style as it did in quality.

If the dramatists' pretensions got in the way of good verse, the conflicts between the playhouses also contributed their part. Then as now, the better companies got the better plays, with only a few exceptions; in the process, they also got the better poetry. We are used to regarding the differences between the theaters as being expressive of economic or class differences, but they also reflected quite different attitudes toward poetry. Actors at the northside playhouses apparently had a looser, prosier, shouting style; those at the Bankside theaters favored a more "musical" style that followed the contours of the verse.[24] When the actor John Shank left the Fortune Theater in 1613 to join the Globe, William Turner satirized his lyrical delivery of the lines, saying that

> Since *Shancke* did leave to sing his rhimes,
>> He is counted but a gull:
> The players on the Bankside,
>> The round Globe and the Swan,
> Will teach you idle tricks of love,
>> But the Bull will play the man.

And writing shortly before the closing of the theaters, Leonard Digges curses the "Vermine" imitators of Shakespeare's "exquisite" poetry by saying "On Gods name may the Bull or Cockpit have / Your lame blancke Verse, to keep you from the grave."[25] You went to the Bankside if you wanted to listen to the verse, to Clerkenwell if you wanted straight heroics, on or off the stage.

At the heart of the interest in dramatic poetry is a concern for the line itself. Audiences could hear the blank verse line emerge and take shape, and their ability to do this gives the point to literally hundreds of speeches and scenes in English Renaissance drama.[26] Consider one familiar example from *As You Like It.* Rosalind is talking as Orlando enters:

Rosalind. And your experience makes you sad. I had rather
              have a fool make me merry than experience
              make me sad—and to have to travel for it too!
Orlando.   Good day and happiness, dear Rosalind!
Jaques.   Nay then God buy you, and you talk in blank verse.

                                                [4.1.27-32]

In order for the joke to work, the audience must have had an instant
grasp of Orlando's line as a rhythmic unit. Not only do we laugh at
Orlando's infatuation, with its unconscious artiness; we also laugh at
Jaques and his exotic sensibilities, which will not permit him to remain
in the presence of metered language. The wit of the whole passage is
then enlarged when we realize that Rosalind too would have heard the
strained music of Orlando's entrance, for she has already commented on
his poetic abilities. In a flagrant case of environmental degradation committed in the name of art, Orlando has been hanging poems in the trees
of Arden, and Rosalind's judgment of these is that "the feet were lame,
and could not bear themselves without the verse, and therefore stood
lamely in the verse" (3.2.169-71). A nice discrimination, closer than the
one that Touchstone had made a few lines before: the feet of Orlando's
verse are not simply monotonous, as they would be if they had "a very
false gallop," but instead are present only to satisfy the prosodic demands
of the line. Rosalind is a keen judge of poetry, but when Orlando enters
in creaking blank verse a few scenes later, she says—virtually nothing
in the way of criticism. She bids the disgusted Jaques farewell, and chides
Orlando for being late. Love tames even the stylistic critic.

In the memorial verses he wrote for the Shakespeare Folio, Jonson
praised Shakespeare's "well torned, true filed lines,"[27] and their accuracy
originates in Shakespeare's instinctive sense of the way verse movement
conveys character and action. His plays offer countless examples of this
gift; we might glance at one that has a degree of self-consicousness rather
higher than that in the lines from *As You Like It*. When Hamlet tells
the Players that "the lady shall say her mind freely, or the blank verse
shall halt for't" (2.2.324-25), we know that the audience Hamlet imagines would be able to hear the lady's meter and tell when it was lame.
If she is to "speak her mind," presumably her language will convey some
agitation or disturbance; and that agitation must be very different from
the agitation of halting and lame meters. Upon numerous details of this
kind turn Hamlet's ideas about emotional excess and the proper bounds
of art.

Even while listening to speeches of great surge and excitement, an
audience could have understood the point Hamlet is making. In Thomas
May's play *The Heir* (1620), one character describes an actor playing
Hieronimo, saying that while he performed, "Ladies in the boxes/Kept

time with sighs and tears to his sad accents."[28] *The Spanish Tragedy* is not a play generally noted for its musical subtlety, but Hieronimo's lament does have a number of expressive variations, which those cultivated ladies could mark like moist metronomes. Certainly the Elizabethan listener's recognition of blank verse lines did not depend upon those lines being regular. A sophisticated audience, like that for which we assume *Love's Labour's Lost* was written, would have been able to hear the meter of the verse and the rhythmic patterns superimposed upon it. The deflation of Berowne's feeble poetry takes no time at all because the audience has independently confirmed Holofernes's metrical analysis:

> Let me supervise the canzonet. Here are only the numbers ratified,
> but for the elegancy, facility, and golden cadence of poetry, *caret*.
>
> [4.2.121–23]

That Holofernes can do no better himself does not invalidate his criticism. As the distinction between "numbers" and "cadence" implies, scholarly audiences had no trouble following the meters and could hear superimposed variations of great complexity. Throughout the Renaissance, Latin plays continued to be acted at the universities, where accuracy in at least "ratifying the numbers" would have been taken for granted; and of course many of the dramatists and players were university men, whose academic concerns affected their understanding of the popular stage. Joseph Hall says that at performances of plays, poets sit up in the better seats and weigh every word like classical scholars:

> Meane while our Poets in high Parliament,
> Sit watching every word, and gesturement,
> Like curious Censors of some doughtie geare,
> Whispering their verdit in their fellowes eare.
> Wo to the word whose margent in their scrole
> Is noted with a black condemning cole.

This is nothing less than instant line-by-line analysis, a form of quick-draw criticism, often performed with a real vengeance. The surest proof that scenes like this took place is supplied by Hall himself, who later in his poem performs exactly the sort of close technical analysis he has ridiculed earlier. Cataloging different kinds of incompetence in dramatic poets, he satirizes the way an inept poet

> scorns the home-spun thread of rimes,
> Match'd with the loftie feet of elder times:
> Give him the numbred verse that *Virgil* sung,
> And *Virgill* selfe shall speake the English tung:
> *Manhood* and *garboiles* shall be chaunt with chaunged feete,
> And head-strong Dactils making *Musicke* meete [,]

> The nimble *Dactils* striving to out-go
> The drawling *Spondees* pacing it below
> The lingring *Spondees*, labouring to delay,
> The breath-lesse *Dactils* with a sudden stay.
> Who ever saw a colt wanton and wilde,
> Yok'd with a slow-foote oxe on fallow field?
> Can right areed how handsomely besets
> Dull *Spondees* with the English *Dactilets*?
> If *Jove* speake English in a thundring cloud,
> *Thwich, thwack,* and *rif raf,* rores he out loud.[29]

That an audience could distinguish among different metrical feet, while hearing lines from the stage for the very first time, might seem to the modern reader a highly implausible fiction. But it is "a ryming age," as Jonson says,[30] which takes in a great amount of information by ear. We can understand better why this might be so if we recall the facts of instruction in the English grammar school.[31] From the Middle Ages, students began with accidence and then proceeded to the pseudonymous Cato's *Distichs,* a set of simple moralizing verses, and this traditional pattern continued into the Renaissance.[32] What came after that most elementary level of study, though, tended to stress poetry far more and in very different ways than was common in earlier centuries. The great Tudor teachers and humanists all emphasized the importance of conducting as much early education as possible through the medium of verse, not only because the "matter" of the study was more easily retained, but also because the study itself was more delightful. John Colet emphasized the use of poetry in the lower forms, and asked Erasmus to give him some verses to use in St. Paul's School; Juan Vives, whose influence upon English education was exceeded among the Europeans only by that of Erasmus, urged the study of poetry in both the classical languages and the vernacular, recommending that it be reinforced with frequent composition of original verses; and Roger Ascham (like Vives) stressed the importance of assigning exercises in double verse translation.[33] Sir Thomas Elyot went so far as to say that up to the age of thirteen, students should study most subjects through poetry alone, because poetry is the language of childhood, both of the race and the individual. Grammar, logic, rhetoric, and above all the great expositions of moral values should be encountered first in poetry, Elyot said, while a student is still in his formative years; prose can come later, after his habits of mind are formed.[34] Although the writers Elyot recommended are suited to a Renaissance taste, the method itself is of some antiquity. In the later Middle Ages and early Renaissance, students had learned grammar, social behavior, and simple ethics not just through the *Distichs* but also through the homely verses of the *vulgaria*; it was only an updated version of one of these that William Lyly offered in 1528, setting out in some eighty Latin verses a concise behavior manual that covers everything from washing in the morning to reading the best authors.[35]

From a student's point of view, poetry was inescapable. You did not have to be a Jaques to hear an incipient line of verse. The youngest pupils, or "petties" as they were called, got poetry in their grammar and catechism, as well as in obligatory readings from the Book of Psalms. Verse composition in Latin was a standard part of the curriculum at all levels, and its pervasiveness may explain why it was a principal target of later attempts at educational reform; John Locke, for example, though he believed Latin to be absolutely necessary, regarded verse composition as both unreasonable and tormenting.[36] Before long, poetry even managed to invade ciphering: in 1600 a schoolmaster named Thomas Hylles actually produced a text of the self-help variety, a full set of rhymed rules for mathematics titled *The Art of Vulgar Arithmetic*.[37] The most rudimentary education for future tradesmen also began with verse lessons of the names of implements, as in Thomas Newbery's *Dives Pragmaticus* (1563):

> I have ladels, scummers, aundyrons and spits,
> Dripping pannes, pothookes, ould cats and kits
> And pretty fine dogs without fleas or nits.[38]

At one point or another in a student's formal education, nearly every subject would be mediated by verse. From the earliest times some *vulgaria* had included metrical vocabularies, and early dictionaries were often designed specifically to be of help in the exercise of double verse translation; as Peter Levins says in his *Manipulus Vocabulorum* (1570), the book was compiled not just "for scholars that want variety of words, but also for such as use to write in English metre."[39] It is encouraging that as a result of this comprehensive program, students would use poetry to deface their books.[40]

The emphasis upon poetry in language instruction was not confined to Latin, or to those schools that were run by the great schoolmasters. Systematic study of English grammar and English poets, which the humanists had recommended, had begun by Jacobean times to employ relatively contemporary materials, such as Meres's *Palladis Tamia* or Allot's *England's Parnassus*.[41] Of course the ideal goal of proficiency in letters remained the study of Latin poets and prose writers, but the rise of the vernacular curriculum, and its use of recent authors, must have affected the way in which classical studies were undertaken.[42] Steeped as we are in modern educational theory, we sometimes need to remind ourselves that at its best the Renaissance curriculum was no less "creative" than our own, and it may have made less distinction than we do between the making of literature and the study of it. Sophisticated as this fundamental identification may seem, it was also recognized outside the major city schools.

When the archbishop of York wrote the statutes for Chigwell Grammar School in 1629, he specified that "the Latin schoolmaster be a Graduate of one of the Universities, not under Seven-and-twenty Years of Age, a Man skilful in the Greek and Latin tongues, a good Poet, of a sound Religion, neither *Papist* nor *Puritan*, of a grave Behaviour, of a sober and honest Conversation, no Tipler nor Haunter of Alehouses, no *Puffer* of *Tobacco*; and above all, that he be apt to teach and severe in his government."[43] The requirement that the applicant be "a good Poet" is of particular interest (although it seems at odds with the bounds put on his private life), for it suggests the extent to which teaching in the language was rooted in "making," or artistic composition; that ability, and the skill in the languages, constitute the only genuine intellectual requirements for the job. The description suggests that poetry was seen as a force in motion, not just a "course" floating autonomously in the curriculum, an educational object for reading or discussion or analysis; when the students read nondramatic poetry—Virgil, for example—they would have been expected to act out the verse in their manner of recitation. When there were no books, students had to listen to the verses under study and copy them down; once more, the poetry demanded active rather than passive assimilation.[44]

The close listening habits of Renaissance audiences seem much more understandable when we recall the aural bias of their early education. With emphasis upon verse as one of the chief means of instruction, no matter what the subject, it follows that even modestly educated persons could hear the meters of poetry as they would occur, on the stage or in everyday speech. Vendors with their street cries, ballad mongers and pitchmen, all thought, spoke, and sang in poetry; even the official guides who escorted visitors around Westminster Abbey recited biographies in doggerel verse.[45] Often we dismiss as convention the Elizabethan use of poetry in conversation, when we ought to ask if it might not have been an easy kind of transference. Ben Jonson was probably being only half facetious when he wondered how a woman could refuse him when

> I'm sure my language to her, was as sweet
> > And every close did meet
> In sentence, of as subtile feet,
> > As hath the youngest Hee,
> That sits in shadow of Apollo's tree.
> > > ["My picture Left in Scotland," 6–10]

We have seen that the Jacobean dramatic audience was well grounded in the formal techniques of poetry, and that many members of it had come to the theater expressly to hear the poetry; but we also know that many came simply for the spectacle. George Puttenham complains that many paid no attention at all to the poetry, which was where the real drama lay;

the common people, he says, "rejoyse much to be at playes and enter-
ludes, and besides their naturall ignoraunce, have at all such times their
eares so attentive to the matter, and their eyes upon the shewes of the
stage, that they take little heede to the cunning of the rime, and therefore
be as well satisfied with that which is grosse, as with any other finer and
more delicate."[46] In Eliot's familiar phrase, they were content with the
meat that the burglar had brought for the dog. Or, to use a more Platonic
metaphor from a decidedly more Platonic poet, one could quote John
Ford, who says that the plot and language of a play are as the body and
the soul:

> The Body of the Plot is drawn so faire,
> That the Soules language quickens, with fresh ayre,
>   This well-limb'd *Poëm*.[47]

The close listening that comments of this sort presuppose often was
difficult because of the noise of those who had come to the theater for
irrelevant though nonetheless professional reasons. In a poem congratulat-
ing Fitzgeffrey for his attack upon the seedier types of playgoers, John
Stephens says that throwing them out would allow us to hear the verse for
a change:

> now the Humours which oppresse *Playes* most,
> Shall (if the owners can feele shame) be lost:
> And when they so converted do allow,
> What they dislik'd once, Players must thanke you,
> And *Poets* too: for both of them will save
> Much in true Verse, which hisses might deprave:
> Since you have so refin'd their Audience,
> That now good *Playes,* will never neede defence.[48]

Ideally an audience would listen for lines while watching a play; they
would also leave with them ringing in their heads. On the lowest level this
memory would batten on the scraps from the clowns, much to the chagrin
of the Puritan opponents of the stage. One "I. H." asks in *This Worlds
Folly* (1615), "What voice is heard in our streetes? Nought but the squeaking
out of those τερετίσματα, obscaene and light Jigges, stuft with loathsome
and unheard-of Ribauldry, suckt from the poysonous dugs of Sinne-sweld
Theaters."[49] The attention of the audience was equally close on higher
levels of taste. Abraham Wright, a minor Anglican divine and a thoughtful
playgoer of Caroline times, noted in his commonplace book that *Othello*
was "a very good play both for lines and plot," although *Hamlet* was "but
an indifferent play, the lines but meane"; in *The White Devil* "the lines are
to much riming," while in Shirley's *The Martyred Soldier* "the lines [are]
indifferent but very good for the presentments."[50] The aesthetic assumptions here are important: Wright may not have been an exceptionally

perceptive critic, but he still knew that the poetry mattered as much as the plot, and he retained a general sense of the verse long enough to get home and find a pen. The remarks of both "I.H." and Wright confirm that poetry was more easily remembered than prose, as Gosson had said long before. The Puritans never forgot that fact, especially as it applied to blank verse on the stage; the "I.G." who refuted Heywood's *Apology for Actors* in 1615 was really concerned about poetry and memory when he ridiculed the false moral authority of dramatic poets, "who pretending a great deale of doctrine and wisdome, are learned, read, heard and borne away in the mind of every man."[51] It was this custom that Dekker laughed at from his own perspective, when he said that any self-respecting gull would come away from a play with the big speeches memorized.[52]

Certainly not all the poetry written for the stage was memorable; an enormous amount of it must have been mere drudge work, executed rapidly to meet no other standard than a deadline. Most theaters or companies employed what was called an "ordinary poet," whose job it was to contribute prologues or prefaces, to revise, add, and update the material bought for performances. As necessary (and often probably as mechanical) as a tailor employed to mend costumes, the ordinary poet dealt in "wit by retail," in Thomas Randolph's words.[53] Often the ordinary poet had an apprentice for help, because the work could be heavy: someone had to work in topical matter to freshen a play that had been out a while, or rewrite as the acting company changed, or launder the dialogue if the authorities found anything objectionable. This is not to say that all the ordinary poets were mere patchers or mechanics; many able playwrights worked under contract in this manner at one time or another, and doubtless they improved much of the material that passed through their hands. It is also certain that more than a few of the ordinary poets were plain hacks, whose names have been lost forever because they had only a job to do. Plays were supposed to be in verse, and it took a certain knack to grind it out. Even the sorriest company must have felt there was a minimum standard that had to be met—none were so flush that they could not have removed one more soul from the payroll—and it would not do to let the players mouth their way through the afternoon. When we look at the inferior plays of the time, it seems safest to guess that the ordinary poets functioned more as editors than artists, and on this account it is easier to understand the contempt with which the better poets regarded them. In plays by dramatists such as Shakespeare, Jonson, and Webster, poets in general and hack poets in particular appear as a ridiculous and affected lot.[54] By such a portrait the good poet flattered the taste and discernment of his audience, assuring them in so many words that poetry did matter, and that if it were filled with errors they would be justified in hooting the stuff off the stage.

THE PLAYER AND HIS ART

If audiences could hear "subtile feet," it was thanks in great part to the better actors, who took pains to convey the movement of the verse in performance. The old debate over how the Elizabethan actor spoke on the stage should not distract us from a related problem that is ultimately more important. As Muriel Bradbrook has focused the matter: "The much discussed question of whether Elizabethan acting was by modern standards conventional or naturalistic may be put in a different way: Did the poets succeed in giving the players a language which allowed the development of sympathetic audience-identification, which replaced 'discourse' and proclamation by the subtler form of introjective and projective art?"[55] The answer to this is yes; that language was simply blank verse, through which the actor could engage most profoundly the minds and feelings of his audience.

Elizabethan acting styles probably varied a good deal from actor to actor and playhouse to playhouse, but within any given style, the boundaries between verse and prose were as clear to the actors as to their listeners. There could be few more concise points of departure here than the 1604 quarto of *The Malcontent*, in which, at one break between a passage of verse and a paragraph of prose, there is the cryptic note "[He] shifteth his speech."[56] This stage direction may have been intended to signal a shift in declamatory manner, but at the least it must have involved a concern for the poetic line. Such awareness was evident in all acting styles, from those in the theaters in the north down to those on the Bankside. The Elizabethan audience would have heard, for example, that Brutus's funeral speech on Caesar was in prose and Antony's was in verse, or that Hero and Claudio spoke verse while Beatrice and Benedick spoke prose, regardless of the styles of the individual actors. Attention to the verse itself, rather than simple shifts in manner, would have been the most direct way of marking boundaries between verse and prose, particularly if we consider the criteria used to judge the proper delivery of verse.

Accuracy, correctness, just weight, discretion, and *tuning* were all terms used to describe the kind of attention the actor should give to the placement of the metrical accent, and in this respect Burbage was acknowledged to be the master of the age. His power with poetry is referred to in almost every elegy produced upon his death. According to John Davies of Hereford, writers in particular would feel the loss:

Poets, whose glory whilome was to heare
Your lines so well exprest, henceforth forbeare,
And write no more.

A few lines later Davies singles out for special notice Burbage's handling of stress or accent: "not a word did fall,/Without just weight, to ballast itt with all."[57] Burbage's close attention to detail is also praised by Flecknoe in his elegy; he describes the difference between Burbage and an ordinary actor as that between "a Ballad-singer who onely mouths it, and an excellent singer, who knows all his Graces, and can artfully vary and modulate his Voice, even to know how much breath he is to give every syllable."[58] A dead-regular iambic tick-tock was the last thing a good actor was after; ideally he would speak instead with that ease and grace of modulation that Sidney refers to as "slidingness of language."[59]

Burbage was not the only actor admired for his careful control of the verse. Michael Mohun, one of Beeston's boys, who began his career in the reign of Elizabeth and ended it well after the Restoration, was praised by the poet Nathaniel Lee, who "vented suddenly this Saying; Oh *Mohun, Mohun! Thou little Man of Mettle, if I should Write a 100 Plays, I'd write a Part for thy Mouth*; in short, in all his Parts he was most Accurate and Correct."[60] Similarly, Elliard Swanston was commended for "his pace, his look, his voice," the first of these probably referring to his speed with individual syllables.[61] Though strictly an amateur, Hamlet too is complimented on his "good accent and discretion" (2.2.466–67), *discretion* being another of those terms, like *just*, that define the weighing and balancing of stresses within a line.

The good actor weighed each syllable in a manner that was quite literally scrupulous. By his delivery he could rescue even mediocre verse: in Thomas Gainsford's words, a "Plaier was ever the life of dead poesie."[62] Jonson makes the same point about Edward Alleyn:

> others speake, but onely thou dost act.
> Weare this renowne. 'Tis just, that who did give
> So many *Poets* life, by one should live.
>
> [*Epigrammes*, no. 89, 12-14]

The poor actors, who according to the dramatists were never in short supply, simply ignored the meters, and thereby destroyed much of the meaning of the poetry. Edmund Gayton, remembering the Jacobean public theater in its heyday, said that "the poets of the Fortune and Red Bull always had a mouth measure for their actors (who were terrible tear throates) and made their lines proportionable to their compass—which were sesquipedales, a foot and a half."[63] Like it or not, everything would come out a roaring fourteener. Both Nashe and Greene have specific and extensive comments on the insolence of the players in destroying the good poetry they are given.[64] According to some poets, the problem is endemic; John Stephens says it is "a *Players* vice to be unjust,/To verse not yeelding coyne,"[65] sentiments with which Dekker agrees in the Preface to *The Whore of Babylon* (1607): "let the Poet set the note of his

Nombers, even to Apolloes owne Lyre, the Player will have his owne Crochets, and sing false notes, in dispite of all the rules of Musick" (ll. 30-32).

Naturally enough then, the clowns got many of their laughs in just this manner, by mangling the verse and doing deliberately what the bad actor did out of sheer neglect. The characteristic drawl of clowns like Tarleton, Singer, and Kempe would drag at the poetry, exaggerating and misplacing its emphases.[66] One good illustration of the foolery to be gained by drawling through the verse occurs in *Volpone*, where Nano is introducing a hermetic song for his master:

> Now, roome for fresh gamesters, who doe will you to know,
>> They do bring you neither play, nor Universitie show;
> And therefore doe intreat you, that whatsoever they rehearse,
>> May not fare a whit the worse, for the false pase of the verse.
> If you wonder at this, you will wonder more, ere we passe,
>> For know, here is inclos'd the Soule of *Pythagoras*.
>
> [1.2.1-6]

The unexpected stress on that last syllable, making a full rhyme with *passe* above it, contributes to the jazzy tone, as do the alternately jigging and dragging meters; the passage is well suited to the perverted dwarf who is speaking.

Many clowns were also able to extemporize doggerel verse; Tarleton and Wilson were two of the most adept at this.[67] Doggerel would have achieved much of its humor by appearing in a context where the manners of conventional verse were known to all. The understanding of the ground rules would have to be firm, for the clowns usually spoke verse in short snips, described by one playgoer as "craps and quibbles."[68] The unrestrained parody of verse in the clowns' routines, with their at times unstoppable jigs, was a cause of despair among legitimate poets, as the clowns gleefully acknowledged; in one play Will Kempe comes forward in propria persona, saying of an earlier play in which he had appeared, "Marry he was no poet that wrote it!"[69]

If the clown stands at one extreme in the delivery of verse, at another stands the actor whose voice approaches the control of music. One term often used to describe an actor's judicious placement of stress was *tune*. Edward Alleyn, for example, was said to have had "a well tun'de audible voyce"; the key word bears down on the way Alleyn observed the metrical accent, as he was not noted for a particularly musical intonation or delivery.[70] Alleyn's speech had that "alteration in the'eare by sound, accent, time, and slipper volubilitie in utterance" that Puttenham calls "outward tuning."[71] Ben Jonson used the term in the same sense in his *English Grammar*, referring to the proper stressing of a word as *tuning*; a misplaced accent makes a word *mistuned*.[72]

At his best, a good actor could bring out the music that was latent in the poetry. We have seen that John Shank was described as "singing" his poetry at the Globe; and there are many other references to the musical qualities of poetry on the stage. John Webster's prose "character" of "an Excellent Actor" is generally assumed to describe Burbage, and it is exact on the transforming power of a good delivery: "[the excellent actor] addes Grace to the Poets labours: for what in the Poet is but ditty, in him is both ditty and musicke."[73] With rather less discrimination, Flecknoe described Burbage's voice as "music to the ear."[74] This use of metaphors from music is not surprising, given the training of many Elizabethan actors. Study in music improves the understanding of verse, particularly the matter of timing, and the combined study of the two was sometimes recommended in the schools. Richard Mulcaster taught music with language; the beneficiaries of this study included not only Lancelot Andrewes but also such distinguished actors as James Whitelocke and Nathan Field[75] (who became himself no mean hand at blank verse, as we may see from his contributions to *The Fatal Dowry*). William Lyly, the headmaster at St. Paul's and to whose emphasis upon verse we have already referred, was said to have known "full well that knowledge in music was a help and a furtherance to all arts," and his pupils included many who went on to become actor-musicians, most notably Thomas Offley.[76] Edward Alleyn was described in one legal document as a "musician"; and Richard Jones, Anthony Knight, and George Vernon were just a few actors from this period who were also accomplished musicians.[77] The usefulness of musical training for a career on the stage was generally accepted, as a contemporary anecdote reveals. In 1600 some players from Blackfriars abducted Thomas Clifton, a boy from Norfolk, while he was walking to school; when he was recovered later, the complaint against the players stated that they had abducted him "well knowing that [he] had no manner of gift in song, nor skill in music."[78] The strong links between verse, music, and acting are summed up in Gosson's *School of Abuse*, which always links "Poets, Pipers, and Plaiers": each trade implies the other.

This was probably the one point upon which both the apologists for drama and its opponents could agree. In his *Defense of Poetry, Music and Stage-Plays* (1580) written in reply to Gosson, Thomas Lodge describes poetry as a musical art, saying it is impossible to separate the two: Allow poetry and you must allow music. Although Lodge's topic is dramatic poetry, he uses Homer as his example:

> Here growes a great question, What musick Homer used in curing the diseased Gretians? It was no dump you say, and so think I, for that is not apliable to sick men, for it favoreth Malancholie. I am sure, it was no mesure, for in those days they were not such good dancers; for soth then what was it? If you require me, if you name the instrument, I wyll tel you what was the musick. Mean while a God's name, let us both dout, that it is no part of our salvation to

know what it was, not how it went? when I speak wyth Homer next, you shall knowe his answere.[79]

To Lodge, poetry is the one essential music. It cures best because it speaks to the religious source of our humanity. What is most interesting about this point is that Lodge chooses to make it in a discussion of poetry in drama. As the music of the intellect, poetry links our imitations in this world with our imitation of the next.

These grand metaphors have an immediate basis in the facts of dramatic employment; the many poetic and musical skills that the actors cultivated were necessary for their professional survival. Elizabethan actors had to develop a hypersensitive ability to respond to each other's methods of handling poetry. This would have been necessary because of economic factors and work schedules; the repertory system of Elizabethan acting companies did not often leave much time for rehearsals. John Russell Brown has pointed out one important consequence of this, in noting that the actors must have been able to make spontaneous adjustments in the poetry of their own speeches: "If an actor has prepared some words with a large and slow delivery, it would matter very much to him at what pace, pitch, and volume the words immediately before his are spoken: he must respond to their rhythms or else his impressive delivery will sound affected, or ponderous, or funny, or unconvincing." In the absence of extended rehearsals, the actor would have to be alert, with his ear ready and his voice responsive to it. As Brown says, performances would have had "an air of improvisation, or danger"[80] when the actors were prepared in this way, and that tension would have been revealed largely in their handling of the verse.

Under the best of circumstances young actors would have had a thorough training in the proper way to deliver poetry. Richard Brome praised William Beeston in terms directly linking poetry with acting, saying that Beeston has

for many yeares both in his fathers dayes, and since directed Poets to write & Players to speak till he traind up these youths here to what they are now. I some of 'em from before they were able to say a grace of two lines long to have more parts in their pates then would fill so many Dry-fats. And to be serious with you, if after all this, by the venomous practise of some, who study nothing more then his destruction, he should faile us, both Poets and Players would be at a losse in Reputation.[81]

Many of the dramatists who worked directly with the companies also would have trained or coached the actors. Greene claimed with his customary outrage that the actors had learned everything from the poets, although they insulted them and took them for granted.[82] Several plays

from this period show dramatists coaching actors, and it is easy to specu-
late that they have some basis in fact; some of the scenes in act 5 of
Bartholomew Fair, for example, may have come out of Jonson's association with Henslowe, and judging from Jonson's literary criticism, we
might safely assume that his attention to verse technique would have been
minute. A German visitor to England observed in 1611 that English actors
"are daily instructed, as it were in a school, so that even the most eminent
actors have to allow themselves to be taught their places by the dramatists."[83] This may be an exaggeration, considering the strong personalities
of some of the actors, but then again it may not be, considering also the
equally strong characters and keen professional sense of some of the
leading dramatists. In either case, nothing could be more erroneous than
to assume that because the modern theater was young and developing at a
rapid rate, the actors were going at the poetry bare-handed. By grammar-
school instruction, by coaching in situ, by spontaneous and sometimes
vegetable criticism from the audience, the actor received an education in
how to make his verse moving. Heywood goes so far as to argue in addition for formal training outside theaters, saying that university study in
rhetoric is ideal for an actor, because it

> not onely emboldens a scholler to speake, but it instructs him to
> speake well, and with judgement, to observe his comma's, colons,
> & full poynts, his parentheses, his breathing spaces, and distinc-
> tions. . . . Actors should be rather schollers, that though they
> cannot speake well, know how to speake, or else to have that
> volubility that they can speake well, though they understand not
> what & so both imperfections may by instructions be helpful &
> amended: but where a good tongue & a good conceit both faile,
> there can never be good actor.[84]

Nonetheless, formal university training in rhetoric appears to have been
the exception for an actor at this time; and not all actors managed to
receive instruction from a Beeston, much less a Lyly or a Mulcaster.
Another index of the actors' understanding of poetic drama would be the
number of actors who wrote plays in verse. The acting careers of many of
the major English dramatists are familiar; what needs to be emphasized
here is the *poetic* aspiration of the actors' plays, particularly those plays
by actors who were several cuts below Shakespeare and Jonson. Dekker,
for one, knew he was far from being a great poet, but still he deplored the
mediocre verse-plays cranked out by actors, and attacked the pride of "a
Player that feedes on the fruite of divine poetry (as swine on Acorns)
that drop from the noble Oke of their mindes, and in the least Winter
of prosperities, will not stick to make their stye in that bosome which
of late releeved them." Worse yet, as far as Dekker was concerned, the

players' bad poetic drama committed the unpardonable sin of pulling in audiences, as least in rural areas:

> O you that are the *Poets* of these sinfull times, over whome the *Players* have now got the upper hand, by making fooles of the poore country people, in driving them like flocks of Geese to sit cackling in an old barne: and to swallow downe those playes for new which here every punck and her squire (like the Interpreter and his poppet) can rand out by heart they are so stale, and therefore so stincking. . . . [85]

Although the idea of recycling worn-out plays for use in the country is not new (nor yet out of fashion), what gives Dekker's complaint a special urgency is its emphasis upon the way poets have taken things lying down; the distinctly poetic failure of the material used by the traveling players should be rebuked by the true poets.

Besides writing plays, many actors also tried their hands at verse, and work of this kind would have added to their understanding of poetic texts. Burbage wrote poetry; Beeston was said to have "most judiciously discoursed of Poesie," which is somewhat amusing for, according to Nashe's witty estimate, he was a feeble poet at best.[86] Prefatory poems were written so often by actors as to make examples unnecessary here; every actor of even moderate distinction could manage to come up with a dozen lines or so to put in front of a new play. Logrolling was not unheard of, and indeed was to be expected when writer and player worked so completely hand in hand. Jonson alludes to this cooperation in *The Devil is an Ass,* where Ingine says, when planning a trick, "Your best will be one o' the players," to which Meere-craft replies, "No, there's no trusting them. They'll talke on't,/And tell their *Poets*" (2.8.60–62). In *Bartholomew Fair* Littlewit puts it more bluntly: "all the *Poets,* and *Poetsuckers* i' Towne . . . are the Players Gossips" (2.1.39–41).

Fluid as were the boundaries between all the literary trades at this time, those between actor, poet, and dramatist are perhaps the most indistinct of all. The reason for this may be found in the heart of the relation between poet and player, poem and play, where there is an important paradox that it is all too easy to reduce. Dramatic poetry in the Renaissance is not something that happens only on the stage, nor does it possess a strictly literary existence in itself. The poetry is neither performance nor literature but both. As contemporaries describe the Renaissance audience, it made a response that was literary, in that it involved analysis, comparison, and judgment by the standards of work existing in print, but that response took place spontaneously and without the printed text before the playgoer. If Hall, Dekker, Jonson, Webster, and the rest are correct in their descriptions of listeners—and they could not have much motive for falsifying the facts in the case—then the attentive playgoer heard the verse as rhythmic, metered speech, not simply as a subspecies of formal rhetoric, or as a vehicle for theme and plot, or as a local diversion. The poetry could, of course, be all these on occasion; however, it always had its own unavoidable work to do, in creating the intellectual and physical rhythms by which the characters lived.

The paradox of performance as literature is inherent in all those metaphors used to describe the actor's basic job of work. Meters or "numbers" in the poetic text become a kind of music in the delivery of the actor, or in the mind of the reader. The process of mediation begins in the poet's mind, and ends in speech that occurs on stage or in the mind of the reader; the second is a sensible apprehension as well as the first, because the residual core of poetry in poetic drama allows the reader himself to recreate the play. Reading should not be a casual process, and indifferent skimming does a verse play no service; as John Earle says in the Fletcher Folio of 1647, these plays are not just to be read

> To passe a fire, or laugh an houre in bed.
> How doe the Muses suffer every where,
> Taken in such mouthes censure, in such eares,
> That twixt a whiff, a Line or two rehearse,
> And with their Rheume together spaule [spit out] a Verse?[87]
>
> [xxxiii]

The reader may in addition create or recreate a proper pitch, intonation, length of syllable, pause, or (the landlord willing) technique of voice production; but all these belong to performance rather than to reading, and constitute an irrelevant part of the literary experience per se, which is bound to and freed by the text. As Sir Richard Baker asked in *Theatrum Triumphans* (1670), "What doth a player else, but only say without book that which we may read without book?"[88]

The literary experience of a play is thus neither gratuitous nor somehow less significant than the experience of a performance; each is really a variant of the other. We have seen that when the dramatists describe each others' work, they assume that poetry does not simply illustrate stage action, but carries that action into the mind of the thoughtful reader. The text contains not only a set of stage directions but also something of the player's *action,* and this term, as Alfred Harbage has reminded us, was used to refer to the player's manner of speech as well as to his gestures.[89] Ideally every one of the actor's gestures originated in the text. John Bulwer, author of the *Chironomia* (1644), that fascinating compendium of actor's manual gestures, says that "gesture must attend upon every flexion of the voice, not scenical, but declaring the sentence and meaning of our mind, not by demonstration, but signification: for it must be accommodated by the hand, that it may agree and have a proper reference, not so much to the words as to the sense."[90] In other words, the actor was no mere pantomimist, repeating with his hands what the speech had made clear in a discursive sense; that would be a fine invitation to laughter. Instead he had to understand the poetry and allow his gestures to convey that understanding, finding equivalents for the intellectual yet sensuous experience of the poetry.

Thomas Gainsford is quite specific on the relation between the actor's gestures and the audience's close listening to the poetry:

> Player must take heede of wrested and enforced action: for if there be not a facility in his deliverance, and as it were a naturall dexteritie, it needes must sound harsh to the auditour, and procure his distast and displeasure.
>
> Player is like a garment which the Tailor maketh at the direction of the owner; so they frame their action, at the disposing of the Poet.[91]

Or as a schoolmaster says of his charges in a play from 1607, "I have taken as much paines with them, *as any poet whatsoever could have don,* to make them answere uppon their Q. with good action, distinction, and deliberation" (emphasis added).[92] Action, voice, and text were fully linked.

The intimate bond between a play's action, language, and structure is perhaps best laid out in Webster's paragraph "To the Judicious Reader" of *The Devil's Law Case* (1623). Commenting upon the music of his "poem," Webster says with great restraint that he will not praise himself, explaining that "A great part of the grace of this [play] (I confess) lay in Action; yet can no Action ever be gracious, where the decency of the Language, and Ingenious structure of the Scaene, arrive not to make up a perfect Harmony."[93] While the reader may not see the action, he can rest assured that the union of language and structure are the sine qua non of drama; as Webster says—in this quoting Horace—if your ears are clean you should have no problems.

It is true that in assuming the rhythms of blank verse could exist not only in performance but also aside from it, Elizabethans accepted a poetic ontology that some modern theorists of meter would not countenance.[94] However, the dramatists had at least one practical reason for insisting on the music inherent in a text or script: If the play is badly acted, the dramatist still knows that it has a poetic existence apart from stage performance. One need not go so far as to accept Dekker's picture of the poet as an oak tree and the actor a hog browsing for acorns beneath it, but the metaphor does imply a distinction worth preserving. If there were no texts or listening readers, bad actors would be a threat to the existence of drama on any but the most primitive level. That may be why Shakespeare, who worked much of the time with one good theatrical company, evident-ly felt less need to see his plays into print than did, say, Jonson, or Web-ster.

The full intellectual claims of poetry in drama, apart from performance, may be seen in the comments of one contemporary if somewhat erratic critic: "Speak the speech, I pray you, as I pronounc'd it to you, trippingly on the tongue, but if you mouth it, as many of our players do, I had as live the town-crier spoke my lines" (3.2.1-4).[95] As Hamlet goes on to say, an actor's failure to convey the meters of poetry is nothing less than a denial of the actor's own humanity. This concern for the accurate trans-mission of the meter makes sense only if dramatic poetry is assumed to have an existence apart from performance. Hamlet is concerned about the philosophical difficulty of representing any human experience, but his deepest concerns also tap into the English dramatic tradition. The actor is responsible for the poetry, and in this respect Hamlet's concern is part of his whole interest in agents and causes: here his view of poetry has met his still-evolving idea of individuals as agents for purposes beyond themselves. This is not to argue that we ought to accept a certain view of the literary existence of poetic drama simply because it adds one more meaning to a passage of *Hamlet*; rather it is to say that this passage—like so many simi-lar ones in Shakespeare—departs from a point that poets had been marking for a generation.

RESTORATION EXCURSUS

One way to see how the Elizabethans were attempting to map the terri-tory of dramatic verse would be to compare their comments with those of their Restoration and Augustan inheritors. What one notices immediately is that after the Restoration, *poem* and *poet* seem to have undergone some subtle shifts in meaning, in the context of drama if no other. Toward the end of the seventeenth century, plays are described ever more consistently as *poems,* but the term now becomes inseparable from its narrower deno-tation of a logical and rhetorical structure. To select one important exam-ple: Dryden's Preface to his and D'Avenant's adaptation of *The Tempest,* published in 1670, refers often to the play as a poem, but Dryden's con-cern is less for the verse than for the building of scenic action or formal structure. There would be no mistaking the concerns of this preface for those in a preface by Jonson, for example, or Webster. Dryden's Prologue then touches on Shakespeare's ability to become Nature for later poets, but he says nothing about the sensuous or intellectual aspects of Shake-speare's verse, and instead spends time divagating on the fact that in his version a woman appears actually dressed as a woman.

Such sensitivity as we find in Dryden for Shakespeare's language is usually directed at a discursive rather than sensuous level of meaning; his chief concern tends to be diction. The well-known pronouncement in the *Essay of Dramatick Poesy* (1668) that Shakespeare's language is, like Jonson's, "a little obsolete," may be qualified by the Preface to *All for Love* (1678), which says that "it is almost a miracle that much of his language remains so pure"; but there is still no readiness there to dwell on the way that Shakespeare's words carry levels of meaning above the strictly discursive level. Dryden's conservatism of response is fully signaled in the Epilogue to the second part of *The Conquest of Granada* (1672); here he says of the Jacobean dramatists that

> were they now to write, when critics weigh
> Each line, and ev'ry word, throughout a play,
> None of them, no not *Johnson* in his height,
> Could pass, without allowing grains for weight.[96]

[13-16]

It is the natural prerogative of every generation to remake the writers of the previous generation; Dryden is only insuring that he will feel no "anxiety of influence." Without feeling any need to beat Dryden with Webster or the late Shakespeare, one can still notice that a curious double shift seems to be taking place. While on the one hand formal criticism of the drama becomes more insistent in its use of the term *poem* to denote a poetic drama—Gerard Langbaine does so, for example, throughout his *Account of the English Dramatick Poets* (1691)—at the same time the poetry itself becomes more the expression of the anaesthetic aesthetic of decorum. The new dramatic laws of aptness and sense make the shift perhaps inevitable, and it should not be surprising that one subject of critical debate should be the question of blank *versus* rhymed verse.[97] One reason for this new scrutiny may be that rhyme is more assessible to discursive analysis, and its effect (or absence) may be easily described in terms of rhetoric. From the new point of view, it is the very absence of constraint that hampers the modern poet. Neander reminds Crites in the *Essay of Dramatick Poesy* that he had once said of dramatic poetry that "we should never find the Audience favorable to this kind of writing, till we could produce as good Plays in Rhyme, as *Ben. Jonson, Fletcher,* and *Shakespeare* had writ out of it."[98] Even the champions of unrhymed blank verse have only a negative authority for their position, Sir Robert Howard objecting that rhyme is generically "unnatural":

> A Poem, being a premediated form of Thoughts upon design'd Occasions, ought not to be unfurnish'd of any harmony in Words or Sound; [a Play] is presented as the present Effect of Accidents not thought of; so that 'tis impossible it should be equally proper to both these, unless it were possible that all Persons were born so much more than Poets, that Verses were not to be compos'd by them, but already made in them.[99]

In all likelihood this defense based upon the alleged demands of realism would have seemed incomprehensible to an Elizabethan.

The limits on the name and nature of dramatic poetry are set forth even more strongly in second-rate critical writing, which always shuts more doors than it opens. John Dennis, in the Prologue to his adaptation of *The Merry Wives* (1702), says that

> As in the mixture of the humane frame,
> 'Tis not the Flesh, 'tis the Soul that makes the Man,
> So of Dramatick Poems we may say,
> 'Tis not the Lines, 'tis the Plot makes the Play.
> The Soul of every Poem's the design,
> And words but serve to make that move and shine.[100]

It is almost as if Dennis had set out deliberately to invert John Ford's comment that the soul of drama is the language, and plot is the flesh. What Dennis offers is a definition of dramatic poetry that splits apart poetry and drama; rhetoric and plot displace not only the immediate sensuous qualities of the verse but also the whole complex relation of verse to the development of character. Writing at about the same time as Dennis, Thomas Rymer is equally assured and direct: "Some go to *see,* others to *hear* a Play. The Poet should please both; but be sure that the *Spectators* be satisfied, whatever Entertainment he give his Audience."[101] Although Rymer is by no means a simple man, it is one sign of the changes in English taste that his contrast between spectators and auditors upholds a view that Ben Jonson had earlier ascribed to the vulgar nutcrackers.

To accommodate Shakespeare to the new definitions, a generation of editors "corrected" his versification and sought ways to rationalize his errors of taste; Pope, for example, generously maintained that Shakespeare's lapses in poetic technique, as seen in the Folio, may in fact be corruptions introduced by actors and compounded by printers.[102] More fanciful explanations abounded, and one intrepid reader even maintained that the "false Numbers and Rhimes" of Shakespeare's early "Dogrel" were an attempt on his part to approximate classical tetrameters.[103] The persistent assumption throughout is that the science of versification has now been raised to its full height, and instinct alone can no longer suffice; the age requires a deeper judiciousness, as Humphrey Moseley had indicated early on, saying in 1651 that "though all *Scholars* are not *Poets,* every *Poet* must be a *Scholar.*" In Augustan times even a defense of the older, looser poetic forms does its damage. Dennis's *Essay Upon the Genius and Writings of Shakespeare* (1712) succeeds in throwing out the baby, the bath, and finally the tub as well: "[Shakespeare] seems to have been the very Original of our *English* Tragical Harmony; that is the Harmony of Blank Verse, diversifyed often by Disyllable and Trissyllable Terminations. For that Diversity distinguishes it from Heroick Harmony, and bringing it nearer to common Use, makes it more proper to gain Attention, and more fit for Action and Dialogue. Such Verse we make when we are writing Prose; we make such Verse in common Conversation."[104] Dennis's common conversation must have been truly dazzling; or perhaps, in Donne's phrase, his blindness too much light breeds. This is the sort of definition that effectively destroys any notion of poetry as something other than a language of discourse. Even Pope himself, a sensitive reader in most respects, falls into line on this, asserting in the Preface to his 1725 edition of Shakespeare that the compositors "did not know prose from verse, and they accordingly printed one for the other throughout the volume."[105] Having said that of the Folio, what would Pope and his age have said of the deliberately mixed prose and poetry of *The Revenger's Tragedy*?

THE RISE OF THE DRAMATIC TEXT

It is easy enough to point out the limited sensibilities of an earlier generation, but it makes dull going after a certain point; the important question now is why the conventions surrounding blank verse changed as fundamentally as they did. The transition was nothing so simple as a change from sensuous blank verse to intellectual prose, from freedom to repression, and beyond these general formulae there are the standard essay-examination answers: the closing of the theaters and the breakup of the old acting companies, with the consequent loss of speaking techniques and manners that had been passed down in apprentice fashion; the later triumph of "scenes," or elaborate sets, and the steady movement of the drama toward spectacular and operatic forms; the historical analyst's own theatrical "engine," the fabled wholesale shift in taste that solves all critical problems; or if none of these convince, one can always point to the degenerate tastes of Charles II and the Restoration court. The portrait paintings of the King, draped in his spaniel curls, and of his flushed and disheveled court beauties, would seem to rebuke any but the most casual view of the drama; possibly common conversation really *was* no more and no less than the language of drama.

Literary surveys often say that the decisive turn from poetic tragedy in English came with George Lillo's *The London Merchant* (1731), but the changes in dramatic poetry and its performance had been noted well before the turn of the century, and the decline—for so the changes were sensed even then—was being explained in terms of the familiar causes just listed. One handy introduction to these explanations is Joseph Wright's bookish dialogue titled *Historia Histrionica* (1699). In some preliminary long-winded speeches, Trueman, "an old cavalier," gives a circumstantial account of English stage history from medieval times down to the present, addressing this to a young friend named Lovewit, who for some inexplicable reason seems nearly unable to contain himself with excitement. The didactic purpose of the conversation is pressed home at several points, as Lovewit takes over enthusiastically, extolling the virtues of old players he saw or only heard of as a child. Trueman says, for example, that "now we have such a crowd of Poets of a quite different Genius; the least of which thinks himself as well able to correct *Ben. Jonson*, as he could a Country School mistress that taught to spell." Lovewit, eager to please, takes up the obvious cue: "We have, indeed, Poets of a different Genius; so are the Plays: But in my Opinion, they are all of 'em (some few excepted) as much inferior to those of former Times, as the Actors now in being (generally speaking) are, compared to *Hart, Mohun, Burt, Lacy, Clun,* and *Shatterel.* . . ." As the dialogue goes on, the two speakers stress above all the speech of the older actors, praising those who were noted in particular for their manner of delivering the lines. Lovewit tells Trueman "I have been told, That those whom I mention'd, were Bred up under the others of your Acquaintance, and follow'd their manner of Action, which is now lost," adding that he wishes the old actors' names had been printed beside the parts they played, "and thus one might have guest at the Action of the Man, by the Parts which we now read."[106] (For Lovewit—if for no one else—would that Thomas Nashe had got around to writing, as he had promised, his study in Latin of players "with the manner of theyr habites and attyre."[107]) Reading the language conveys the drama: reading reveals *action,* in that special sense of the term. But as Trueman replies to Lovewit, newfangled stage machinery and elaborate sets have taken the place of drama: "the Plays and Actors, of the last Age . . . cou'd support themselves merely from their own Merit; the weight of the Matter, and goodness of the Action, without Scenes and Machines."[108] Several years before this dialogue Richard Flecknoe's *Short Treatise of the English Stage* (1664) had come down to this very point: "[Our stage decorations] now for cost and ornament are arriv'd to the heighth of Magnificence; but that which makes our Stage the better makes our Playes the worse perhaps, they striving now to make them more for sight than hearing, whence that solid joy of the interior is lost." This is the fulfillment of Puttenham's warning that too many come to plays to look rather than to listen, and from Flecknoe we could trace a line through Wright down to Collier, who says in 1831 that "The introduction of scenery gives the date to the commencement of the decline of our dramatic poetry."[109]

    To these explanations we might add another interconnected cluster of causes. One is the dramatist's need for economic protection: printing was advisable given the frequency with which plays were pirated. To judge from the number of times bad editions are mentioned in prefaces by both authors and printers, the *concern* for self-protection (as perhaps separate from the necessity for it) must have been deep, and there are two important aspects of that concern. The fact that pirated or corrupt editions could be sold at all while the original play was still even intermittently on the stage suggests that there was a definite *reading* market for the plays. (One illustration of this would be the "good" quarto of *Hamlet*.) References to piracy also may have served another purpose more social than economic. Tudor and early Elizabethan plays often were printed, as their prefaces assure us, in order to educate us in virtue or to provide some edifying diversion;[110] disclaimers of this kind must have been old hat by Jacobean or Caroline times, for they appear much less frequently in front of the later plays. There the stated motives for publication become more complex, as the author or printer will be found lamenting the economic, legal, or personal necessities that have driven the work into print, while still maintaining that the experience of the play is a satisfying end in itself. From one point of view, publication was still awkward for someone with gentlemanly pretensions; allusions to piracy and forced printing of correct copy might cover an unseemly desire for fame or profit. One hesitates, though, to assign too much *pudeur* to these professionals, and on balance it seems likely that economic forces probably did compel many to go to publication when stage performance had been the original goal.

The dramatist's use of publication to protect his investment has some definite effects upon his readers as well as his art; those shifts that Ian Watt observed some time ago in relation to the novel have analogues in the history of drama,[111] and one could argue that the later rise of fiction was made possible by the economic changes that had occurred earlier in the production and reception of printed plays. Muriel Bradbrook and Gerald Eades Bentley, among others, have demonstrated the rise of economic independence in both players and dramatists, although work still remains to be done in relating the socioeconomic changes to changes in the dramatic forms themselves.[112] Numerous examples of economic mobility are depicted in the characters and action of Jacobean plays—Middleton is of special interest here—but many larger questions of tone and genre remain to be treated. How, for example, was the rising use of pathos in the drama an expression of social and economic changes within the audience? These and related questions can remind us that our work still has its tentative aspects.

From the standpoint of the present study there is a case to be made for another factor, besides these socioeconomic pressures, which was instrumental in the shift to a drama with less expressive poetry. The economic problems caused by the pirating of texts must have diminished rapidly after 1642; even by the time of Charles I, the repertory of the better-known acting companies tended to rely heavily upon "old" plays from before 1625.[113] What was it then besides money that kept pulling dramatists into print? To put the strong word first and make qualifications later: on the part of the dramatists, there seems to have been an increasing desire to make plays imperishable as literature rather than perishable as performance. In many ways this impulse is quite separate from the matters we have discussed up to this point. Despite the large shifts in the economic bases of English society, despite the changes in the reading public, despite the changing economic status of writers in particular, the poetic dramatist still was confronted with the job of writing verse if he were to get through a play. As the seventeenth century came to a close, he tended increasingly to see a relation between the fact of print, the chances of literary permanence, and the supposed laws of verse.

It is quite likely that at the height of Jacobean stage writing, enormous numbers of plays must have been assembled willy-nilly, the playwright and actors cobbling blank verse and songs around that notorious Italian courtesan or the late murder in Whitechapel. It is also evident that the topicality and immediacy of drama, including the very rapidity of its production, comprised a good part of its aesthetic. This right happy and copious industry reflects a common social stance, and just as any true gentleman should have been able to reel off a sonnet with easy nonchalance, so even a hardened professional like Jonson could admit with more than a trace of self-satisfaction that he had tossed off *Volpone* singlehandly in five weeks.[114]

The existence of this cult of facility does not imply that other standards did not exist too or that authors were unaware of them. When the chance for publication appeared, the playwright could and did arrange and rewrite, setting his verse in order. Heywood's *If You Know Not Me You Know Nobody* was first published in 1605 and was performed and reprinted frequently after that, though it was not until sometime around 1636 or 1637 that Heywood had a chance to put it right:

> [The play]
> Did throng the Seates, the Boxes and the Stage
> So much; that some by Stenography drew
> The plot: put it in print: (scarce one word trew:)
> And in that lamenesse it hath limp't so long,
> The Author now to vindicate that wrong
> Hath took the paines, upright upon its feete
> To teach it walke, so please you sit, and see't.[115]

That veteran pun on *feet* assures the reader that Heywood has paid close attention to his verse technique; as Heywood senses, precision and the marking of boundaries increasingly have become a sign of valuable and permanent dramatic poetry. Hemminge and Condell did not claim Shakespeare to be a champion of this kind, but Jonson deliberately assumed that role from the first, and after 1616 other playwrights become more and more emphatic about the tightening that was thought necessary before dramatic poetry went onto the page.

It would be impossible to fix an exact date for the rising awareness of the relation between the printed page and poetic form in drama. Today pessimistic critics forecast the total extinction of the print sensibility; in 1600 no dramatist was guilty even of optimism about its enlargement. Consider again the example of Shakespeare, who did not bother to print nineteen of his own plays; that list would include *1 Henry IV, Twelfth Night, Measure for Measure, Othello, Macbeth, Coriolanus, Antony and Cleopatra, The Winter's Tale,* and *The Tempest*—hardly works a writer would overlook if he were concerned with establishing a permanent reputation in print. In early Jacobean times the question would have been mooted whether drama was even literature at all; Donne did not regard the dramatists as providing enough material for a good jibe, and he was, again, "a great frequenter of plays." Drama was not literature. Or not yet. Although one could cite individual Elizabethan readers (like Sir John Harington) who had unusually large collections of printed plays,[116] their enthusiasm must not have been contagious among the wealthy and influential. When Sir Thomas Bodley, for example, laid the foundation for his great library at Oxford, he specifically excluded plays and other "baggage books."[117] With the advantage of our hindsight we can see that the really important point about Bodley's judgment is its date: 1612. Within another generation, his attitude would be as unthinkable as that of a modern librarian refusing to purchase *The Wasteland* or poetry like it. Possibly Hemminge and Condell had an access of solicitude for readers by 1623; and it is almost certain that the example of Jonson's Folio provoked their assembly of Shakespeare's plays. We do know that Hemminge and Condell realized what Shakespeare himself was evidently indifferent to, that the experience of the drama was available to readers and not merely to spectators and direct auditors. To be sure Jonson's motives in the publication of his Folio were complex, but one component must have been his awareness that drama had to defend itself from irrelevant producers, bad actors, and stupid audiences. (In this light we can understand how Jonson's second "Ode to Himselfe" begins with the injunction "Come leave the loathed Stage" and ends by saying that henceforth his audience can *read* his tributes to the just King.) Jonson's running feud with Inigo Jones over the proper uses of poetry and spectacle has a bearing upon the discussion here, for in it too we can see Jonson's stress upon drama as literature in performance.[118] Like much else besides the printing of the Folio, this celebrated quarrel indicates the developing conception of the *dramatic text*, a conception which earlier would have been regarded as a contradiction in terms.

Some of the older dramatic poets of Jonson's time made no bones about their antipathy to this newfangled sort of publication; as Thomas Heywood says in the Preface to *The English Traveller* (1633), "my Playes are not exposed unto the world in Volumes, to beare the title of Workes, as others . . . it never was any great ambition to me, to bee in this kind

Volumniously read"[119] Heywood might have regarded "volumnious" publication with more interest had he been a better poet; he seems to have
known well his limits as a writer. Others with greater talent or less self-
knowledge had no fear of appearing in volumes, and indeed the evolution
of the printed dramatic text has an intimate connection with such matters
of mind and awareness. Jonson's high seriousness in presenting his Folio—
never before had popular literature dared to present itself with such dignified credentials[120]—not only gives a date to the rise of the intellectual and
professional spirit of playwrights, but also makes a new claim for the
reader, sitting alone with what had originated as a social document, a
formula for a public performance.

It is still possible to see one point, however, at which the claims for
printed dramatic poetry are being advanced with a new and consolidated
directness, and that is in the Beaumont and Fletcher Folio of 1647. Its
extended prefatory apparatus says little in any one place that is entirely
new; what it does is to stress with great clarity and repetition that the
printing of *poetry* enables the reader to recreate the *drama*. This is not a
claim that was advanced earlier with such insistence in either the Jonson
or Shakespeare folios, and if we analyze its elaboration, we can see a
remarkable uniformity of attitude among the thirty-three writers who
contributed encomia to the collection. Much of what is said about Fletcher's verse points ahead to standards of judgment for the next several
generations, yet at the same time the attitude toward the experience of
the drama sums up all that had happened between playwrights and audiences since the 1570s. The prefatory poems to this Folio mark a pivotal
moment in English literary history.

By writing the poetry of his drama with readers in mind, Fletcher
allows them to recreate the plays in their *own* minds, and thus assures
himself a place in literary posterity. The process begins in the technical
perfection of Fletcher's verse: James Shirley says that "not one indiscre-
tion hath branded this Paper in all the Lines" (p. xi); Henry Howard
pictures Fletcher going to Elyzium and drawing large audiences with his
"even numbers" (p. xv). References to the ease and control of Fletcher's
versification are extended in a manner neither easy nor controlled; the
taste for this quality heralds the coming emphasis upon "numerousness,"
as Dryden called it, or the use of smoothly flowing meters.[121] To the
encomiasts of the Folio, Fletcher's next of kin may be traced without
difficulty: as Berkenhead remarks, "*Johnson* made good Poets and right
Verse" (p. xliii). The Jonsonian goals of tightness and precision in language and versification may be seen in Alexander Brome's condemnation
of all other plays as "Witts Stenographie"; Brome adds that in the collection we are about to read we will never find "words, as voyd of Reason,
as of Rithme, / Only caesura'd to spin out the time" (p. xlix). The increasing emphasis upon decorum and the new stricter legislation of verse is

one great difference between the comments here and those before either
the Jonson or Shakespeare folios. Thomas Palmer says "ev'ry word has
weight and yet no Noise" (p. xlviii); like the references to Fletcher's even
numbers, this praise foreshadows the coming poetic, as may be seen in
Pope's reference much later to Shakespeare's "most pompous rhymes, and
thundering versification."[122]

Although Fletcher's polish and ease may not appeal to modern tastes
as they did to those of Caroline readers, it is important to notice that his
contemporaries did not see his virtue as a writer in his mere inoffen-
siveness. The refinement of his poetry did not just contribute to the
design of his plays: that seamless quality best *revealed* the design. Praising
the "smoothnesse from his file and eare," Joseph Howe says that

> Not the most strict enquiring nayle
> Cou'd e're finde where his piece did faile
> Of entyre oneness; so the frame
> Was Composition, yet the same.
>
> [xlvii]

Robert Herrick concurs with his usual aptness, while taking his line of
thought one step further. In Fletcher's plays the control of an entire act
originates in the choice of individual words:

> Here's words with lines, and lines with Scenes consent,
> To raise an Act to full astonishment.
>
> [xli]

In verse drama as in other forms of life, ontogeny repeats phylogeny.

By printing a play, then, Beaumont and Fletcher have made it possible
to re-create the experience of a performance. This idea sounds familiar
enough, but not even our friends Trueman and Lovewit—despite the much
later date of the *Historica Histrionica*—went as far with the implications
of it as do the poets in the Folio. They have begun to move the setting
of the drama into the mind of the playgoer or reader; in studying these
comments in the Folio; we realize (what will be fully apparent by 1700)
that we are seeing nothing less than the extinction of the poet's role
as a creator of mystery and enchantment, with himself the victim of
a fine frenzy. Instead he becomes a manager of responses, an objective and subtle therapist. In a passage most important to the development of English literary aesthetics, James Shirley says that in these
plays

> you may find here passions raised to that excellent pitch and
> by such insinuating degrees that you shall not chuse but consent,
> & go along with them, finding your selfe at last grown insensibly

the very same person you read, and then stand admiring the subtile Trackes of your engagement.

(xii)

A similar process can occur during reading; in his labored commendatory
poem, Roger L'Estrange echoes Shirley on this point, saying that a good
dose of Beaumont and Fletcher will take us out of ourselves, purging our
assorted vices: gallants forget their women, "*Poets* their *Wine;* the *Usurer*
his *Pelfe;* / The *World* its *Vanity;* and *I* my *Selfe*" (p. xxix). In all these
comments, print is not held to be just the best way of conveying the
poetry, or even the best way of recreating a performance; more importantly, it is the best way for us to enter the fictive world of the poet—
which is nothing less than our own minds, as they experience the text
itself. It would not be possible to overestimate the significance of this
change, which is one step past Sidney and the Elizabethan theorists; many
of the root assumptions of modern fiction may originate in this shift we
have been observing.

The new emphasis is enthusiastically codified in Restoration dramatic
criticism. Out of the many possible illustrations of this, we might look
at one that sheds light back to the Elizabethans. In his Dedication to *The
Spanish Friar* (1681), Dryden comes out boldly against the performance
of drama in favor of reading: "'Tis my ambition to be read: that I am
sure is the more lasting and nobler design." It is true that this attitude has
some very deep classical roots; Dryden may be echoing Aristotle, who
insists, at several places in the *Poetics*, that plays should be judged not
only by their performance but also as texts. In Aristotle's view "The
tragic effect is quite possible without a public performance and actors,"
and stage performance may be distracting or positively objectionable:
the public "cannot see the meaning, unless they add something themselves, that causes the perpetual movements of the performers—bad flute
players, for instance, rolling about."[123]

While the roots of Dryden's attitude may be deep, his uses of the
attitude are quite at odds with Aristotle's. There is a difference between
a critic who prefers to read a play rather than see it marred by vulgarity
and a dramatist who prefers to write a play for readers. Aristotle presupposes one copy of the play, preferably in his own hands; Dryden
presupposes thousands, preferably in the hands of a discerning public
(although that is not an absolute requirement). Aristotle wants to escape
from the flute players; Dryden would have no objection at all to their
buying his plays. Yet when we look back at the comments on Beaumont
and Fletcher's dramatic poetry, they line up unequivocally on Aristotle's
side. Reading is the form of dramatic experience—both for the actor, who
creates the role from the text, and for the reader (no different from a
physically present listener) who creates it in what is another kind of

performance in its own right. The two merge into one response imagined and foreseen by the dramatist; neither actor nor reader requires the other, yet there is no question of trying to pull one response out of the dramatist's creating audience, or to reject one altogether.

The decline of poetry as a means of direct exposition in drama seems linked with the rise of a "print culture," and the transition becomes visible after the Restoration. Dryden's stand implies a drama-reading public large enough that it could be reached only by a volume of printing undreamed of in 1590.[124] These changes, in the absence of a firm continuity in dramatic companies, contributed to the decline of verse as a means of direct sensuous contact. A reader after 1700 might make every effort to hear the lines and the drama within them, but he would have only indirect ways of checking his reading against performances of the old kind. The old plays were no longer popular except in revisions and adaptations; and even when the stage was held by someone who learned from someone who learned from Burbage, the plays were not the same because the texts had been changed. While the theaters had been closed before (as in 1592, because of the plague) and had undergone some shifts in organization before reopening, never had the theatergoing public been thrown upon reading as the principal means of experiencing plays. Increasingly visualizing and abstracting, the attention of that public also conceives of "numbers" in progressively stricter sense, preferring the symmetry and authority of lines that scan regularly. The best rhythmic patterns become those that can be seen, traced with an inquiring nail. This carries us further than our present story, however; the dramatists with whom we are concerned now were all accessible in print in their own times, and yet were not so restrained by that fact that they felt forced to write in "smooth numbers" that had to pass an ocular inspection. What, and how, they had the actors speak we still can share if we wish.

3

THE REVENGER'S TRAGEDY

In few plays are the major speeches so obviously and self-consciously set as they are in *The Revenger's Tragedy*; even in the unlikely case that we might miss them, Tourneur is usually thoughtful enough to have bystanders remind us of the merits or importance of what we are hearing. But oddly enough, all of Vindice's great speeches occur in the first two-thirds of the play: the exposition of act 1, scene 1; the temptation speeches in act 2, scene 1; the descriptions of night in act 1, scene 3, and act 2, scene 2; and the silkworm speech to Gloriana in act 3, scene 5. These are indeed splendid, yet by consent of critical silence there is nothing on their level in the latter third of the play. In fact, after act 3, scene 5, Vindice speaks a much larger proportion of his lines in prose,[1] and he seldom speaks more than three or four lines of verse at a time. He does rise to sustained poetry in his last speech and (more briefly) in the six-and thirteen-line speeches to the nobles in the next-to-last scene; but except for these, his longest speeches in verse in the last third of the play are only seven and nine lines long.[2] In short, something goes out of Vindice *as a poet* after he has killed the Duke. We could change the emphasis and say that Vindice's achievement of his primary revenge against the Duke (as distinct from his secondary revenge against the sons) has something to do with diminishing his interest or abilities in poetry. The kind of verse he spoke at first, which the critics have all rightly admired, is no longer an adequate mirror of his self. What is there in Vindice's great verse that leads us to accept his dropping it later? And how is his later style a truer image of his changing self?

If one of the main concerns of the play is the way Vindice regards himself, there is probably no better description of his thinking than a passage by Paul Valéry, in a section of the *Analects* headed "Moralities":

> *The man who has hurt himself.*
> We collide with something: hurt and rage. After the shock come

pain and anger, intermingled; one a wave, the other foam, each reinforcing each. We fling ourselves on the innocent cause of our mishap, trying to destroy it. By its inertia it has injured us; we even credit it with memory, malice, sensibility (a deeply significant mistake).

A whole drama is enacted, usurping reality but arising from it. Little by little our feelings subside. Little by little we come to see the sheer stupidity of this crazy nightmare; of our fit of temper. Sometimes we laugh. But when we think back over what has happened we can't help recommencing the vicious circle of our "brain storm"—in an abridged form. The net result is: we have hurt ourselves, smashed something, wasted time and energy, come up against our own absurdity; and we now proceed to blot from our minds what has taken place—and is sure to repeat itself next time, on the next occasion.

What has happened is that a tidal wave has welled up from the depths, spread havoc, caught the quiet dweller on the foreshore off his guard. Every big upheaval takes the form of a dream, for it's a dream to try to reconcile the scheme of things with chance; a dream all the more total, the greater the upheaval. It keeps pace with the eddies, revives, dies out; it thrives on anything and everything—naively. An overexcited brain does what comes naturally to it: personifies, sees itself as an outsider, fails to recognize itself.

Here, then, is the cycle. First the psyche goes the round of the nervous system: pain, sensation, reversion to the moment before the shock, blind rage: an excess of stupidity, stupidity in action, stupidity in the state of agonized sensation, the stupidity of rage, but also of our remorse—a new cause for rage. The successive terms, though periodic, are phases of our recognition of absurdity stepped up to ever higher "powers."[3]

Valéry's description sums up the pattern of Vindice's development. In laughter and dream, in the mind seeing itself as an outsider, and in the widening waves of his stupidity, which finally takes in remorse as well as rage, Vindice gradually extends his capacity to wound himself. Two generations ago readers confirmed that Vindice was not a very admirable person and therefore no hero of a tragedy.[4] He lacked stature, which is probably true if one reads the play on the level of narrative alone, but quite untrue if one pays attention to Vindice's self-conception and his verse. As a character he develops steadily through the play, and his verse is the means by which we learn of his psychological enlargement. More recently, critics who have complained that Vindice does not grow have not looked at the way his verse changes over the course of the play.[5] This oversight is related in turn to some misconceptions of Tourneur's social vision, as the passage from Valéry might imply. It is hardly necessary to explain how T. S. Eliot confused Tourneur with Vindice when he said that the play expresses Tourneur's "cynicism, . . . loathing, and disgust of humanity."[6] But we need not say on the other hand that Vindice is obsessed by the Duke and the assorted degenerates in his court. More exactly, Vindice is obsessed by his own *experience* of the court, which is a very different thing. He is not a close observer of the villains, and as we shall see, often his judgment of them is not borne out by what they say or do. He has been horrified by his own experience and not by the characters themselves, who are variously stupid, comic, and ineffectual. Vindice is willing to credit more memory, malice, and sensibility to his enemies than we ever could. Only the self-persuasive changes in his own verse can allow him to regard others as he does.

The easiest way to begin pursuing some of these matters would be to go immediately to Vindice's first speech. These forty-nine lines conduct their exposition in so direct and breathless a manner that we could almost overlook their primary subject, the mind of Vindice. Establishing the movements of that mind, in its varied rhythms and tones, the speech is a showcase for Tourneur's metric virtuousity, and it is worth examining in some detail for the precedents it can offer.

The speech involves three subjects, the Duke and his train, Gloriana and her relation to the Duke, and Vindice's vow to seek revenge. But despite the changes in subject, the style remains consistent in its variations. The first line is a metrical tour de force, typical in its unusually high stress levels and light eleventh syllables:

Duke: royal lecher; go, grey-hair'd adultery.

The long vowels, numerous pauses, and high levels of stress make this the slowest line in the whole speech, yet within it there is still some speed and compression in the two long elisions; the combination of speed with pauses is one of Tourneur's favorite metrical devices. Vindice builds again toward a similar effect, first with three regular lines, which underline his mockery and sarcasm:

And thou his son, as impious steep'd as he:
And thou his bastard true-begot in evil:
And thou his Duchess that will do with devil.

He then draws out another line like the first, with high stress levels and long elisions, leading into some unusual displacements that indicate his tension:

Four excellent characters—O that marrowless age,
Would stuff the hollow bones with damn'd desires,
And 'stead of heat kindle infernal fires,

Within the spendthrift veins of a dry Duke,
A parch'd and juiceless luxur. O God! one
That has scarce blood enough to live upon.
And he to riot it like a son and heir?
O the thought of that
Turns my abused heart-strings into fret.

[1.1.8-16]

Vindice's excitement is evident in the way he moves into and out of the couplet pattern, as if the effort of organizing his thought continuously required a distancing he cannot sustain. At the end he drops into a line that leaves him silent for the space of two feet, in the middle of a thought: from this he moves quickly into a line that is mostly short vowels and frontal stops. The speed of the last line above suggests in itself the dexterity of fingers upon frets.

The extreme nervousness of the style, its movement from short lines to overflowing, from self-consciously regular stressing to irregular, all help convey directly the character's manic instability. While shifting in rhythm, the lines also shift constantly in their presumed audience: first the Duke and his family, then anyone at all, then God, and finally Vindice himself. Coming as rapidly as they do, and in lines of such varied rhythms, these shifts immediately establish a mind that has trouble focusing its attention for long in one place.

As Vindice begins to speak to Gloriana's skull, the motion of his thought becomes more regular and controlled, enforcing his generally meditative stance; he can even distance the skull before him by offering two hypothetical examples of the power of Gloriana's beauty:

the uprightest man, (if such there be,
That sin but seven times a day) broke custom
And made up eight with looking after her.
O she was able to ha' made a usurer's son
Melt all his patrimony in a kiss,
And what his father fifty years told
To have consum'd, and yet his suit been cold.

[1.1.26-32]

But at the end of this second movement Vindice falls back into two more spasms of anguish, though now he self-consciously pulls his thoughts together in a couplet:

But O accursed palace!
Thee when thou wert apparel'd in thy flesh,
The old duke poison'd,
Because thy purer part would not consent
Unto his palsy-lust, for old men lustful

Do show like young men angry, eager violent,
Outbid their limited performances—
O 'ware an old man hot, and vicious:
"Age, as in gold, in lust is covetous."

[1.1.33–41]

By the time Vindice reaches the next-to-last line he has already thought of the last line, and deliberately sets it up. His control here seems sure enough, yet he seems unaware of the strange comparison he has made between the Duke and himself, in terms of their violent impotence. We learn that the Duke is changeable, "sudden" (4.1.97): His mercurial disposition seems matched only by Vindice's. As we shall see, the link between Vindice and the Duke will constitute one pole of the tragedy.

But the sense of surface control continues as Vindice winds up the speech, vowing revenge:

Vengeance thou murder's quit-rent, and whereby
Thou show'st thyself tenant to Tragedy,
O keep thy day, hour, minute, I beseech,
For those thou hast determin'd: hum: who e'er knew
Murder unpaid? faith give Revenge her due
Sh'has kept touch hitherto—be merry, merry,
Advance thee, O thou terror to fat folks
To have their costly three-pil'd flesh worn off
As bare as this—for banquets, ease, and laughter,
Can make great men, as greatness goes by clay,
But wise men little are more great than they.

[1.1.42–52]

Some tensions are still visible beneath the surface order; as in the first part of the speech, Vindice's attention starts to shift. He addresses first a personified Vengeance, then asks a question at large, then advises those below to be merry, then speaks to the skull, then shifts away from it, referring to it as "this," and then moves still further away by moralizing at large. Although the lines remain generally regular, the metric still has its surprises; as we have seen, Tourneur's use of pause is especially varied and keeps the actor or reader from settling into any repeated rhythmic pattern. One curious feature of the lines, and a characteristic of Tourneur's more passionate verse, is the high number of secondary stresses, which slow the lines in which they appear and make the other lines with fewer secondary stresses seem much faster by comparison.

The verse technique of the speech is important for its metaphoric significance. In its breathless turns and returns, stops and starts, Tourneur gives an immediate impression of Vindice's tension and his tendency to aggravate the very thoughts that cause him the most pain. (That is why verse of this sort always seems somehow on the edge of self-parody.) These are the habits, we learn later, of nine years, but we can also see that Vindice's imagination has transformed many of the characters around him from what they actually appear to be. This is especially true of the Duke, to whom Vindice attributes memory, malice, and sensibility that the Duke does not have and probably never did have. As we see later, the Duke is neither astute nor subtle in his management of the courtroom; he seems quite duped by his wife; although he can see the ambition of two of his sons, he seems to have no idea that Lussurioso is less than fully competent; he forgets that he has sent the youngest son to prison; and he shows a lack of judgment in not protecting himself in the assignation with Gloriana, when he knows already that his life has been threatened. He also allows the Duchess's youngest son to be hanged, although he had been reluctant to see that happen earlier. In several places he refers to his own faults and sins, but these gestures are just interior decoration, and he does not seem to remember the outlines of anything specific. He is rather easily manipulated on account of his own belief in his wickedness, his probing of which he restrains with little difficulty.

It is this old dog-fox that Vindice credits as the source of his pain, and the source is inadequate enough that we can be sure Vindice will hurt himself again; he will fail to recognize himself in his rhetoric, and will start the whole process over again. For this reason, to treat Vindice primarily as a moral commentator would be to move him into an area of discourse where large parts of his character development would be inaccessible. This emphasis may have begun with Eliot's reading of the play as a view of society, but whatever the source, later critics who read the play as a sort of fictive sociological study, usually with a satiric or moral bias, are perhaps forced to ignore Vindice's development. If we regard a dramatic character as a personified commentary on society, we may exclude from consideration the dramatist's creation of an individual mind—which in this particular case is defined by the development of Vindice's poetry.[7] Vindice has an individual psychology, and he differs from the other moral defectives in the play simply in the quality of his verse. The completeness of his characterization also shows in the discrepancies between his and our perceptions of the things around him. To take an obvious example, when he says of the Duke, "who e'er knew/Murder unpaid," he does not seem to realize that he too will be repaid. This obtuseness has a more sinister and interesting side, as when he says that Gloriana "was able to ha' made a usurer's son/Melt all his patrimony in a kiss." By an imaginative jump he makes her unfaithful to him; he redeems this in a second thought, when he says "yet his suit been cold," thus suggesting that the basis of his feeling for Gloriana was the passion she inspired in others.[8] This is the first sign of a triangle of desire in Vindice's imagination, and another suggestion that he may need the Duke more than he realizes.

Vindice's next set speech occurs just two scenes later, in act 1, scene 3. After Vindice and his brother Hippolito have readied his disguise as a pander, Lussurioso enters: Hippolito introduces them to each other and steps out for a breath of air. Vindice then launches a string of one-liners and innuendo in a style by now familiar: unusually short lines, unstressed final syllables, slow lines with high stress levels alternating with fast lines, although as before the syntax is always simple and direct. Now that Vindice has begun to unfold as a dramatic character, these techniques seem to be promoting certain types of thinking and suppressing others. Let us trace some examples.

> *Luss.* Thou hast been scrivener to much knavery, then?
> *Vind.* Fool, to abundance, sir; I have been witness
> To the surrenders of a thousand virgins,
> And not so little,
> I have seen patrimonies wash'd a-pieces
> Fruit fields turn'd into bastards,
> And in a world of acres,
> Not so much dust due to the heir 'twas left to
> As would well gravel a petition.
>
>   [1.3.53–61]

Vindice's racy jokes and jumpy manner succeed in convincing Lussurioso that he is the saucy knave he was said to be; but the numerous affinities between Vindice's style here and that of his opening soliloquy should make us wonder if the disguise has actually displaced Vindice's character. His prospectus for bankrupts seems not so much the move into "another" that he had announced at the end of act 1, scene 1, as it does an unwitting exercise in self-parody. That tendency appears again when Vindice warms to his big speech for the scene:

> *Luss.*   —Then thou know'st
> I'th'world strange lust.
> *Vind.*   O Dutch lust, fulsome lust!
> Drunken procreation, which begets so many drunkards;
> Some father dreads not (gone to bed in wine) to slide
>   from the mother,
> And cling the daughter-in-law,
> Some uncles are adulterous with their nieces,
> Brothers with brothers' wives, O hour of incest!
> Any kin now next to the rim o'th'sister
> Is man's meat in these days.
>
>   [1.3.63–72]

A number of strange things have begun to happen, both in the verse and in Vindice's mind. The sense of expanding evil is conveyed directly in the lengthened lines, as it is in the parallel and coordinate clauses; phrase is stacked upon phrase, and emphasizing this, most of the lines are end-stopped, except for the brilliant contraction of line 68.

Vindice's evocation of drunken lust is inventive and meticulous. But why *incest*? Lussurioso had only said that Vindice would have known "strange lust," which then as now could involve several options besides incest. The peculiarities do not stop there. Vindice has been observing Lussurioso's family for nine years, and yet he forgets that Lussurioso has no sisters or nieces, and is not interested in his mother. Nor is Lussurioso likely to be interested in his brothers; that hardly seems his style either. One might argue that Vindice is worried about having to solicit his sister Castiza, but Lussurioso has not said yet that he has his eye on her, nor had he mentioned her in his commission to Hippolito. Of course this is not the first mention of incest in the play; in the previous scene the Duchess accosted the bastard Spurio. But Vindice was not present then, and this is the first time in the play that the concept has entered into his mind. The speech might be the expression of his own mingled fear and desire for his sister; but still it is very odd that his consciousness seems to have surfaced suddenly with something he has not seen or experienced, and an incident like this is probably one source of the common amalgamation of Vindice and Tourneur himself.[9]

This unusual management of a character's consciousness, coupled with the stylistic richness of the lines, creates some sense that the character is shifting uncertainly around us. But suddenly the whole technique becomes extremely convincing because of what Vindice now does. As if to repress or punish this whole train of thought, the speech takes a sudden moralistic turn:[10] "Who can perceive this, save that eternal eye/That sees through flesh and all." Vindice now proceeds to become more and more shrill, only barely retaining his balance:

> well:—if anything be damn'd,
> It will be twelve o'clock at night; that twelve
> Will never 'scape;
> It is the *Judas* of the hours; wherein,
> Honest salvation is betray'd to sin.

> [1.3.75-79]

Because most of the lines immediately preceding have been longer than usual, the contrast of the short line is conspicuous, but it introduces no new matter and seems to be present for rhetorical heightening alone—an odd thing to do for Lussurioso's benefit, as if Vindice has been sent for as a visiting curate. The final couplet is also peculiar in intention and unclear in meaning. *Salvation* is the key word; if it were switched for something like *young virgins* or *sweet innocence*, the couplet would make more sense but would say much less about Vindice's imagination and the short circuits it is making.[11] The style of the outburst emphasizes its flat inappropriateness to either Lussurioso or "Piato," but naturally Lussurioso notices none of this; his stupidity has to know no bounds. The audience, however, can see Vindice becoming visibly less reflective as the rhythmic patterns of his speech accelerate, and can feel him losing control over the surging movement of his mind.

The tensions and conflicts we have seen in this speech are linked to those in the temptation scenes. Because Vindice's appeal to Castiza is a solid failure, he quickly goes to work on the mother, building his temptation around three extraordinary set speeches. These are conceived and scaled as a group, and as a group they can tell us much about Vindice's growth, for they show him trying to master the movements of his mind.

Gratiana immediately refuses to encourage Castiza for "the riches of the world," and Vindice replies, suavely and with great patience,

> No, but a thousand angels can;
> Men have no power, angels must work you to't,
> The world descends into such base-born evils
> That forty angels can make fourscore devils,
> There will be fools still I perceive, still fools.
>
> [2.1.98–102]

The short line here is very much under control, working with the longer line below it, and the couplet that follows is a neat device, padded perhaps by *base-born evils* (what other kind is there?) but clear enough in thought. One wonders at its appropriateness in the mouth of a pander, unless it is an aside, but it would be more consistent to consider that the lines are *not* an aside. Vindice's holding up a higher standard, or what he thinks might imply a higher standard, is one more slip of his mask, as in the conversation with Lussurioso. It would be reassuring to think that Vindice was actually coaching his mother, but he is hardly exhorting her to virtue; his intentions seem blurred to himself, even as his voice comes more under control, and this potentially dangerous situation will occur again at the climax and in act 5.

As Vindice begins to work Gratiana into prostituting her daughter, he appeals first to her sense of ownership:

> Would I be poor dejected, scorn'd of greatness,
> Swept from the palace, and see other daughters
> Spring with the dew o'th' court, having mine own
> So much desir'd and lov'd—by the duke's son?
> No, I would raise my state upon her breast
> And call her eyes my tenants, I would count
> My yearly maintenance upon her cheeks:

Take coach upon her lip, and all her parts
Should keep men after men, and I would ride
In pleasure upon pleasure.

[2.1.103-12]

The reduction of the daughter to income-producing property allows some specious arithmetic (How can she be Lussurioso's mistress and still keep "men after men"?); it also allows the "pleasure" to be shifted finally to the mother, in a vision of vicarious sexuality, which Vindice emphasizes with the short last line and its galloping rhythm. Vindice then concludes by invoking the pangs of childbirth:

You took great pains for her, once when it was,
Let her requite it now, though it be but some;
You brought her forth, she may well bring you home.

[2.1.113-15]

Implying that nothing, not even the daughter's "maintenance" of the mother, could requite that agony, Vindice discreetly leaves out any reference to the source of the requital. The speech has a well-modeled appeal, not so detailed in its reference to the daughter's sexuality that the mother could be repelled, yet vague enough in its suggestion of "pleasure" for the mother as to allow her sexuality to enter by another door. The grotesque details of the imagery[12] show Vindice's moral bias; eyes as tenants could appear in any number of sonneteers, but maintenance upon cheeks and coach upon lip depict in contrast the grossest soil and misuse. This obscenity does not offend Gratiana, though, and the pressure of the metric does not allow any lingering upon details except that undefined "pleasure." The caesuras fall very irregularly, and as the meter accelerates there is an abrupt change in grammar:

I would count
My yearly maintenance upon her cheeks,
Take coach upon her lip and all her parts
Should keep men after men. . . .

The momentary suggestion of taking coach on "all her parts," before the next line picks up the change in subject, shows great persuasive skill; but the end effect is still rather puzzling because of Vindice's initial problem of not knowing what he is speaking for and why. This confusion becomes worse as the scene goes on.

Warming to his role as tempter, Vindice has more and more difficulty controlling his verse. First he is back to implying strongly all the arguments against his proposition. The extent of his emotional commitment to the ethical ideal is evident in the breakdown of the meters:

'Tis honesty you urge; what's honesty?
'Tis but heaven's beggar; and what woman is so foolish to keep
    honesty,
And not be able to keep herself? No,
Times are grown wiser and will keep less charge,
A maid that has small portion now intends,
To break up house, and live upon her friends.

                                                        [2.1.204-9]

It is hard to imagine the sort of woman whom remarks like this would seduce, and harder still to understand why Vindice later feels he has made an unequivocal statement for evil.[13] Whether he knows it or not, he is implying that the women could and should reject Lussurioso on every ground.

As Vindice describes the joys of being Lussurioso's mistress, he returns as before to a more measured pace, using it to build toward a sudden climax:

How bless'd are you, you have happiness alone;
Others must fall to thousands, you to one,
Sufficient in himself to make your forehead
Dazzle the world with jewels, and petitionary people
Start at your presence.

                                                        [2.1.210-14]

It would be hard to overpraise the sheer skill of this; the grand line on the jewels secures its impact by Tourneur's characteristic manner of counting only stresses, and packing in syllables (in this case thirteen) to increase the speed. The rhythm is almost dactylic:

Dázzle the wórld with jéwels, and petítionary péople
Start at your présence.

Tourneur's control of the syntax and enjambment, placing the strong verbs at the start of the lines and shifting the grammar in the second, creates a sense of sudden movement, as if the transformation of Castiza is just taking place before our eyes; at the same time the lines are tied together by the alliterated *p*'s.

The dazzling technique secures an immediate impact on the mother: "O if I were young, I should be ravish'd" (2.1.215). Doubtless funny on stage, this is followed by the daughter's sarcasm, which extends the laughter: "Ay to lose your honor" (2.1.216). Tourneur is deliberately deflating Vindice's powerful verse, for at least a couple of reasons. On the surface there would seem to be little reason for Vindice to continue working on the two women; although he has succeeded all too well with Gratiana, Lussurioso was not especially interested in her, and Castiza seems to be even more rigid than she was at first, if that is possible. Vindice might have some reason for continuing if he were really interested in seeing that the two remain (or in the mother's case, become) virtuous. But Vindice's problem is that while he wants them to choose what is good, the only arguments he can think of in its favor are negative: the terror of damnation and the loathsomeness of evil itself.[14] Having tried to point out the first, he drives his case home now with the second:

> O think upon the pleasure of the palace,
> Secured ease and state; the stirring meats,
> Ready to move out of the dishes, that e'en now quicken when
>   they're eaten;
> Banquets abroad by torchlight, musics, sports,
> Bareheaded vassals, that had ne'er the fortune
> To keep on their own hats, but let horns wear 'em.
> Nine coaches waiting—hurry, hurry, hurry.
>
> [2.1.222-28]

The zestful bad taste of this—especially that pornographic cartoon shot of the meat—could hardly persuade Castiza to accept Lussurioso when she has already rejected him and her mother's solicitations as well. Yet the material is enormously satisfying to Vindice himself, quickening when it is spoken, although it contains some of his usual self-evident hokum. Why should Castiza *hurry* to court if it is a life of *"secured* ease and state"? The word *fortune* also suggests rather strongly that this is not the sort of life in which one has the freedom to make individual choices. But again, in spite of this fuzziness, Vindice seems to be nearing the peak of his energy as a poet. The first two lines are regular, but the second is run on, into a phrase that is short one syllable and whose strong stresses occur in such a way as to produce a jump in the middle of the line:

Ready to move out of the dishes.

The strong stresses in the next phrase animate the meat:

That e'en now quicken when they're eaten;

the line demonstrates an expansion suitable to the subject. Vindice then moves to more stable patterns, but ends in a line heavy with six stresses:

Nine coaches waiting—hurry, hurry, hurry.

The self-preoccupied way in which this dazzling display of technique pours out, without regard for its audience, helps create the sense of Vindice's increasing unbalance.

The speech falls strangely flat, though; once again Castiza says dully "Ay, to the devil" (2.1.229), and we are left looking at Vindice, wondering at the reason for his great agitation. Why does he keep it up? Of course he must do so if the play is to have any excitement, but is there any cause for it? Perhaps the most common explanation is simply that he is alienated; he loses his own identity when he becomes Piato, and then his values go all topsy-turvy until he is, by the end of the play, no better than the hoodlums he is murdering.[15] But this just begs the question, for we still have to go beyond this explanation and ask why he became alienated in the first place. Was it only because Tourneur wanted him to? And why is he later so convinced of the total depravity of his arguments here? As they are usually offered, the terms *alienation* or *transformation* seldom reach these problems.

Perhaps we could understand more about the sources of Vindice's excitement if we looked more closely at his language. One notable aspect of the scene we have just been discussing is the shuffling of Vindice's references to Lussurioso and the Duke. As Vindice describes Lussurioso over the course of the scene, he becomes the Duke; how much this is the result of Vindice's attempt to seduce Castiza and how much it is an unconscious confusion on his own part would be hard to say. At the start of the scene Vindice is specific in his references to "the Duke's son" (37), "the next of Italy" (65). But as the scene goes on, Lussurioso becomes "our sudden Duke" (70), and at the conclusion of the appeal to Gratiana the change is complete:

> *Vind.*   —hurry, hurry, hurry.
> *Cast.*   Ay to the devil.
> *Vind.*   Ay to the devil, to th' Duke by my faith.
> *Grat.*   Ay to the Duke.
>
> [2.1.229-31]

Vindice's thinking of himself as pandering for the Duke has two implications. The first is that Lussurioso's desire to seduce Castiza is connected in Vindice's mind with the Duke's seduction of Gloriana. The second is that in pandering for Lussurioso, Vindice also identifies himself as a son of the Duke.

The emotional logic behind this identification is easy to trace. While Vindice says that he reveres the memory of his father, there seem to be some serious contradictions in the father's life. Vindice praises his father's noble mind, but he must have had a weak character, for when the Duke "did much deject him" (1.1.138), he seemed to lack any philosophical resources; he simply gave up without a word, exhibiting none of the Christian toughness that Vindice goes around recommending later. He may have been a religious phony but it is hard to tell, for he was more secretive than Vindice and the Duke put together.[16] Vindice never uses the term *despair*, but it seems to describe what he calls "discontent: the nobleman's consumption" (1.1.143).[17] The tendency of the oppressed mind to wound itself appears in the father as in the son. Throughout the play, good does seem to wilt before evil: there is the mother, of course, and also Antonio's wife, who is talked about in the trial scene of act 1, scene 2, as if she were alive, but then has committed suicide by act 1, scene 4. The mental failure of Vindice's father—*spinal* failure might be more accurate—is linked with the moral obtuseness of the mother, whose assessment of her late husband is very curious: "Indeed he was a worthy gentleman/Had his estate been fellow to his mind" (1.1.136–37). Maybe the irony is unconscious, but the suggestion is certainly strong that the father was better than he needed to be. The mother would never make that error; as she says, "O if I were young, I should be ravish'd."

These considerations profoundly affect Vindice's development in the play. As Gratiana weakens, Vindice begins to retreat from the awful knowledge that her sellout seems to imply:

> O suff'ring heaven with thy invisible finger,
> E'en at this instant turn the precious side
> Of both mine eyeballs inward, not to see my self!

[2.1.142-44]

When he tells Lussurioso later that he has succeeded with Gratiana, he fears the results of his "success": "Now must I blister my soul" (2.2.41). And the note is repeated later when he confronts Gratiana with her action: "O I'm in doubt/Whether I'm myself, or no" (4.4.31-32).

It is extremely important for an audience to realize that there is more at stake here than Vindice's feeling cut off or estranged; nor is his anguish merely a fear for his mother. Gratiana's weakening forces Vindice into the intuition or subconscious fear that he may be a son of the Duke. His pimping for Lussurioso transforms him into the son onstage, and the relationship is significantly established by his own mother. Castiza has just refused Vindice, who is standing there with the two women; Gratiana then says to her daughter:

> You cannot come by yourselves without fee.
> And 'twas decreed that man should keep the key!

And then, while Vindice is standing there before them, she exclaims, "Deny advancement, treasure, the Duke's son!" (2.1.179). With Vindice the only other person onstage, this appeal could not fail to suggest that the duke is Vindice's father. Coupled with Vindice's own questions as to who he is, and our own doubts about the capacities of his father, the identification is dramatically established.

The connection is echoed throughout the play. When Vindice offers Lussurioso a "character" of the Duke, it is that of "a usuring father to be boiling in hell, and his son and heir with a whore dancing over him" (4.2.90-91). Yet earlier, in describing his own relationship with Gloriana,

Vindice had said that "she was able to ha' made a usurer's son/Melt all his patrimony in a kiss." In this imaginative figure of the usurer[18] (the sexual connotations of which are familiar), Vindice and Lussurioso are joined to the Duke. Indeed Vindice complains that the Duke riots it "like a son and heir" in the same speech where he compares old lechers to violent young men.

The most brilliant connection that Tourneur makes between Vindice and the Duke, however, is in the killing of "Piato." When Vindice runs the dead Duke through from behind, he realizes beforehand the significance of the act:

> That's a good lay, for I must kill myself.
> Brother that's I: that sits for me: do you mark it,
> And I must stand ready here to make away myself yonder—I must
>   sit to be kill'd, and stand to kill myself.
>
> [5.1.3–6]

The nervous repetitiveness of this, the drop into loose prose, suggests that the "murder" means a great deal to Vindice. In killing the Duke he is irreparably wounding himself, his poetic self.[19] Having lived so long for the Duke, then having killed him, he has taken away his own center (as the Elizabethans would say), the man who has ordered his life. After he kills the Duke, Vindice has only three things to do: first, to kill the self that killed the Duke, then to kill anyone who would attempt to become a new duke, and finally to kill the killer. In effect then, the plot has three poles (like that of *The Duchess of Malfi*): the murder of the Duke, the murder of Piato, and the suicide of Vindice. This last is the step back through the mirror, the final destructive self-revelation. All these levels of dramatic meaning are latent in the remurdering of the disguised Duke.

This is getting somewhat ahead of the narrative, however, and we might return to Vindice's discovery of his parents' critical weaknesses. That discovery occurs just as his soliciting for Lussurioso begins to lay open his identification with the Duke. Much of the tragedy of Vindice lies in the fact that he does not discover his identification with the Duke until after he has killed him, and that he has to kill him to discover it.

Once we understand the nature of Vindice's bond to the Duke, we can make sense out of his outrage at discovering that the Duke is being cuckolded. To Vindice's brother Hippolito it is a great joke, "knavery faith" (2.2.119), but to Vindice it is something very serious indeed: "O sin foul and deep,/Great faults are wink'd at when the dukes asleep" (2.2.126–127).[20] If Vindice's sole purpose were revenge, it would be difficult to explain why he should become so wrought up after seeing Spurio go to the Duchess. Certainly his speech at that time is one of the strongest in the play, opening with a tense line full of high stresses and moving in such a way as to give a shape to the action it describes:

Mark, there, there, that step, now to the Duchess,
This their second meeting writes the Duke cuckold
With new additions, his horns newly reviv'd:
Night! thou that look'st like funeral herald's fees
Torn down betimes i'th' morning, thou hang'st fitly
To grace those sins that have no grace at all.
Now 'tis full sea abed over the world;
There's juggling of all sides; some that were maids
E'en at sunset are now perhaps i'th' toll-book;
This woman in immodest thin apparel
Lets in her friend by water, here a dame
Cunning, nails leather hinges to a door,
To avoid proclamation.
Now cuckolds are a-coining, apace, apace, apace, apace.
And careful sisters spin that thread i'th' night,
That does maintain them and their bawds i'th' day!

[2.2.146-61]

This must be one of the most extraordinary and masterful verse paragraphs in the Jacobean drama. The steady movement of the first three lines, with only one metric substitution (the reversed foot in the first line) emphasizes Vindice's sobriety; as he shifts to vice on a global scale he becomes more excited. The lines are difficult to discuss in terms of a two-stress metric, as we see in

Now 'tis full sea abed over the world.

We can account for the metric in traditional terms by saying that it employs two reversed feet, but against this reading there is a tension best shown in a four-value scansion:

Now 'tis full sea abed over the world.

The high tide of fornication requires and gets a line full of stresses. Vindice becomes progressively more excited now; the lines, by requiring long elisions, begin to gather speed:

some that were maids
E'en at sunset are now perhaps i'th' toll-book.

As he continues, many of the lines take only four strong stresses and a minimum of pauses:

This woman in immodest thin apparel
Lets in her friend by water, here a dame

Cunning, nails leather hinges to a door
To avoid proclamation.

He ends with his usual gesture toward haste, but follows it this time with the steady beat of the spinning wheel:

Now cuckolds are a-coining, apace, apace, apace, apace.
And careful sisters spin that thread i'th night
That does maintain them and their bawds i'th day!

The effect is of the possessed mind employing, using, its great energy; no wonder Hippolito comments, "You flow well brother" (2.2.162). This is Vindice's last sustained speech before the play's dramatic climax in the poisoning of the Duke (2.5.) and it marks an important point in his development. Comparing its imagery with that of the earlier speeches, we note that there is simply more of it; there are fewer polysyllabic abstractions and instead whole series of metaphors in layers. Consider the last of these, for example. Referring to the Fates as *sisters* conveys Vindice's own fear for his sister; and the image of the thread made at night to support the bawds by day suggests an inversion of the chaste Penelope, who undid her work at night to hold her suitors away by day. The *thread* of lust is related in turn to the other fabrics in the speeches: the thin apparel, the funeral herald's fees (or *pheese,* black hangings), the three-pil'd flesh of the first speech, the new gowns of the temptation scene, and above all the clothes and fabric in the silkworm speech that is to come. One could go through nearly every image in the speech in this way, relating it to others in the speech and in the play as a whole. This coalescence of imagery goes with the fuller lines and the mastered hysteria. Vindice is anything but sane, just as he is anything but out of control; he has almost finished preparing his voice, as an instrument, for the climax of the play.

Between the speech we have just studied and the climax of the play, Vindice has almost no speech of any length; he has only two three-line speeches later in act 2, scene 2 (lines 237–39, 241–43). Most of the time the stage is occupied instead with the plot of the youngest son. In spite of his bravado the youngest son is, unlike Vindice, afraid of death. Vice does not excite his imagination; it is simply fun. With the youngest son onstage at this crucial point in Vindice's development, we can see that part of Vindice's depth originates in his grasp of the uniquely personal relation between the murderer and his victim. The youngest son has absolutely no conception of his relationship to the woman he raped; as he says in his happy way, "Well then 'tis done, and it would please me well/Were it to do again" (1.2.67–68). Vindice, on the other hand, has been moving closer to an understanding of the symbiotic relationship between himself and his victims, as if he had been reading D. H. Lawrence on the bond between the murderer and the murderee. It is Tourneur's understanding of this bond, and his artistic apprehension of it, that constitutes one of the play's enduring achievements. In readying himself to strike the Duke, Vindice will be preparing to wound himself yet again, this time with a psychologically fatal blow. He realizes this in the silkworm speeches of act 3, scene 5.

Upon first reading or hearing these speeches, one is immediately aware that many strands of meaning are being pulled together. This is partly a result of the imagery; like some of the earlier speeches, these focus the major trains of imagery, the patterns of light-breaking-out-of-darkness, fabrics and clothes, and most obviously "the skull beneath the skin." The metrical ordering of the speeches is another such strand of meaning. As Vindice describes his rendezvous with the Duke, then produces the skull and speaks to it, his poetry reveals the extreme excitement that we saw earlier, which he has gradually mastered. As he progresses toward the murder, performs it, and moves on, his meters and rhythms become more regular and controlled. (This will be demonstrated more closely in a moment.) These two levels of style, the metaphors and the verse, are both aspects of the chief organizing agent, Vindice's mind.

The immediately satisfying coherence of the speeches in this scene should not, however, prevent our asking some questions about its presence in the first place, or its formal cause. When and how did the duke solicit Vindice, and why did Tourneur not show their encounter? In all the criticism of the play, one seldom if ever meets this fairly obvious question, yet the answers to it carry us far into the play and its central character. In the first place, any encounter between the two onstage prior to the murder would have made the murder anticlimatic—or so a certain sort of theatrical criticism might say.[21] But do we need to sell Tourneur short in this way? It is not hard to imagine a scene of verbal sparring between the two on a higher plane than that which Vindice does with Lussurioso. Under the circumstances, with the execution of the youngest son occupying so much time onstage, a preliminary encounter between Vindice and the Duke could conceivably heighten the horror of the murder. However, Tourneur is working for one main sort of recognition in Vindice himself, and for dramatic reasons he wants that recognition to occur immediately prior to and during the murder. It is also essential to this recognition that the Duke remain somewhat vaguely characterized and not have a chance to exhibit much wit or intelligence; again, the play involves Vindice's attribution of these qualities to the Duke. In the speeches of act 3, scene 5, Vindice's identification of himself as a corrupt character is complete. Such a recognition might plausibly have occurred in a scene where the Duke would enlist Vindice as a pander; yet to have the murder follow after such a recognition would have obscured the fact that in murdering the Duke, Vindice murders part of himself.

The speeches themselves clarify these remarks. The speeches in which
Vindice announces his meeting with the Duke convey his self-preoccupied
excitement of both memory and anticipation:

> *Vindice.*   O sweet, delectable, rare, happy, ravishing!
> *Hippolito.* Why, what's the matter, brother?
> *Vindice.*   O, 'tis able to make a man spring up, & knock his
>   forehead
>   Against yon silver ceiling.
>
> [3.5.1–4]

The first and third lines are good examples of the way Tourneur counts
five strong stresses and lets the other syllables take care of themselves; the
speed and surprise that this allows are familiar by now. Vindice collects
himself as he begins to explain the plan to Hippolito, but soon loses his
self-control:

> The old Duke
> Thinking my outward shape, and inward heart
> Are cut out of one piece; (for he that prates his secrets,
> His heart stands o'th'outside) hires me by price:
> To greet him with a lady,
> In some fit place veil'd from the eyes o'th' court,
> Some darken'd blushless angle, that is guilty
> Of his forefathers' lusts, and great folks riots. . . .
>
> [3.5.10–17]

Line 11 is regular with a conventional substitution, but in line 12 Vindice
starts to hurry the syllables in, then tucks in his parenthesis; in the next
line he ends the parenthesis and scrabbles the line together only to come
up short in line 14, with just two firm stresses holding together seven syllables. The line is characteristically Tourneur's in its hurrying to a pause,
Vindice hugging himself mentally in the space of the missing syllables. The
lines then become more regular, to set up the next disturbance at the end
of the speech:

> The Bastard and the Duchess have appointed
> Their meeting too in this luxurious circle,
> Which most afflicting sight will kill his eyes
> Before we kill the rest of him.
>
> [3.5.23–26]

In a later line, Vindice talks about the violence of his joy; it is evident in a
line like the last one above, with its tension between the expected iambic
pattern and the logical emphasis required on *we* and *rest*. When he plans the
use of Gloriana's skull, the frequency of irregularly stressed short lines rises:

Hippolito. Ay, but where's that lady now?
Vindice.   O, at that word
          I'm lost again, you cannot find me yet
          I'm in a throng of happy apprehensions.
          He's suited for a lady; I have took care
          For a delicious lip, a sparkling eye—
          You shall be witness, brother;
          Be ready, stand with your hat off.

                                          [3.5.30-37]

The last two energetic lines, each with only three strong stresses, help convey that breathless manner of the early speeches, but now the manner is employed for the contemplation of his particular joy. The equation subtly indicates that Vindice's joy will become part of his suffering.[22]

It is in this excitement, then, that Vindice—after a brief speech pausing, starting again, and pausing again—finally unmasks the skull:

Art thou beguil'd now? tut, a lady can,
At such all hid, beguile a wiser man.
Have I not fitted the old surfeiter
With a quaint piece of beauty? age and bare bone
Are e'er allied in action; here's an eye,
Able to tempt a great man—to serve God,
A pretty hanging lip, that has forgot now to dissemble;
Methinks this mouth should make a swearer tremble,
A drunkard clasp his teeth, and not undo 'em,
To suffer wet damnation to run through 'em.
Here's a cheek keeps her color; let the wind go whistle,
Spout rain, we fear thee not, be hot or cold
All's one with us; and is not he absurd,
Whose fortunes are upon their faces set,
That fear no other God but wind and wet?

                                          [3.5.54-68]

For those fifteen lines Vindice controls himself in fairly regular verse; there is a sober concern for the skull's familiar properties, and his own acceptance of those properties. The skull will lead sinners of all shapes and sizes to serve God: "we" cannot fear natural change, and if we do worry more about our own complexions than our relations to the true God, the consequences are clear.

If Tourneur were to end here and bring on the Duke for his poisoning, both Vindice's revenge and the play as a whole would be very different. But now Vindice begins to probe behind the conventional uses of the skull as an emblem, and finds another cave opening up out of the first:

> And now methinks I could e'en chide myself,
> For doting on her beauty, though her death
> Shall be reveng'd after no common action;
> Does the silkworm expend her yellow labors
> For thee? for thee does she undo herself?
> Are lordships sold to maintain ladyships
> For the poor benefit of a bewitching minute?
> Why does yon fellow falsify highways
> And put his life between the judge's lips,
> To refine such a thing, keeps horse and men
> To beat their valors for her?
> Surely we're all mad people, and they
> Whom we think are, are not; we mistake those,
> 'Tis we are mad in sense, they but in clothes.

                                        [3.5.72–85]

The steady and gathering movement of the lines is partly a result of the syntax and enjambment; the prepositional phrases in particular tend to draw the sense out from one line to another.[23] These create the sense of a mind moving by stages toward a conclusion, yet at the same time Tourneur has done everything possible to keep the lines from falling into a recurrent or hypnotic rhythm. The speaker's consciousness is rising, and the alertness of the rhythms is evident in the way Vindice balances regular lines with lines that are very subtly modulated. To take just two examples:

> Are lordships sold to maintain ladyships
> For the poor benefit of a bewitching minute?
>
> And put his life between the judge's lips,
> To refine such a thing, keeps horse and men
> To beat their valors for her?

The incredulity expressed in the last line, for example, is conveyed in great part by the pause of three syllables' duration that ends it, and the slight delay before *her*, caused by the addition of an extra lightly-stressed syllable. In the first example, *poor benefit* is set in apposition to *bewitching minute*, and the two are not only linked by their alliteration and near rhyme but also by their similar falling rhythmic pattern. Endlessly meticulous, Tourneur's art should be studied line after line in such detail.

   Several commentators have unpacked the speech word by word, and if they are correct, nearly every noun and verb in the passage carries two or three meanings.[24] It is doubtful, though, that so many multiple meanings could be sensed on the stage at once, and a reading in terms of these ambiguities also risks ignoring the logic of the speech. In reading something this rich, we simply have to consider our options, selecting those that provide the cleanest and longest line of connection between the principal incidents and speeches of the play. The logic behind the speech as a whole can provide a means of dealing with individual details in the phrasing and vice versa. Consider, for example, that little connective *though* in line 73, which controls the meaning of the first three lines. With it Vindice is implying that although he should not have been so in love with something purely transitory, he will make up for those misplaced values in the killing of the Duke. He thinks he can atone for that shame by sacrificing the Duke in as ingenious a manner as possible.

The main force of Vindice's imagination returns to contemplate the absurd and self-destructive actions people commit for the sake of fugitive sexual pleasures. He does not and cannot think about the resemblance between his own desire to kill the Duke and the behavior of the people he describes. Logically speaking, there would be no reason to kill the Duke if all mankind were mortal and undoing itself anyway; under these circumstances the best approach might be to follow Escalus's advice to Elbow in *Measure for Measure*: "Let him continue in his courses till thou knowest what they are" (2.1.186–88). The speech never considers that possibility; Vindice would rather elaborate his amazement that people destroy themselves for transitory pleasure. Vindice, of course, is such a person himself; as Bradbrook was the first to note, the "bewitching minute" Vindice refers to here resembles the vengeance he is soon to "crowd into a minute" (3.5.126).[25] But because Vindice sees his madness in this respect does not mean he sees farther into the heart of his own relation to the Duke. And what he says about human behavior simply does not hold up in the play: Castiza and (finally) Gratiana are pat examples of virtue, but there is also Hippolito, who seems not so much a lecherous monster as a yes-man in the tow of a stronger brother. Vindice's father, far from being seduced by evil, withdrew from it neurotically to mourn. Even Lussurioso honors his father. As we saw first in his conception of the Duke, Vindice is not a careful observer of others, and when he justifies his actions to himself he needs to adopt a desperate view of the people around him.

The narrow focus of the silkworm speech can be seen in Hippolito's typically cute comment on it: "Faith and in clothes too we, give us our due" (3.5.86). Vindice's hypnotic vision could not take much of this sort of commentary, although it does distance us from Vindice at a crucial point, revealing that he has adopted a stance rather than a complex point of view. The latter would require that he understand better his relation to the Duke; instead, Vindice takes off like a jet for the second part of the speech, contrasting vice with his noble purpose:

Does every proud and self-affecting dame
Camphire her face for this? and grieve her Maker
In sinful baths of milk,—when many an infant starves,
For her superfluous outside, all for this?
Who now bids twenty pound a night, prepares
Music, perfumes, and sweetmeats? All are hush'd,
Thou may'st lie chaste now! It were fine methinks,
To have thee seen at revels, forgetful feasts,
And unclean brothels; sure, 'twould fright the sinner
And make him a good coward, put a reveler
Out of his antic amble
And cloy an epicure with empty dishes.
Here might a scornful and ambitious woman
Look through and through herself,—see ladies, with false forms
You deceive men, but cannot deceive worms.

[3.5.87–101]

Controlling the rhythm here, the regular iambic pattern is closer to the surface than it was in Vindice's earlier set speeches. The one short line, with its falling rhythms and final pause, neatly imitates the arrested motion it describes:

                    put a reveler
Out of his antic amble.

Of particular interest are the two alexandrines, the first in the service of sensual excess: "In sinful baths of milk,—when many an infant starves." The second creates and embodies a long introspective glance, followed by an insistently repeated pressure against the meter:

Look through and through herself,—see, ladies with false forms
You deceive men, but cannot deceive worms.

As the final *t* of *cannot* becomes the *d* of *deceive,* the first syllable of *deceive* could almost be dropped by an actor speaking at a moderate pace; a simplified scansion of the line would thus be / x / / ∥ x / x / / . The second half repeats the first and emphasizes the link between men and worms.

Vindice's rhythmic balance is hard-won and precarious, but it is impossible to regard it without a certain alarm. By its blocklike weighting of rhythm and syntax, it attempts to validate an insanely illogical conclusion: that women are mortal in some way proves they are untrue. Another problem is that Vindice's steadily increasing control does not coincide with his insight into his own nature. That insight occured in the previous speech, and was undercut by Hippolito's simple wisecrack; now this speech is given the lie by the uses to which it is put, for Vindice himself is hardly put "out of his antic amble" by the sight of Gloriana. If anything, there seems to be a net decrease in his self-knowledge.

It is as if the restrained tension of his verse were trying to supply an equilibrium and stabilizing force that his logic and actions lack; Vindice seems ridden with a form of autosuggestion, which originated in an almost compulsive set of mental rhythms that he has finally learned to control and use, with little regard to context or audience. Marvelous as this last speech is, it ignores the penalties for the murder Vindice is about to commit, and it can hardly justify the killing of the Duke, who, whatever his other vices, is not known to bathe in milk or camphor his face. (While there *are* perfumes stealing through the air as the Duke enters, these have been provided by Vindice and not by the Duke.) The sliding irrelevance of the speech is, then, an important factor in Vindice's characterization: It helps confirm our sense that Vindice has other more personal reasons he cannot name for wanting to kill the Duke. In some respects the problem is similar to that in *Richard III*, where Richard, like Vindice, blurs the lines between an irrational and illegal revenge upon others for the pain of his own existence and a single-handed cleansing of a rotten society—which may be a rational task, but is equally forbidden. Richard, however, does not use the power of verse to justify himself and obscure his own understanding of his motives.

The ironies of the murder are readily apparent: In whoring his own mistress, Vindice becomes the type of pimp he has condemned, which could hardly happen if he had honored Gloriana's memory.[26] To judge by much recent criticism of the play, this is an article of faith: Vindice prostitutes the woman he loved and falls to the level of the villains in the piece. But perhaps this is rather strained; to identify that skull as a woman is visually absurd, inasmuch as Vindice himself emphasizes repeatedly the hideousness of bare bone. In one sense, Vindice has been able to achieve the poise of his great speeches precisely *because* the skull is no more Gloriana for him than it is for an audience. Under the circumstances, it is hard to see how the skull could be a woman on the stage, except as a sort of puppet that would emphasize by distortion its very distance from a woman.[27] As Vindice says, "I could e'en chide myself / For doting on her beauty." Given his disgust for the skull, it should be hardly surprising that after the murder of the Duke, Vindice shows no concern whatever for the skull; we never do learn what happened to it.[28]

The murder of the Duke is, by contrast, both anticlimactic and casual, for us and for Vindice as well. The poisoned kiss is an apt means for the revenge because it literally eats the Duke; just as he had been a sexual cannibal, so is he consumed by that final cannibal, the death's-head. If the corrosive is appropriate for the Duke, it is equally suited to Vindice, who has been practicing his own gradual self-disintegration; after the murder, Vindice becomes rather preposterous as a tragic character, not so much because he says funny things as because the murder of Lussurioso is not required by the wrongs that he has committed upon Vindice. Lussurioso has assayed Castiza's virtue, but that only indirectly, and his appetite has not led him as far as rape; that was more the youngest son's style, and at this point in the play he has only a few minutes to live. In general Vindice begins to devote his energies to killing a group of imbeciles who have a more than passing interest in the job themselves. The decline of Vindice's character after act 3, scene 5, is due to his running on indignation alone, and to his lack of an antagonist whom he (and we) could consider immorally worthy; he spends the last third of the play in what is essentially a mopping-up operation.[29] Once his action and thought lose a central organizing agent (an agent whose capacities were largely of his own creation), his movement loses its line, becoming more a series of jokes larded with false confrontations. When the Duke dispossessed Vindice of his mistress and his father, he assumed their combined importance for Vindice; and under the pressure of his own poetry, Vindice even sees, momentarily, the Duke as the would-be seducer of his sister. By trying to wipe out his deep investment in the duke, Vindice bankrupts himself spiritually; it is fitting that his poetry should thin out radically from this point on.

Vindice's increasing use of prose after act 3, scene 5, indicates the shift in his character, and is related to one of the more puzzling textual problems in the play, that being the uncertain division between the prose and the poetry. How much prose *did* Tourneur actually write? Of course the uncertainty is in the reader rather than the text (a point sometimes forgotten), and there may actually be more logic to the arrangement of the Quarto text than many readers have allowed. Most editors—Allardyce Nicoll is the notable exception—have created difficulties in the interpretation of Vindice's character by their own reluctance to accept the Quarto. The bibliographical arguments against it begin with its erratic punctuation (especially in its profusion of question marks) and an occasionally misattributed speech. Other objections include several missing stage directions, and the compositor's failure to leave space between stage directions and dialogue.[30] Many short lines are also set on the right-hand side of the page, as in this example from G4^r:

> *Vin.*   Ime couetous,
> To know the villayne,
> *Lus.*   You know him that slaue Pandar,
> *Piato* whome we threatned last
> With irons in perpetuall prisonment;
> *Vin.*   All this is I.   *Hip.*   Ist he my Lord?
> *Lus.*   Ile tell you, you first preferd him to me.

Vin. Did you brother.   *Hip.* I did indeed?
Lus. And the ingreatful villayne, . . .

The immediate appearance of the play thus suggests, as Foakes says in his Introduction to the Revels edition, "a printinghouse job done with the utmost economy" (p. lvii), which is typical of play texts printed by George Eld.[31]

What many editors regard as verse is also set as prose in the Quarto, although this is not a bibliographical fact but a critical judgment—What is verse?—which we will consider separately. One last objection to the Quarto is that it is simply unattractive, being printed on coarse stock with narrow margins. It is not the sort of book to bring one to the British Museum's North Library for an aesthetic experience.

No one has stated, however, the arguments in favor of the Quarto text and against its rearrangement. The punctuation is a minor problem; many of the liberally sprinkled question marks are obviously intended as exclamation points, and the remainder are no more confusing than the second in the passage quoted above. Generally the pointing of the Quarto is light. Nor is there much difficulty caused by the misattributed speeches, which involve those of a noble in act 5, scene 1 (the discovery of the old Duke's body) and of Spurio in act 5, scene 3 (the masque of the intended revengers). Far more serious misattributions occur in other texts that are regarded as good.

More substantial problems begin with the missing stage directions, particularly entrances and exits. George R. Price has treated these omissions in detail in his study of the play's authorship;[32] by themselves they shed little light on the question of whether the compositor deleted lines of dialogue or printed Tourneur's verse as prose. There is always the possibility that some stage directions were missing from the compositor's copy-text: certainly a few of the Quarto's stage directions are quite full, such as those relating to the masque. The suggestion that the compositor deleted stage directions remains only a hypothesis, and again it would not seem to illuminate questions concerning the lineation of the play.

Nor does the occasional lack of space between the stage directions and the text provide any clue about the reliability of the Quarto's lineation. Pointing out the way the compositor has huddled together some stage directions and dialogue, most editors convey the impression that the text as a whole is unusually crowded. In fact, most of the stage directions are indented as least as far as the speech headings (except of course for the first word, which begins at the left margin); a few are laid out quite generously, some even being centered with progressively smaller lines.[33] Neither is a practice that a compositor intent on saving space at all costs would be likely to do. In short, the stage directions seem inconsistent

enough to prevent our drawing inferences *from them* about the compositor's having altered Tourneur's poetry or prose.

   Criticism of the compositor's manner of setting short lines seems to
have ignored several of his habits. Let us reexamine the passage quoted
above, which contains two distinct problems. In these lines the compositor had a good opportunity to set Vindice's first speech as one line instead
of two, but inexplicably (if we accept the argument of "utmost economy")
he failed to. For some reason, however, he did set Hippolito's two short
speeches over to the right. R. A. Foakes, in the Revels edition, makes
very heavy weather of all this by printing it as follows:

> *Vind.*   I'm covetous
>   To know the villain.
> *Luss.*   You know him, that slave-pander,
>   Piato, whom we threatened last
>   With irons in perpetual prisonment.
> *Vind.*   [Aside] All this is I.
> *Hipp.*   Is't he, my lord?
> *Luss.*   I'll tell you,
>   You first preferr'd him to me.
> *Vind.*   Did you, brother?
> *Hipp.*   I did indeed.
> *Luss.*   And the ingrateful villain. . . .
>   [4.2.127–33]

First we are to suppose that the compositor followed the copy-text, then
that he *failed* to cramp the text enough, so the first three words of Lussurioso's speech ("I'll tell you") can be divided from the rest of the speech
and indented to form a "complete" poetic line. Thus we are also expected
to assume that "All this is I. Is't he my lord?" is not a "complete" line, as
it has only eight syllables and four stresses, although the line just above—
presumably it is Tourneur's—has exactly that meter (and note how the
Quarto's disyllabic *threatned* has become *threatened*, with its suggestion
of an additional syllable).

   If we study the entire text, we can see several of the compositor's
habits. First, he rarely sets a speech to the right if it continues into the
next line. There are only twelve occasions when speeches set on the right
continue into the next line, and every time the short line obviously com-
pletes a verse line to the left of it—so obviously that no editor has noted it
in his apparatus.[34] Unless a short phrase was a complete speech in itself,
or demonstrably completed a line of verse, the compositor never set it to
the right, even when it would have been much more economical of space
and paper to set more short lines on that side. Nowhere does a passage of
verse end with a short line offset to the right. And not once in the text
does a prose passage begin with a short line on the right. The compositor

seems to have set speeches on the right only when they would not be confused with the lines around them, and in this he was consistent. In other words, there seems reason to believe that the compositor knew when he was setting verse and when he was setting prose.

Further, while every editor mentions the compositor's way of setting short lines (usually as support for rearranging the text), none has remarked that there are many places in the text where two short lines could have been pulled together, had the compositor wanted to do so.[35] We might assume that the casting off has produced some of the problems in spacing, but generally the compositor seems to observe line divisions even when he would have had reason to squeeze the text together. Some lines in the Quarto do look suspiciously long, and some are indeed very short; but before recomposing Tourneur's pages, we should consider whether the lines as they stand have their own literary integrity. R. A. Foakes has discussed the lineation in his essay on the authorship of the play, and in the process has defined many of Tourneur's strengths as a poet. But valuable as that study is, it reveals how easily problems can arise in marking the borders between critical and textual analysis. Consider this: "One characteristic of the original printing is the placing of an extra half-line of verse on the same line as the full pentameter which should precede or succeed it." The word *extra* is misleading, for not all the lines set off to the right are "extra" in the sense that they fail to fit the metrical pattern of the lines above and below, although they may be extra in the sense that it is uncommon to find a speech set to the right. Or this: "In these examples quoted from the original text a line runs on far beyond its natural length, and is brought to an end by some mark of punctuation. It would appear that the compositor in each case printed the line according to its meaning, not its metre, and carried on until he came to a pause."[36] But as we have seen, there are many cases in which the compositor did *not* ignore the meter, and set his lines consistently.

Under the circumstances, there seems to be no way that the compositor's practice of setting short lines to the right can be used as evidence of his general unreliability in lineation. And the presence of numerous short lines that could have been cramped together and were not—even in the last two sheets, where the compositor would presumably be looking for space to save—tends to argue against the theory that he assembled long lines out of Tourneur's short lines. If the compositor thus begins to appear more reliable than editors have made him out to be, we may then have less justification for assembling longer lines of verse from the Quarto's short lines, or for breaking up lines that are more than ten syllables long.

Some editors' difficulties in handling the Quarto's verse seem to come back to the modern practice of line division by indention. Staggering portions of lines across a page may create a superficial impression of order, but it is an order imposed by the editor alone. It would be well to remember here that the practice of beginning all speeches to the left, by the speech headings, is observed even in texts that were prepared with relative care. Line division by indention is of relatively recent origin, and its nearly universal acceptance at the present would seem to have begun with the rise of the modern notion of a literary text as a visual rather than an aural artifact. The old Penguin Shakespeare from 1937, edited by G. B. Harrison, was perhaps the last popular text to begin all the speeches over by the speech headings; it may be only a coincidence that the book dates from about the same time that modern ideas about visual media were being formed. Line division by indention rests in part upon a visual analogy, although Elizabethan and Jacobean audiences *heard* the text. As we saw in the opening chapters, a play had for them an auditory existence, and the audiences—either as spectators or as readers—did not need to have the speeches arranged across the page to tell them when a character had completed a line of verse. This does not imply that as a modern audience we do not or cannot obtain a similar experience; but we need to remind ourselves often that as a generation of readers we depend upon more visual signals from the text than did our predecessors. This dependence has led to some interesting hybrids, such as old-spelling texts arranged with line division by indention. The result is somewhat unsettling, like a Charles Eames house furnished entirely in Louis Quinze.

Basically the same difficulties obtain when we consider rearrangement of the Quarto's prose. Because much of the prose can be made to scan, and because the compositor has supposedly revealed his incompetence by setting many short lines on the right, it has seemed appropriate to most editors that any scannable prose might be available for setting as verse. The practice has been honored since Dodsley's eighteenth-century editions, and when it comes to the resetting of the Quarto's prose (as in the reformation of its long and short lines), the only restraint on an editor would be his own ear. Not surprisingly, a passage that one editor prints as verse will often be printed as prose by another, usually without explanation by either.

Throughout the play Tourneur uses prose to relax the tensions created by the poetry.[37] Thus when Vindice reports back to Lussurioso about his soliciting of Castiza he speaks in tense verse, but once that is past and they begin to talk about Vindice's payment, both speak in a loose, jazzy prose. Similarly, after the great speeches of act 3, scene 5, and the murder of the Duke, Vindice drops back into prose, which is appropriate for someone who has begun to lose the focus of nine years of his life.

The editorial and critical problems begin, however, with those speeches in the Quarto in which characters shift into and out of prose, sometimes more than once in the same speech. These shifts often create a good deal of tension, as when Lussurioso enters to Vindice in act 1, scene 3, or when

Vindice goes back to Lussurioso after tempting the two women. As might be expected, the technique is used to great advantage in the climax of act 3, scene 5, where Vindice gathers his thoughts up then lets them out again. At other times the prose is studiedly casual, as when Vindice sells Gloriana to the Duke with some offhand chitchat:

> *Vind.* Privately rid forth,
>   He strives to make sure work on't—your good grace?
> *Duke.* Piato, well done; hast brought her, what lady is't?
> *Vind.* Faith my lord a country lady, a little bashful at first as
>   most of them are, but after the first kiss my lord the
>   worst is past with them; your grace knows now what
>   you have to do; sh'has somewhat a grave look with
>   her—but—
>
> [3.5.137–43]

Versifying editors have their greatest test in the confrontation itself, where the shift to prose controls the tone precisely, as the old man becomes gallantly impetuous:

> *Duke.* How sweet can a Duke breathe? age has no fault,
>   Pleasure should meet in a perfumed mist.
>   Lady sweetly encounter'd. I came from court, I must
>   be bold with you, oh, what's this, oh!

The Quarto's shift into prose at the third line goes perfectly with the Duke's adoption of a more informal—one might say unbuttoned—manner.

A passage like the last should remind us what a limited view of Tourneur's metric most editors would give us by way of their emended lineation. Most want to assemble regular iambic pentameter lines, although Tourneur's interest in sustaining this pattern without variation is apparently rather limited. At the other extreme, we have a view of Tourneur's metric like that in some of the edited examples, where the playwright's judgment is represented as being so porous that he will call anything poetry. In the Quarto all the great passages of verse show a movement into, out of, and back into regular verse, which the compositor could apparently recognize. The wonderfully reckless single lines that we admire—

> Ready to move out of the dishes

> O sweet, delectable, rare, happy, ravishing!

> For the poor benefit of a bewitching minute

all occur in predominantly regular iambic contexts. As this implies though, it is a mistake to try to manufacture either the reckless lines or, as nearly all editorial relineations aspire to, the completely regular lines. No editor would offer an emended passage as daring metrically as any one of Vindice's major speeches, and that is just the point: one of the reasons we read Tourneur is because he is *not* a smooth versifier, with five beats and ten syllables always at hand. With this play, one constantly has to bear in mind the saying of art historians, that a major work of art can sustain the greatest damage but not the smallest restoration.

If the common editorial view of Tourneur's metric is somewhat limited, so is the implied view of the function of poetry in drama. The impulse to reshape the prose and irregular verse of *The Revenger's Tragedy* often proceeds from a well-meaning desire to have all of the play as sweet as its best single moments, as if one would want a meal with nothing but desserts. Certainly many lines in the play are neutral or flat, yet they are needed to set off the strong lines. Because there are lines or passages that could be improved does not mean we have to improve them, and even small changes can have large implications. In his notes to the New Mermaid edition, Brian Gibbons notes his "adjustment" or "realignment" of the Quarto's lineation,[38] but the problem with this is that changing the lineation of a speech can change both the character and the conflict. We may hear verse movements in Tourneur's prose, or hear the prose shading into verse, but wherever possible we might try first to accept these as aspects of Tourneur's characterization.

A brief illustration might conclude this section. Vindice's accent is unmistakably his own; there is no one else in the play who can or does employ it. But there is one approximation, and that is the speech of Spurio. It is significant that the one character whose style most resembles Vindice's should be the bastard son of the Duke, as if Tourneur could hear the two voices at once. The distinctive note is coming from a similar but more limited instrument, though we might miss it unless we use the lineation of the Quartos:

> *Spur.*   I'faith 'tis true too; I'm an uncertain man,
> Of more uncertain woman; maybe his groom o'th'stable begot me, you know I know not; he could ride a horse well, a shrewd suspicion marry—he was wondrous tall, he had his length i'faith, for peeping over half-shut holiday windows,
> Men would desire him light; when he was afoot,
> He made a good show under a penthouse,
> And when he rid, his hat would check the signs, and clatter
> Barbers' basins.
> *Duch.*   Nay set you a-horseback once,

        You'll ne'er light off.
Spur.   Indeed I am a beggar.

                            [1.2.153-64]

Hazlitt was the first to set the prose of this passage, not very successfully, as verse; more recent editors, swallowing camels elsewhere in the text to produce verse, often lump the whole speech in prose, even though Spurio's verse is no more irregular than Vindice's in his undisputed poetic lines. [39]

One of Tourneur's more imaginative touches in the creation of the character is Spurio's own wondering reflection that he may *not* be the Duke's son. The humid pleasures of incest that he and the Duchess later cook up with such delight may well be imaginary, much like Vindice's rhapsodies on evil. Thoughts of this fiction and of his father's anatomy tumble from Spurio in unreflective prose. As he begins to shape his thought in verse, the subject changes, and the shift from prose to verse allows for two types of comedy, two types of perception, just as it does in Vindice. More to the point thematically, Spurio's pleasures of imagined parentage and incest parallel Vindice's. Whether he is the son of the Duke or not, Spurio has a sharply developed moral sense—he would have to, or incest in this case would hold no pleasure for him—and he is the only villain endowed with a proper soliloquy. In terms of his verse style, the character of his thought and the rhythms of its motion, we might regard him as Vindice's poetic half brother. The resemblance of his verse to Vindice's confirms our sense of Vindice's bond to the Duke. [40]

After the Duke's death, Vindice dries out his style and assumes the disguise of a lawyer, providing some typical Jacobean satire upon the law; the subject has a general thematic appropriateness to revenge tragedy, as well as an immediate appeal to the audience (perhaps a large part of it, for the play was written for the King's Men). Beyond that, there is a personal appropriateness in Vindice's disguise as a civil lawyer, or as a middle-aged law school dropout; the distinction is not clear in the play and probably is not important, for an air of frustration and failure hangs over the whole pose: "I have known those that have been five and fifty," he says, "and all about pullin and pigs" (4.2.59-60). Not only withdrawn from immediate human concerns, these lawyers have so isolated themselves by their own preoccupations that they have no grasp of divine law: "They cannot so much as pray but in law, that their sins may be removed, with a writ of error, and their souls fetched up to heaven, with a sasarara" (4.2.66-68). Their law has become a kind of fiction, and thus the appropriateness of the role to Vindice: for him the law of retaliation also is a fiction, as he implied in his first speech ("Who e'er knew murder unpaid?") and later realized consciously at the play's climax ("Surely we are all mad people").

This progress helps explain why Vindice can assume so readily the law-yer's tone of resentment and failure.

These matters are all focused in the scene in which Gratiana is exposed by Vindice and then tested by Castiza (act 4, scene 4). Vindice is hardly in a position to be chiding Gratiana so fervently; she at least has no blood on her hands. The irony, then, is that while Vindice is manifestly unfit to ad-minister the law in a religious sense, he is all too well qualified to admini-ster a corrupt and self-serving civil law. His fervor for religious law, for its undeviating moral standards, is apparent in the sententious and height-ened blank verse that he speaks to Gratiana. There could be no greater contrast with the racy prose of his earlier comments on law in the pre-vious scene:

> For honest women are so seld and rare,
> 'Tis good to cherish those poor few that are.
> O you of easy wax, do but imagine
> Now the disease has left you, how leprously
> That office would have cling'd unto your forehead.
> All mothers that had any graceful hue,
> Would have worn masks to hide their face at you:
> It would have grown to this, at your foul name,
> Green-color'd maids would have turn'd red with shame.
>
> [4.4.68–76]

In passages like these, the modern reader is likely to be concerned about the state of Tourneur's engagement. The problem seems to involve the verse itself, which conveys no suitable terror or even awe at the vision of a higher law. While it might be said that the problem lies in the couplets, we also recall that there are moralizing couplets in the passages that are, by general consent, the finest in the play. The difficulty would seem to lie in the general lack of metrical variety, coupled with the thinness of imag-ery. In several places the meter approaches a monotonous falling pattern: all but two of the polysyllables have their strong stresses on the first syllables, and only two lines have the light eleventh syllables that usually appear in the passages where Vindice is even slightly animated. Is the problem Tourneur's or Vindice's? Should we think that Tourneur's ca-pacities failed, or that the verse reflects Vindice's own uncertain commit-ment to virtue?

At this stage neither answer seems satisfactory; it would make more sense simply to keep on reading, letting the verse establish its own con-text. And as we read on, we see something familiar beginning to happen again: When it comes to picturing the virtuous and their censure of vice, Vindice does not catch hold; but let him start picturing vice directly, and he is off straightaway. Here it is especially important to follow the linea-tion of Quarto text:

Vind.	Green-color'd maids would have turn'd red with shame.
Hipp.	And then our sister full of hire, and baseness.
Vind.	There had been boiling lead again,
	The duke's son's great concubine:
	A drab of state, a cloth o'silver slut,
	To have her train borne up, and her soul trail i'th'dirt;
	great.

[4.4.76–81]

After Hippolito's line, Vindice's line is short one foot, while he pauses, gathering for the full effect of the next line. His second line is simply incredible, one of the reasons why we return to this drama, which can prepare for and deliver such moments; the absence of unstressed syllables slows the line, and the heavy sibilants enforce the distance between the words, to sustain the jeering tone:

The dúke's són's gréat cóncubíne.

Vindice now speeds up; the next line is paced conventionally as an iambic pentameter, and then the final line takes a leap ahead, the voice speeding over the numerous unstressed syllables to space the stresses out:

A drab of state, a cloth o' silver slut,
To have her train borne up, and her soul trail i'th'dirt; great.

The antithesis is between the dress carried high and the soul dragged down; the imagery suddenly draws on that whole network that deals with clothes and the corrupt soul. Here a special passion animates the imagery because of Vindice's rhythmic excitement, from the slow first line on out to the final swift exclamation. The rise in his dramatic temperature is so rapid as to suggest that he is very nearly out of control; indeed, Hippolito says a little later, after Vindice has spoken some choppy and muscular couplets, "O brother, you forget our business" (4.4.91).

Vindice's mounting hysteria is conveyed directly in the texture of the verse, and the organization of the passage is easy to see if we simply listen for Tourneur's five stresses and resist imposing our own notions of metric norms. Vindice's orderly and schoolbookish exposition on the one hand and his gathering energy on the other, with its exaggerated emphases, seem to be the result of a deliberate choice on Tourneur's part, to emphasize the continuing development of Vindice's character.[41] Concerned as he is with right conduct and unchanging law, he is still more excited by evil. Unable to sustain his initial rage, and unwilling to probe his own recognition, he can only succeed now in exciting himself (and his mother) in these short passages.

By this time, however, his recognition begins to have some psychological consequences, and the killing of "Piato" is one of them. We have already seen some of the thematic connections of that "murder"; here we should note the way that it is carried off quickly in laconic prose with quick verse interludes. These show another side of Tourneur's variety, in the comic double take, though again it is significant that Vindice should be reduced in his verse to this level:

> *Luss.*   that villain *Piato*
> Whom you thought now to kill, has murder'd him,
> And left him thus disguis'd.
> *Hipp.*   And not unlikely.
> *Vind.*   O rascal was he not asham'd,
> To put the Duke into a greasy doublet?
>
> [5.1.70-75]

The droll effect of Vindice's speech is produced partly by his short first line, which makes one joke as it stands, the pause with the missing foot emphasizing it; the next line compounds the joke, in one of Tourneur's usual eleven-syllable, five-stress lines. The result is funny enough for slapstick, but this low sort of *poetic* wit seems about all that Vindice is capable of at this point in the play. In acts 4 and 5 he has many good one-liners, but most readers are apt to become impatient with a tragic character who does this:

> That nobleman has been i'th' country, for he does not lie.
>
> [5.1.118]

> Could you not stick? see what confession doth.
> Who would not lie when men are hang'd for truth!
>
> [5.1.141-42]

> Courtiers have feet o'th' nines, and tongues o'th' twelves;
> They flatter dukes, and dukes flatter themselves.
>
> [5.1.148-49]

In certain respects the degeneration of Vindice's character resembles that of Marlowe's Faustus: Faustus declines from his stated programs into a practical joker, while Vindice declines from his achievement as poet and visionary. Vindice's situation humor may be a long way from the great verse of the play, but it still has many connections with it. In the silkworm speech as in these one-liners and couplets there is a similar use of the frisson. The difference lies in the working out of the implications. For the later Vindice, it is evidently sufficient in itself to have had the momentary perception alone; further reflection seldom modifies the original insight. The earlier Vindice was not satisfied simply with the frisson, but would allow the current of his verse to carry him toward a conclusion and, by the center of the play, toward insights into his own nature. By not speaking sustained verse, the later Vindice avoids painful reflection; the impulse to start the line is still there, but the pressure to sustain it is gone. If we can see that the impulse is present, and can recognize it in the squibs, then we shall have no problems in seeing where Vindice's final long speech comes from. We only have to understand what it is that lets him sustain that speech once it is launched.

Vindice's motivation in the final scenes is more comprehensible if we go directly to the discovery of the murders, and work back from that point. After the bloodbath of the masque is over and Antonio has restored order, he wonders that all the villains could have exterminated themselves so neatly. Only the Fourth Lord is left at the apparent end of the chain, and Antonio orders him borne off to "bitter execution" (5.3.108) before anyone can be confused by the facts. Antonio has no idea that Vindice was the mastermind of the masque, and there is no reason to suppose that he would approve of that wild justice. But we do know that in time Vindice would have been revealed anyway as the murderer of Lussurioso, for in act 5, scene 2, he had organized the nobles, including Piero—who had been identified in act 1, scene 4, as Antonio's friend and personal agent in the revenge for his raped wife. In other words, Vindice's confession at the end could be supplemented by evidence from Piero, who is still onstage with the other first masquers. Piero wisely says nothing, since one innocent man has already been taken away for execution; in the moral murk at the end, there is a conspiracy of silence that Vindice recognizes, looking at those around him:

> if we list, we could have nobles clipp'd,
> And go for less than beggars.
>
> [5.3.165-66]

Does Vindice realize, in the preparation of the masque and the murders, that he will end as he does later? Certainly by the start of act 5 a new element has entered Vindice's verse, and his speeches now resemble his last speech far more than they do the prose and snippets he has been speaking since act 3, scene 5. Consider the first speech to Piero and the other nobles:

> My lords; be all of music, strike old griefs into other countries
> That flow in too much milk, and have faint livers,
> Not daring to stab home their discontents:
> Let our hid flames break out, as fire, as lightning,
> To blast this villainous Dukedom vex'd with sin;
> Wind up your souls to their full height again.
>
> [5.2.1-6]

As we might expect, he begins in prose, but then by an active effort gradually pulls together his rhythms and imagery. While nominally regular, the metric is full of cross-currents against the iambic pattern:

Lèt oùr hîd flaḿes brèak oût, aš fîre, aš lîghtnǐng.

The faculty to integrate the imagery and rhythms of his mind has not been active in Vindice lately; in act 1, scene 1, he told his mother that his life had become unnatural after his father's death, but his verse did not begin to come apart until after the Duke's death. Here, as he sets up what will be his own death, it comes together again.

The speech describing the preparation for the masque shows a rising pressure in Vindice's concentration:

> Revels are toward,
> And those few nobles that have long suppress'd you,
> Are busy'd to the furnishing of a masque:
> And do affect to make a pleasant tale on't,
> The masquing suits are fashioning, now comes in
> That which must glad us all—we to take pattern
> Of all those suits, the colour, trimming, fashion,
> E'en to an undistinguish'd hair almost:
> Then ent'ring first, observing the true form,
> Within a strain or two we shall find leisure,
> To steal our swords out handsomely,
> And when they think their pleasure sweet and good,
> In midst of all their joys, they shall sigh blood.
>
> [5.2.12-24]

The organization and development of these speeches, Vindice's longest since the silkworm speeches, show a mind thinking precisely, even obsessively, as Vindice elaborates point-device on all the details of his scheme. The speeches are not just flat exposition, which would be the easy thing for Tourneur to have done if he had lost interest in Vindice's character. On the surface Vindice seems less conspicuously self-centered here than in most of his other speeches, yet many of his details are not strictly required by the deeds to come; it hardly seems necessary to mention, for example, that Lussurioso affects "a pleasant tale," or that the suits "must glad us all." The final couplet also exhibits some rather heavy smacking of the chops. None of this is necessary for persuasion, for as one noble has already said, "our wrongs are such,/We cannot justly be reveng'd too much" (5.2.9-10). Much of Vindice's increased pressure and concentration are thus directed toward pleasing himself; yet even while he begins to reassert himself as a poet, he ignores himself as an agent. This is the same fatal division we saw in act 3, scene 5, and in the revelation of his final speech he will go on to recognize the wound he has given himself, seeing also its ultimate source.

After the masques and Antonio's entry with the guard,[42] there are revelations all around, some specious; it is here that the hapless Fourth Lord, who was not one of Vindice's accomplices, is carried off as the murderer of Lussurioso. This is frightening business from Antonio, who is pleased to see himself as a force for moral order in the play.[43] The incident draws from Vindice one of the controlling lines for the scene: "New marrow! no I cannot be express'd" (5.3.109). Earlier, when Lussurioso had wrongly executed another noble, Vindice had managed a wisecrack; now he says he "cannot be express'd." The last word is puzzling; it seems to carry its Latin sense of something forcing its way through, and may be related to other such images in the play: Lussurioso, who must fly out (1.1.92), the French mole heaving up (1.1.110), the faults of great men breaking through their cerecloths (1.2.19), meats that move out of dishes (2.1.223), the heads of the dukedom peeping up (3.5.240), murder peeping out (4.2.236), the murderer bringing forth himself (5.1.159), the hid flames that break out (5.2.4), and swords that steal out (5.2.22). These associations carrying into *express'd* suggest both the danger of Vindice's telling all, and the danger of keeping close.

But within only a few lines of this recognition, Vindice suddenly volunteers that he murdered the old Duke. His motivation in doing this is seldom explained satisfactorily; the overreaching revenger with pride in his craftsmanship may be a stock property, but that hardly makes him plausible or even interesting.[44] However, Tourneur is at pains to emphasize the way in which Vindice differs from the overreaching revenger. This special emphasis shows up in one far-reaching statement that Tourneur gives to Vindice. After Lussurioso has died, Antonio remarks, in his usual inflated manner,

> It was a deadly hand that wounded him.
> The rest, ambitious who should rule and sway,
> After his death were so made all away.
>
> [5.3.120-22]

Vindice's brief comment on this is enigmatic: "My lord was unlikely" (5.3.123). This remark reflects the several layers of Vindice's thought and helps clarify the motive behind his self-revelation. Lussurioso was unlike his brothers (who were actually only half brothers, sons of the Duchess) in that he was not especially ambitious: he had no designs upon the old Duke. He was also unlikely as an assassin; completely lacking in physical courage, he could not face Piato after the mixup in the Duke's bedchamber, and later he tries to cover his cowardice, saying he beat and threatened him. (Lussurioso's preferred form of violence is to watch while his henchmen kill his victim.)

Vindice's remark also carries another meaning that ought to be clear on the stage. When Antonio says *his death*, Vindice also thinks of the old Duke, to whom he had often referred as "my lord" or "the lord."

When he sees Lussurioso as the new duke, Vindice telescopes the two deaths; he has tended to identify Lussurioso with the Duke from the beginning, when he solicited Castiza by using the ambiguity of the Duke's name. The compression in Vindice's thought is emphasized by the truncated line, which stands out because of Antonio's regular iambics.

It is a tense moment for Vindice. Hippolito—always the less imaginative of the two—rallies immediately, changing the subject: "Now the hope/of Italy lies in your reverend years"(5.3.124-25). At this cue Vindice seems to pull himself together, in a platitudinous couplet that Antonio rounds upon in turn:

> *Vind.* Your hair will make the silver age again,
>   When there was fewer but more honest men.
> *Ant.*   The burden's weighty and will press age down;
>   May I so rule that heaven may keep the crown.
>
> [5.3.126-29]

But Vindice is unable to stick with the pieties, and forcibly pulls the talk back to his private interest, revenge: "The rape of your good lady has been quited/With death on death" (5.3.130-31), a rather tactless point to make to the man who sees himself as the clean new candidate for the dukedom. Antonio stops him with a briefer and more emphatic platitude, then asks the question that catches Vindice completely off guard:

> *Ant.*   Just is the law above.
>   But of all things it puts me most to wonder,
>   How the old Duke came murder'd.
> *Vind.* Oh, my lord.
>
> [5.3.132-35]

Antonio pursues the question, and Hippolito tries to cover, in the moralizing tone that has gone over well so far:

> *Ant.*   It was the strangeliest carried, I not heard of the like.
> *Hipp.* 'Twas all done for the best my lord.
>
> [5.3.136-37]

And then out of Vindice's distracted state the answer suddenly tumbles, in bemused and gabbly verse, the very antithesis of Vindice's conscious manner:

> All for your grace's good; we may be bold to speak it now,
> 'Twas somewhat witty carried though we say it.
> 'Twas we two murdered him.
>
> [5.3.138-40]

Vindice is so relaxed, so off guard in his distraction, that he babbles on, bemused by his own rapid connections between Lussurioso and the old

Duke, forgetting that Antonio has had Lussurioso's murderer (or whom he thinks to be the murderer) borne off to "bitter execution," and that he had also told himself to stay quiet. The lack of metric control in his verse indicates well his mental abstraction at this point.

When Antonio reacts in his sudden yet thoroughly predictable manner, Vindice hardly seems to know what has happened, although Hippolito is not surprised:

> *Ant.* Away with 'em; such an old man as he,
> You that would murder him would murder me.
> *Vind.* Is't come about?
> *Hipp.* 'Sfoot brother you begun.
>
> [5.3.147-50]

Vindice's last speech then rolls out as freely as his confession:

> May not we set as well as the Dukes son?
> Thou hast no conscience, are we not reveng'd?
> Is there one enemy left alive amongst those?
> 'Tis time to die, when we are ourselves our foes.
> When murd'rers shut deeds close, this curse does seal 'em,
> If none disclose 'em they themselves reveal 'em!
> This murder might have slept in tongueless brass,
> But for ourselves, and the world died an ass;
> Now I remember too, here was *Piato*
> Brought forth a knavish sentence once—no doubt, said he,
>   but time
> Will make the murderer bring forth himself.
> 'Tis well he died, he was a witch.
> And now my lord, since we are in forever:
> This work was ours which else might have been slipp'd,
> And if we list, we could have nobles clipp'd,
> And go for less than beggars, but we hate
> To bleed so cowardly; we have enough.
> I'faith, we're well, our mother turn'd, our sister true,
> We die after a nest of dukes, adieu.
>
> [5.3.151-69]

In some respects we are back where we began, in the irregular rhythms of the first speech. But Vindice has come a long way since then, and the differences are perhaps greater than the parallels. As the speech unfolds, Vindice's comic tone controls it all, even when he acknowledges the murder of Lussurioso. Everything in the style of the speech keeps it close to parody of his earlier passionate manner. The short, highly stressed lines juxtaposed with longer lines containing many unstressed syllables create the alternate speeding and slowing that is almost Tourneur's trademark. Some other characteristic touches include the jaunty feminine rhymes in one of the couplets, a habit Vindice has in his self-consciously witty moments, and the alexandrine in the next-to-last line, which is followed by a line that is very fast, having only four strong stresses instead of the expected five. These several different techniques all practiced together seem responsible for what Eliot called—in the essay referred to earlier—"the peculiar abruptness, the frequent change of tempo"[45] that characterizes the whole play.

It would be easy to mistake this as the speech of

> one that had been studied in his death
> To throw away the dearest thing he owed
> As 'twere a careless trifle.
>
> [*Macbeth*, 1.4.9-11]

But there is no suggestion that Vindice's life is dear to him; quite the contrary, and he also sees how paltry are the "nobles" around him. Their triviality, and ultimately his, is carried in that image of "a nest of dukes." One's first thought is that the figure refers to vipers,[46] but it may just as likely refer to fledglings: Lussurioso, Ambitioso, Supervacuo, and Spurio were all new little dukes, in that order. The image ridicules their domesticity, and also suggests the duke's paternal role; Renaissance naturalists knew that the male eagle tends the nest.[47] The verse style of the last line also carries some of the mockery, in its shortness, with the pause for the missing foot before *Adieu*, the alliterative *d*'s and the internal rhyme of *dukes/Adieu*; in terms of technique, *Adieu* works almost as a line in itself, parodying Vindice's incessant couplets.

The tone in the end is not simply derisive, however, for in these lines Vindice achieves a legitimate form of self-regard, which does not consist simply of knowing he is evil: he had realized that quite a while ago. Instead his concern is for the identity he has finally been able to acknowledge, and for the fact that evil is in a profound sense irrelevant. The first line establishes that knowledge: "May not we set as well as the Dukes son?" His identification with, his identification *as*, a son of the Duke is now complete and conscious: it is the voiced expansion of the frisson in his earlier cryptic comment, "My lord was unlikely." Vindice increasingly masters his poetic medium at the same time that his mind goes out of control; this conjunction allows him to kill the Duke, but that in turn makes him lose control of the medium, for he had failed to realize the extent of its—and his—dependence upon the Duke. Vindice's intellectual struggle to become the great man, with sweeping powers and privileges,[48] swings from poetry to action and back, and it is one sign of Tourneur's genius, his complete grasp of Vindice's tone, that Vindice's conscious recognition of his own desire should embrace suicide as a form of wit.

4

CYMBELINE

When Iachimo first meets Imogen, he recognizes, with the quickness which he alone seems to possess in this play, that she looks like all that Posthumus had claimed her to be:

> If she be furnish'd with a mind so rare,
> She is alone th' Arabian bird; and I
> Have lost the wager.
>
> [1.7.16–18][1]

In an instant he conceives a daring plan whose purpose we grasp a few moments later. As Imogen reads Posthumus's introductory note, Iachimo launches into a wildly exaggerated "Elizabethan world-picture":

> What! are men mad? Hath nature given them eyes
> To see this vaulted arch, and the rich crop
> Of sea and land, which can distinguish 'twixt
> The fiery orbs above, and the twinn'd stones
> Upon the number'd beach, and can we not
> Partition make with spectacles so precious
> 'Twixt fair and foul?
>
> [1.7.32–38]

We know this is not Iachimo's usual manner because his earlier speeches in the wager scene, though in prose, were nowhere near as obscure metaphorically, nor was his initial aside in this scene.[2] He is trying to see if Imogen has "a mind so rare," although his approach is only partly successful; Imogen's mind is not as rare as her soul, but she *is* smart enough to reply that she does not understand him:

> What makes your admiration? . . .
> What is the matter, trow? . . .

What, dear sir,
Thus raps you? Are you well? . . .
          I pray you, sir,
Deliver with more openness your answers
To my demands.

[1.7.38, 47, 50–51, 87–89]

As Iachimo's speeches go on, they reveal the poets' "dark wit" as well as
a general nastiness quite odd for a wooer:

                          apes and monkeys,
'Twixt two such shes, would chatter this way, and
Contemn with mows the other. Nor i'the judgement:
For idiots in this case of favour, would
Be wisely definite: nor i' th' appetite.
Sluttery, to such neat excellence oppos'd,
Should make desire vomit emptiness,
Not so allur'd to feed.
          . . . The cloyed will—
That satiate yet unsatisifed desire, that tub
Both fill'd and running—ravening first the lamb,
Longs after for the garbage.

[1.7.39–46, 47–50]

Before offering any specific details about Posthumus's alleged infidelity,
Iachimo has made a great imaginative leap,[3] and begun with weirdly
illustrated generalizations about unfaithful lovers. The prosody of the
passage—which consists of two speeches, interrupted by Imogen's extra-
metrical "What is the matter, trow?"—shows Shakespeare's habit, common in the later verse, of allowing some of the nominally stressed syllables
to carry almost as little weight as the nominally unstressed syllables;[4]
and and *would*, at the ends of the second and fourth lines, are conspicuous examples, as is

Should make desíre vómit emptiness.

The diphthong in the second syllable of *desire* almost adds another
syllable, putting only the briefest space before the sudden lurch into the
verb and its object. The effect is astonishing in its larger context too,
because up to this point the pauses in Iachimo's lines have occurred
earlier and earlier; this last pause before *vomit* then occurs later and with
more violence than anyone could have expected. The rhythms of the
verse are one of Iachimo's chief means of seeming in a state of "admi-
ration," and the technique is now allied, still without specific charges, to
images of labor, dirt, and disease:

                          Had I this cheek
To bathe my lips upon: this hand, whose touch
(Whose every touch) would force the feeler's soul
To th'oath of loyalty: this object, which
Takes prisoner the wild motion of mine eye,
Firing it only here; should I (damn'd then)
Slaver with lips as common as the stairs
That mount the Capitol: join gripes, with hands
Made hard with hourly falsehood (falsehood, as
With labour): then by-peeping in an eye
Base and illustrous as the smoky light
That's fed with stinking tallow. . . .
                          A lady
So fair, and fasten'd to an empery
Would make the great'st king double, to be partner'd
With tomboys hir'd with that self exhibition
Which your own coffers yield! with diseas'd ventures,
That play with all infirmities for gold
Which rottenness can lend Nature! Such boil'd stuff
As well might poison poison!

                                   [1.7.99–110, 119–26]

The imagery seems to take off on its own, without any overt plan, as a cheek becomes a basin, lips become stairs, hands develop apparently psychosomatic callouses, and eyes smoke like the wicks of poor candles. There is a strictly logical contrast with Iachimo's first speech on order, but in terms of poetic style, and the way the imagery functions, the two speeches fit together and complicate his tone marvelously. In his unrelenting pressure against the expected iambic pattern,[5] in the frequent and irregularly spaced pauses, the syntactic units broken across line-ends, the bizarre diction, and the zigzagging in ideas from ideal to real and back, Iachimo mystifies Imogen while suggesting some truth just out of reach.

One thing is certain: if Iachimo were trying to seduce Imogen, he could not have chosen a method less likely to succeed. She would have to have the interpretive quickness of a Coleridge even to know she is being propositioned; she does not understand Iachimo until line 137, when he finally mentions her bed. Deliberately astounding and incomprehensible—there would be no reason to doubt that Shakespeare conceived of Iachimo as a pupil of Marino—Iachimo's verse style is calculated to put Imogen on her guard. He knows what he is doing: as he had told Posthumus earlier, "I am the master of my speeches" (1.5.137). If (and this is his long shot) she is quick enough to understand him but does not feel the need to remain faithful to Posthumus, he may win the wager directly; if she cannot understand him until he becomes explicit, and then rejects him, he can appeal soberly to her own sense that the confusion is now past. And sure enough, when he reveals that it was all just a plot to test her, he returns to smooth and flat blank verse. His earlier use of the astounding style becomes a way of affirming his ethical conventionality now:

> O happy Leonatus! I may say:
> The credit that thy lady hath of thee
> Deserves thy trust, and thy most perfect goodness
> Her assur'd credit. Blessed live you long!
> A lady to the worthiest sir that ever
> Country call'd his; and you, his mistress, only
> For the most worthiest fit. Give me your pardon.
>
> [5.7.156-62]

Now the good honest fellow, when he goes on to praise Posthumus his poetic manner becomes naive and clumsy, full of "unintentional" rhymes and tongue-twisting stumbles, standing with his poetic feet together:

> He sits 'mongst men like a descended god;
> He hath a kind of honour sets him off,
> More than mortal seeming. Be not angry,
> Most mighty princess, that I have adventur'd
> To try your taking of a false report, which hath
> Honour'd with a confirmation your great judgement
> In the election of a sir so rare,
> Which you know cannot err.
>
> [1.7.169-76]

In this, his most sincere voice, Iachimo abandons imagery altogether, straightens out his syntax, and smooths his meters. As surely as Jaques in *As You Like It,* he knows when he is hearing blank verse, and he knows that his verse style also has a special relation to the problems at hand.[6]

By this time Iachimo realizes that if he plays fairly he has lost the wager, and the next time we see him, climbing out of the trunk in Imogen's bedroom, we might expect some nominal anguish. But there, although Iachimo is speaking only to himself, questions of sincerity or moral intent seem even more irrelevant than they might have in his first speeches:

> The crickets sing, and man's o'er labour'd sense
> Repairs itself by rest. Our Tarquin thus
> Did softly press the rushes, ere he waken'd
> The chastity he wounded. Cytherea,
> How bravely thou becom'st thy bed! fresh lily!
> And whiter than the sheets! That I might touch!

But kiss, one kiss! Rubies unparagon'd,
How dearly they do't: 'tis her breathing that
Perfumes the chamber thus.

[2.2.11-19]

The first two sentences set the hypnotic tone (for Iachimo's own benefit) through the alliteration of metrically stressed key words (*sing-sense,
repairs-rest*), the suggestion of internal rhyme (*thus / rushes; softly / chastity / bravely / lily / dearly; waken'd / wounded*), the many sibilants, the enjambment, and the varied caesurae that keep the steady iambics from
falling into a singsong. Until the last two lines there are no reversed initial
feet to disturb the pickup of a steady beat at the start of each line. In the
apostrophe to Imogen, the alliteration becomes stronger (*bravely / be-
com'st / bed*) just as the tension in the meter also curves to a peak, with
four end-stopped lines and pressures in each against the last two feet. The
style matches perfectly Iachimo's fascination with Imogen's place in an
imagined setting. The Victorian critics who flew into rhapsodies over
Imogen forgot that at least her appearance is actually Iachimo's creation,
and Iachimo is very aware of his own role in the creative process.[7] No one
else in the play goes into such ecstasies over her beauty—certainly not her
husband, and her brothers are more taken by the way she trims vegetables.
Her beauty is Iachimo's creation: one might append, as a gloss on the
whole scene, Wallace Stevens's poem "So-and-So Reclining on Her Couch."
Too much of the passage reflects upon itself for it to be a lyric cri de
coeur; the opening line alludes to the way he worked upon Imogen earlier,
and comparison of himself to "our Tarquin" only underscores the differences between the two—the rapist physical and the rapist imaginary. Even
his kiss is qualified, for himself and for us, by the way he lays on the imagery of touch, sight, and sound, in a remote kind of self-titillation. As the
visual images become steadily more ingenious, they receive a conscious
termination:

The flame o' th' taper
Bows toward her, and would under-peep her lids,
To see th'enclosed lights, now canopied
Under these windows, white and azure lac'd
With blue of heaven's own tinct. But my design.
To note the chamber: I will write all down:
Such, and such pictures: there the window, such
Th'adornment of her bed; the arras, figures,
Why, such, and such; and the contents o'th'story.

[2.2.19-27]

The conventional prettiness of a partly cloudy sky (Imogen's blue and
white eyelids) hiding the sun (her eyes) is immediately distanced by his

melodramatic return to his task: "But my design." Abandoning pauses, parallels, and images, his colorless "such, and such" recreates, in its own quick irregular rhythms, the indifference of the rapid notetaker; the alternation of metric expansion and density satisfies us that three hours elapse during the scene. As he removes the bracelet, Iachimo then returns to the language of an overheated sonneteer:

> On her left breast
> A mole cinque-spotted: like the crimson drops
> I'th'bottom of a cowslip. Here's a voucher,
> Stronger than ever law could make; this secret
> Will force him think I have pick'd the lock, and ta'en
> The treasure of her honour.
>
> [2.2.37–42]

The much-admired natural detail raises a number of questions. Some readers have seen in this and similar passages a Shakespeare "reverting" to the style of his earlier work, particularly the poems, but the remembered passages must be the critic's and not the artist's; what mature poet sits down to reread, much less imitate, his earlier poetry? One can readily imagine, though, an accomplished poet looking at a slightly faded mode and seeing in it some ways of shaping fresh material, in this case a poetic voice unlike any he had created before.[8] If we wished to understand Iachimo better, we could begin with these "Elizabethan" passages, for curiously enough, some of these delicious details never find their way into the temptation of Posthumus. Consider that mole, for example. In the source for this scene, the prose tale *Frederyke of Jennen,* the heroine was identified by a black wart on her arm. Shakespeare's shift to the spotted mole is important because of its effect on Iachimo, who never tells Posthumus the mole is spotted and never uses on him the simile of the flower. Iachimo is describing Imogen for his own pleasure, and that pleasure has its origins less in sexual desire than in the use of a poetic style, tried out for effect upon himself alone.

Self-regard is fundamental to Iachimo's character, and after the passage just quoted he turns again, as if to catch his own image in a mirror:

> No more: to what end?
> Why should I write this down, that's riveted,
> Screw'd to my memory?
>
> [2.2.42–44]

Iachimo's nervous reflection upon his own memory comes out in short, irregularly stressed clauses, and the next detail is an even greater step back from "literature":

> She hath been reading late,
> The tale of Tereus, here the leaf's turn'd down
> Where Philomel gave up.
>
> [2.2.44-46]

A master's stroke, that: the Elizabethan best-seller has put the heroine to sleep at the very height of the narrative. It is a fine satiric touch that leads nowhere, another detail that Iachimo never mentions. But it tells us much about the limits of Imogen's romantic imagination, while it distances still further Iachimo's Elizabethan manner.[9]

It would be pointless to object that none of Iachimo's verse leads to self-knowledge, for he is not in search of any self that can be detached from the pleasures of his different voices. His self-depiction involves no reaching after recognition:

> Swift, swift, you dragons of the night, that dawning
> May bare the raven's eye! I lodge in fear;
> Though this a heavenly angel, hell is here.
>
> [2.2.48-50]

Possibly these lines contain a backward glance to *Romeo and Juliet, Macbeth,* or even Marlowe's *Faustus*; but Iachimo's "hell is here" involves no probing of his own depths, if he has them; few villains on the Jacobean stage are less tormented than Iachimo.

The care that Shakespeare has put into Iachimo's surface may be seen by comparing him with the villain in *Frederyke of Jennen*. John of Florence hardly thinks at all, but goes straight to his work; he speaks only once, when he sees that unfortunate wart on the heroine's arm: "O good lorde! What great fortune have I. For now have I sene a pryvy token, wherby he shall byleve me that I have had my pleasure of his wyfe; and so I shall have the money of hym."[10] In his simpleminded declaration John shows no concern for the effect of the deception upon himself, whereas that is almost entirely Iachimo's concern. Iachimo has, after all, undertaken the wager not to make a profit but to prove that human nature is not fixed: "I make my wager rather against your confidence than her reputation" (1.5.107-8).[11] If Iachimo had to acknowledge that there really *is* one woman true and fair, he would have to revise his ideas on human nature in particular and the universe in general.[12] His own pleasure in his poetic style will hold off that knowledge until act 5.

Returning to Rome, Iachimo springs the trap on Posthumus in a casual, almost unconcerned way. He knows he has legitimately lost the wager, and points out as much to Posthumus:

> my circumstances,
> Being so near the truth, as I will make them,

Must first induce you to believe.

[2.4.61-63]

Creating a fiction, he half expects to be exposed; when he shows Posthumus the bracelet and Posthumus says "May be she pluck'd it off/To send it to me," he asks nervously "She writes so to you? Doth she?" (2.4.104-5). Suppose Imogen had not been asleep as Iachimo thought? Letting him go back to Posthumus with an explanatory letter would be the best way to set up a punishment, and Iachimo has an anxious moment after his sketches of Imogen's room. But except for the description of the mole, Iachimo scores his telling points briefly and with no poetic heightening: "By Jupiter, I had it from her arm," "Will you hear more?," "I'll be sworn," "I'll deny nothing" (2.4.121, 141, 143, 146). Taking over the deception for himself, Posthumus does not even require much elaboration on the mole:

> under her breast
> (Worthy her pressing) lies a mole, right proud
> Of that most delicate lodging. By my life,
> I kiss'd it, and it gave me present hunger
> To feed again, though full.

[2.4.134-38]

Iachimo's mind is still fabricating (he moves the mole from *on* her breast to *under* it, thus requiring a more intimate perusal), but if he can deceive Posthumus without using his battery of lyric detail, so much the better: It is a greater victory against the upstart notions of confidence and constancy.

Posthumus reaches his own impasse at the same time as Iachimo, although his path to it is less connected with Iachimo's than it might seem at first. From the beginning of the play, Posthumus has a tone entirely different from Iachimo's mimic facility. He speaks in a manner direct and unaffected at its best, but abrupt and inconsiderate at its worst. His farewell to Imogen is a model study in curtness:

> Should we be taking leave
> As long a term as yet we have to live,
> The loathness to depart would grow. Adieu!

[1.2.37-39]

Posthumus's wooden stance is apparent in the unvaried rhythms, the unintended rhyme of *leave/live*, and his tendency to package his syntax in units that coincide with line-ends. The rigidity of the final product is emphasized by its lack of imagery. As Imogen complains affectionately, "Were you but riding forth to air yourself,/Such parting were too petty"

(1.2.41–42); she passes over his rather brutal suggestion that they might spend the rest of their lives saying goodbye.

When imagery does appear in Posthumus's first speeches, it usually jars in the context, with reverberations that Posthumus does not hear and cannot control:

> Write, my queen,
> And with mine eyes I'll drink the words you send,
> Though ink be made of gall.
>
> [1.2.30–32]

As Nosworthy says, this is more the language of Troilus parting from Cressida;[13] both lovers place all their emphasis upon their own experience: Posthumus stresses, for example, not the beauty of Imogen's words but the bitterness of his own reading, in a metaphor quite as strained as one of Troilus's. Posthumus's reserve originates partly in his desire not "to be suspected of more tenderness/Than doth become a man" (1.2.25–26); the stiff rhythms of his verse thus reflect his coolness as well as his conviction of his own merits. It is not surprising that when Cymbeline commands him to leave, he can manage only a farewell that suggests his own priggish self-concept: "The gods protect you,/And bless the good remainders of the court!" (1.2.60).

Posthumus's combination of reserve and self-regard appears even more strongly in the wager scene. Although conducted entirely in prose, this scene tells us much about the development of Posthumus's poetry. The clumsiest member of the group at Philario's, Posthumus tries the witty and graceful Roman manner, but takes himself so seriously that he is easily thrown off balance; he invites antagonism by being alternately deferential and obtrusive. It is a wonder that Philario puts up with him; as we see later, he is the sort of nightmare guest we have all come close to having, who makes fulsome apologies for imposing (thus ignoring a long friendship), but at the same time makes virtually no plans to leave until he is carried out feet first:

> in these fear'd hopes,
> I barely gratify your love; they failing,
> I must die much your debtor.
>
> [2.4.6–8]

No other gentleman in the play (including in that term Philario, Lucius, Belarius, and Cornelius) goes to such lengths to emphasize his unworthiness as does Posthumus in the early scenes of the play. In the wager scene he says with typical extravagance to the Frenchman, "I have been debtor to you for courtesies which I will be ever to pay, and yet pay still" (1.5. 34–35). This shows the ambivalence of Posthumus's submission: the last time they met, the Frenchman had separated Posthumus from quarreling

with another Frenchman, again over Imogen's virtues.[14] Despite Posthumus's protestations of indebtedness now, he still believes the fight
was worth it: "Upon my mended judgement (if I offend not to say it is
mended) my quarrel was not altogether slight" (1.5.44-46). The elabo-
rately apologetic manner does not conceal a repetitive insistence upon
his own rectitude (*not* upon Imogen's), and the conspicuous self-esteem
that is part of Posthumus's public manner must be fairly evident in order
for Iachimo's sarcasm in this scene to have effect:

> *Iach.*   Either your unparagon'd mistress is dead, or
>   she's outpriz'd by a trifle.
> *Post.*   You are mistaken: the one may be sold or given,
>   or if there were wealth enough for the purchase, or
>   merit for the gift. The other is not a thing for
>   sale, and only the gift of the gods.
> *Iach.*   Which the gods have given you?
> *Post.*   Which by their graces I will keep.
>
> [1.5.77-84]

Posthumus is not quick enough to rally off Iachimo's claim that the
woman is dead, or else the world would be enjoying her; instead he de-
personalizes Imogen as "the other," "a thing," "a gift." Posthumus's
final retort is of course intended to be ironic, but at the moment it
has an offensively complacent ring to it.

Posthumus's public self-regard gives his speedy rejection of Imogen a
great psychological validity. In one sense, Posthumus *needs* to believe
that Imogen is false because of the large claims he has made upon himself. In public he is the self-confident and competent courtier; in private,
he is intensely conscious of his own deficiencies. Imogen notes after he
had left that

> When he was here
> He did decline to sadness, and oft-times
> Not knowing why.
>
> [1.7.61-63]

Posthumus knows that Imogen has married beneath her station, and also
knows of the gossip that says "his virtue/By her election may be truly
read" (1.1.52-53). He tells Imogen himself that "I my poor self did exchange for you/To your so infinite loss" (1.2.50-51); even at the start
of act 5 he asks, "how many/Must murder wives much better than themselves"(5.1.3-4). His continued protests about his inadequacy become
a chewing on the sore gum, a more or less socially acceptable way of
favoring his tic; they also help explain why he wants to, why he must,
reject Imogen. He is a character born guilty; as his name constantly
reminds us, he has already been the cause of one woman's death. His

own consciousness of his failings and his distinct sense of being Imogen's inferior are attitudes he must shake, and by suspecting her of being unfaithful, that whole great weight can be canceled, that sense of perpetual obligation removed.[15] One could call it a form of projection, Posthumus's sexual jealousy being a reflection of his own sense of unworthiness, but a formulation like this would not imply the liberating health, the full love, that finally comes out of this particular sickness.

Many details in this outline can be clarified by a careful reading of Posthumus's poetry, especially the scene of the deception and the soliloquy immediately following. Immediately before the deception Posthumus and Philario have been talking about the Roman-British political situation, and Posthumus has been holding forth in a manner more pompous than usual:

> I do believe
> (Statist though I am none, nor like to be)
> That this will prove a war. . . .
>
> [2.4.15-17]

Into this conversational desert comes Iachimo, and for a brief moment Posthumus's verse flourishes with imagery:

> The swiftest harts have posted you by land;
> And winds of all the corners kiss'd your sails,
> To make your vessel nimble.
>
> [2.4.27-29]

Agreeing to Iachimo's initial statement that Imogen is fair, Posthumus begins by saying that she is

> therewithal the best, or let her beauty
> Look through a casement to allure false hearts,
> And be false with them.
>
> [2.4.33-35]

As he thinks of what she can do with her beauty if it prove false, the rhythms become uncertain and groping, the first sign of the crack-up:

> Loók through a cásement to allúre false heárts,
> And bé false with them.

The image of the prostitute at the window is strangely uncalled-for, as if Posthumus expects (or wants) to lose the wager; a fond husband might reassert his belief in his wife's constancy at this point. Iachimo's arrival, and with it the prospect of Imogen's infidelity, seems to have stimulated Posthumus's poetic imagination as conversation with Philario could not. Now when Posthumus reasserts the terms of the wager, the imagery begins to fade and the rhythms once more strain against the iambic pattern:

> If you can make't apparent
> That you have tasted her in bed, my hand
> And ring is yours. If not, the foul opinion
> You had of her pure honour gains, or loses,
> Your sword, or mine, or masterless leave both
> To who shall find them.
>
> [2.4.56-61]

The meter becomes impacted at two points crucial to meaning:

> Her púre hónour gains

and

> Masterless leáve bóth.

The logical and metrical ambiguity of *both* is a brilliant touch; both swords *and* both lovers will have to go their separate ways.

When Posthumus concedes the wager and gives Iachimo the ring, his verse runs out of imagery altogether and becomes quite uncertain in its meters:

> The vows of women
> Of no more bondage be to where they are made
> Than they are to their virtues, which is nothing.
> O, above measure false! . . .
> 'Tis true, nay, keep the ring, 'tis true: I am sure
> She would not lose it: her attendants are
> All sworn, and honourable:—they induc'd to steal it?
> And by a stranger? No, he hath enjoy'd her:
> The cognizance of her incontinency
> Is this: she hath bought the name of whore, thus dearly.
>
> [2.4.110-13,123-28]

Mentally Posthumus is wobbling among concepts that are never defined or given concrete form in imagery.[16] His mingled dogmatism and distrust are echoed in his ambivalent rhythms, which fall into iambics but take an unusual number of light endings, often combined with reversed initial feet in the lines immediately following. The speech sounds off-balance, tilting unpredictably as it struggles to approach an orderly rhythmic pattern. The first major rift in Posthumus's control appears in the last line quoted above, and from that point on he is unable to control the movement of his mind and voice. His first soliloquy is a bravura passage for his wildly dislocated style:

> Is there no way for men to be, but women
> Must be half-workers? We are all bastards,

And that most venerable man, which I
Did call my father, was I know not where
When I was stamp'd. Some coiner with his tools
Made me a counterfeit: yet my mother seem'd
The Dian of that time: so doth my wife
The nonpareil of this. O vengeance, vengeance!
Me of my lawful pleasure she restrain'd,
And pray'd me oft forbearance: did it with
A pudency so rosy, the sweet view on't
Might well have warm'd old Saturn; that I thought her
As chaste as unsunn'd snow. O, all the devils!
This yellow Iachimo, in an hour was't not?
Or less; at first? Perchance he spoke not, but
Like a full-acorn'd boar, a German one,
Cried "O!" and mounted; found no opposition
But what he look'd for should oppose and she
Should from encounter guard.

[2.4.153-71]

The imagery that tumbles out now is radically mixed and only barely under rational control. Coining and tools, sun and snow, the "yellow Iachimo" and the "full-acorn'd boar"—it is as if Posthumus's belief in Imogen's infidelity had released a flood of images, the sheer quantity of which he could not have managed before. As for the imagery itself, one recent reader describes the passage as "Othello reorchestrated,"[17] but that is to miss the point: Othello never does come up with an image of Desdemona in flagrante delicto; Iago plants these images, and Othello never reaches the loquacious sort of verbal rage that Posthumus soars into here. The passage on the boar would make us think of Othello only if we forgot who was speaking. Here imagery is a function of characterization, and it matters greatly that these lines come from a mind that has been terse and generally abstract up to now. And graphic as the imagery is, it is still as notable for what it leaves implied as for what it pictures directly. Imogen's "pudency so rosy" in having restrained Posthumus of his "lawful pleasure" has occasioned some comment,[18] but the thought is clear enough: Posthumus thought that she was reluctant because of her chastity, but now that she has been proved to be lustful, her restraint must have had some other motive. That epithet "full-acorn'd"[19] would seem to imply a fear on Posthumus's part that he has been unable to satisfy Imogen sexually.

Horrified by what he sees in this welter of images, Posthumus returns to abstractions, running through a catalog of vices:

Could I find out
The woman's part in me—for there's no motion

That tends to vice in man, but I affirm
It is the woman's part: be it lying, note it,
The woman's: flattering, hers; deceiving, hers:
Lust, and rank thoughts, hers, hers: revenges, hers:
Ambitions, coveting, change of prides, disdain,
Nice longing, slanders, mutability;
All faults that name, nay, that hell knows,
Why, hers in part, or all: but rather all. For even to vice
They are not constant, but are changing still;
One vice, but of a minute old, for one
Not half so old as that. I'll write against them,
Detest them, curse them: yet 'tis greater skill
In a true hate, to pray they have their will:
The very devils cannot plague them better.[20]

[2.4.171-86]

The great agitation of rhythms in this passage is expressive, in that it mirrors Posthumus's racing mind; at the same time it is also functional, in that it positively blocks any realization on his part that these are his own vices, too. The purpose of the speech can be unfolded in part from the last line, which has a curious history in the Variorum. Many editors have tried to justify dropping it, and thus have the soliloquy end neatly with a couplet. However, the thought is not complete without the last line, and Posthumus is hardly in any state of mind to be thinking—or rhyming—precisely. By concluding with a line that is falling in rhythm and has an extra light syllable at the end, Posthumus emphasizes the triteness and bathos of the curse, which is only a variant on "This hurts you more than it does me." He is enjoying the pleasures of his own rant, just as Iachimo in his long soliloquy enjoyed the pleasures of his own lyricism. In more than one sense, Shakespeare has freed Posthumus through the shifts in his imagery and rhythmic intention.

From the standpoint of technique, the most significant element in the passage is its use of pauses, which will take on a major role in Posthumus's characterization. Posthumus seems continually to break off, qualify, or chop at what he has just said, and he always does this by an abrupt shift in rhythm. Someone who is distraught does not automatically speak blank verse with a great many pauses; the verse might just as well tumble out in long gushes. Of all the other characters in the play, only one speaks in short bursts like this, and that is Cloten. (If we did not notice Cloten's choppy habit of speaking, Belarius later points to "the snatches in his voice/And burst of speaking" [4.2.105-6].) It is appropriate that Posthumus should assume the accents of Imogen's archpest, for at this point both men want to shame and humiliate her. The resemblance between them is later stressed, of course, by the scene in which Imogen discovers

Cloten's headless body. There, surveying all his anatomy with a wifely eye, she is convinced he is Posthumus, and it is possible that the two parts were played by the same actor, for Cloten and Posthumus never appear in a scene together.[21] Given their physical identity the doubling would have been natural, and the stylistic resemblances between their manners of speech at this point reveal Shakespeare's understanding of Posthumus's degradation.

After this speech, his own impasse, Posthumus drops out like Iachimo, not reappearing until act 4;[22] like Iachimo's, Posthumus's style has obvious limitations, and Shakespeare has done all he wants to within them for now. The relationship between Iachimo and Posthumus is also designed to be dropped by the middle of the play, freeing the stage for the development of Imogen and the subplot of Belarius and the two sons. But there is finally more than a little Shakespearean humor in Posthumus's departing to become a satiric poet, this man who knows himself so little and whose verse is stiff and preoccupied when not raging. The humor is like that in Imogen's being put to sleep by Ovid. At least we *saw* her asleep over the book, but the extent of Shakespeare's interest in satiric poetry is evident in the way that Posthumus has to write it and speak it all offstage.

With Posthumus and Iachimo safely stowed until the last act, Shakespeare begins to develop Imogen and her own unique idiom. His problem with her character is simple: how can he make health and balance appealing as verse, without lapsing into a stiff pattern of correctness? To describe her in a negative way, Imogen has none of the tendencies toward self-regard that we saw in the two men, even though she has a fertile romantic imagination. She enjoys experience itself, yet unlike many mental travelers, she is constantly weighing and judging. We have already noted her gentle admonition to Posthumus upon his stiff and ungenerous goodbye; consider also her miniature of Posthumus's departure:

> I would have broke mine eye-strings, crack'd them, but
> To look upon him, till the diminution
> Of space had pointed him sharp as my needle:
> Nay, followed him, till he had melted from
> The smallness of a gnat, to air: and then
> Have turn'd mine eye, and wept.

[1.4.17–22]

The point overlooked by many readers is that she did *not* see him leave; this is all a superbly evoked and conscious creation. The rhythmic structure of the passage as a whole shows Imogen's organizing intelligence, because the lines gather to the actual point of Posthumus's disappearance; the rhythms build to that delicate line with two strong stresses, spaced and surrounded by pauses, evoking the almost tangible *feel* of an object isolated in immense space. Perhaps a four-stress scansion would indicate best the balance of tensions in Imogen's mind:

The smallness of a gnat # to air # and then . . .

Imogen is more aware of her own dependence upon words than is any other character except Iachimo; as she says in this same scene, "I did not take my leave of him [Posthumus], but had/Most pretty things to say" (ll.25-26); she had even planned her parting kiss to appear "Betwixt two charming words" (l.35). And not long after Posthumus has left, she rebuffs Cloten, telling him "You put me to forget a lady's manners,/By being so verbal" (2.3.104-5). She knows from the first that words have a potency and value that should not be used lightly.

Imogen's attitude toward her own poetry is especially evident in her first long speech, in which she plans with Pisanio to go to Milford Haven. Here we see her interest in sensation, not for its own sake, as is the case with Iachimo, but rather as a means of understanding her own ideals and ultimate desires. Always sampling and testing, she often moves toward a tentative and aphoristic phrasing, which further restrains her essentially plain style:

> You good gods,
> Let what is here contain'd relish of love,
> Of my lord's health, of his content: yet not
> That we two are asunder; let that grieve him;
> Some griefs are med'cinable, that is one of them,
> For it doth physic love: of his content,
> All but in that! Good wax, thy leave: blest be
> You bees that make these locks of counsel! Lovers
> And men in dangerous bonds pray not alike:
> Though forfeiters you cast in prison, yet
> You clasp young Cupid's tables. Good news, gods!
>
> [3.2.29-39]

The first unusual and unexpected stress on *relish*, and then the final shift onto *pray*, keeps us from any feeling that she might be repeating a formula. Savoring her own excitement at the letter, she nonetheless realizes that separation from Posthumus could be a way of purifying and strengthening both their loves. Her interest in the sensation of the moment is not purchased at the expense of her judgment.

She can immerse herself in sensation when she wants to, for after she has read Posthumus's letter, she releases a glorious passage of huddle-duddle, in broken syntax and rhythms. Halfway through, she even gives the style a name:

O, for a horse with wings! Hear'st thou, Pisanio?

He is at Milford Haven: read, and tell me
How far 'tis thither. If one of mean affairs
May plod it in a week, why may not I
Glide thither in a day? Then, true Pisanio,
Who long'st, like me, to see thy lord; who long'st
(O let me bate) but not like me: yet long'st
But in a fainter kind. O, not like me:
For mine's beyond beyond: say, and speak thick,
(Love's counsellor should fill the bores of hearing,
To th' smothering of the sense) how far it is
To this same blessed Milford.

[3.2.49-60]

"Thick speech": this is the closest Imogen ever comes to indulging herself in a stylistic romp for its own sake, yet she still knows exactly what she is doing. After talking then about the time it takes to get to Wales, she concludes,

But this is foolery:
Go, bid my woman feign a sickness, say
She'll home to her father; and provide me presently
A riding-suit; no costlier than would fit
A franklin's housewife.

[3.2.74-78]

Recovering her balance, weighing and judging again (as in the wit of her last remark), she knows well what her strengths and temptations are; but the game of style is not one of them, and it is left to the men.

Where Imogen is deeply tested, however, is in her discovery of Posthumus's real intent in sending her to Milford Haven. The temptation would be for her to reject Posthumus in turn, and to emphasize the selflessness of her own devotion. Instead she goes into a deeper understanding of their relationship, though at first her reaction is the healthy one, simple anger:

False to his bed? what is it to be false?
To lie in watch there, and think on him?
To weep 'twixt clock and clock? If sleep charge Nature,
To break it with a fearful dream of him,
And cry myself awake? That's false to's bed, is it?

[3.4.41-45]

After running through some charitable but realistic explanations—the first being that Posthumus was betrayed by "some jay of Italy" (3.4.50)—she starts to generalize about men, as Posthumus did about women. There is a great difference in their two approaches:

> so thou, Posthumus,
> Wilt lay the leaven on all proper men;
> Goodly and gallant shall be false and perjur'd
> From thy great fail.
>
> [3.4.62-65]

Imogen's interest is in the way men are regarded, and her point of view is much more sophisticated than Posthumus's; he was less concerned with attitudes than with what he took to be objective truth about the evil of women. Imogen's self-concern, when it appears, involves no stylistic adornment. She acknowledges the facts of her family and her former suitors, then admits that her disobedience to her father might figure in Posthumus's estimate of her (actually they do not; he cannot reason that far past himself). At the same time she avoids self-pity, thinking exactly and turning her verse with care. Notice in particular the firm stressing of the verbs here:

> I grieve myself
> To think, when thou shalt be disedg'd by her
> That now thou tirest on, how thy memory
> Wilt then be pang'd by me.
>
> [3.4.94-97]

Hardly thick speech. The dominant terms all concern physical appetite (*disedg'd, tirest,* a term from falconry meaning "to tear", and *pang'd*); the metaphor of eating returns later, when she says of Posthumus "Now I think on thee,/My hunger's gone" (3.6.15-16). Imogen's critical sense applies to herself as well as to Posthumus; she sees the interdependence of their love and more, that Posthumus tried to use her as if she were a commodity, and that she accepted that role. In the speech above, her meters tie her thoughts together, rising on *myself* and *disedg'd,* then coming down on *tirest*; all have the sibilant and thin *e*-sound, shaped by frontal consonants, physically giving the sense of her exactness; the darker vowel and nasals in *pang'd* prolong that word and allow time for us to grasp the realization behind it. However much her consciousness may be manipulated in some scenes, here it is demonstrably full.

Imogen's attitudes continue to grow after this; otherwise Shakespeare would have sent her off sooner to wait for act 5, as he did with Iachimo and Posthumus. Her further characterization is again most easily described in negatives. She does not cease to consider and discriminate; she does not lose her sense of humor or her ironic view of herself. Even under the stress of her pastoral trials,[23] she retains her essentially critical mind:

> To lapse in fulness
> Is sorer than to lie for need: and falsehood
> Is worse in kings than beggars. My dear lord,

Thou art one o' th' false ones! Now I think on thee,
My hunger's gone; but even before, I was
At point to sink, for food.

[3.6.12–17]

The thought of Posthumus can relieve hunger, but only for about three lines. Because of the rhythmic flexibility-within-order of these lines we feel no doubt of Imogen's fundamental balance and sanity. Even in circumstances like these she has no tendency to rant, and her accusation of Posthumus is brief, though it swells the line with two elisions: "Thou art one o'th'false ones! Now I think on thee, . . ." Though firm, the accusation needs only light control, and even when she is surprised by the aristocratic mountaineers, she says to herself, with light but pointed emphasis,

'Mongst friends?
If brothers: would it had been so, that they
Had been my father's sons, then had my prize
Been less, and so more equal ballasting
To thee, Posthumus.

[3.7.47–51]

Here she uses her present experience to understand better her bond to her husband, and the fine metrical shading in the last two and a half lines emphasizes her growing knowledge. Had Cymbeline not had only one child to dote upon, her defection would not have been so heinous: because she would have been prized less, Posthumus would have seemed a more suitable husband. The wonderful thing about the lightness of the meters here is that it keeps us from feeling even a trace of condescension in her attitude. That her meditation is addressed to Posthumus shows that she has now understood more fully his own sense of shamed insufficiency.[24]

It is necessary to insist upon the depth of Imogen's awareness here if we are to regard her next scene, in which she discovers Cloten's headless body, as something besides a grotesque joke at her expense. Most immediately, her concern over Posthumus when she meets her brothers helps to prepare us for her anguish in the next scene: just as she begins to understand why he has rejected her, she discovers him dead. Her speech over the corpse also gives us something by which to judge Posthumus's later speech, in which he thinks he has killed Imogen and reached a new self-understanding. Not just a lament, these lines show her thinking forcefully, admitting and discarding first one set of possibilities and then another. When she believes she may be having hallucinations, the rhythms are accordingly tentative.

If there be
Yet left in heaven as small a drop of pity
As a wren's eye, fear'd gods, a part of it!

> The dream's here still: even when I wake it is
> Without me, as within me: not imagin'd, felt.

[4.2.303-7]

She comes out of her concentration in an alexandrine, which prolongs the moment of balance between dream and waking; what follows is not an elegy (that comes later) but a passage of mental discovery and fabrication, more important than mourning, in which Imogen convinces herself that Pisanio was hired by Cloten to deceive her and Posthumus both. Appropriately enough, the next passage is more excited than anything else that Imogen speaks in the play; often putting extra syllables in a line, her voice gains in urgency, the biggest jump occurring as she suddenly imagines the conspiracy of Cloten and Pisanio:

> Pisanio,
> All curses madded Hecuba gave the Greeks,
> And mine to boot, be darted on thee! Thou,
> Conspir'd with that irregular devil, Cloten,
> Hast here cut off my lord. To write, and read
> Be henceforth treacherous! Damn'd Pisanio
> Hath with his forg'd letters (damn'd Pisanio)
> From this most bravest vessel of the world
> Struck the main-top!

[4.2.312-20]

Of all the plausible explanations for things, it is surprising that Cloten should pop in here, for there were others in the play besides Cloten who disliked Posthumus. Why does she think of him? One cannot go so far as to conclude that Imogen subconsciously loved Cloten, in the manner of Beatrice and DeFlores in *The Changeling*; the point of the confusion is that without their reason—that is, their heads—men may have much in common.[25] No opportunity is lost to identify Cloten with Posthumus; when Imogen concludes that Pisanio forged Posthumus's letters and led her to Wales where Cloten could kill Posthumus, she calls out Cloten's very name as she embraces the corpse: "This is Pisanio's deed, and Cloten, —O!/Give colour to my pale cheek with thy blood" (4.2.329-30). This parody of unselfish forgiveness removes some responsibility from Posthumus; in a narrow sense, he was no more responsible for his deception in the first place than Cloten was for his noble appearance.

Imogen has been a measured speaker before, but now her verse leaps at every crucial point in her fiction of Pisanio and Cloten; in the passage quoted above, she stresses Pisanio's name two different ways in two consecutive lines. Distraught as she is though, her own impulse to live is never threatened in these lines; at the end she even thinks directly of "those/ Which chance to find us" (4.2.331-32).[26] When she goes with Lucius, she never once suggests or implies that she will not continue living. Having none of Posthumus's tendencies toward self-deception, she never can become intoxicated by the theme of honor.

Imogen's knowledge runs deeper than she herself realizes, for one side effect of her speech on Cloten-Posthumus is to qualify the dirge ("Fear no more the heat o' th' sun") that her brothers had just spoken.[27] As elsewhere in the play, the lyrical moments in an Elizabethan style are all followed by more grotesque passages in a mode we usually think of as Jacobean: Iachimo's reverie over the sleeping Imogen is tinged by his own posturing, not to mention his dastardly intentions; and the short song "Hark, hark" of act 2 is surrounded by vulgarities from the ineffable Cloten.[28] (This song and the dirge are so familiar that quotation should be unnecessary.) In a lesser artist, the practice would seem like a failure of nerve, an unwillingness to risk the lyric description of nature without the addition of an ironic context. Here the juxtaposition implies that the lyric response is an unsatisfactory mirror of the world in which it appears; in each case the lyric moment fails to describe with even momentary accuracy the situation before it. Iachimo is not so taken with Imogen's beauty that he repents of his vile behavior; "Hark, hark" has only the most perversely idealized connection with Cloten's desires; and the dirge cannot account for the way that Imogen and Posthumus are still alive, or the fact that the only dead body present is Cloten's, and he is hardly a "golden lad."[29]

In terms of the play's poetic, two provisional conclusions emerge. The coherent lyrical manner cannot resist the thick speech, which Iachimo, Posthumus, and Imogen all employ to disastrous effect at one time or another. However, the lyric moments do give the audience a way of evaluating the fineness of the characters' sensibilities. We recognize the nobility of Guiderius and Arviragus as much by their dirge as by their martial zeal, and we find Iachimo disturbing not because he is a cad simple but because he can recreate Imogen's beauty and still do evil deeds in spite of this ability. (If Shakespeare were not interested in Iachimo's lyricism he could just as easily have made him a two-dimensional Don John.) Poetry of the pretty sort makes nothing happen; yet in this play as in few others, it is our chief means of understanding *why* things happen.[30]

Posthumus's second soliloquy begins act 5 and announces that his rehabilitation is to be one of the main subjects of the act. Since we last saw him, he has schooled his voice; he now speaks neither woodenly, as in his early private moments with Imogen, nor in the erratic and inflated manner of his first soliloquy. Somehow he has found a plain and spontaneous tone:

> Gods, if you
> Should have ta'en vengeance on my faults, I never

> Had liv'd to put on this: so had you saved
> The nobel Imogen, to repent, and struck
> Me, wretch, more worth your vengeance. But alack,
> You snatch some hence for little faults; that's love,
> To have them fall no more.

[5.1.7-13]

On one level Posthumus is still confused: he has not forgiven Imogen, but only wishes she had lived to repent, which he would do his best to encourage by his own death, an added punishment for her. His sense of responsibility is still woolly, since he blames first Pisanio and then the gods for Imogen's death, going on to note "my faults" without the unpleasant bother of any precision: his saying that the gods have snatched her hence is the excellent foppery of the world.

None of this accounts for the tone of the passage, which could hardly have come from Posthumus's vow to write invective.[31] The diction and syntax of the lines are plain; in most lines a long phrase leads out, followed by a short phrase that in turn draws the sense into the next long phrase. With his thoughts thus linked, even though his imagery is sparse, Posthumus has none of the close-lipped constriction that had marked his style in the early scenes. As important as the syntax and line-endings, however, is the new freedom in his meters. Abandoning the heavy iambics of his first speeches and the jumble of his first soliloquy (just as he also abandons the abstractions and surreal imagery that went with these), Posthumus is now moving into cadences, patterns repeated from line to line. They appear in the lines quoted above, and continue as he resolves to reform and sacrifice himself:

> I'll disrobe me
> Of these Italian weeds, and suit myself
> As does a Briton peasant: so I'll fight
> Against the part I come with: so I'll die
> For thee, O Imogen, even for whom my life
> Is, every breath, a death: and thus, unknown,
> Pitied, nor hated, to the face of peril
> Myself I'll dedicate. Let me make men know
> More valour in me than my habits show.
> Gods, put the strength o' th' Leonati in me!
> To shame the guise o' th' world, I will begin,
> The fashion less without, and more within.

[5.1.22-33]

Most of these lines contain a similar rhythmic pattern, descended from that in Posthumus's early speeches; it consists of two phrases separated by a pause, each pause containing two strong stresses, the first arranged

roughly / x x / , the second a sort of extended pair of iambs, of the form
x x / x / . Here is one line that shows it clearly:

       x x   x   x x   x
Gods, put the strength ‖ o' th' Leonati in me!

And here are two in a row:

  x   x   x   x   x
Is, every breath, a death: ‖ and thus, unknown,
    x   x   x   x x   x
Pitied, nor hated, ‖ to the face of peril. . . .

Posthumus's vow to retreat into anonymity and fight to the death may be
a somewhat limited program for building character, but the new poetry in
his voice suggests that he will grow into a larger attitude.[32] Posthumus is
at last beginning to sound like someone who is educable, a condition that
none of his earlier speeches had suggested. The play shows a division between the poetic characters of Posthumus, who is reluctant either to let
his poetic style grow or to trust it; of Imogen, who uses it to deepen her
understanding; and of Iachimo, who regards it as an end in itself.

Posthumus's lingering desire not to relinquish his claims on himself has
a parallel in his own family history. Because his father, Sicilius Leonatus,
lost his first two sons in wars, he despaired even while his wife was preg-
nant with Posthumus. He was "fond of issue," the gentleman in act 1,
scene 1, tells us, but not, apparently, fond enough of his wife or the child
his wife was carrying. Like Posthumus, he was unable to grow out of the
past and into a future. It is precisely this ability that we have seen in
Imogen. Both Posthumus and Imogen began in similar circumstances:
Posthumus's brothers died before he was born, and Imogen's brothers were
kidnapped before she was born.[33] As we have seen, she is aware of the
burden this puts upon her in relation to her father, but she is still able to
direct and control her own feelings of insufficiency toward Cymbeline.
The great discrepancy between Imogen's and Posthumus's resources is
evident most of all in Posthumus's suicidal plan for dealing with his loss.

Posthumus's description of the battle (which follows the soliloquy and
Iachimo's perfunctory confession that he has "belied a lady"—a knavish
pun) might seem at first to be exposition and little else. Its style shows,
however, that Posthumus has begun to open his closed mind. Like the
soliloquy in act 5, scene 1, this descriptive speech shows a great resourcefulness in imagery and metric. The battle has had a decisive influence on
Posthumus; one of its chief effects has been to remove his tendency to
speak abstractly in a frozen rhythmic pattern—what might be called the
rigidity of a virtue shaped only by a sense of shame. Now, with more
positive accomplishments to his credit (the defense of his country—in
other words, his mother) he can move beyond that shame to a final acceptance of his own limits.

The battle itself is a metaphor for the change in Posthumus. What happens to the Britons is nothing less than a total change of personality;

cowards before, they become all the more valiant by having grown out of cowardice: "having found the back-door/Of the unguarded hearts, heavens, how they wound!" (5.3.45–46). For a speech describing such a reversal in character, a stylistic upheaval would be appropriate; and one sign of Shakespeare's craft in this play is that he has developed the character of Posthumus in such a way as to make the speech dramatically plausible. In some ways the speech is closer to the huff-snuff that was still popular on some Jacobean stages than it is to narrative poetry circa 1610:

> [these three] with this word "Stand, stand,"
> Accomodated by the place, more charming,
> With their own nobleness, which could have turn'd
> A distaff to a lance, gilded pale looks;
> Part shame, part spirit renew'd, that some, turn'd coward
> But by example (O, sin in war,
> Damn'd in the first beginners) 'gan to look
> The way that they did, and to grin like lions
> Upon the pikes o' th' hunters.
>
> [5.3.31–39]

The imagery is thoroughly conventional and almost Spenserian in its formal qualities; there are no unexpected juxtapositions, and the heroic scale is insisted on throughout, with the harts, lions, and eagles. Later the losers even flee like chickens in the approved epic manner. Archaism is just the point in a description that extols old-fashioned values.

At the same time, as with Iachimo's Elizabethan speeches over the sleeping Imogen, the style has the late Shakespearean tint, so that we never fear we might be listening to Hamlet's player. The enjambments, for example, contain reversals of a sort seldom found in earlier Elizabethan narrative:

> three performers are the file when all
> The rest do nothing. . . .
> their own nobleness, which could have turn'd
> A distaff to a lance. . . .
>
> [5.3.30–31,33–34]

In each case the focus suddenly moves from an agent to the things worked upon. By means of such shifts, and the metrical sophistication, the speech creates the effect of an older rhetoric viewed through a refracting prism; in this remodeling of heroic narrative, the dramatist holds up an ideal and emphasizes its distance at the same time. Self-conscious the manner may be, yet it is not merely Shakespeare's self-consciousness but that of Posthumus as well. He knows he is close to parody of the heroic style, admitting at the end that one could "vent it for a mockery" (5.3.56).

This enlargement of Posthumus's awareness leads directly to his final repentance: within fifteen lines of his battle speech he delivers his last soliloquy, forgiving Imogen for her alleged lapse. Now he has come around to a language at once fully conscious, plain, and spontaneous:

> Most welcome bondage; for thou art a way,
> I think to liberty: yet am I better
> Than one that's sick o' th' gout, since he had rather
> Groan so in perpetuity than be cur'd
> By th' sure physician, Death; who is the key
> T' unbar these locks. My conscience, thou art fetter'd
> More than my shanks and wrists: you good gods, give me
> The penitent instrument to pick that bolt,
> Then free for ever.
>
> [5.4.3-11]

The metric organization of the speech, like its logic, conveys a sense of directed energy rather than disorganized, line-by-line tension. The stress pattern identifies *bondage* with *liberty*, each taking more weight than the other words in its line. An extended comparison then flows over three line-ends to make a double pause around *Death*; the next firm stress falls on *key*, and then in one short pause he is back where he began, the locks he now wears. The unexpected weight on *my conscience* helps emphasize that the word here carries its double meaning of awareness as well as moral sense. (Jupiter, when he enters, is much more interested in Posthumus's knowledge than he is in his moral development.) Posthumus's formal repentance that follows is convincingly personal, because the rhythms are broken around each of the three stages of penitence, that is, sorrow, repentance, and satisfaction:

> Is't enough I am sorry? . . .
> Gods are more full of mercy. Must I repent, . . .
> Desir'd more than constrain'd: to satisfy,
> If of my freedom. . . .
>
> [5.4.11,13,15-16]

The natural and unforced displacements reveal a man without affectation and pretense; his self-knowledge is complete enough that he seems neither impatient for his recognition nor humbly frozen. He ends in the firm cadences we heard before:

> and so, great powers,
> If you will take this audit, take this life,
> And cancel these cold bonds. O Imogen,
> I'll speak to thee in silence.
>
> [5.4.26-29]

Finally his educated voice coalesces with his awakened moral sense; his development is substantially complete, and he has achieved it by himself, before the intervention of Jupiter.[34]

Editors since Pope and Johnson have had a low opinion of the speeches by the spirits in Posthumus's dream, but their poetic and dramatic relevance has been so well established in recent years that there is no need to repeat what has already been said by G. Wilson Knight and others.[35] Briefly, the characters of Posthumus's mother, father, and brothers all speak (as one sign of their great age) in stanzas of fourteeners, with short two-stress codas. This dated form suits both their age and their lack of poetic sophistication; the rustic simplicity of the generation just past has always been a cherished fiction. Jupiter answers the spirits in alternately rhymed, stolidly Senecan couplets, half in imperatives; most of the speech is heavy-handed and sententious—both desirable qualities in this case, for he would be a very shallow monster indeed if he descended speaking light verse. In Jupiter's speech as in the speeches of the spirits, the poetic technique is consistent with that in the rest of the play, since the play's verse repeatedly gestures toward conventions and styles outside the experience of the character himself. In this play the poetic style of any given character is liable to become something without himself as within, something other than what he literally seems to be on the stage. All of the characters—including Jupiter and the spirits—are ventriloquists, particularly at the crucial moments in the play.

Posthumus's manner of speaking does not change greatly after the vision; as in his second soliloquy, the metaphors are vivid but not mixed, and the flexibility of his metric remains unimpaired. Like Imogen when she thought she had discovered that Posthumus was dead, he trusts what he sees, accepts the inexplicable without irritation or impatience:

'Tis still a dream: or else such stuff as madmen
Tongue, and brain not: either both, or nothing,
Or senseless speaking, or a speaking such
As sense cannot untie. Be what it is,
The action of my life is like it.

[5.4.146-50]

That calm is tested in the final scene, which is so full of peripeteia—twenty-four, in all—that the reader is apt to ask, with Posthumus, "How comes these staggers on me?" Yet as far as the three principals are concerned, the plotting still remains an extension of character. Imogen naturally feels no necessity to come forward and explain why she is not dead; nor does Posthumus, who is still dazed after the battle, and although he sees Iachimo early in the scene, before Iachimo confesses, he remains beyond all thought of revenge or recrimination.[36] Perhaps Shakespeare's cleverest dovetailing of plot and character, however, appears in the way that the restoration of Posthumus's moral sanity is finally revealed in his striking Imogen. There would be every reason for him to suppose that the page (as Imogen appears to be) was one of Iachimo's cohorts; no one else present would have understood the significance of Iachimo's ring. The blow that Posthumus strikes is the sort of unequivocal response he should have made to Iachimo's taunts in the first place.

The elements of *cuisine opera* in Posthumus's final confession should not blind us to the real alterations that have occurred in his mind and speaking voice; these appear, once again, in his extraordinary line to Imogen, after the confusion has been cleared away:

> Hang there like fruit, my soul,
> Till the tree die."
>
> [5.5.263-64]

"The tree" is the body, their one body, and the appropriately strong rhythm suggests anything but melting abandon; it is also very distant from the abstract and rhythmically mechanical phrases Posthumus spoke at the beginning. This sentence, one of the few he has after the concluding revelations, shows that his imagery and verse style have become means of understanding, not simply techniques for concealment or decoration.

But it is Iachimo's development that shapes and controls the act; the conclusion of the romantic plot itself is one side of Iachimo's development. After Posthumus disarms him, Iachimo claims to know the reason for his own weakness, but his final confession gives the lie to that. If Shakespeare is to play fair with Iachimo, he cannot let him change; he has been out of sight since the play's initial action, and there would be no middle term for his growth. The growth of Posthumus is dramatically justifiable because of Imogen's exploration of Posthumus's problems. She supplies the middle term for his growth, and through her we realize that all—all!—Posthumus has to do in order to come around is to identify the reason for his rejecting her. If we accept Imogen's judgment of him, we must accept that all he needs is enough time and aggravation, neither of which requires that he be onstage. Iachimo is another matter, and because we gain no insights into his character in the middle of the play, we are reluctant to believe that he has changed at the end.

If we ignore Cymbeline's two half-line interruptions, Iachimo's confession is the longest speech in the play (ll. 153-209); it obviously fascinated Shakespeare, even if it does not do the same for many modern critics.[37] So elaborate that it seems more an aria than a speech,[38] it lets all of Iachimo's old habits reappear, in a form more highly polished than before. Imogen may have invalidated Iachimo's ideas about human nature, and he may claim to be in a state of neurasthenic collapse, but he still has the pleasure of his poetic creation to fall back on. (That pleasure, incidentally, revives him long before Posthumus gets around to forgiving him.)

Iachimo's self-conscious tone is signaled early, as he calls for Cymbe-line's attention, and then requests first aid:

> *Iach.*   Wilt thou hear more, my lord?
> *Cym.* All that belongs to this.
> *Iach.*   That paragon, thy daughter,
>   For whom my heart drops blood, and my false spirits
>   Quail to remember—Give me leave! I faint.
>
>   [5.5.146-49]

How finely absurd: the character with the most presence in the play about to faint; Cymbeline thinks Iachimo is dying, although he has suffered no worse in battle than acute embarrassment. Far from quailing or drooping, any one of Iachimo's lines above would show his old control returning. It is as if Shakespeare wanted to try the instrument one more time, showing a reassertion of self in poetic rather than psychological terms (as in the tragedies); it would have been an easy matter to have unraveled the story circumstantially rather than poetically, as Shaw's revision showed. Iachimo's baroque tone seems highlighted by the salubrious and self-congrat-ulatory atmosphere of the British victory:

> Upon a time, unhappy was the clock
> That struck the hour: it was in Rome, accurst
> The mansion where: 'twas at a feast, O, would
> Our viands had been poison'd (or at least
> Those which I heav'd to head) the good Posthumus
> (What should I say? he was too good to be
> Where ill men were, and was the best of all
> Amongst the rar'st of good ones) sitting sadly,
> Hearing us praise our loves of Italy
> For beauty, that made barren the boast swell'd
> Of him that best could speak.
>
>   [5.5.153-63]

As before, his rhetoric employs interminable interruptions, shifts in tone, striking of poses, and sudden intrusions of unexpected and racy meta-phors. Beyond these there is also the prosodic luxuriance that we associate with Iachimo; against the dominant iambics he often slides into trochaics at the beginnings of lines ("Those which I heav'd to head," "What should I say?" "Hearing us praise our loves"), which the frequent light endings reinforce. This sense of being suspended between two ways of thinking is typical of Iachimo; his manner insists upon the listener's concentration, because the heavy internal rhymes and alliterations often link contraries, as in *poison'd/Posthumus* or *beauty/barren* and *boast/best*. Iachimo extends his matter as far as he can, offering paradox and logical redun-dancy in metrically exotic settings: "beauty that made barren the swelled boast," or "Fairness, which strikes the eye" (5.5.168). The phrase-by-phrase pyramiding of the passage also adds to the tension:

Upon a time	unhappy was the clock		
That struck the hour	it was in Rome	accurst	
The mansion where	'twas at a feast	O	would

Raising the tension by enlarging one basic pattern, he goes on to ransack his full magazine of effects, and he does not use the same rhythms and pauses in any two lines of the speech.

Critics who complain about Iachimo's interruptions can join Cymbeline, who responds just as Iachimo wants: "I stand on fire. / Come to the matter" (5.5.168-69). Iachimo proceeds economically for a few lines but then, in spite of himself, slides back to more extreme variations, gross images formed in grosser vowel contrasts:

> This Posthumus
> Most like a noble lord in love and one
> That had a royal lover, took his hint,
> And (not dispraising whom we prais'd, therein
> He was as calm as virtue) he began
> His mistress' picture, which, by his tongue, being made,
> And then a mind put in't, either our brags
> Were crak'd of kitchen-trulls, or his description
> Prov'd us unspeaking sots.
>
> [5.5.170-78]

When Iachimo comes to "his mistress' picture" he can no longer restrain himself, and sails off into a longer line that introduces the most telling distortion of all. Claiming to be a defender of Italian womanhood, he reveals that his real concern was—as we knew all along—to show how well *speaking* really could be done.

For someone listening closely this is the heart of the matter, but Cymbeline, with his usual brash irrelevance, exclaims, "Nay, nay, to th' purpose" (5.5.178), and Iachimo then begins his last and fullest display of artistry. He describes, at about equal length, the wager, his British interlude, and his deception of Posthumus; the transitions are marked with unusual deliberation, and show Iachimo's conscious organization of his material. Although as he speaks he is surrounded by people, his prime audience remains himself, and many of the details in the speech would be comprehensible to Iachimo alone. At first he leans toward self-justification, impugning Posthumus's integrity while claiming to uphold it, but then he makes some surprising turns:

> Your daughter's chastity (there it begins)—
> He spoke of her, as Dian had hot dreams,

> And she alone were cold: whereat I, wretch,
> Made scruple of his praise, and wager'd with him
> Pieces of gold, 'gainst this (which he then wore
> Upon his honour'd finger) to attain
> In suit the place of's bed, and win this ring
> By hers and mine adultery: he, true knight,
> No lesser of her honour confident
> Than I did truly find her, stakes this ring,
> And would so, had it been a carbuncle
> Of Pheobus' wheel; and might so safely, had it
> Been all the worth of's car.

> [5.5.179-91]

According to this version, the reference to Diana's "hot dreams" seems to be a metaphor from Posthumus, while Iachimo's picture of himself as a miserable outcast ("I, wretch") who had small reservations ("made scruple") bears little resemblance to the Iachimo we saw. There is also that preposterous detail of "his honour'd finger." The humanized digit must be related to Imogen's "right proud" mole, and in both cases the detail ends up diminishing its object rather than enlarging it. These distortions accompany some most distracting imagery: the gold coins, the finger, the bed, the diamond, the rubies of the sun and the imagined wheel they form—all shift and move as if they were props in an animated display. The rhetorical uses of meter are especially evident in the contrast between "I, wretch" and "he, true knight"; *whereat* holds back the expected two stresses that would finish the line, then deposits them both on *I, wretch*; Iachimo then lands firmly on *scruple* and *wager'd*, but gives *him* almost no weight at all, as if Posthumus were an ignorant accessory. The wager then unfolds in two lines of alliteration, consonance, and unexpected pauses, becoming regular again at *attain* and stressing even more heavily *win this ring*, as if to emphasize his own preoccupation with the symbol itself. Posthumus's confidence and Imogen's honor are described, by contrast, in unvaried iambics, but when Iachimo describes the ring for a third time, the meters loosen again; as the ring becomes a celestial gem, the line slows to take up the slack of a missing stress:

> And would so, had it been a carbuncle.

Plunging through to a flourish, he pauses briefly on *wheel*, but (sign of his gallantry) he does not mention Imogen, instead moving quickly over two pauses with unstressed syllables before each (*and might so safely, had it/* . . .), then making her honor even more remote by the emphasis of the open vowels at the end: *All the worth of's car.*

The speech takes some odd turns for a confession, endorsing and sympathizing uncertainly in the verse and imagery; but this is only the start.

The second (and slightly longer) section concerns the scenes in Britain, and the description here is notable for not containing one image, in contrast to the description of the wager; the cosmic scale is gone too, with its deities and myths. In this colorless atmosphere Iachimo's meters almost dissolve as he describes his encounter with Imogen; it would be hard to tell where to place stresses in either of the full lines here:

> I was taught
> Of your chaste daughter the wide difference
> 'Twixt amorous and villainous. Being thus quench'd
> Of hope, not longing. . . .
>
> [5.5.193–96]

Because we already know the story and its ending, the main focus for the audience is the sheer evasiveness with which Iachimo's style can work upon a matter for simple narrative. To us, all of this seems only a buildup for the deception of Posthumus, yet when Iachimo comes to that, he drops it flatly, saying that he is subtle but hardly showing his trade secrets:

> I return'd with simular proof enough
> To make the noble Leonatus mad,
> By wounding his belief in her renown,
> With tokens, thus, and thus: averring notes
> Of chamber-hanging, pictures, this her bracelet
> (O cunning, how I got it!) nay, some marks
> Of secret on her person, that he could not
> But think her bond of chastity quite crack'd,
> I having ta'en the forfeit.
>
> [5.5.200–208]

Metrically regular with no suggestion of ambiguity (there is only one light ending, and not until the end does Iachimo change the initial foot), the speech comes out as a quick, simplified view of the event. Elisions in *simular* and *Leonatus* speed the first two lines along, the "evidence" is swept up in enjambed lines that allow minimal pausing (*notes/bracelet/ marks*), and the conclusion is enjambed as well, as if it were inevitable: *he could not/But think.* Iachimo tactfully avoids pointing out that Posthumus wanted to doubt Iachimo even before Iachimo had presented all his "evidence."

For us the main question is why the poetic organization of Iachimo's speech heightens the account of the wager, lowers the tone of his encounter with Imogen, and finally dismisses what was psychologically the most important part of all, the deception of Posthumus. We seem to run very quickly into questions about the nature and mode of Iachimo's dramatic existence. If self-justification were Iachimo's dominant motive, he could have done much better than he does: he could have presented Posthumus in a much less favorable light merely by telling the truth. One might explain the emphases of his speech as partly the result of habit, or partly the operatic occasion at hand, the stage having, by conservative estimate, twenty-one people on it at the moment.

But more than either of these, Iachimo seems to be led on by the variety and delight of his own voice, and in this he remains thoroughly consistent. As we saw earlier, many of the details he alludes to would be appreciated or understood by himself alone: his self-distanced longing for Imogen, his knowledge that his attempt to seduce her was instant theater for her benefit, his ingenious way of getting into her room. These details, unstated but hinted at, suggest that Iachimo is highly conscious of what he is doing at that moment. Similarly, the intricate organization and rich poetic texture of his confession satisfy him as a poet and justify his self-depiction as an "Italian brain," although none of this is of much interest to the uncouth Britons, who are "on fire" to follow the mere narrative.[39]

Certainly of the three characters whose poetic development we have followed, Iachimo is the least changed at the end.[40] This comes across well on the stage; in the 1974 Royal Shakespeare Company production of the play, there was barely restrained laughter in the audience when Posthumus forgave Iachimo, not so much because of Posthumus's earnest boy-scout manner—"Live / And deal with others better"—as because Iachimo so obviously finds his own performance of more interest than anyone else's forgiveness.[41] No one could believe in his reformation on the basis of his five-line repentance:

> now my heavy conscience sinks my knee,
> As then your force did. Take that life, beseech you,
> Which I so often owe: but your ring first,
> And here the bracelet of the truest princess
> That ever swore her faith.

[5.5.414–18]

By offering the ring and bracelet after asking for death, instead of before, Iachimo gallantly leaves the emphasis upon Imogen's endurance, just as his request for death follows a generous reference to Posthumus's force (which no gentleman would use now on a captive). Like the exaggeration and pathos of "so often," it all goes with the conspicuously falling rhythms, which add to the precious atmosphere; of the eight disyllabic words in the passage, seven have the stresses on the first syllables. Whatever truth the speech contains (Is he repentant, or is he angling for a reprieve?) must finally lie in its poetry and not in its sentiments.

Having begun with Iachimo, we will find him the best place to end; he is the one character whose stylistic variation does not lead him out of himself. But that may be a misplaced criterion with Iachimo in any case: the notion that there is one "sincere" self back of all the masks becomes the final illusion. Trying on one voice after another, he is the play's chief poetic ventriloquist, and because the play is a romance, he can be spared in order to exhibit his villainy fully at the end, now neutralized and harmless to the community. Iachimo is a kind of living nightmare through which the other characters have traveled; if their transformations are to seem convincing, he will have to be alive and present at the end, not simply dead, or worse, silenced.

5

THE WHITE DEVIL AND
THE DUCHESS OF MALFI

It is probably no exaggeration to say that in a typical Webster play the conflict is not so much between one set of characters and another as between Webster and his own notebooks. Yeats's comment that we make poetry out of our quarrels with ourselves is nowhere more true than with Webster, whose commonplace books and reference files continually threaten to take over his plays yet are thrust finally into the background by his verse, which holds the plays together and allows them to offer coherent versions of experience. The problem can be described most easily in terms of characterization: how can Webster fragment a character's consciousness enough to justify feeding into his speeches all manner of tidbits from the author's voracious reading,[1] yet still make the character seem real enough to be a plausible factor in the play's action? The difficulties are enormous, and are perhaps most familiar in a certain kind of modern novel. If the writer makes his central characters polymorphous enough to let them utter all the different lecture notes that the writer took in graduate school, then the characters become almost impossible to propel into action; as a result, events in the novel often take the form of dream or hallucination, as if to convince the writer that they occurred at all. That a play by Webster triumphs over these obstacles and can offer in the end a world coherent in its own terms, with characters who focus the action rather than move about at its requirements, is thanks largely to the poet's mastery of his blank verse. The shifting and turning currents of Webster's poetry encircle territories of experience that might not otherwise seem to adjoin each other.

In *The White Devil* and *The Duchess of Malfi* the conflict is especially evident in the central characters of Flamineo and Bosola. It is apparent that Webster regarded these two as the centers of their respective plays: *The White Devil* concludes with an Epilogue in which Webster praises the acting of Richard Perkins,[2] who created the role of Flamineo, and the Quarto of *The Duchess* appeared with a cast list—the first in printed English drama, which is headed by the part of Bosola. Similarities between the two characters have often been noted; each stands in a special relation to the love plot of his respective play, although Bosola's relation to the villains in *The Duchess* is much more ambiguous than Flamineo's relation to Francisco, Monticelso, and Lodovico. Flamineo and Bosola both develop as characters in their own right, and it would probably be an oversimplification to regard either as a mere commentator or chorus; however, the differences between the two are not just a function of the different actions that they are given to perform, or of their presumably different states of mind, but involve the relative depths of their dramatic existence. Each is endowed with a different kind of reality, and this is emphasized by the different kinds of verse they are given.

The earlier play makes a good beginning for our purposes, because the author's control of the central character is both more open and less risky. Webster seldom seems in doubt as to what he wants from Flamineo, for he has done much to place specific limits upon his character: Webster silences him in certain situations, cuts back on his knowledge and consciousness, and reduces his connivance, thus simplifying his mind and responses. Unlike Bosola in *The Duchess of Malfi*, Flamineo has little direct knowledge of the counterplots against him; he is not an especially effective intelligencer. He never does manage to probe Lodovico, for example, and never realizes that Lodovico loved Bracciano's wife Isabella. Flamineo also fails to see through Francisco's disguise, in spite of several tedious conversations and the obviously comic potential of the disguise itself. When a plain lack of information does not limit Flamineo's character enough, Webster will simply bank him down, as in the trial scene for example. (We will return to this scene later.) In short, despite Webster's massive injections of learned references, Flamineo's depth as a character is shifting and uncertain, unlike that of his sister, whose psychological depth and plausibility seem fairly consistent throughout the play. One could trace the movements of her mind with some sureness,[3] but it would be hard to do so with Flamineo.

There is nothing especially subtle in the way that Webster shields Flamineo from too much knowledge. To mention only two scenes: at line 62 of act 5, scene 1, Flamineo exits abruptly in order to let the conspirators reveal their plans, and then when they are through he reenters just as abruptly at line 86. Webster takes him off again at line 209 so he will remain unaware of the plot complication involving Francisco and Zanche. Similar manipulations occur in act 5, scene 3, in which Flamineo is conspicuously present as the "Capuchins" chant over the dying Bracciano, then is sent out so they can reveal themselves to the victim, and then is brought back to see Bracciano dead. As in act 5, scene 1, these adjustments reduce Flamineo's intellectual options by not allowing him to see events that might prompt fuller reflection and awareness. Needless to say, they also simplify greatly the moral dilemmas he faces.

On the other hand, Webster is equally direct in bringing Flamineo into scenes where his tone is needed, or where Webster wants that tone to change. Flamineo's allusive mockery functions as a running *continuo* in the scenes with Vittoria and Bracciano (act 1, scene 2, and act 4, scene 2); the inevitability and the physical basis of their love are thus emphasized both at its beginning and at its ending. But in two scenes in particular, the dramatic structure of the play is manipulated much more frankly for Flamineo's sake, as Webster works rapidly to heighten the character's awareness. These are the consecutive scenes of Bracciano's death and the winding of Marcello's corpse (act 5, scenes 3 and 4). In the first of these, Bracciano fights, goes out for a short interval (in which his armor is removed and the poison begins to work), and then is brought back onstage to die. There is no explanation as to why he should be brought back out of his cabinet to die on the tilting ground, unless it is that the rest of the cast is assembled there, and getting them into a discovery space or something similar would involve their crowding upstage. However, Webster is not interested in this aspect of stage architecture; *where* Bracciano dies is not so important as the fact that he should die in public, while alluding to Flamineo as an accomplice whose loyalties are in doubt. The exposure of Flamineo is necessary in turn for his own development, because it explains his behavior in the next scene. Here in act 5, scene 4, Webster again loosens up the play's mechanics in order to develop Flamineo: never mind that for convenience's sake Marcello's corpse is being wound in Bracciano's house,[4] or that Gasparo is left onstage to express an incongruous pleasure with the young prince Giovanni (who, incidentally, orders Gasparo off to torture at the end).[5] What Webster wants—and he is very direct about it— is to have Flamineo view Marcello's corpse immediately after the young prince has rejected him. As in the earlier scene, some light revision could have made the transition here less obvious, but in neither case does Webster mind if his indifferent underpainting shows through.[6] The scenic structures are as transparent as those in the late Shakespeare, and for the same reason: the dramatist is more interested in the voice of his character than in the circumstances that have allowed it to speak.[7]

The limits and controls on Flamineo's knowledge are related to the limits on his verse. In the beginning Flamineo seems more a character of prose comedy than a verse-speaking tragic principal. Up to the trial scene he is close to being merely a stand-up comedian; most of his comments are predictably satiric, and much of his verse consists of throwaway lines. His patter in the first two acts shows us what sort of ironies the play will accommodate, for his language is at once erudite and stylistically flat. The effect is of a powerful and energetic mind playing—or wasting itself, to

be more exact—entirely on surfaces. A typical passage is the early dialogue
with Camillo, in which Flamineo's racy prose and metrically loose verse
help establish the lower range of his tone:

> *Flam.* And so you should be certain in one fortnight,
>   Despite her chastity or innocence
>   To be cuckolded, which yet is in suspense:
>   This is my counsel and I ask no fee for't.
> *Cam.* Come you know not where my night-cap wrings me.
> *Flam.* Wear it a'th'old fashion, let your large ears come
>   through, it will be more easy,—nay I will be bitter,—
>   bar your wife of her entertainment: women are
>   more willingly and gloriously chaste, when they
>   are least restrained of their liberty. It seems you
>   would be a fine capricious mathematically jealous
>   coxcomb, take the height of your horns with a
>   Jacob's staff afore they are up.
>
>   [1.2.83–94]

The spread between the verse and the prose is slight, partly because of the
very irregular meter and the indifferent disposition of pauses; the turns
and counterturns in the verse continue into the prose. Both depend upon
simple surprise and contrast to hold the audience's interest, since the
pleasures of seeing Camillo gulled are not inexhaustible.

After establishing Flamineo's ordinary working manner, Webster goes
on in the same scene to show a more passionate level in the character
when he confronts his mother. The following verse speech is supposed to
be strong enough to make Cornelia flinch, and she is pictured as a tough
customer indeed:

> I would the common'st courtezan in Rome
> Had been my mother rather than thyself.
> Nature is very pitiful to whores
> To give them but few children, yet those children
> Plurality of fathers,—they are sure
> They shall not want. Go, go,
> Complain unto my great lord cardinal,
> Yet may be he will justify the act.
> Lycurgus wonder'd much men would provide
> Good stallions for their mares, and yet would suffer
> Their fair wives to be barren.
>
>   [1.2.334–44]

The jumps and sudden pauses in the rhythm demonstrate Flamineo's emotion, although the jerky violence of the verse seems at odds with the formality of the appeal to Nature's laws and Plutarch. This mixture of metrical choppiness and pedantic elaboration is one of Webster's ways of making his notebook bits seem plausibly uttered; the disturbed rhythms in passages such as this show us how intense is Flamineo's resentment of his mother and their social class. The literary range of the passage is slightly broader than that in the exchange with Camillo,[8] and the rapid reversals in the syntax of the earlier prose have now been translated, as it were, into the dotted verse rhythms. But the movement of Flamineo's mind remains essentially the same, in the sudden aphoristic interjections and scholarly diction; the verse has only increased the pressure.

Both speeches have another signature peculiar to Flamineo. Despite his proclaimed resentment, his speech has no special pressure; it never really takes off, and to see how Webster has kept Flamineo back we need only compare his speech to Cornelia with another speech of rejection, Bracciano's outburst to Isabella in the very next scene. Here Bracciano's fury reaches for a lyric dimension:

> Because your brother is the corpulent duke,
> That is the great duke,—'Sdeath I shall not shortly
> Racket away five hundred crowns at tennis,
> But it shall rest upon record: I scorn him
> Like a shav'd Polack,—all his reverend wit
> Lies in his wardrobe, he's a discreet fellow
> When he's made up in his robes of state,—
> Your brother the great duke, because h'as galleys,
> And now and then ransacks a Turkish fly-boat,
> (Now all the hellish Furies take his soul,)
> First made this match,—accursed be the priest
> That sang the wedding mass, and even my issue.
>
>   [2.1.180-91]

Although close to hysteria, grammatically incoherent, and rapidly associative in imagery, the speech still has a wild kind of form and music. Besides the formal bracketing of the two *becauses*, there are parallel figures in the rhythms, repetitions that almost ring like refrains:

the great duke,   a shav'd Polack,   a discreet fellow.

Some of these refrains are longer, as in

Racket away five hundred crowns at tennis

or

And now and then ransacks a Turkish fly-boat.

A similar patterning exists in the metaphors; the two parts of the speech both end with pictures of hieratic figures, the duke in his robes of state and the priest singing the wedding mass, both cursed, both defied; paired with each are the symptomatic recklessness of court tennis and the casual bravado of piracy "now and then," the two activities linked in sound as well as function (*racket* and *ransack*). The passage as a whole has a lyric integrity as fine as that of the Webster songs that get into poetry anthologies, and yet the resonance of it is something that Webster never allows Flamineo.[9]

Up to the climax of the play in the trial scene, Flamineo's speeches all continue to fall into his distinctive and narrow mold: the rapid-fire chatter with Doctor Julio, clearly a relative of Harpo Marx (act 2, scene 1), takes place in prose similar to that in the scene with Camillo; raising the tension somewhat as the trial approaches, the scene between Flamineo, the Lawyer, and Marcello (act 3, scene 1) is another in loosely mixed prose and prosy verse. As noted before, however, it is in the trial scene that we first become directly aware of the way Webster is shaping and holding back Flamineo's character, for although Flamineo is present throughout the scene, he says almost nothing. He makes no comment when his hand-picked lawyer is rejected, or when Francisco and Monticelso describe the murder of Camillo (not even an aside here), or when his sister scores her most telling points, or when his master, Bracciano, storms out. He speaks three short, separated lines when Monticelso hands down the sentences, but has a full speech only at the end of the scene, and that is an aside. Much of this silence is just good theatrical sense on Webster's part; any ridicule or sarcasm from Flamineo would detract from Vittoria's heroics, which are dependent upon some brutal ironies that would not be improved by one more layer of jest.[10] Nonetheless, it is still strange that the play's leading chatterbox should be quiet for over 250 lines without any evident reason, even though the matter of the trial is of personal concern to him. Certainly there is room to interpolate some nonverbal mugging, but like joking dialogue, this might undermine the force of Vittoria's rhetoric.

Getting Flamineo's boundaries straight at this crucial point can only lead us to admire Webster's integrity as a dramatist, for however much he might have limited Flamineo's knowledge and his opportunities to speak, he did not alter the qualities of Flamineo's thought or voice in midstream. Having heard them, one supposes, in his own mind, Webster let them grow and play out to the end on their own, becoming steadily more intense, even if this kind of development would mean some odd features in the structure of the play. After the trial scene Flamineo appears only twice, in act 3, scene 3, and in act 4, scene 2; the first is the strange scene in which he is scouting Lodovico, and the second is the delivery of the letter to the house of convertites. For a main character neither scene involves many lines, but as Webster organized the play, Flamineo was not likely to be of much use in the middle action, where neither his knowledge nor his range of tones was needed. The actions of Francisco and Monticelso could not be advanced or retarded by anything Flamineo would do; and Bracciano is so mercurial that he might have been allowed to reconcile himself to Vittoria without Flamineo's help. Flamineo's role in these scenes is not designed to set up or justify any deep changes in his character. Naturally, this sort of limitation also controls the verse he can speak; and after the trial Flamineo's verse flickers along as it did before, never rising to lyricism or extending to meditation.[11]

After setting up Flamineo's voice and its limits, Webster puts him away poetically until act 5, where events will exhaust in one rush the possibilities of Flamineo's mind. Webster's stalling is especially apparent in the scene at the house of convertites in act 4, where Flamineo has a brief showdown with Bracciano. Convinced that Vittoria is a whore, and half-determined to kill her, Bracciano meets some unexpected opposition from Flamineo, but Webster is careful not to let Flamineo's verse rise to the occasion:

> *Brac.*   Do you brave? Do you stand me?
> *Flam.*   Stand you? let those that have diseases run;
>   I need no plasters.
> *Brac.*   Would you be kick'd?
> *Flam.*   Would you have your neck broke?
>   I tell you duke, I am not in Russia;
>   My shins must be kept whole.
>
> [4.2.51–56]

The short, snappy phrases and the ingrown joke about Russians (Dekker had used it a few years before)[12] keep Flamineo's speech on the level of the quip rather than the lie direct, but the reminder about the murder of Camillo ("Would you have your neck broke?") is the last straw, and when Bracciano responds by asserting the sheer fact of his ego, Flamineo wilts under his master's imperious *I am*:

> *Brac.*   Do you know me?
> *Flam.*   O my lord! methodically.
>   As in this world there are degrees of evils:
>   So in this world there are degrees of devils.
>   You're a great duke; I your poor secretary.
>   I do look now for a Spanish fig, or an Italian sallet daily.
> *Brac.*   Pander, ply your convoy, and leave your prating.
>
> [4.2.56–62]

Prating has all the force of a stage direction; Flamineo has simply dropped back into babble, his rhyming "sentence" trailing off into two lines in which the meter finally disappears. The dilution and softening of his resistance is conveyed directly in the contours of his blank verse. Scenes such as this suggest that Webster is restraining Flamineo's voice in order to secure a stronger effect in the last act, where all the potential of that voice can be released while one catastrophe is piled upon another.

The chief merit of Richard Perkins's portrayal of Flamineo, as Webster saw it, was that it "did crown both the beginning and the end," and it is in act 5 that Webster raises Flamineo to his full height and in the process gives him all his best lines. At the heart of act 5 is Flamineo's attempt to gain some control over his own life, and in this attempt we may understand his change from prattle to a more intense style. The decisive speech in this regard is the one that is organized around his vision of Bracciano's ghost. It is Flamineo's only long meditative speech, and it is related to the ironies that Webster unfolds at the end; it is remarkably like the other sustained meditation in the play, that by Francisco in act 4, scene 1. Comparison of the two speeches is natural, if not inevitable, considering that a ghost appears in each; they are also linked because Flamineo's speech occurs immediately after he has been talking to Francisco. The very positioning of the two meditations thus makes a comment on the structure of the play: while Webster is doing little with Flamineo in act 4, he gives us our longest look at Francisco, whom he will link with Flamineo at the end. If Francisco is taken as a key to Flamineo's development, the puzzles in both characters become more understandable, and it is important to note the contrasts and resemblances between the meditations that Webster has given them. (Here quotation must be selective because the speeches are long, but the elements stressed in the following pages would only be seen at greater length in full quotation.) Flamineo begins by recognizing his own guilt in a calm and preoccupied manner, as reflected in the generally steady meters:

> This night I'll know the utmost of my fate,
> I'll be resolved what my rich sister means
> T'assign me for my service: I have liv'd
> Riotously ill, like some that live in court;
> And sometimes, when my face was full of smiles
> Have felt the maze of conscience in my breast.
>
> [5.4.116–21]

The evenness is reinforced by the number of words with more than one syllable, which admit less metrical variation than a succession of monosyllables.[13] When the ghost appears, Flamineo becomes very jumpy, often failing to complete lines, or making them too long:

> Ha! I can stand thee. Nearer, nearer yet.
> What a mockery hath death made of thee?
> Thou look'st sad.

In what place art thou? in yon starry gallery,
Or in the cursed dungeon? No? not speak? . . .
No answer? Are you still like some great men
That only walk like shadows up and down,
And to no purpose? say:—   *The Ghost throws earth upon*
                              him and shows him the skull.
What's that? O fatal! he throws earth upon me.
A dead man's skull beneath the roots of flowers.

                              [5.4.124-28,133-37]

The irregularity of the verse conveys directly Flamineo's mixture of queasy courage and wit; as he says, mockery must be one component of the ghost's stage appearance, and there is an undeniable pathos in this cossacked figure who has an interest in organic gardening. But when the ghost throws earth upon Flamineo the fun is over, and the verse at the end is cryptic and metrically dense:

I do dare my fate
To do its worst. Now to my sister's lodging,
And sum up all these horrors; the disgrace
The prince threw on me; next the piteous sight
Of my dead brother; and my mother's dotage;
And last this terrible vision. All these
Shall with Vittoria's bounty turn to good,
Or I will drown this weapon in her blood.

                              [5.4.144-51]

Flamineo now seems to have forgotten his earlier attack of compassion, while gaining an unlikely new solicitude for his brother and mother; he seems to be looking for emotional weapons to use on Vittoria, or justifications for his extortion threats, and we might well doubt the extent of his reformation.[14]

Francisco passes through the same general stages of guilt, vision, unease, and determination, but behind this resemblance in pattern, the differences are great. While holding Monticelso's black book, he thinks not of his own guilt, but of an entire society's, in contrast to Flamineo's personal scale:

                   That in so little paper
Should lie th'undoing of so many men!
'Tis not so big as twenty declarations.
See the corrupted use some make of books:
Divinity, wrested by some factious blood,
Draws swords, swells battles, and o'erthrows all good.

                              [4.1.92-97]

The calm with which Francisco pictures moral anarchy contrasts with Flamineo's attitude, although the dramatic focus is blurred; Francisco never does make use of the book, and "scheming divinity," at least as exemplified by Monticelso, neither "o'erthrows all good" nor has much impact upon any of the action. However, the tone of this opening is everything; the steady gaze into chaos is necessary for the contrast that will follow, and the measured pace of the verse (especially the drawn-out last line) is proof of Francisco's mental control. Because he now summons consciously the ghost of Isabella, he can carry his contemplative tone into the vision, shaping the spirit itself:

> Now I ha't—how strong
> Imagination works! how she can frame
> Things which are not! methinks she stands afore me;
> And by the quick idea of my mind,
> Were my skill pregnant, I could draw her picture.
>
> [4.1.102–6]

Sounding for a moment like Theseus on the poet, Francisco's aesthetic generalizing accords with his lines on the black book, and his mastery of the verse is almost flaunted; *idea*, for example, takes it full weight as a trisyllable, with the whole line carrying an unusual emphasis because alone among this group it has no caesura. The great duke is a connoisseur of poetry. However, when the ghost of Isabella goes out of control, he becomes as nervous as Flamineo with his uninvited guest:

> 'Tis my melancholy,—
> How cam'st thou by thy death?—how idle am I
> To question my own idleness?—did ever
> Man dream awake till now?—remove this object—
> Out of my brain with't.
>
> [4.1.109–13]

Unlike Flamineo, Francisco can dismiss his ghost by an effort of the will, and then can lay his plot in an aria buffa full of turns and fillips:

> My tragedy must have some idle mirth in't,
> Else it will never pass. I am in love,
> In love with Corombona; and my suit
> Thus halts to her in verse.—
> I have done it rarely: O the fate of princes!
> I am so us'd to frequent flattery,
> That being alone I now flatter myself.
>
> [4.1.119–25]

As soon as Francisco has mentioned idle mirth, the verse begins to stumble and turn irregularly, which is appropriate considering that he is writing a letter to Vittoria in halting verse. Webster's unexpectedly deft touch, in the wry, self-mocking way Francisco regards not just the parody but also his own pleasure at it, does more to create the sense of a full character than any number of ingeniously contrived murders.

The ambiguous role of the ghosts in the two scenes can indicate the movements that Flamineo and Francisco both make toward self-knowledge. Flamineo thinks he achieves it, but even before his speech is over we suspect he has not, and later events only confirm this sense. Francisco, on the other hand, hardly makes any effort toward self-knowledge, and his suave lines on flattery suggest that although he may possess it, he is hardly interested in surveying its boundaries like a Hamlet. The two soliloquies stand in an ironic relationship; Flamineo's poetry rises in tension as he mistakenly believes he has plunged deeper toward self-understanding; Francisco's shows an easy control, while he finds self-knowledge tiresome and instead organizes the catastrophe.[15] One hesitates to say that this pattern represents a skeptical conclusion on Webster's part as to the advantages of self-knowledge, although it may be relevant that Flamineo dies suffering while Francisco survives with all his schemes having prospered.[16]

To sustain this contrast between the two characters, Webster must run great risks with the character of Francisco, and chief among these is his tendency to make him look ridiculous while still stressing his considerable powers. One major element of Francisco's character, one source of his political strength, is his apparent indifference to his public image: he has no desire to present himself as a prince with a just grievance,[17] and he can afford the ludicrous disguise as a Moor because he has no vanity. (Lodovico finds Francisco's pose aesthetically offensive—"You have most ridiculously engag'd yourself" [5.5.2] —because it makes his hero-worship more difficult, as we will see in a moment.) By giving Francisco his speeches of self-analysis, and by letting them reflect upon his poetry, Webster lifts him out of the mold of the stock revenger and provides some prima facie evidence of an individual consciousness. We cannot push this reasoning so far as to exalt Francisco into a genius of evil, an interpretation that might work in the library but would be impossible onstage, with the fat duke in disguise and never granted a soliloquy or summing-up after one of his masking scenes. The cumulative effect of Francisco's scenes with Flamineo is a net lowering of the duke's dignity; seeing him protest against the extremes to which he will go, and then going to them nonetheless, almost invites our comparison of him with Marlowe's Barrabas. The devil remains an ass, even if he has a high level of awareness. In the same way, Webster faces up to his risks with Flamineo, who could easily have become the servant-pander of a dozen other plays, the stock figure whose pedigree begins with the parasite of Latin comedy. By limiting Flamineo's knowledge (compare him to Mosca, the brainiest pander on the Jacobean stage), and by having the currents in his poetry coincide with his late-rising awareness of his limited knowledge, Webster endows the character with a vitality that not even Mosca possesses.

At this point we can turn directly to Flamineo's poetic growth in act 5. Except in his vision of Bracciano's ghost, Flamineo is given prose for the opening scenes of the act; at several points his verse is also interrupted by lines of offhand prose. In this way Webster makes Flamineo's final bursts of poetry all the more astonishing and reduces any rhetorical heroism that might accumulate to him before the very end. Secondly, by plotting as he has, Webster can write two sets of death speeches for Flamineo, the first (with the pistols) joking and casual, the second more somber and probing, its jokes heightened by those in the first "death." The first death scene serves the even more practical expedient of letting Webster flush out his notebook bits, as Boklund and Dent have shown; by the time Flamineo gets to the second death, Webster is ready to work in terms of situation and poetry alone.

The final death scene has not been too much admired, and much of its power lies in the way Webster poetically counterpoints the deaths of Flamineo and Vittoria. Terse to the end, and as usual more sardonic than Flamineo, Vittoria says only what she must, and her self-control is evident in the presence of the many couplets throughout her last speeches. When she defies Lodovico to strike, she reveals her resolution in terse monosyllables, with strong pressures against the meter:

> I will not in my death shed one base tear,
> Or if look pale, for want of blood, not fear.
>
> [5.6.225–26]

Her first speech after they stab her shows some brilliant animation:

> 'Twas a manly blow,
> The next thou giv'st, murder some sucking infant,
> And then thou wilt be famous.
>
> [5.6.232–34]

Webster recreates Vittoria's death spasm by running two strong stresses together at a pause:

> giv′st # múrder.

A similar contraction appears in her brief recognition:

> O my greatest sín # láy in my blood.
>
> [5.6.240]

Her final words produce the expected couplet, but the immediacy of the second line brings us up short: "O happy they that never saw the court,/ Nor ever knew great man but by report" (5.6.216–62). The falling rhythms

of the first line suggest that we are about to hear a commonplace, but the
metrical punctuation of the second line makes it seem a gesture toward
order wrenched out at terrible cost:

> Nor éver knéw gréat mán but by repórt.

Knew of course carries a special emphasis because its double meaning involves her recognition of her *blood; great* must also take a stress, because
it is hardly knowledge of man per se that has caused her ruin (if anything,
great has slightly more weight than *man); ever* and *report* carry what are
logically and metrically the lightest stresses in the passage.

Between and around Vittoria's understatement, Webster has set Flamineo's looser, more expansive speeches. The ground rules for these are
clear. Given the previous development of Flamineo's character, Webster
will not be able to allow him any excursions in a grandly lyrical or meditative manner; and he cannot give him any tender sympathy for Vittoria,
much less Zanche, for although Flamineo left the winding of Marcello's
corpse in a state he uncertainly called compassion (5.4.113-15), his
jeering interlude with the women suggests that he could not tell compassion
from fear. (After all, before act 5, scene 6, he had not felt *that* emotion
either, not even in confronting Lodovico.)

It is customary to point out the bravado of Flamineo's last speeches,
but little attention seems to have been paid to their poetry and its place
in Flamineo's development. Our sense of his tone is perhaps surprisingly
dependent upon our view of Lodovico; many readers fail to distinguish
adequately between Flamineo's tone and that of Lodovico, whom Webster
has provided with a crazily humorless and limited intelligence. Lodovico is
essentially a coward, as seen in his nervousness after Flamineo slaps him
about (3.3.126-36); he also has an adolescent delight in his vision of
conspiracies all around him. He is moved to kill Flamineo not so much out
of desire for revenge as because his vanity has been wounded and, perhaps
more importantly, Francisco has paid him. He is talked out of the murders
once by Monticelso's trite exhortation (4.3.116-27) and then back into
them in a moment when he receives more money, thinking (mistakenly)
that it has come from Monticelso. Francisco's trick appeals to Lodovico's
childish notion of how a great man ought to behave (4.3.141-51).[18]

Lodovico's tone at the end can tell us much about Flamineo's. He
never tells Flamineo—if he even remembers—that he knows Flamineo
killed Isabella;[19] instead he says "You once did strike me" (5.6.190), to
which Flamineo replies by baiting him further:

> *Flam.*   Thou'lt do it like a hangman; a base hangman;
>   Not like a noble fellow, for thou seest
>   I cannot strike again.
> *Lod.*   Dost laugh?
>
>   [5.6.192-94]

Lodovico's deadpan amazement shows up well in the way he cannot complete the line. Gasparo's entrance is necessary at this point, since Lodovico is obviously failing to terrorize the victim properly, and the dialogue is worth watching at a bit more length. An intimidating piety from Gasparo, in brisk iambics, is countered by Flamineo's looser line, a cribbing from Montaigne; Lodovico, running out of patience, describes his own very high threshold of boredom and asks a variant on "Aren't you scared yet?":

> *Gasp.* Recommend yourself to heaven.
> *Flam.* No I will carry mine own commendations thither.
> *Lod.* O could I kill you forty times a day
> And use't four year together; 'twere too little:
> Nought grieves but that you are too few to feed
> The famine of our vengeance. What does think on?
>
> [5.6.196–201]

Flamineo's reply is the last thing he says before he receives his death wound:

> Nothing; of nothing; leave thy idle questions,—
> I am i'th'way to study a long silence,
> To prate were idle,—I remember nothing.
> There's nothing of so infinite vexation
> As man's own thoughts.
>
> [5.6.202-6]

His preoccupied, almost musing answer draws every line out with a final, unstressed syllable; pausing twice in the first line, not once in the second line, and finally running on the last line and a half with no break, Flamineo's mind is moving in a way we have not seen before. There is none of the "prating," the witty gab, that has marked his style up to now. The perfect rightness of "I remember nothing" is a stroke for which Webster is, as far as we know, beholden to no one. Flamineo has learned everything—and forgotten everything. If we understand him to be rejecting the idle chatter that Lodovico wants to draw out of him, we probably have half the meaning, but on top of that there is something closer to Francisco's earlier statement that

> Thought, as a subtle juggler, makes us deem
> Things supernatural, which have cause
> Common as sickness.
>
> [4.1.107-9]

Flamineo's desire is nothing less than the annihilation of consciousness, and in a moment we will see him rise out of this in such a way as to affirm his own authentic self.

With Flamineo sunk in thought, the killers dispatch Vittoria, at which point Flamineo's final words come back in an heroic assertion of his own mixed nature, in the chatter, the racy prating, the whole simultaneous, self-detached, and ironic vision that has marked his voice from the beginning. It is an affirmation of idleness, of scattering, of limitation, not the least of which is Webster's own consistent restraint with the character.

> Art thou gone
> And thou so near the bottom?—false report
> Which says that women vie with the nine Muses
> For nine tough durable lives: I do not look
> Who went before, nor who shall follow me;
> No, at myself I will begin and end:
> While we look up to heaven we confound
> Knowledge with knowledge. O I am in a mist.
>
> [5.6.253-60]

The occasional rapid run of syllables between stresses is suited both to the thrusts of Flamineo's wit and his gasps as a dying man. As he weakens, logical connections become telescoped, and metrically regular lines seem the result of conscious effort; the syntactic muddle of some lines is appropriate. As they tumble out, his last lines complement his earlier recognition in "I remember nothing," for his praise of Vittoria is a kind of solipsism à deux. The two die apart, with neither interest in nor compassion for each other, and it is the consistency of this indifference that Flamineo praises in her: "I remember nothing" must include finally his own sister, must include nothing less than the fact of his own birth. Against that nihilistic insight, Flamineo now launches a final battery of wit, prose rallying verse, as if in the face of it all, the energy of his own style were eternal delight:

> I recover like a spent taper, for a flash
> And instantly go out.
> Let all that belong to great men remember th'old wives' tradition, to be like the lions i'th'Tower on Candlemas day, to mourn if the sun shine, for fear of the pitiful remainder of winter to come.
> 'Tis well yet there's some goodness in my death,
> My life was a black charnel: I have caught
> An everlasting cold. I have lost my voice
> Most irrecoverably: farewell glorious villains,—
> This busy trade of life appears most vain,
> Since rest breeds rest, where all seek pain by pain.
> Let no harsh flattering bells resound my knell,
> Strike thunder, and strike loud to my farewell.
>
> [5.6.263-76]

The dramatic function of the metric irregularity should not require comment, but the order beneath it may not be so apparent. Flamineo's last chunk of verse begins with a prosy transition line, and three lines of highly broken rhythms stop on *irrecoverably,* which recreates in itself the sound of a cough. One could note the way in which the last four lines are laced together by repetition in diction and syntax, end and internal rhyme, and consonance; more interesting are the immediate uses of these techniques, for the dragging pace of the whole performance constitutes Flamineo's last taunting of his impatient and uncomprehending assassins.

The wit of the final couplet is based upon Flamineo's own perception as much as upon the play's pervasive storm imagery; the couplet comes with credentials, so to speak, but in its larger context it is also enormously ironic.[20] The lines glance at a heroic farewell, and then reject it in a fashion that seems all the more heroic. if we notice exactly what the vigorous meter of the last line is introducing: it is another voice, calling "This way, this way, break ope the doors, this way" (5.6.277). This is not thunder but only the English ambassador knocking down the door. Flamineo's devastating self-concept can transform that knocking into the final thunder—as indeed it is, for Lodovico and Gasparo.

Flamineo's departure in a joke is emphasized by Lodovico's unintentionally comic remarks after he is apprehended. Gloating with imbecilic pride, he says "I do glory yet, / That I can call this act mine own" (5.6. 293-94), a pseudoinsight that fails to show any recognition whatever that he is Francisco's tool.[21] Lodovico's limited mentality here supplies one more proof (if more were needed) that Flamineo was being sarcastic when he called Lodovico and Gasparo "glorious villains." Virtually the whole current of the play would have to be reversed in order to take this remark seriously, as many critics say we should.[22]

Naturally, there is an element of the preposterous in Flamineo's end; how could it be otherwise, given the strict limits that Webster put upon Flamineo's knowledge and tone? Within those limits the character is taken about as far as possible, and his speeches at the end, knowing yet skeptical, insisting on his and his sister's solitary strength while laughing at themselves and at their murders, seem a consistent and heroic assertion of his essentially trivial character. Yet that consistency alone cannot explain the warmth of our response to him: somewhere in that response we know that although Webster set limits upon Flamineo's knowledge and voice, the character was still permitted to explore these as fully as possible and finally to understand them for himself. Flamineo's poetry is the means of both the exploration and the understanding, as if the carriage in which one were riding had become itself the destination. Maybe that can only happen on the stage; and it certainly is not to say that *The White Devil* is an early forerunner of a Pirandello play, with the characters all very aware of their own borders. It is rather to suggest that Flamineo's vision of life finally coincides with Webster's view of his character.

Comparing the territory embraced by Flamineo and by Bosola, we see immediately that Webster is attempting something very different and much more ambitious in the later play. Because we are aware from the beginning that Bosola knows everything that is going on around him (or is in the process of digging it out), we expect more self-understanding from him. Webster also has thoughtfully provided him with a criminal past and, more importantly, a reputation among the other characters; he is unlike Flamineo, whose past consists of a stereotyped poverty and who has the reputation of only an insignificant pander. Bosola is learned in evil, and was evidently a precocious scholar; Flamineo is what we would now call a slow learner. As one sign of his knowledge, Bosola is established early as a strong speaker of verse; and eventually he becomes less the spokesman for Webster's library, most of those duties in this play devolving, with ironic appropriateness, upon the heavy villains. Like Flamineo, Bosola is sometimes kept ignorant, but these occasions are both fewer and shorter, and Bosola's recognitions are almost always allowed to occur in verse. As a rule he is also less nervous than Flamineo; he seldom shifts between verse and prose in the same speech, the only examples of this in the Quarto being one of the speeches to the Old Lady, and the (verse) speech in which he finds the (prose) horoscope. He is more the master of his thoughts, and he finds them much less a source of vexation than does Flamineo. Flamineo jokes his way to the end in choppy verse and prose, but for Bosola the gags must have a stop; it is he whom we recognize, with hindsight, as the Eliotic sermonizer. And though Bosola may have more long speeches, these are still not all the story: Flamineo cannot sing, but Bosola uses a lyric voice quite naturally, and to him is given one of the finest dirges in Renaissance drama. All of this returns to the way that Webster lets the character *know* more.

Indeed, the plan of the play almost requires that Bosola be a creature of his poetry, for (to the chagrin of many critics) after the death of the Duchess he becomes the central character: except for one sentence (at 5.2.315), he stops speaking prose after killing the Duchess. To make this shifted center convincing, though, Webster does not simply rely upon heightening Bosola's style late in the play; rather he has written up Bosola's character from the very beginning. The use of a shifted center is hardly novel in itself—*Antony and Cleopatra* is without doubt the most lyrically splendid example in English drama—but Webster's solutions of its difficulties are characteristically dogged and ingenious. If Webster is to convince us of Bosola's growth; if we are not supposed to feel that Webster blundered and inadvertently killed the Duchess at the wrong time, thinking he was finishing act 5 when he was really on act 4;[23] if we are not to experience the play as being too form-ridden, with Bosola steered into place mechanically for the sake of the waxworks alone; then Webster will have to convince us that Bosola sees he is called into a special relationship with the Duchess by the end of the play. The easiest way to see this recognition occur is by listening to the verse.

From the beginning Webster seems to be flushing the conventional elements out of Bosola. He does nearly all his railing as a malcontent in the first half of the play, using his prose as a vehicle for Webster's library. The poetry rises through and out of this prose, often with quite deliberate effect. For an illustration of the process one need look no farther than the first scene, when after some initial railing to Antonio and Delio, Bosola returns to Ferdinand, responding to his gift of "the provisorship o'th'horse":

> I would have you curse yourself now, that your bounty,
> Which makes men truly noble, e'er should make
> Me a villain: O, that to avoid ingratitude
> For the good deed you have done me, I must do
> All the ill man can invent! Thus the devil
> Candies all sins o'er; and what heaven terms vile,
> That names he complimental.
>
> $\qquad\qquad\qquad\qquad\qquad$ [1.1.271-77]

The prosiness, the almost total lack of tension against the meter, does not coincide with Bosola's professed anguish. His uneasiness sounds feigned, a pose that, though eloquently maintained, is a pose nonetheless. To the question of whether he is sincere we could ask in reply: Does it matter? After all he is a self-admitted murderer, and his protests have at least one evident goal, in reaching which they succeed: they have raised his price, for now he is to receive a salary and is no longer paid merely for piecework. When Bosola accepts the charge, he can imagine its responsibilities with an experienced eye:

> $\qquad\qquad\qquad$ I have seen some
> Feed in a lord's dish, half asleep, not seeming
> To listen to any talk; and yet these rogues
> Have cut his throat in a dream.
>
> $\qquad\qquad\qquad\qquad\qquad$ [1.1.282-85]

He first muses his way semiabstractedly through three run-on lines, pausing twice in the same place at the middle of the lines, to end on a lingering phrase with irregular stressing. Now he can jump abruptly to the question which, he thinks, identifies him finally:

> what's my place?
> The provisorship o'th'horse? say then, my corruption
> Grew out of horse-dung: I am your creature.
>
> [1.1.285-87]

Pausing and turning on rising pitches and then falling, he is the creature in the excrement that is Ferdinand. The verse shows a sinuousness that reflects Bosola's intelligence; unlike Flamineo, he makes no excuses for what he has become, and finds his self-acknowledgment a source of strength.

The pattern of movement from public railing to private exposure is repeated in act 2, scene 1. Here Bosola gives some gull's hornbook advice to Castruchio, and then rails violently and self-consciously in prose at the Old Lady. Beginning with a long catalog of sores, spittle, and ordure, he finally shifts into a verse meditation:

> in our own flesh, though we bear diseases
> Which have their true names only ta'en from beasts,
> As the most ulcerous wolf, and swinish measle;
> Though we are eaten up of lice and worms,
> And though continually we bear about us
> A rotten and dead body, we delight
> To hide it in rich tissue: all our fear—
> Nay all our terror—is lest our physician
> Should put us in the ground, to be made sweet.
>
> [2.1.52-60]

This is where readers usually quote Eliot's "Whispers of Immortality"; but we do the passage no service to take it out of context, for it seems designed to have virtually no dramatic occasion. Bosola himself administers the coup de grace, saying anticlimactically that Castruchio and the Old Lady should elope to Rome and take the waters. Certainly the tension between Webster and his library could not be lower; the poetry is rhythmically flat and not much different in that respect from the prose catalog that precedes it. There is little reason for the Old Lady to be onstage, except to give Webster the chance to work out the images through Bosola. The scenes have, it is true, an obvious thematic logic; the imagery of decay suggests the pervasive moral corruption in the court. But we need no Old Lady come from the grave to tell us that. If we limit ourselves to talking only about the play's themes, Bosola might just as logically have stepped forward and recited both of Donne's *Anniversaries*, which would be only a little less flat dramatically.[24]

Between the two speeches to the Old Lady are Bosola's speeches on the apricots he has purveyed for the Duchess. The contrast in Bosola's poetic manners could not be greater, especially when he springs the trap on the Duchess:

I forgot to tell you the knave gard'ner
(Only to raise his profit by them the sooner)
Did ripen them in horse-dung.

[2.1.138-40]

As in the lines to the Old Lady, the thematic connections are plain (most importantly, the link between self-interest and excrement), but now the wit is animated by the verse lines; first the adjacent stresses on *knave gard'ner* slow that line, then the quick parenthesis sweeps the words together in a rapid jumble, as if what will follow is of little importance; and finally the joke blossoms in the last, short, evenly stressed line. Bosola's manner of speaking is immediately responsive to the situation at hand, dramatically appropriate for his stage listeners, and not imposed from without as in the lines on living death that he delivers to the Old Lady.

In this brief contrast we see how Bosola will grow. Over the course of the play he begins to respond more to the dramatic moment and becomes more sensitive to the accidents in his own poetry and that which he hears. As this happens, he imposes less set verse from Webster's library. In one respect his development thus may seem rather mechanical, because the situations in which he ventilates his learning are patently manufactured and have little dramatic necessity. But since he does not appear in those situations after the middle of the play, Bosola seems then to be escaping from a mechanical plan. Once the plot of the play is established, there is less time for set railing, and as Bosola begins to live more by improvisation, his responsiveness is mirrored in his verse.

Rather than multiply examples, we might go directly to another turning point in the action, past the time lapse between acts 2 and 3 and into the scene in which the Duchess discloses that her husband is Antonio. It is in act 3, scene 2, that Bosola first senses what is to happen between the Duchess and himself. After appearing to dismiss Antonio, the Duchess asks Bosola's opinion of Antonio's condemners, a rabble of four officers. Bosola replies in an energetically nasty condemnation of flatterers and pickthanks, his verse unusually full of pauses and extra syllables, emphasizing the overflow of feeling:

These are rogues, that in's prosperity,
But to have waited on his fortune, could have wish'd
His dirty stirrup riveted through their noses,
And follow'd after's mule, like a bear in a ring.

[3.2.228-31]

Yet when he goes on to praise Antonio, the imagery disappears and the lines have no movement of their own to propel them. There is no sense of tension against the meter, and the lines often lengthen in irregular gestures toward prose:

> he was an excellent
> Courtier, and most faithful, a soldier that thought it
> As beastly to know his own value too little
> As devilish to acknowledge it too much:
> Both his virtue and form deserv'd a far better fortune.
>
> [3.2.250-54]

The rest of his description is equally abstract, being ornamented with only two well-worn images, the virtuous man as a whispering room or a stately cedar. The discursive and prosaic qualities of the verse are appropriate because Bosola has only a qualified respect for Antonio, thinking him a bawd who poses as a "precise fellow."

Bosola's feigning is not apparent to the Duchess, however, who responds only to the praise and not to the indifferent manner in which it comes out. When she impulsively reveals that Antonio is her husband, Bosola responds gallantly, and the Duchess, happy at last to share her secret, is altogether above doubts; but now something strange starts to happen to Bosola's verse, and we realize that this is the first stage of the play's climax. He replies with an effusion upon the Duchess herself:

> You have made your private nuptial bed
> The humble and fair seminary of peace:
> No question but many an unbenefic'd scholar
> Shall pray for you for this deed, and rejoice
> That some preferment in the world can yet
> Arise from merit.
>
> [3.2.281-86]

Everything comes to life: his mind moves rapidly, one image coming in upon another and the pressure rising against the meter. Bosola was an "unbenefic'd scholar" himself, though he did not prosper as well as his colleague Delio, perhaps because his studies appeared to concentrate on the criticism of poetry.[25] It is important for his tone that the line beginning "No question," with its long bridges between the stresses drawing out his barely concealed sarcasm, has a colloquial immediacy quite lacking in his praise of Antonio and his condemnation of sycophants. The crowning touch nearly shows Webster coming through Bosola:

> Last, the neglected poets of your time,
> In honor of this trophy of a man,
> Rais'd by that curious engine, your white hand,
> Shall thank you, in your grave, for't; and make that
> More reverend than all the cabinets
> Of living princes.
>
> [3.2.291-96]

In Webster's time as now, a trophy is (inter alia) a prize taken in hunting; and Antonio's being thus raised by an engine suggests that the Duchess's hand is nothing less than a gallows. These metaphors link strongly with the crucial phrase in the sentence. *In your grave*: the noun takes great weight in a line that is otherwise vague but full of pauses. And above Bosola's glimpse of the Duchess's fate is yet a glimpse of another, that of the understanding but "neglected" poets. Later we will hear Bosola die claiming that his own good nature has been "i'th'end/Neglected" (5.5.86–87); one object of the play is to make Bosola into that neglected poet.

Though Bosola may see now what lies ahead for the Duchess and himself, there is little sign that she comprehends any of it, absorbed as she is in her thoughts of Antonio: "As I taste comfort in this friendly speech,/So would I find concealment" (3.2.299–300). The naïve accents of this, in the even fall of stresses after *comfort*, reveal how little she has understood of Bosola's own speech and its peculiar emphases.[26] In the contrast between the two voices Webster clarifies much that has gone before; Bosola's irregular drive and engagement as a speaker of poetry are linked directly with his attitudes toward Antonio, the Duchess, and himself.

For most readers the climax of the play is nearby, in act 3, scene 5, when Bosola summons the Duchess and she replies in an assertion of her full dignity.[27] For that scene to have its full effect, Bosola's recognition had to come first (it would hardly do to have him not realize until later what he was doing; that would be like dropping Nick Bottom into the middle of the tragedy), and thus scenes 2 and 5 of act 3 are linked in a number of ways; the attitudes we have seen developing in the second scene receive their final extension in the fifth scene. Scene 5 is also important to Bosola's development, for in his exchange with the Duchess he comes to accept his role as her murderer. His imagery conveys his knowledge, as does the somber progress of his verse, which follows the time signature of the Duchess's opening line:

> *Duch.* What devil art thou, that counterfeits heaven's thunder?
> *Bos.* Is that terrible? I would have you tell me
> Whether is that note worse that frights the silly birds
> Out of the corn, or that which doth allure them
> To the nets? you have hearken'd to the last too much.
>   [3.5.100–104]

The first line spreads its twelve syllables over five stresses; Bosola's lines continue the same motion, the stresses on the lines' first words acting as a *retard*; the last line makes the longest pauses of all, slowing into anapests: *To the nets? you have hearken'd to the last too much.* As Bosola's speed and fluency wane, the Duchess starts to speak in fancier figures and more intricate verse. Bosola, however, is beginning to have trouble shaping the verse line:[28]

> *Duch.*   O misery! like to a rusty o'ercharg'd cannon,
>   Shall I never fly in pieces? come: to what prison?
> *Bos.*   To none:—
> *Duch.*   Whither then?
> *Bos.*   To your palace.
> *Duch.*   I have heard that Charon's boat serves to convey
>   All o'er the dismal lake, but brings none back again.
> *Bos.*   Your brothers mean you safety, and pity.
>   [3.5.105-10]

Bosola's feeble last line has only four beats, as if he were choking; the uncertain rhythm suggests his lack of conviction. The more his resolution falters the more the Duchess's verse flares up, filling out the pentameter pattern in strong, metrically complete lines.

> *Bos.*   Fie, madam,
>   Forget this base, low fellow
> *Duch.*   Were I a man
>   I'd beat that counterfeit face into thy other.
> *Bos.*   One of no birth–
> *Duch.*   Say that he was born mean:
>   Man is most happy when's own actions
>   Be arguments and examples of his own virtue.
> *Bos.*   A barren, beggarly virtue.
> *Duch.*   I prithee, who is greatest, can you tell?
>   [3.5.116-23]

Bosola's rhythms start to drag against the meter; saying less, then falling silent, Bosola has started to see what he has become. All through the play his rationale for his actions has had its basis in a self-concept whose legitimacy he alone could vouch for; now he is confronted by someone whose self-concept he must also acknowledge.

It is little wonder that when act 4 begins, Bosola should be describing the Duchess as a heroine, Webster borrowing from the *Arcadia:*

> She's sad, as one long us'd to't; and she seems
> Rather to welcome the end of misery
> Than shun it:—a behaviour so noble
> As gives a majesty to adversity;
> You may discern the shape of loveliness
> More perfect in her tears, than in her smiles.
>   [4.1.3-8]

The final horrors of act 4 often make us forget what Webster is doing by means of speeches such as these. Reticent and poetically awkward as he is in the presence of the Duchess, Bosola is composed and orderly in the presence of an intellectual and moral inferior like Ferdinand, with whom he is speaking here. The irony of this alternation makes Bosola's eventual assumption of the central role seem more plausible and even necessary: it supplies firsthand evidence of his inner conflict, and allows him to speak in a more complex tone at the end.[29]

Yet for all Bosola's role as Master of the Revels, he takes no direct account of his own reactions to events until Ferdinand finally commands him to kill the Duchess. At that time, Webster does a most extraordinary thing in the way of psychological realism. When Bosola comes to sentence the Duchess, he instinctively returns to his old tone in order to assert the primacy of the soul over the body:

> Thou are a box of worm-seed, at best, but a salvatory
> of green mummy:—what's this flesh; a little crudded
> milk, fantastical puff-paste; our bodies are weaker
> that those paper prisons boys use to keep flies in;
> more contempible, since ours is to preserve earth-worms.
>
> [4.2.124-28]

Though not far removed from his earlier harangues to the Old Lady, Bosola's prose sermon has a new dramatic relevance in this context. He knows what he has come for and so does the Duchess; this elaborate shrift is no shrift at all, as she points out herself. Having been pulled into verse before by the Duchess, and having wilted under the force of her rhetoric, Bosola is now trying one last time to assert the easy confidences of his prose—and of Webster's library.[30]

Once more the Duchess forces him back into verse. At first, in the face of the Duchess's insistence upon her individual identity, Bosola tries to continue with his pedantic repetition in prose, and when he tries to rise to a verse "sentence," the lines are followed by a conspicuous tag, identifying and limiting their tone:

> *Bos.* That makes thy sleeps so broken:
> *Glories, like glow-worms, afar off shine bright,*
> *But look'd to near, have neither heat, nor light.*
> *Duch.* Thou art very plain.
>
> [4.2.143-46]

By this time the verse has begun to stand in a very odd relation to the moral sermonizing, and the tension between the two has a bearing upon Bosola's final development. In the first place it is unclear why he is lecturing the Duchess at all; he had said earlier that when he went to her again "the business shall be comfort" (4.1.137), but now he persists long after it is obvious he brings no comfort whatever, and he does not refer to his earlier intention at any time. As his speeches go on, then, he seems more likely to be giving the Duchess such elaborate shrift because Webster wants him to, specifically wants him to have the worm-seed speeches, and so forth, in the same way that he had planted Bosola with the earlier speeches to the Old Lady. These sermons to the Duchess have little dramatic necessity in terms of the plot, as the two characters acknowledge themselves. Each knows why the other is there.

The lack of motivation and structural necessity behind these speeches is emphasized by their being in prose rather than verse; this is the last major victory for Webster's library. When the final confrontation between killer and victim takes place, both speak in poetry, and, as we have noted before, from that time forward Bosola has to live with the rhythms of his own mind. In other words, when Bosola does *not* return to prose homiletics after the murder of the Duchess, it suggests that Webster is trying to have Bosola work out his state of mind directly in terms of poetry rather than in discursively accessible moral systems.

Naturally, the use of poetry does not preclude the presence of a coherent ethical schema behind a play; but in this particular case it is striking that the moralizing passages tend to be (*a*) in prose, (*b*) victories for Webster's library at the expense of motivation and the logic of event, and (*c*) almost invariably followed by passages of brilliant poetry, in which the motivation and logic of event are revealed and heightened by the verse itself. Maybe the tension is Webster's after all, because he wants to use the strong prose from his commonplace book, and yet senses somehow that this will not work, that if the characters are truly to come to life, it will have to be in *spite* of the imported reading and not by means of it.

As evidence of this, one could observe that Bosola's sermons have little effect upon the Duchess. Once he sees that he is neither consoling nor frightening her, he drops back into irregular verse, hesitating and piecing his matter out with pauses, lagging reluctantly again in anapests. When the Duchess decides to humor this implausible tombmaker with a question, Bosola's reply, as it appears in the Quarto before Dyce relineated it, shows clearly his halting state of mind:

> Duch.   Why, do we grow fantastical in our death-bed? do we
> affect fashion in the grave?
> Bos.   Most ambitiously: princes' images on their tombs
> Do not lie, as they were wont, seeming to pray
> Up to heaven, but with their hands under their cheeks,
> As if they died of the tooth-ache; they are not carved
> With their eyes fixed upon the stars, but as their
> Minds were wholly bent upon the world,
> The selfsame way they seem to turn their faces.
> [4.2.154-62] [31]

Most of this odd illustration turns inward to Bosola, especially in his stress upon this world as an ache in the teeth (the diseased mouth again), a preparation for the next world, into which one is taken while looking in another direction. The verse too conveys Bosola's uncertainty, his fumbling and almost self-hypnotized way of confronting the Duchess; it supplies a dramatic tension almost wholly lacking in the earlier sermons. Bemusedly falling into and out of iambics, Bosola is now committed to a world of wandering in uncertain verse: again, it is appropriate that after this speech he has only one brief sentence in prose.

With an instinctive feel for the coincidence of plot, character, and poetry, Webster marks the turn in Bosola's character with the brilliant dirge "Hark, now everything is still" (4.2.178-95). This is so well known that quotation here is probably unnecessary; what we should observe is the placement of the dirge, for it marks the emergence of Bosola as a character who lives in and through the medium of his poetry. Moreover it signals, by its very presence, that Bosola's style will now find its basis in improvisation. Even the Duchess sees that the song is extemporized: "Even now thou said'st/Thou wast a tombmaker" (4.2.175-76).

The dirge frees Webster almost as much as it does Bosola. As if by an economy of energy, the Duchess's blank verse gathers momentum once the mournful song is over; but Bosola is becoming more uncertain, fumbling to get some purchase on the verse he now has to speak:

> *Duch.*   Now what you please—
> What death?
>   *Bos.*   Strangling: here are your executioners.
> *Duch.* I forgive them:
> The apoplexy, catarrh, or cough o'th'lungs
> Would do as much as they do.
>   *Bos.* Doth not death fright you?
> *Duch.*   Who would be afraid on't?
> Knowing to meet such excellent company
> In th'other world.
>
>   [4.2.205-12]

Boggled again, Bosola thinks, pauses the better part of a line, and starts yet again:

> Yet, methinks,
> The manner of your death should much afflict you,
> This cord should terrify you?
>
>   [4.2.213-15]

Although one is reluctant to place too much emphasis upon the Quarto's final question mark, it does emphasize what is apparent in the verse itself: Bosola has lost his way. Where, for example, does one place the stresses in Bosola's last line? The verse texture conveys his own bewilderment, and contrasts strongly with the resolution and muscular drive of the lines given the Duchess:

> What would it pleasure me to have my throat cut
> With diamonds? or to be smothered
> With cassia? or to be shot to death with pearls?
> I know death hath ten thousand several doors
> For men to take their exits; and 'tis found
> They go on such strange geometrical hinges,
> You may open them both ways—any way, for heaven-sake,
> So I were out of your whispering:—tell my brothers
> That I perceive death, now I am well awake,
> Best gift is they can give, or I can take.
> I would fain put off my last woman's fault,
> I'd not be tedious to you.

[4.2.216–27]

The authority of this is rooted less in its "ideas," which are all commonplace, than in its consistently varied rhythms and their relation to the syntax. One factor that gives the speech a steady momentum is the way lines that seem to be complete syntactic units in themselves are followed by lines that "draw the sense out"; the result is an effect of continual surprise and enlargement, as if the Duchess has begun to sense one death opening out of another. Her moral resourcefulness, her ability to draw upon deeper resources of strength, is as much a creation of the verse movement as it is a direct statement of belief. Webster has succeeded in communicating directly the very arc of her feeling.[32] This magnificent rejoinder by the Duchess also provides us with a handhold on Bosola's development. Her reference to his "whispering" describes not just his manner of speech but also his attitude; one sign that his character must begin to develop now or never is the Duchess's open impatience with Webster's library. It is finally a bore; Bosola—and Webster—are going to have to go one last long act without it. There are few scenes in the tragic drama of the time in which the author confronts so directly his own usual methods of work.

After the Duchess rebukes him, Bosola enters a paralysis so complete that he does not speak again until after the executioners have strangled her (he does not kill her himself, and were he to have done so, Webster would have forfeited our engagement with the character in act 5). Bosola's isolation at this point is emphasized by the Duchess's final speech, which virtually ignores her murderer:

> Come violent death,
> Serve for mandragora to make me sleep!

> Go tell my brothers, when I am laid out,
> Then they may feed in quiet.
>
> [4.2.234-37]

The ghoulishness of the final line is deftly underplayed by its brevity and the slightly askew rhyme; it is the expression of a mind more intent upon the idea than the form, even impatient of the form.[33]

The other strangulations go off according to schedule, Cariola's resistance slowing matters somewhat, the lower orders traditionally being reluctant to assume their place in tragedy; when Ferdinand then comes in to view the Duchess's body, Bosola picks up her cosmic imagery, using it now in his own hesitant accents:

> *Bos.* Other sins only speak; murder shrieks out:
> The element of water moistens the earth,
> But blood flies upwards, and bedews the heavens.
> *Ferd.* Cover her face: mine eyes dazzle: she died young.
> *Bos.* I think not so: her infelicity
> Seem'd to have years too many.
>
> [4.2.261-66]

Every line of Bosola's is either short or has nominally stressed syllables that carry little actual stress; their pausing and uncertain fumbling is counterpointed by Ferdinand's splendid single line, whose short phrases (from a character usually quite garrulous) suggests the gaps beginning to open in his mind. As Ferdinand leaves in the first stages of madness, Bosola begins to recognize his own dependence upon the Duchess, and when she momentarily revives, he realizes that if she dies he is damned. She is not like any of his earlier victims, as his kissing her emphasizes:

> Return, fair soul, from darkness, and lead mine
> Out of this sensible hell:—she's warm, she breathes:—
> Upon thy pale lips I will melt my heart
> To store them with fresh color:—who's there?
> Some cordial drink!—Alas! I dare not call:
> So pity would destroy pity:—her eye opes,
> And heaven in it seems to ope, that late was shut,
> To take me up to mercy.
>
> [4.2.342-49]

The kiss seals the bond between Bosola and Antonio, who kissed her last, and in the same way it signs Bosola's own *quietus est.*

Our sense that Bosola's excitement is genuine is confirmed by his rush of phrases and syllables, after his earlier silence and tongue-tied stumbles. He is loosening up and starting to respond more immediately to events, and the speeches with which he concludes the act prepare us by their poetic manner for the sort of physical action that he undertakes in act 5. Bosola's final speech in act 4 has much in common with Flamineo's near the end of act 5 of *The White Devil;* both characters are moved to what they recognize as a new state of mind, after contemplating a death they had not previously thought important. In Flamineo's case, the feeling was unlocated and incorrectly defined; finally he did not exhibit any of the compassion he proclaimed in his earlier recognition after seeing the ghost. In *The Duchess*, Webster has Bosola begin his self-understanding much earlier, thus giving the character time to verify his recognition by later experience. This pattern in *The Duchess* is directly connected with the early death of the Duchess herself. Any recognition offered on behalf of Flamineo in the short space allotted him at the end of *The White Devil* would have seemed specious; but with Bosola we have such a scene occurring one act earlier. Because we soon realize (even if we have not read or seen the play before) that the plots around Bosola will take some time to be completed, and that he is at least partially aware of their existence, we listen to his soliloquy in act 4 knowing that more development will follow it:

> O she's gone again: there the cords of life broke.
> O sacred innocence, that sweetly sleeps
> On turtles' feathers, whilst a guilty conscience
> Is a black register, wherein is writ
> All our good deeds and bad, a perspective
> That shows us hell! That we cannot be suffer'd
> To do good when we have a mind to it!
> This is manly sorrow:
> These tears, I am very certain, never grew
> In my mother's milk. My estate is sunk
> Below the degree of fear: where were
> These penitent fountains while she was living?

> [4.2.354-65]

Whatever we may think of the sentiments—and there is a good deal of evasiveness in them—this is still verse that is quite new for Bosola, growing as it does out of an immediate situation instead of the author's library. In Webster's design Bosola does not know yet what he is going to do, nor is there any reason why he should, at this particular point; however, one ominous note in the passage above is that once Bosola goes past his notice of the problem of will, his poetry becomes limp and aimless, which does not promise much for the firmness of his resolution in the few scenes left. Called into a world of verse, in which reaction and movement are the rules, his set lectures and harangues no longer come to hand. He is beginning to anticipate his later rashness.[34]

As if to stress Bosola's uncertainty, Webster keeps him offstage or quiet at the start of act 5; he does not appear in the first scene, and during that part of the second scene in which Ferdinand's madness is exhibited at happy length, Bosola speaks only two lines of commentary. It is after this interlude that Webster shows the first result of Bosola's stumbling resolution, in the death of Julia. This murder intensifies Bosola's rising jitters, as he resolves to help Antonio:

> Well, good Antonio,
> I'll seek thee out, and all my care shall be
> To put thee into safety from the reach
> Of these most cruel biters, that have got
> Some of thy blood already. It may be
> I'll join with thee, in a most just revenge.
>
> [5.2.338-43]

Thinking by fits and starts, Bosola's instability is increasing, and the movement of the verse reflects his woolly ideas; revenge is the last thing in Antonio's mind, and it would seem to have little relation to "safety." The sharp emphases in such phrases as

> *mŏst crúel* or *mŏst jŭst*

appear to keep Bosola from realizing that he was the agent of the "cruel biters," and that the best revenge for Antonio might be the death of Bosola. The lurches in the prosody show Webster's meticulous detail in documenting his character's moral anxiety.

The end comes soon in a marvelous confusion. When Bosola enters at act 5, scene 4, and overhears the Cardinal, his adrenalin can be heard to rise suddenly in two lines:

> Hah? 'twas the cardinal's voice: I heard him name
> Bosola, and my death: listen, I hear one's footing.
>
> [5.4.32-33]

In the first line his voice speeds over the unstressed syllables to pick up the five stresses, and in the second the three pauses reverse the tempo and demonstrate Bosola's catlike jumpiness. As he braces himself to kill the Cardinal—or Ferdinand, for both are moving and talking in the dark—he realizes that this is a prelude to his own death:

> My death is plotted; here's the consequence of murder:
> *We value not desert, nor Christian breath,*
> *When we know black deeds must be cur'd with death.*
>
> [5.4.39-41]

His realization mounts to the last line, heavy with stresses: *Know* and *black* both carry a logical weight, but so does *we*, which establishes a witty and courageous distance from Christian ethics. The couplet also has a plausibility in terms of the character, because we have seen the origins of this insight from some distance back; it is the kind of recognition that Webster never did permit Flamineo, even though Bosola still has no clear idea of what he is going to do.[35]

Now another concise murder, with a minimum of small talk at the moment; what matters again is what comes after. When Bosola tells Antonio of the deaths of the Duchess and their children, he makes the murder seem, to the victim, a form of spontaneous euthanasia; it is a brilliant improvisation that also happens to be true. Bosola's hedging to himself, though, shows the dull underside of his wit:

> —Antonio!
> The man I would have sav'd 'bove mine own life!
> We are merely the stars' tennis-balls, struck and banded
> Which way please them—.
>
> [5.4.52–55]

After the one-line raid on Christian values Bosola tries one on classical atomism, in up-to-date imagery; but the prosaic qualities of the line on tennis balls reflect his own ultimate lack of conviction, as the action will soon demonstrate. After Antonio dies, Bosola still dodges the realization that his fumbling overreaction soon must come to an end. A servant tells Bosola that he had brought Antonio to be reconciled to the Cardinal, to which Bosola replies sharply, "I do not ask thee that" (5.4.75). And there he stops; not a complete line, nothing thought through; a quick dodge, as what could have been an opportunity for insight just grazes by. Unable to accept his own responsibility, and unable to grasp the significance of events as they occur, Bosola tries to shift the ground of his action back into his own mental integrity, saying "I will not imitate things glorious,/ No more than base: I'll be mine own example" (5.4.81–82).

Bosola's inability to "be his own example" has been amply revealed since the Duchess's death; he is instead the complete opposite, the clay that takes any print. The pointlessness of seeking revenge against the Cardinal never occurs to Bosola, and he forgets that it was Ferdinand who stood by while *he* managed the murder. Stepping back farther from these last two lines, we see also that they come from someone who not only acts like the central character but even *thinks* he is: to Bosola, the murder of Antonio is only a sign of his *own* fate. At this point he inherits the full burden of awareness he took on when he murdered the Duchess.

Entering to the Cardinal with Antonio's body, Bosola first kills Antonio's servant, even though he has been loyal to both Antonio and Bosola. The indiscriminateness of the murder confirms that Bosola's sense of improvisation has crossed into the irrational; presumably a faithful servant could have defended Bosola against Ferdinand's later attack.

Bosola's inmost impulse now is toward suicide; barricaded in with the Cardinal, he has no plan whatever for getting out.

His speeches to the Cardinal before killing him are brief enough to convince us of his resolution, and strict enough as poetry to indicate the madness of his reasoning. After all his poetic fumbling when he had tried to do some good, he now asserts himself with sudden energy:

> Card.   Antonio!
> Bos.   Slain by my hand unwittingly:—
>   Pray, and be sudden; when thou kill'd'st thy sister,
>   Thou took from Justice her most equal balance,
>   And left her naught but her sword.
>   [5.5.38-41]

In terms of compression these lines would be difficult to improve upon; they illustrate perfectly what Graham Greene has called "the keen, economical, pointed oddity of the dialogue" in Webster's plays.[36] The tension of the verse is suggested by the nearness to, and resolute distance from, the even iambic lines that precede it. Consider for example

And léft her naúght but her swórd,

which literally gathers all its weight upon *sword*. The authoritative displacements in the speech reflect Bosola's new and clearer image of his self.

As Bosola finishes with the cardinal he calls upon one last perfectly ambiguous image:

>   I do glory
> That thou, which stood'st like a huge pyramid
> Begun upon a large and ample base,
> Shalt end in a little point, a kind of nothing.
>   [5.5.75-79]

Vanishing as he ascends, the Cardinal—in his mental outline—is a permanent and religious monument to self-annihilation. Yet solemn as the lines are—the stresses piling up as before at the end, this time on

húge pýramid

—one cannot help noticing that they apply equally well to Bosola, whose actions since the middle of the play have all moved him further toward self-destruction. Again, he naturally projects his own vision of himself onto those who have used him, although now he seems finally to be moving toward a new and authentic self-understanding:

> Rod.   How comes this?
> Bos.   Revenge, for the Duchess of Malfi, murdered

> By th'Arragonian brethren; for Antonio,
> Slain by this hand; for lustful Julia,
> Poison'd by this man; and lastly, for myself,
> That was an actor in the main of all
> Much 'gainst mine own good nature, yet i'th'end
> Neglected.
>
> [5.5.80-87]

That long-delayed word *Neglected* is an acknowledgement not only of his action but of the existence of the will itself: the participle has its subject in the implied *I*, the "actor in the main of all." Bosola's final speech builds upon this tide of awareness, as he explains how Antonio died:

> *Mal.* How came Antonio by his death?
> *Bos.* In a mist: I know not how—
> Such a mistake as I have often seen
> In a play:—O, I am gone!—
> We are only like dead walls, or vaulted graves,
> That ruin'd, leaves no echo:—Fare you well—
> It may be pain, but no harm to me to die
> In so good a quarrel. O, this gloomy world!
>
> [5.6.93-100]

The ironies are rich, uniquely Websterian: of course graves *do* yield echoes, at least in plays like this (in act 5, scene 3, to be exact), and this makes Bosola's reference to the world of plays strangely reflexive; the end effect is to suggest that the murder of Antonio was *not* the sort of thing that happens in a play. His tendency to sermonize and then break off is focused for the last time in four words:

> In what a shadow, or deep pit of darkness,
> Doth womanish and fearful mankind live!
> Let worthy minds ne'er stagger in distrust
> To suffer death, or shame for what is just—
> Mine is another voyage.
>
> [5.6.101-5]

However much the admonition may describe the failure of the Duchess and Antonio to reveal their marriage, its field of view is still narrow enough to focus upon Bosola as well. He knows he has failed to emulate the Duchess and be his own example; up to now his only shame has been that of being a poor intelligencer. Realizing now that integrity can work in other ways, his last half-line is a heroic assertion of his own tinkering nature. Marring the neatly phrased and nicely stressed couplet, Bosola's last four words with their abrupt break in rhythm jerk him back into his own native strain of improvisation. The logical contrast between *stagger* (suggesting stumbling) and *voyage* (suggesting a conscious choice of direction) is part of that wrench; by a felt effort in the verse, he recognizes that his own wavering has an inner consistency of its own. In breaking the poetic form as he does, Bosola concludes his own always-uncertain excursions into tragic poetry.

Bosola's emergent occasions are finally linked to Webster's improvisations with the form of the play itself. The shifted structure of the play is nothing less than an aspect of its characterization. In playing off poetry arising out of the dramatic moment against poetry drawn out of the library and handed to the characters, Webster creates a double reality that we apprehend directly as we hear the play: the development of the poetry *is* the structure of the play.[37] Bosola may enter the Duchess's world and leave his prose behind, but he has no passport to a mind unburdened and imposing its own restraints. For the characterization of the Duchess, poetry gives Webster a way to show her achieving her own authenticity; for the characterization of Bosola it ensures that he remain true to his own wavering nature.

Knowing more throughout his play than Flamineo, Bosola appropriately falls harder at the end. Flamineo dies in a corner, still coughing out jokes and squibs; in Bosola, though, there is a rising willingness to tinker with, respond to, and tinker again with the world in which he lives. His own improvisation is analogous to Webster's with the play itself. The form suddenly takes a jump, seeming to capitalize upon chance, accident, a switch in the subject at the fourth act: Webster knew what he was doing, and had enough artistic integrity to leave the final product seeming spontaneous, which is perhaps the hardest kind of planning.[38] To keep Bosola's poetry alive at his fingers' ends was to underscore in the strongest way the planning and care that had gone into the creation of the Duchess.

6

THE BROKEN HEART

To judge by the criticism of the last forty years or so, the quietness of Ford's poetry is canonical; it is possible to see how much of this notion originates in T. S. Eliot's own needs as a dramatist. Ford is in some ways the most unfortunate beneficiary of Eliot's interest in the relation between blank verse and the quieter forms of colloquial speech, because the consequences of that interest have seemed to reduce both the range of Ford's poetry and the essential relation of it to his characters and plots. It is true that the poetry of *The Broken Heart* is quite formal: virtually every line of the play is in verse; there are no lines over eleven or less than nine syllables except for the songs and a few alexandrines; and although every line has its nominal five stresses, there are seldom the extreme variations in stress levels that we find in the poetry of Webster, for example.[1] Thus it is not surprising that it has seemed safest to advertise Ford's quietness and to imply (if only by critical omission) that he is a poet with basically one tone, either masterly or monotonous, depending upon the reader's tastes.[2]

It is also widely admitted, however, that the formality of much of Ford's verse in this particular play corresponds to the two levels of Spartan life that he dramatizes. Beneath the quiet surface of the poetry there is usually an emotional turbulence in the characters, most of whom talk incessantly about manners and good form, but still behave toward each other with the utmost brutality.[3] The facts of Ford's style thus have a tidy metaphoric significance here, and one that has the advantage of being at least a partial truth in our own experience. The only trouble with such an admission is that it is all too easily made for Ford's other plays too, and for that reason it does not take us very far in understanding the uses of poetry in this particular play. Indeed, no one metaphor or relationship can describe the poetry of *The Broken Heart*; with its various tones, in all likelihood designed to appeal to the educated tastes of a particular audience, the play represents the culmination of the whole practice of writing dramatic verse for the ear, because here the poet has secured a great range of tone by the utmost rigor and economy of means.

One could start with Ford's humor, the dry irony of which is linked with his control of the iambic line. *The Broken Heart* is sometimes regarded as the most humorless product of the age's most humorless poet,[4] but in fact it has many comic scenes that enlarge our understanding of the major conflicts in the play. The problem with Ford's humor is its purity. In *The Broken Heart* there is no tragic satire, no critique of a merchant or moneyed class, no ridicule of London lowlife. Instead Ford offers moments of comedy based on distancing and inversion, especially as they occur in speech itself.[5] We might note two instances. After Ithocles has been welcomed home as a hero, the interlude with Groneas and Hemophil and the girls they left behind shows the ridiculous obverse of Spartan decorum. In Sparta even the lesser nobles speak with as much control as their betters, with the result that there is a discontinuity between their expression and their racy propositions:

Philema.   Indeed I dare not stay.
Hemophil.   Sweet Lady,
      Soldiers are blunt—your lip.
Christalla.   Fie, this is rudeness;
      You went not hence such creatures.
Groneas.   Spirit of valor
      Is of a mounting nature.
                            [1.2.106-9][6]

When physical details enter the speeches, the brief lines with their tightly controlled meters disinfect the subject matter and keep it at a distance:

Christalla.   Where are your spoils,
      Such as the soldier fights for?
Philema.   They are coming.
Christalla. By the next carrier, are they not?
Groneas.   Sweet Philema,
      When I was in the thickest of mine enemies,
      Slashing off one man's head, another's nose,
      Another's arms and legs—
Philema.   And all together—
Groneas. Then would I with a sigh remember thee,
      And cry, "Dear Philema, 'tis for thy sake
      I do these deeds of wonder!" Dost not love me
      With all thy heart now?
Philema.   Now as heretofore.
                            [1.2.115-24]

The sense of play is conveyed partly in those short sarcastic clauses, cutting above the sense of sense—"Such as the soldier fights for," or "are they not?" The terseness of the women's comments is countered by the crazy precision of Groneas's butchery, like that of Thurber's homicidal fencer crying "Touché!" The gruesome recitation is extended by Philema's "And all together," evidently the start of a rejoinder on the various detached members, as if she has been reading Donne's "To your scatter'd bodies go." A related factor controlling the exchange is the steadiness of the verse; the careful dislocations in the rhythms suggest a civilizing control that is at odds with the violence of the imagery. Suppose we rewrite the lines as prose, with just enough changes in syntax to obliterate the meters:

> *Groneas.*   My sweet Philema, when in the thickest of mine
>   enemies,
>   I was slashing off one man's head, or another's nose,
>   or another's arms and legs—
> *Philema.*   Together, all these—
> *Groneas.*   Then I would remember thee, crying "Dear Philema,
>   I do these wondrous deeds for thy sake." Now will
>   'ee love me with all your heart?

The detail itself changes once the rhythms are transformed. When the horrors are recited in verse, there is more sense that they are being manipulated for a response; without the meters, there is less sense of an intelligence dissociated from the flat detail. The verse helps trivialize the violence, and reveals in the process the bluntness of the courtiers' motives.

Certainly no one is laughing, except the women; our responses are far from simple.[7] The passage as a whole retains a simultaneous harshness and sophistication that is entirely peculiar to Ford. Perhaps a modern work like *Der Rosenkavalier* best approaches this tone, particularly in those passages where a certain punitive humor is distanced by the artistic form itself.

Some of the same things happen in the very next scene, in which Orgilus is disguised as the zany scholar Aplotes. His inkhorn speeches are great fun on the stage, and the verse has many built-in directions for performance:

> Say it: is it possible
> With a smooth tongue, a leering countenance,
> Flattery, or force of reason—I come t'ee, sir—
> To turn or to appease the raging sea?
> Answer to that. Your art? What art to catch
> And hold fast in a net the sun's small atoms?
> No, no; they'll out, they'll out; ye may as easily

Outrun a cloud driven by a northern blast
As fiddle-faddle so. Peace, or speak sense.

[1.3.102–10]

Here the effects of cacophony and metric surprise are much broader than those in the previous scene, but taken with what we know of Orgilus's character they prevent any kind of simple laughter. We know that Orgilus detests Prophilus and is trying to control his sister's marriage; as a result, we can hardly join their merriment at his pedantry, although we can see why they should find him so amusing. And naturally our ironic pleasures are heightened by Orgilus's brisk soliloquy of revenge once the two lovers leave.[8]

As these two comic scenes show, Ford's technical resources are not small, and the effects he secures are both local and largely metaphoric. *The Broken Heart* is a play that "lives along the line" more than, say *The Revenger's Tragedy,* in which expanded rhythmic structures take on meanings of their own.[9] If there are metaphoric meanings in the poetry of *The Broken Heart,* they originate in Ford's verse technique, which helps to limit and intensify the characters. Ford's control of tone is virtuoso work at its best, achieved by hearing the characters' voices with remarkable consistency; every line shows the result of close attention to what the character has said before. By the end of the play, most of the characters have become more intense without having changed fundamentally. The technique would seem merely arbitrary if it did not have, as its object, the highlighting of the two characters who *do* have psychological complexity, Penthea and Bassanes. Thanks to Ford's scrupulous attention to detail, these two blossom out as characters in some unexpected and exciting ways.[10]

We might first see Ford's plan of limitation in the paired characters of Orgilus and Ithocles, beginning with Orgilus's request to his father for permission to go to Athens. His motives are laudably Spartan, based as they are upon voluntary self-repression; because he cannot marry Penthea he will join the foreign legion of Athenian philosophy. Orgilus's description of Bassanes shows Ford indicating, through the verse, Orgilus's own firm self-disicpline:

Orgilus. So much out of a self-unworthiness
His fears transport him, not that he finds cause
In her obedience, but his own distrust.
Crotolon. You spin out your discourse.
Orgilus.   My griefs are violent.
For knowing how the maid was heretofore
Courted by me, his jealousies grow wild. . . .

[1.1.68–73]

His griefs may be violent, but Orgilus is having little trouble keeping them under control. His inhibitions are all in good shape, especially as they exclude concrete nouns or specific verbs. Because both speakers also achieve the iambic measure with so little evident strain, and never break that pattern forcefully, we are convinced that their self-control is almost complete. Thus while Orgilus goes on to extract Euphranea's promise not to marry without his consent, he seems restrained and polite, even when engaged in the same sort of meddling he condemned in Ithocles. Right up to the time the father and sister say farewell to Orgilus, the even beat of the meter is seldom disturbed:

> *Crotolon.*   I will prove
>   A father and a brother to thee.
> *Euphranea.*   Heaven
>   Does look into the secrets of all hearts.
>   Gods, you have mercy with 'ee, else—
> *Crotolon.*   Doubt nothing
>   Thy brother will return in safety to us.
>
>   [1.1.112–16]

There is nothing mysterious in the way Ford manages the tone; there is of course the understated diction, but that alone could not supply the *pace* of the lines. The frequent use of an unaccented eleventh syllable, along with the reversal of the initial foot that follows it, keeps the speaker from falling into any rhythmic currents longer than one line. As a result, such emotions as the characters feel seem to be twinges rather than sustained passion.

This steadiness is especially suited to the development of Orgilus, because his one-way mentality is completely consistent, from the surface of his verse to his reduced and simplified psychology. Orgilus's narrow attitude toward Euphranea's marriage may be detestable, but in itself it is a source of dramatic conflict as good as any other. The problem for us, if we want to read plays that involve the high tragedy of the will, is that Ford never has Orgilus wonder why he has this violent antagonism.[11] He objects to Prophilus as Ithocles' "creature," but later he drops those objections abruptly at his father's insistence (act 3, scene 4), and makes no further attempt to hinder their marriage.

The static quality of Orgilus's character is tested most by his repentance to his father, for if that repentance is genuine, then his character may be said to have undergone some change. But although Crotolon thinks that Orgilus gives up his hatred for Ithocles, in fact Orgilus promises nothing of the sort. What he says is shifty and sinister:

>   I will rather
> Be made a sacrifice on Thrasus' monument,

Or kneel to Ithocles his son in dust,
Than woo a father's curse.

[3.4.46–49]

Later he actually does grovel before Ithocles, until he traps and kills him.[12]
In the end Orgilus has no second thoughts about the attitude toward Ithocles that he first revealed in act 1, scene 1, and generally he has no interest
in studying his own motives. At one point he says that

Ingenious fate has leapt into mine arms,
Beyond the compass of my brain. Mortality
Creeps on the dung of earth and cannot reach
The riddles which are purpos'd by the gods.

[1.3.178–81]

As a commitment to the primacy of his irrational mind, nothing could be
more direct. What gives the statement a personal note is the regular
rhythm that breaks down twice, first in the buried alexandrine of the second
line; Orgilus's imagination overflows at the prospect of reducing himself
to a zombie. Then after energetically expressing his contempt for mortal
life, he can end in solid iambics that here underscore his regressive mentality. If Orgilus is a fixed character, it is not because Ford has attempted
to make him something else and has failed.

Orgilus never wavers in his love for Penthea, even though it is apparent
to her, if not to him, that his continued presence aggravates her misery
and will contribute to her breakdown. Thoughts of this sort never intrude
on his concentration, and it never occurs to him simply to leave her
alone:

Revenge proves its own executioner.
Con it again; for what? It shall not puzzle me;
'Tis dotage of a withered brain.—Penthea
Forbade me not her presence; I may see her
And gaze my fill. Why see her then I may;
When if I faint to speak, I must be silent.

[4.1.152–57]

Illustrating both the self-gratification at the heart of Orgilus's love and the
emptiness of his "sentences," the speech also raises a serious question
about his stage presence in the latter part of the play. How can Orgilus
convince us of his simultaneous love for Penthea and hatred for Ithocles?
In the total absence of a reflective component in his nature, we might
be forced to conclude that he is inconsistent or stupid or both. How does
Ford solve the problems that this love-hate division causes? Does Orgilus
simply switch on his nastiness when he thinks of Ithocles, and then switch
it off when he thinks of Penthea? Admittedly, both feelings are grounded

in a general kind of self-gratification, but is the bond between them demonstrated in the text?

The connection is established most fully in Orgilus's poetry, which has a certain wooden and thick quality; it is as if by making his thought denser and less responsive to the language of those with whom he speaks, Orgilus could avoid any awkward self-reproach. From a different standpoint, one might say that by writing speeches for Orgilus that become progressively more illogical and metrically leaden, Ford can convince us that this character can love Penthea and still be jealous of Euphranea, or can find himself unfailingly in the right and still hate Ithocles.

Orgilus's crucial speeches all occur in the second half of the play, and show his muddle ascending to great heights. His dubious repentance to his father in act 3, scene 4, his murder of Ithocles, and his final apologia are the key speeches in his development, and they contain some remarkable writing. When he is talking with his father, for example, he sets up a cloud of clogged syntax and meter that leaves the father asking for something more direct. The king has just asked that the marriages of Calantha and Euphrania be celebrated with all due haste, and here is Orgilus's reply:

>   were it lawful to hold plea against
> The power of greatness, not the reason, haply
> Such undershrubs as subjects sometimes might
> Borrow of nature justice, to inform
> That license sovereignty holds without check
> Over a meek obedience.
>
> *Crotolon.*   How resolve you
> Touching your sister's marriage?
>
>   [3.4.2–8]

The father asks only what the rest of us are wondering. The distinction Orgilus draws is invalid (the existence of power cannot be separated from its exercise), and he uses it to claim that insubordination is the best way to affirm sovereignty. Crotolon accepts this double-talk quietly; after all, he thinks that for the last few weeks Orgilus has been studying philosophy in Athens. But it is probably the last line and a half, in which the muddle of ideas simply swamps the meter altogether, that best shows Orgilus's mad self-absorption. The term *mad* is not used lightly; Orgilus's father suggests it himself when he asks what brought Orgilus so quickly from Athens:

>   I fear
> Thou has brought back a worse infection with thee,
> Infection of thy mind, which, as thou say'st,
> Threatens the desolation of our family.
>
>   [3.4.42–45]

A Faulknerian notion of cumulative madness is perfectly at home in the closed Spartan society, and the overwhelming effect of Orgilus's poetic style is to give us an immediately felt experience of the infection that Crotolon is talking about. The feeling that the course of events is fixed or doomed is borne out by the intensification of Orgilus's style. Of course this stylistic development alone cannot go so far as to provide Orgilus with some internal complexity or even a self-consciousness; but the remark about the family helps explain why Ford gave Orgilus the poetry of a monolithic consciousness.

Orgilus's later speeches show his gathering descent into a dense non-language. When Penthea goes mad, Orgilus finds Bassanes and summons him mysteriously:

> I have found thee,
> Thou patron of more horrors than the bulk
> Of manhood, hoop'd about with ribs of iron,
> Can cram within thy breast. Penthea, Bassanes,
> Curs'd by thy jealousies—more, by thy dotage—
> Is left a prey to words.
>
> [4.2.39–44]

The problems with logic are severe, and the style of the speech—like that of others throughout the mad scenes—forces the logical disjunctions to the surface. The first sentence could be unpacked for paragraphs by a modern linguist; briefly, Orgilus seems to be saying that Bassanes contains either *(a)* more horrors (vices?) than can be crammed within him, or *(b)* more horrors in addition to those that others have tried to impute to him. Neither reading makes much sense, yet the form of the expression is highly portentous, as is usual with Orgilus. As a pseudostatement it is topped only by his breathless revelation at the end. That Penthea is "left a prey to words" could mean, as one editor suggests, that she is now a subject of scandal,[13] but that would be implausible, for Penthea and Bassanes had long been shown as the subject of gossip. (They even carry their differences into public themselves, as in act 2, scene 2.) It would be critically fashionable to wonder if Penthea has been taken over by the forms of language itself, but unfortunately the play has no similar references to language that could justify our seeing Orgilus as a Spartan precursor to Wittgenstein. One is left with the feeling that Orgilus has looked for the biggest rhetorical bomb he can find, without considering anything in the words beyond their sound or portentous effect.

Orgilus habitually employs a language that carries its own gravity, with no necessary reference to the moral or psychological forces around him. By the time he kills Ithocles, the manner is so far advanced in him that no return seems possible:

> Farewell, best spring of manhood; henceforth welcome
> Best expectation of a noble suff'rance.
> I'll lock the bodies safe, till what must follow
> Shall be approv'd.—Sweet twins, shine stars forever.—
> In vain they build their hopes whose life is shame;
> No monument lasts but a happy name.

> [4.4.71-76]

The portentous manner is marked by "henceforth welcome," as if Orgilus were actually seeing and acting from a conscious awareness. We know from his earlier speech, welcoming an anaesthetized brain, that his mind lacks that full awareness; and his usual obscurity creeps in with the dense abstractions and the use of words as if they were code.[14] When he says, for example, that he will conceal the bodies "till what must follow/Shall be approv'd," there is no way of knowing whether he is referring to the acclaim with which he thinks the murder of the ambitious Ithocles will be greeted or to his own criminal prosecution for having committed the murder; he may be thinking higgledy-piggledy of both, and that possibility is strengthened by the last couplet, which could also apply either to Ithocles or to himself. The obscurity of Orgilus's thought is enhanced by the way the meter gives us no clear guide for understanding. The undirected strength of Orgilus's passion is evident in every line, most of all in the last line before the couplet. The instant myth in the heavenly twins gives the line an unusual stressing, which sweeps out of the way the preceding clause, *shall be approv'd*, as if it were a foregone conclusion. The energy of the last line

> Nó monument lásts ‖ but a háppy náme

rushes him past any nagging questions as to what a happy name *is,* and past any memory of his statement that he would be a sacrifice on Ithocles's family monument. The ironies of the speech run deep, but by raising the tension in his voice, Orgilus makes sure he will hear none of them.

To the end Orgilus remains unaware of the murk of his speeches. When he is finally condemned to die and then opens his veins, he senses no gathering clarity, and his last speech shows the confusion that has increasingly come to saturate his thinking:

> I feel no palsies.
> On a pair-royal do I wait in death:
> My sovereign, as his liegeman; on my mistress,
> As a devoted servant; and on Ithocles,
> As if no brave yet no unworthy enemy.
> Nor did I use an engine to entrap
> His life, out of a slavish fear to combat
> Youth, strength, or cunning, but for that I durst not

Engage the goodness of a cause on fortune,
By which his name might have outfac'd my vengeance.

[5.2.135-44]

The evasiveness of this is extraordinary even by Orgilus's standards.[15] He
explains that he used the mechanical chair not because he was afraid to
fight, but because he did not want to trust fortune; the absurdity of this is
nicely given away by the hemming and hawing of "but for that I durst
not," a jumble of clumsy fillers and connectives with which he pads out the
meters and stalls for an excuse. Orgilus also ignores the belief (articulated
in many places throughout the play) that the gods control fortune,[16] and
thus would have controlled a free and open encounter, in which a military
hero like Ithocles doubtless would have pulverized a philosopher like
Orgilus. To justify the murder rhetorically, Orgilus elevates Ithocles as an
antagonist while degrading him at the same time, implying that he might
have resorted to "cunning" in a fair fight; Orgilus never does manage to
sort out his attitude toward Ithocles. After saying that he could not trust
fortune, Orgilus goes on to claim he bears it out:

Ah Tecnicus, inspir'd with Phoebus' fire,
I call to mind thy augury; 'twas perfect:
Revenge proves its own executioner.

[5.2.145-47]

With the stage thus set for Orgilus's last utterance, Ford gives him a daring
outburst:

So falls the standards
Of my prerogative in being a creature.
A mist hangs o'er mine eyes; the sun's bright splendor
Is clouded in an everlasting shadow.
Welcome, thou ice that sitt'st about my heart;
No heat can ever thaw thee.

[5.2.150-55]

It is a cliché of Ford criticism that this speech is indebted to Flamineo's
last speech in *The White Devil*,[17] yet the resemblances between the two
are only superficial. The first sentence is brilliant nonsense, with no
parallel in Webster; it is Orgilus's typically inflated way of saying "I
cease to live as a creature when I die." The advantage that a creature
enjoys as compared, say, to a rock or a cloud, have played no discernible
part in his thought up to now (as they would have for a Hamlet). As before, the essential prosiness of the speech (Where will the principal stresses
fall, if there are any?) betrays Orgilus's willful obscurity. In his farewell
everything happens at one remove, as compared to Flamineo's: Flamineo

is *in* a mist, while Orgilus's mist hangs before his eyes; Flamineo has "caught an everlasting cold," with its explicit reference to disease and the recognition of moral illness, while there is nothing wrong with Orgilus's heart except that it is surrounded by ice. The cold is neither a disease nor a quality of his heart that is working its way from the inside out, and the final image more describes a shrimp cocktail than an organ suffering a fatal trauma.

By no means should this be construed as a hostile critique of Ford's characterization. Orgilus has always kept understanding at a distance, and it is appropriate that he should end by seeing his own death as something imposed upon him from the outside, like a mist before him or ice around him. It is also fitting that his speeches should lack the immediacy of Flamineo's. The flaccid elements in this speech (*bright splendor*, for example) are well suited to someone who feels that his own humanity is signaled externally, as by a *standard* or ensign.

In terms of his characterization and poetry, the matchless Ithocles is another whose transit is all one way. His breezy manner never allows him to be bothered for long by second thoughts or scruples. When he first considers marriage to Calantha, he makes a perfunctory speech on ambition, which begins with stock comparisons and steady rhythms altogether lacking in conviction:

> Ambition? 'Tis of vipers' breed; it gnaws
> A passage through the womb that gave it motion.
> Ambition, like a seeled dove, mounts upward,
> Higher and higher still, to perch on clouds,
> But tumbles headlong down with heavier ruin.
> So squibs and crackers fly into the air.
>
> [2.2.1-6]

After mentioning firecrackers, Ithocles goes on to another worn simile between morality and musical harmony. The lack of urgency in the speech is also apparent in the wordiness that is present to satisfy the meter, as in "the womb *that gave it motion*," "mounts *upward*," "tumbles *headlong down*," or "*heavier* ruin." Unlike Orgilus, Ithocles always speaks clearly (if shallowly) and in even rhythms; his poetic correctness bears out his own complacent awareness that he is a paragon. Here he suddenly realizes that his moralizing is forced, and he concludes that action is more his style:

> But this is form of books and school tradition;
> It physics not the sickness of a mind
> Broken with griefs. Strong fevers are not eas'd
> With counsel, but with best receipts and means.
> Means, speedy means and certain; that's the cure.
>
> [2.2.11-15]

The sureness of Ford's characterization is especially evident here. In the even spacing of the sounds and the jogging rhythms that are disturbed only once, Ithocles hardly sounds broken with grief; we know that Ford is capable of stronger accents if he wants to hear them in a character. Thus it comes as no surprise that the "speedy means" never materialize; Ithocles never does come up with a plan to ease Penthea's misery, and as if to emphasize this, Orgilus makes a similar resolution himself in the next scene.[18] Ithocles' narrowness is not a failure on Ford's part; instead, it is, like having Orgilus reduce himself to a machine with one fixed gear, the result of a deliberate artistic decision. The limits of Ithocles' mind are calculated to coincide with the ironies of the play's politics.

Here we might note briefly the social setting of the play, for much of the characterization cannot be separated from it. The first thing to establish is that for all their polished manners, the Spartans are culturally and politically second-rate. As they themselves admit, the Athenians have better philosophy, drama, science, and medicine; the Spartans even have to import their prophecies. Further, despite all the fanfare given to Ithocles' victory over an outlying province, there is no question of the military superiority of Argos, who can make Sparta submit to its decrees, as King Amyclas admits (3.3.1–3). Nearchus, the Prince of Argos, has compelled Amyclas to give him his daughter Calantha in marriage, but when Nearchus sees that Calantha and Ithocles are in love, he offers a gentlemanly comment (in private) about not tampering with true affection; besides, it is in his best interests to relinquish his claim upon Calantha. He already controls Sparta without her anyway, but if he persisted and married her, Ithocles and his army would be a nuisance. By giving up Calantha to Ithocles, he makes sure that the obviously infatuated general will have his hands full. At the same time, by appearing still to want Calantha, yet not stopping her marriage to Ithocles, he can placate the Spartans, who have this almost Chinese insistence on form and saving face.[19]

Because of the larger political ironies, the verse as it unfolds can diminish or adjust our perspective on the events that the principals take so seriously. Ithocles has, of course, only the vaguest understanding of the action around him, and his character remains as fixed to the end as Orgilus's. Neither breaks through his limited attitudes, and nothing comes of their resolutions—certainly nothing of benefit to Penthea, upon whom some of the political ironies are focused. At the climax of the play Ithocles tells Penthea that he is prostrate with pity for her, but he seems unable to separate that pity from his melancholy or his ambitious love for Calantha. In his conversation with Penthea there is an embarrassing moment when she realizes that Ithocles is truly more concerned about Calantha than about her, and he never even has a shiver when Penthea sees what he is doing. The transition is marked nicely in the poetry. With Penthea's encouragement, Ithocles is elaborating upon his guilt feelings:

Death waits to waft me to the Stygian banks
And free me from this chaos of my bondage.
And till thou wilt forgive, I must endure.

[3.2.90-92]

The mechanical and repetitive thump of this is interrupted by Penthea's short question, whereupon Ithocles becomes flustered and loses the beat:

Penthea.   Who is the saint you serve?
Ithocles.   Friendship, or nearness
          Of birth to any but my sister, durst not
          Have mov'd that question. 'Tis a secret, sister,
          I dare not murmur to myself.

[3.2.93-96][20]

The anticipated iambic pattern—the intellectual matrix over which the emotions move—proposes a stress on *is*, which is Penthea's most important question: Whom precisely *do* you love? For Ithocles the answer is the first person singular, with some assorted third persons as accessories to the fact. When spoken, the question tends almost inevitably to raise the stress on *who*, which involves a far simpler question: *Whom* do you love? implies that there are others one *can* love, while the other, more complex question asks if one can love another person at all. The mind entertains both possibilities, just as the spoken question can make the stresses nearly level. It is a brilliant stroke of Ford's to have found this situation, so to speak, in his poetry; the effect is almost that of Ford talking to the characters through the poetry itself, and perhaps it is that which gives the question the shudder of recognition. But Ithocles never notices what Penthea has asked, never realizes that Penthea might have wanted to hear him answer "Penthea" (which also would have fit the meter). Instead he is merely embarrassed. He misses the beat on *Friendship,* then blusters his way through the rest of the speech with a vague threat. Gradually Penthea worms the rest of the story out of him, even while she is trying to arouse whatever guilt may decently linger within him. When he tells her to desist, her answer is as sinister as it is—possibly—loving:

Ithocles.   Trouble not
          The fountains of mine eyes with thine own story,
          I sweat in blood for't.
Penthea.   We are reconcil'd.
          Alas, sir, being children, but two branches
          Of one stock, 'tis not fit we should divide.
          Have comfort, you may find it.

[3.2.109-15]

In the ensuing dialogue there is no suggestion that the irregular emphases of Penthea's speech register even slightly with Ithocles; when she says she may have a plot, he is delighted and has no more concern for her misery.

Ford goes to some lengths to demonstrate the sheer obtuseness of Itho-cles. It never occurs to Ithocles to speak to Bassanes and rebuke him directly until he becomes violent; and although he then takes Penthea away from Bassanes, Ithocles still spends all his time in the Spartan court, trying to score points with Calantha and put down Nearchus. Ithocles' lack of introspection is pinpointed when Armostes rebukes him for his ob-noxious remarks to Nearchus, saying that "He deserves small trust/Who is not privy counsellor to himself" (4.1.77-78). Like Orgilus, Ithocles re-mains so caught up in his own suavity that he never notices some obvious jokes at his own expense. The most amusing of these is Orgilus's fulsome praise of Ithocles not long before he murders him. Magnanimously com-manding Orgilus to "call me thine own," Ithocles soaks up two lines of singsong jeering, to hear only the last word:

> Orgilus.   Most right, my most good lord, my most great lord,
>   My gracious princely lord, I might add, royal.
> Ithocles.   Royal? A subject royal?
>
>   [4.3.102-4]

As elsewhere, much of the humor lies in the varied music of the lines, the tensions against the meter in the first line resolved in the deliberately trite falling rhythms of the second.

Ithocles' lack of political awareness is especially notable. His difficulty in separating his political ambition from his love is so great that he distorts the facts of the Spartan succession, calling Calantha the "sole heir of Sparta" (3.2.100-101), when everyone else knows that Nearchus is not only her suitor but also the nearest male heir (3.3.7-8).[21] When Ithocles thinks of the marriage, he always manages to keep it separate from the political facts of the Argonauts' dominance.

If Ford does not want Ithocles to examine his motives at the climax of the play, he also does not want him to see them at the moment of his death. Although there are elements in Ithocles that would divide any nor-mally constituted person, Ford never allows them room to work within his character. At the end, when Ithocles trades insults with Orgilus after being "catch'd in the engine," neither looks fully into his own or the other's motives. Ithocles' confidence would seem to give him a psycholog-ical edge in the flyting, if only Orgilus were listening:

> Penthea, by thy side thy brother bleeds,
> The earnest of his wrongs to thy forc'd faith.
> Thoughts of ambition, or delicious banquet
> With beauty, youth, and love, together perish
> In my last breath, which on the sacred altar

Of a long-look'd-for peace—now—moves—to heaven.

[4.4.65-70]

This has none of the problems evident in the speeches of Orgilus; the
metaphors sort themselves neatly, and the rhythmic pattern clarifies the
ideas rather than obscures them. Ithocles sees again what he did to
Penthea, and recalls that ambition played a part in his love, but he still
feels no conflict between the two. His ambition is coequal with his love
(notice *or* in the third line), and it is under Calantha that both drives are
subsumed—consumed, rather, as Ithocles describes her literally as a delicious dish.

Calantha herself is not complex, although she is more decorous and certainly more decorative. She never has any conflict with the will of her
father, Amyclas; she is all pliability and affective faculties. In the beginning she acquiesces in the decision that she should marry Nearchus, but
even after she has met Ithocles and has found him attractive, she still vows
to serve Nearchus (3.3.21-25) until she can obtain permission to marry
Ithocles. Her obedience is accompanied by generous sympathies, as may
be seen in her warm greeting to Ithocles and later in her conversation with
Penthea. In the light of her obedience and sympathy, both her death and
her concealment of the mortal blow itself seem relatively plausible, or no
less implausible than many other incidents in the play and in received
Spartan folklore. The great calm of Calantha's last poetry has been much
admired,[22] but it is, even more conspicuously than the last poetry of
Orgilus and Ithocles, a natural extension of qualities seen in her poetry
and character from the beginning.

Enclosed by these comparatively unchanging characters, the relation of
Penthea and Bassanes lies at the center of the play and generates its most
interesting poetry. The play could almost be viewed as struggling to free
itself from this pair, and indeed all the relationships in the play are tangled
in theirs. We have already had a glimpse of Penthea in action, and the lines
of her conflict with Bassanes may be sketched quickly. She wants to
honor him and at the same time to hurt him; she wants to love Ithocles
and at the same time to kill him for betraying her; and she wants to aid
Calantha in her love while using her as an instrument of revenge. Bassanes
is similarly divided. Much of the roaring and comedy in the play focuses
on him, but so does much of the pathos; neither Ithocles nor Orgilus has
much claim on us for the latter, as each dies in a haze of self-deception
and special pleading. At first Bassanes may look like a stereotyped comic
figure, but we soon see that he is, more than anyone else in the play, a
human protagonist. Critics who maintain that the character is only a stock
property might have wondered why, when Sir Laurence Olivier came to
stage the play, it was the part of Bassanes that he took for himself. Clearly
the character has more contours to it than the standard Caroline cuckold.[23]

The irony—perhaps even the tragedy—of his relationship with Penthea is
that once he is cured of his jealousy he is also cured of his love, although
his affections continue in a frantic desire to help her by any means possible.

From the first time we see him, Bassanes is speaking an extraordinary
poetry:

> I'll have that window next the street damm'd up;
> It gives too full a prospect to temptation,
> And courts a gazer's glances. There's a lust
> Committed by the eye, that sweats and travails,
> Plots, wakes, contrives, till the deformed bear-whelp
> Adultery be lick'd into the act,
> The very act. That light shall be damm'd up;
> D'ee hear, sir?

> [2.1.1–8]

In its vigorously irregular rhythms and dense imagery this is unlike anything elsewhere in the play; its vigor is on a plane with the surreal para-
noia granted Leontes in *The Winter's Tale,* and it immediately establishes
Bassanes as something other than a comic butt or a ludicrous, horn-mad
husband. The beastliness of his imagination finds full expression in his
verse, unlike the beastliness of the other characters, whose verse smooths
over their willingness to hurt. Bassanes' violent language is no mere expression or condition of his jealousy; he talks that way at other times too.
Either he has not been provided with the inhibitions of the others or the
passion of his jealousy must be assumed to have stripped them off before
the play begins, in the process laying bare many emotions besides jealousy
alone. In one sense he is thus the impacted double of the two other male
principals, and it is interesting to note that during the first half of the play
Ford consistently places him close to Ithocles, whose actions start the
play's basic conflict, and in the second half places him close to Orgilus,
who initiates the catastrophe. Later we will see some of Ford's other
reasons for doing this, but for now we might note that although Bassanes
seems completely distracted by the end of the play, he alone has been
close enough to the sufferers to understand what each has been through.

Bassanes' complexity is most apparent in his attitude toward his wife.
We never do see Penthea regarding him with anything resembling affection—a legalistic deference is all she can manage—but when he sees her,
something happens to his jealousy and he tries to become a poet:

> She comes, she comes. So shoots the morning forth,
> Spangled with pearls of transparent dew.
> The way to poverty is to be rich;

> As I in her am wealthy, but for her
> In all contents a bankrupt.
>
> [2.1.68–72]

This spontaneous response to the beauty of his wife is not designed for any listeners around him (at this point there are none). Perhaps it is the hush of the second line that most carries his conviction: the meter requires that *pearls* take up the time of two syllables, and while the image may be familiar, it comes out with a personal accent that would not seem possible for a man dominated solely by animal jealousy.[24] This lyric passage and others like it suggest that the relationship between Penthea and Bassanes is a variation on the ancient stories of the beauty and the beast. Throughout the play Bassanes is usually characterized as an offensive animal, yet he is more than deeply affected, he is *charmed* by Penthea. Unlike the beauty, however, Penthea never recognizes the effect she has on Bassanes, and the result is a considerable sense of pathos that finally is focussed on Bassanes.

One side of Bassanes' love does well by a Platonic system of accounting, for he seeks what is good for Penthea; he is glad to hear that Ithocles has returned safely, because he knows this will please her. At the same time his love also has a selfish edge; he wants her to please him, although here too he is contradictory:

> We will to court, where if it be thy pleasure,
> Thou shalt appear in such a ravishing luster
> Of jewels above value, that the dames
> Who brave it there, in rage to be outshin'd,
> Shall hide them in their closets, and unseen
> Fret in their tears, whiles every wond'ring eye
> Shall crave none other brightness but thy presence.
>
> [2.1.77–83]

In contrast to his earlier desire to imprison Penthea, Bassanes now wants to show her off. There was nothing in Orgilus's initial description of the two that could have prepared us for this, but Orgilus can never afford to admit that Bassanes might love Penthea as much as he does himself (and incidentally, Orgilus never becomes lyrical at her presence). Bassanes does not just want to be envied, although that figures in his feelings; rather he wants to have his wife be satisfied by her own choice, as the rest of the speech goes on to show, and that is not an uncommendable desire, even if the pleasures he suggests are not ones that Penthea would choose. Indeed his imagination is stirred by his suggestion, as in the line,

> ´ x x ´   ´
> Of jewels above value, that the dames
> Who brave it there, . . .

That two-syllable evocation of the jewels is a personal note, another part of his ambivalent affection for Penthea. When the whole group is getting ready to leave for court, he has an exchange with Grausis, in which the old lady makes a shrewd comment on his complexity. He has tried to rebuke her, and she retaliates with a pointed insight:

> You dote,
> You are beside yourself. A politician
> In jealousy? No, y'are too gross, too vulgar.
>
> [2.1.149-51]

Dote sums up both Bassanes' foolishness and his fondness, but still more suggestive is Grausis's comment that Bassanes is "beside himself." Orgilus made a similar comment at the start, when he described Bassanes as transported by a sense of "self-unworthiness" (1.1.68). Jealousy is not the only or even the dominant component in his suffering, as he discovers when he brings Penthea to court.

Court life in Sparta, when it does not involve executions and ritual dancing, seems mainly to consist of insults delivered in temperate language. When Calantha welcomes Ithocles and says that Penthea has made them all happy by her presence, Ithocles responds with a gratuitous dig at both his sister and Bassanes:

> Sister, wedlock
> Holds too severe a passion in your nature,
> Which can engross all duty to your husband
> Without attendance on so dear a mistress.—
> 'Tis not my brother's pleasure, I presume,
> T'immure her in a chamber.
>
> [2.2.65-70]

The rebuke is linked with a call to public-spiritedness and a joke at Bassanes' expense. But it comes off smoothly, the verse hardly ruffling (notice how the primary stresses do not appear until the middle of a line, thus creating a sense of Ithocles' restraint). Bassanes' response is a brief and crude attempt to save face: "'Tis her will,/She governs her own hours" (2.2.70-71). Bassanes' more rugged meters indicate his bluntness, as in "She governs her own hours." Penthea can play the game too, and when Ithocles asks her how she feels, she replies, "You best know, brother,/From whom my health and comforts are deriv'd" (2.2.75-76). Considering that he has been gone for some time, and that she is wasting away and unhappy (2.2.142-43), the reply is a straight rebuke that Ithocles must understand, for he then falls silent. Bassanes senses her implied criticism: "I like the answer well; 'tis sad and modest" (2.2.77). Penthea's role as unsmiling Patience on a monument is emphasized by the steady beat of the line, "From whom my health and comforts are deriv'd," which immediately conveys both her resistance and her resignation.

Although the Spartans are always taking shots at each other, no one really seems to listen to anyone else, nor do any of them seem to *remember* what the others say. This is one side of Ford's controlled thinness of characterization. (Again the exceptions are Bassanes and Penthea.) Crotolon and Armostes discuss the marriage of Euphranea and Prophilus as if they were trading horses (Euphranea herself says that Prophilus is "in all points worthy," 2.2.98), but despite their exhaustive debate, they admit that no one has seen Orgilus, let alone secured his permission to the match. Crotolon himself had been eager to insist upon that, but with his usual obtusity he forgets it now, even though he knows that Prophilus is Ithocles' best promoter. Not listening to each other or engaging their problems directly, these characters seem more intent on striking postures, the consequences of which they all feel later.

The eruptions begin in act 3, scene 2, and continue to the end. After that scene, Ithocles snaps out of his melancholy (in more than one sense Penthea bears it away), and goes on to pursue Calantha with an almost canine concentration; Penthea starts to fall apart, and when we see her next she is making her will to Calantha; and Bassanes puts a stop to his jealousy, but only after threatening to kill Ithocles. Because we have also learned in the meantime that Orgilus is becoming more desperate, we realize that Ithocles' removal of Penthea will push Orgilus further toward revenge.

The climax of the play is act 3, scene 2, which has a tightly knit structure, beginning with Ford's stage direction for "soft music," progressing through orderly, set speeches by Penthea and Ithocles into short, impassioned give-and-take, and culminating in the sudden appearance of Bassanes. He is followed in by Grausis, Groneas, and Hemophil, whose remarks form a crude counterpoint to his suffering and humiliation; the scene ends with Ithocles leading Penthea off and Bassanes vowing to conquer his jealousy. The whole scene has an upward curve to its action and language, from the elegant melancholy of the opening, to the coarse jokes of the courtiers, to Bassanes' being charmed like a bear by the music of Penthea's voice. The progress of the verse, Penthea's in particular, helps establish this contour of event.

Ithocles begins by wishing he had never been born, and Penthea agrees that would have been pleasant:

> Then had you never known that sin of life
> Which blots all following glories with a vengeance
> For forfeiting the last will of the dead,
> From whom you had your being.
>
> [3.2.39–42]

This magnificent sentence running over three lines before a pause is one of Ford's more splendid technical achievements, showing too that his genius for the verse form can encompass much more than the short, understated phrase. One crucial clause is remarkable for its metric telescoping:

For forfeiting the last will of the dead.

Those sudden compressions at *forfeiting* and *last will*, with slack syllables trailing out behind them to be brought up at *dead*, convey more clearly than any direct announcement that Penthea's mind is beginning to weaken. To Ithocles' claim that his heart is breaking for having broken hers, her reply is savage and heated:

Not yet, heaven,
I do beseech thee! First let some wild fires
Scorch, not consume it. May the heat be cherish'd
With desires infinite but hopes impossible.

[3.2.46–49]

The insanity of this prayer is conveyed largely in the unexpected stressing and pausing; up to now the characters have kept their brutal sentiments contained in rhythmically smooth lines.[25] When she asks Ithocles to kill her, he replies with a question about Bassanes, and the dialogue is worth following for several lines:

Ithocles. How does thy lord esteem thee?
Penthea.   Such an one,
As only you have made me: a faith-breaker,
A spotted whore. Forgive me. I am one
In art, not in desires, the gods must witness.
Ithocles. Thou dost belie thy friend.
Penthea.   I do not, Ithocles;
For she that's wife to Orgilus and lives
In known adultery with Bassanes
Is at the best a whore. Wilt kill me now?

[3.2.68–75]

As Ithocles points out, Penthea is not being honest; Bassanes' love is profound in spite of his jealousy, and at the end of the scene he finally does believe her when she says she is faithful. Bassanes' feeling for her should not be underestimated, although Penthea feels so dirtied that she is unable to respond to it, and is also unwilling to admit how much power she has over him. These problems are intensified by her sexual relations with Bassanes ("I am one/In art, not desires"): her feelings of guilt also have another related source, however, as we learn later in the mad scene. But

Ithocles can make no rebuttal; Penthea vigorously closes the door on the subject, in another long sentence that runs on without pause, the regular rhythm of the first line followed by a jump in the second:

> For she that's wife to Orgilus and lives
> In known adultery with Bassanes
> Is at the best a whore.

The power of the second line derives from the sudden acceleration of tempo, the run of light syllables after that very important word *known*. Her "adultery" is known only to herself, and the word is accessible only in terms of a paranoid sensibility.

When Ithocles reveals that he loves Calantha, he reasonably expects the worst from Penthea, but instead of threatening to expose him, she makes the enigmatic comment we have already noticed:

> Alas, sir, being children, but two branches
> Of one stock, 'tis not fit we should divide.
> Have comfort, you may find it.

Since Penthea is absolute for death, there is only one way they can remain undivided and Ithocles can still love Calantha: that would be for all three to die. The wandering emphases in *Have comfort, you may find it* show perhaps better than anything else just how short-lived Ithocles' pleasures will be.[26]

By having Bassanes then enter suddenly, Ford leaves the bond between Ithocles and Penthea to be explored later; but while Bassanes lunges in with his accusations, Penthea tries to silence Ithocles with a very strange question.

> *Bassanes.*   I blush more
>   To name the filthiness than thou to act it.
> *Ithocles.* Monster!
> *Prophilus.*   Sir, by our friendship—
> *Penthea.*   By our bloods—
>   Will you quite both undo us, brother?
>
>   [3.2.151-54]

In what sense could they be undone by Ithocles' calling Bassanes a monster? One clue to Penthea's thinking lies in the peculiar organization of her verse. The inside-out syntax of her question makes the placing of stresses somewhat uncertain, but the line seems to work this way:

> Will you quite both undo us, brother?

The sense is clear enough; it is the dramatic relevance of the question that is puzzling. If *both* takes a strong stress, as seems likely, the reason for the question becomes clear; by antagonizing Bassanes, Ithocles might make him kill them both, and thus deprive her of that pleasure. She wants to die and achieves it soon enough; but along the way she wants to claim certain prerogatives with regard to her brother.

Bassanes is as distraught as ever, and if the others were inclined to listen to him, they would see that his speeches point up the real nature of his love as well as his sickness. In answer to Penthea's protest that she has "ne'er studied [his] vexation," he says

> Light of beauty,
> Deal not ungently with a desperate wound.
> No breach of reason dares make war with her
> Whose looks are sovereignty, whose breath is balm.
> O that I could preserve thee in fruition
> As in devotion.
>
> [3.2.161-66]

In all the Jacobean drama there is probably no other jealous husband like this, who calls for his wife's continued fruition.[27] It is important that he should say *preserve*, and not *defend* or some other word implying struggle. Bassanes has put the very word on his fears: he knows that Penthea is failing, and probably will not live much longer. The metrical stress on *preserve* is central in every way, for in the presence of *fruition* the word makes a profound and touching appeal, to which Penthea responds with a warmer defense of her chastity than usual. Ithocles, however, has not understood the exchange, for he says with the usual Spartan courtesy, "Purge not his griefs, Penthea" (3.2.171).

But Bassanes is already kneeling, "charm'd with sounds celestial" (3.2. 174). The Spartan nobility standing by are unmoved, and the canny old maidservant alone responds: "Alas, kind animal" (3.2.178). For all his abuse of Grausis, she alone seems to understand Bassanes; she alone can hear the angel beating his wings within the beast, to use Yeats's phrase. Platonically angelic in wanting what is good for Penthea, he has a beastly inability to want it with a constant heart.

Ford heightens the pathos of the situation by bringing in Groneas and Hemophil. Their vulgar lack of sympathy increases our awareness of Bassanes' pain:

Grausis.	Out on him.
	These are his megrims, firks, and melancholies.
Hemophil.	Well said, old touchhole.
Groneas.	Kick him out at doors.

[3.2.154-56]

When Grausis tries to excuse Bassanes' behavior, the courtiers' ridicule of her makes our sympathies go out to both the servant and her master. As before, a cruel sort of humor seems inseparable from these two courtiers.[28] Neither of them understands Bassanes' pain:

>   Rip my bosom up,
> I'll stand the execution with a constancy.
> This torture is insufferable.

                                              [3.2.188-90]

It is a convincing speech of resolved helplessness; much of its plangent note is carried in that second line, another of Ford's quiet alexandrines, lengthened by the many nasal consonants. The man's frustration and despair are even more apparent as Ithocles takes Penthea away, and he realizes too late that he must "try/To outdo art and cry a jealousy" (3.2. 205-6). Yet the wrench in his voice, especially as he says he must

>   try/To outdó árt

does not give us much hope for a balanced self-cure. He has lost his wife just when he has recognized for the first time the shortness of love and fruition.

Ford's problem with Bassanes begins with this recognition. A jealous husband's anxiety can start a great deal of action on the stage, and can provide a framework for tense and energetic poetry. The uses of a stoic husband are not so certain. After being exposed and humiliated in the scene with Ithocles and Penthea, Bassanes determines to be as impassive as possible, and even dares others to upset him emotionally. Ford must have sensed the problems in having Bassanes remain undivided, and he makes the character's stoicism collapse under the pressure of Penthea's illness.[29] The desperation of Bassanes' attempts to find a cure for her invalidate his composure from the start, and also make him a rather ludicrous bustler in the process. Ford also has Bassanes' attitude toward Penthea undergo a basic change. After he is purged of his jealousy, she plays a very different role in his emotional life, for although he remains obsessed with his search for a cure, his sensual response to her as a woman is gone, even before he sees that she has gone mad. After his reformation she excites not his passion but only his pity, and by the end we realize that the purging of his illness has taken with it his only consolations.

This would seem an ideal recipe for a very dull ending, at least as far as Bassanes is concerned, and some readers have admitted freely to Ford's accomplishment here.[30] Certainly Bassanes is a letdown if we come to him in search of an aspiring hero. However, Ford goes on to lead Bassanes to a peculiarly satisfying end, accomplishing this through the great control of his verse and the sustained metaphor of the beast. Abandoned by Penthea, Bassanes attempts to withdraw into himself and control at least his own mind. After his exposure, he admits in act 4, scene 2, that he has offended the gods, asks Grausis' pardon for abusing her, and then arranges his thoughts in one of the play's most fascinating soliloquies. Although Bassanes has lost one kind of madness, his jealousy, he may only have exchanged it for another:

> Beasts, only capable of sense, enjoy
> The benefit of food and ease with thankfulness;
> Such silly creatures with a grudging kick not
> Against the portion nature hath bestow'd.
> But men, endow'd with reason, and the use
> Of reason, to distinguish from the chaff
> Of abject scarcity the quintessence,
> Soul, and elixir of the earth's abundance,
> The treasures of the sea, the air, nay, heaven,
> Repining at these glories of creation,
> Are verier beasts than beasts. And of those beasts
> The worst am I.

> [4.2.18-29]

Bassanes becomes progressively more furious as he exalts reason over bestiality, and the rising gorge can be felt in the verse itself. There is a gathering coincidence of harsh consonants, difficult junctures, irregular stresses, and jammed syntax in phrases such as *with a grudging kick not / Against the portion,* or *distinguish from the chaff / Of abject scarcity the quintessence.* If reason can distinguish the chaff, why are the lines so rough? Neither the sweetness nor the substance of reason is heard here. Bassanes has simply reduced his demands to a new and fanatical minimum, tipping over all the Renaissance commonplaces; he is proud to see himself as the nadir of the universe. The selfishness that motivated his jealousy has been transformed into something more savagely comic, and the distortions of his thinking become more pronounced as he continues, saying

> I, who was made a monarch
> Of what a heart could wish for, a chaste wife,
> Endeavor'd what in me lay to pull down
> That temple built for adoration only.

> [4.2.29-32]

The disorder is evident from the beginning: he never was the "monarch" of Penthea's heart, but his emphasis on *chaste wife,* with its two emphatic stresses, controls and directs his fantasy. There is a confusion of meter and syntactic movement in the third line, and when he attempts to pull his thought together in the fourth line, he says something neatly regular yet wholly absurd. In his fanaticism he is repudiating not simply jealousy but the whole field of adult sexuality.

There is a pathetic appropriateness in having the beast descend into himself, determined to become an angel and leave his beastliness behind, and it makes for a splendidly ironic scene when Bassanes meets Penthea after she has gone mad. As she comes in with her hair about her ears, his composure is manically extreme; the meeting between the two is sheer black comedy, this confrontation between the wildly unbalanced wife and her husband, who has retreated for the moment into rocklike catatonia, and who greets her with the good news that he is sane at last.

The pathos of the situation is typical of Ford, and it would have been easy for him to have left Bassanes in a corner while the rest of the play whirled on about him. But Ford is still interested in the divisions within Bassanes' character, the sentient heart within the animal, and as a sign of this he makes Bassanes unable to maintain his stoic fixity. Before Penthea's mad scene is even over, his composure has begun to crack:

> Fall on me, if there be a burning Aetna,
> And bury me in flames! Sweats hot as sulphur
> Boil through my pores! Affliction hath in store
> No torture like to this.
>
> [4.2.95-98]

The spontaneous and natural syntax of these lines, sustained by the lightly varied meter, gives an immediate sign that his stoic immobility will not hold, and the three speeches that follow show him trying to hang onto his resolve but weakening nonetheless.[31]

As Bassanes breaks down, Penthea becomes only more steady. The composure of her madness has been widely rediscovered, ever since Eliot fastened onto the rose garden passage as the epitome of Ford's verse. Penthea's raving, of course, discloses the desire for revenge that she had concealed earlier (most of all from herself).[32] When she tells Orgilus that he was really the one who lost his wits in the rose garden, or calls him a married bachelor, she implies that he has failed to revenge the wrong done to them by Ithocles. Orgilus understands her perfectly, and chides himself like the conventional revenger: "She has tutor'd me;/Some powerful inspiration checks my laziness" (4.2.124-25). Thus Penthea's quiet formality is another example of the way Spartan violence is shown working beneath the good manners of the poetry.

Her madness also has more than method to it; many of Penthea's remarks go well beyond hints to Orgilus that he should kill Ithocles, and lead into the central conflicts in her character. Consider, for example, the movement of two typical passages. The first is her description of Ithocles, just before the lines on the rose garden:

too much happiness
Will make folk proud, they say—but that is he;

Points at Ithocles.

And yet he paid for't home. Alas, his heart
Is crept into the heart of the princess;
We shall have points and bride-laces.

[4.2.115-19]

The second is her speech to Ithocles and Bassanes:

Take comfort,
You may live well and die a good old man.
By yea and nay, an oath not to be broken,
If you had join'd our hands once in the temple—
'Twas since my father died, for had he liv'd
He would have done't—I must have call'd you father.

[4.2.138-43]

It is very important—and very easy—to hear the line-by-line movement of
the verse in both passages, in which each line reverses or sharply modifies
the idea of the line before it. In the first passage, the plan is something
like this: "The proud and happy Ithocles/Will get his due, and get it in his
heart,/By loving this important and powerful woman in secret/And then
marrying her later with ceremony." The second passage has the same tips
and turns, and accentuates them by being addressed to two people: (to
Ithocles):[33] "Cheer up/You may reform and live long,/While I am irre-
versibly married;/But if you (Bassanes) had joined me and Orgilus in the
temple/(For my father, now dead,/Wished us to marry), you would have
been like a father to me." As in the first passage, the shifts are abrupt yet
steady in progression, like the musical development of a funeral march;
the switchbacks in the ideas, meshing with the line-by-line organization of
the poetry, suggest the inevitability of her derangement, and suggest it in
a manner we experience immediately, of reversals and turns within an
anticipated development. Penthea's mad verse is very different from the
photomontage that most Jacobean dramatists present as madness. (One
could usefully contrast Penthea's style with Ophelia's.) Because of her
constant turning and balancing, her madness gives the impression of
having more sources than simple unhappiness in marriage. Much of her
agony has to do with her hardly understood desire for revenge, which the
composure of her verse always reins in.

Penthea's madness also reveals another motive for her marriage to
Bassanes, and that is her feeling (as expressed in the quotation above)
that Bassanes has assumed the place of a father. Her vigorous rejection
of Orgilus is more understandable if we see that she is looking for a

relationship that he could never join. The curious stressing in the last clause quoted above carries all the ironies:

Í mûst hăve call'd yôu father.

The options for emphasis are many, but the inescapable accent on *must* reinforces her own puzzlement at the contradictory things she has expected of Bassanes; it also helps explain why she never could afford to admit consciously that she had a sensuous power over him.

The contrast between Penthea's composure and Bassanes' hectic energy extends to their verse. A cold eye on death is not for Bassanes, and while he bustles in search of a cure for his wife, his verse becomes as headlong and repetitive as it had been when he wanted to coffer her up. The reader who wants to see him as undergoing a successful trial by fire during Penthea's mad scenes will be hard put to account for his dotty movements now:[34]

> Foh! I am busy; for I have not thoughts
> Enow to think. As shall be well anon;
> 'Tis tumbling in my head: there is a mastery
> In art to fatten and keep smooth the outside,
> Yes, and to comfort up the vital spirits
> Without the help of food; fumes or perfumes,
> Perfumes or fumes.
>
> [4.2.160-66]

His perfume cure is not necessarily irrational in itself, but his attitude toward it is, and the self-absorption of his rapture is especially evident when he leaves, saying to no one in particular,

> I grant t'ee, and will put in practice instantly
> What you shall still admire. 'Tis wonderful,
> 'Tis super-singular, not to be match'd.
> Yet when I've done it, I've done it; ye shall all thank me.
>
> [4.2.170-73]

The nervous repetition of this is completely appropriate, as is the tension against the iambic line. Another of Ford's buried alexandrines, the first line in its unusual length works wonderfully against the idea of Bassanes' achieving an instant cure; and in the last line the rhythm nearly dissolves in his jumpy thinking. Bassanes goes beyond the stoic ideal.

Ford's emphases are especially evident if we consider that he does not present a scene is which Bassanes sees Penthea die, or a scene in which Bassanes comes in to see her dead in the chair beside her brother. If the depiction of a stoic convert were Ford's main interest, it would have been logical to include scenes such as these. Instead, as if to stress that Bassanes' stoicism has collapsed and that his character is still in motion, Ford immediately puts him into a scene (act 5, scene 1) with Orgilus, whose character has not changed but has instead become only more intense. Bassanes has, like Orgilus, a firsthand experience of the homicidal mentality, having contributed to his wife's death and having almost killed Ithocles himself before Orgilus could coax him into his chair. The emotional logic alone in this pairing does not create a dramatic necessity; it would have been natural for Ford simply to have Orgilus present Bassanes to the two bodies, and let Orgilus's summons be taken for granted. But rather than settle for that easy pathos, Ford seems to have been trying to gauge still more deeply Orgilus's rising madness and Bassanes' evolving self-concept.

When Orgilus enters to Bassanes in act 5, scene 1, there is an immediate contrast between Orgilus's inflated, portentous manner and Bassanes' colloquial energy. Bassanes is now speaking with the same tone he had when we first saw him:

> *Orgilus.* Noble Bassanes,
>   Mistake me not.
> *Bassanes.* Phew, then we shall be troubled.
>   Thou wert ordain'd my plague; heaven make me
>   thankful.
>   And give me patience too, heaven, I beseech thee.
> *Orgilus.* Accept a league of amity; for henceforth,
>   I vow by my best genius, in a syllable
>   Never to speak vexation. I will study
>   Service and friendship with a zealous sorrow
>   For my past incivility towards 'ee.
> *Bassanes.* Heyday, good words, good words! I must believe 'em,
>   And be a coxcomb for my labor.
>
>   [5.1.19-29]

Bassanes' colloquial and blunt replies hardly constitute an endorsement of the stoic ideal, and his verse, in contrast to Orgilus's, has the same animated variations it had at the end of his last scene. He has never achieved the polished surface manners that seem to come naturally to everyone else in Sparta, and in spite of his wishes he cannot restrain his emotions. After Orgilus takes Bassanes out to see Penthea and his handiwork with Ithocles,[35] the deaths are reported to Calantha and the marriage party; and when their dancing is over and all assess their losses, Bassanes silences everyone, telling Armostes in particular not to mourn for Ithocles:

> Continue man still;
> Make me the pattern of digesting evils,
> Who can outlive my mighty ones, not shrinking
> At such a pressure as would sink a soul
> Into what's most of death, the worst of horrors.
>
>   [5.2.57-61]

This begins a march out on solid feet, but Bassanes cannot sustain it, and starts to stumble as he ends:

> But I have seal'd a covenant with sadness,
> And enter'd into bonds without condition,
> To stand these tempests calmly.—Mark me, nobles,
> I do not shed a tear, not for Penthea.
>
> [5.2.62-65]

His stoic program collapses in the last line, the hesitation of the last clause choking out his wife's name. As he says to Calantha when she takes over, "wherefore should I pule, and like a girl/Put finger in the eye?" (5.2.95-97). Bassanes' tears only confirm what was evident from the start in the accents of his verse.

Because he has long pondered on murder and violence, there is a rightness in the almost paternal care Bassanes takes in helping with the ritual suicide of Orgilus; such logic in the choice of an executioner would not have seemed strange to Elizabethans.[36] When Bassanes assists in opening Orgilus's veins, he knows exactly why he is there:

> I am for 'ee.
> It most concerns my art, my care, my credit.
> Quick, fillet both his arms.
>
> [5.2.107-9]

Rather than outdoing art, as he had hoped earlier, he is now a practitioner himself, professionally qualified by his worry and the gains of trial and collapse. Helping Orgilus open his veins, Bassanes dilates upon the principle involved:

> O, I envy not a rival fitted
> To conquer in extremities. This pastime
> Appears majestical; some high-tun'd poem
> Hereafter shall deliver to posterity
> The writer's glory and his subject's triumph.
>
> [5.2.130-34]

Turning Orgilus's suicide into art, Bassanes' stoicism is finally an aesthetic stance; for him the order of surface and manner cannot be lived, but ends only in art.

That the end of life is its transmutation into art occurs to no one else in the play, and Bassanes repeats it later, as Calantha is disposing of her affairs. His outburst then is a self-dramatizing catalog, placed where it is, one suspects, to gratify the contemporary desire to sum up the horrors. But it is personally fitting besides, and consistent with Bassanes' character and its divisions:

Give me some corner of the world to wear out
The remnant of the minutes I must number,
Where I may hear no sounds but sad complaints
Of virgins who have lost contracted partners,
Of husbands howling that their wives were ravish'd
By some untimely fate, of friends divided
By churlish opposition, or of fathers
Weeping upon their children's slaughtered carcasses,
Or daughters groaning o'er their fathers' hearses,
And I can dwell there, and with these keep consort
As musical as theirs. What can you look for
From an old, foolish, peevish, doting man
But craziness of age?

[5.3.25-37]

Bassanes would "outdo art" by transforming his own life into the arrangement of ghastly actions they have all been living through. The beast turns further within himself, but by that descent he has *become* the play.[37] The artificial nature of Bassanes' whole outburst is emphasized by its unusual reliance on falling rhythms, which give the passage a monotonous and even silly quality: *virgins, husbands, children, daughters, hearses, howling, ravish'd, weeping, slaughter'd, groaning,* and so on. This pattern establishes the conscious aesthetic shaping in Bassanes' feeling.

There are a number of puzzles in Calantha's recommendation that Bassanes become marshal of Sparta, because "The multitudes of high employments could not/But set a peace to private griefs" (5.3.47-48). It seems plausible enough therapy, although in some ways Calantha's charge bears out Penthea's desire for vengeance: as a marshal Bassanes would be about as competent as Hieronimo at the end of *The Spanish Tragedy*, and the end of the play does not imply much restoration of order. Calantha is saying in effect that life is so painful the intelligent person gives it up; only madmen with conventional minds (like Prophilus or Euphranea) would want to carry on. But whatever her own motives, we still have to ask why Bassanes, alone among the principals, is left alive and weeping at the end. And here it might be appropriate to return to the old beast myths, for with everyone around him dead, Bassanes' desire to relive the play is only a desire to return perpetually to that moment when he might have awakened the consciousness of his mistress and bound her forever to him.

It is a suitably equivocal ending for the character who has had the most varied poetry in the play. Dependent as Ford's blank verse is upon high tensions within narrow limits, it has a power especially appropriate to a character with a shifting and subterranean spirit. Of course this description fits all the characters to some degree. Their exquisite manners (Orgilus even thanks Bassanes as he helps him open his veins) mask a great insensitivity toward each other and justify their preoccupation with their own drives. As a result most of the characters seem caught as rigidly in their attitudes as Ithocles in his chair. The formality of their verse emphasizes this enclosure, just as the range of the verse given to Penthea and Bassanes mirrors their own divided minds. In the Spartan world where social codes and the unconscious are in permanent conflict, those who feel the struggle most deeply have art but not understanding to guide them.

EPILOGUE:
THE METAMORPHOSIS
TRANSFORMED

The plays with which we have been here concerned are tangent at many points, and connecting these should help us understand the drama of the period as a whole. We may want to cut across considerations of genre or tone by looking first at resemblances that have their origin in the similar handling of dramatic poetry. With this in mind, two plays that seem improbable companions in most respects may have much in common. *The Revenger's Tragedy* and *The Broken Heart* are obviously worlds apart in tone and action: while Tourneur's overflowing verse emphasizes his melodramatic situations with impassioned soliloquies, Ford's poetry secures its effects by the starkly simple presentation of the horrors of revenge; in contrast to the happily sadistic murders and mutilations in *The Revenger's Tragedy*, the death of Calantha is purely psychosomatic, the suicide of Orgilus no more violent than the attentions one might receive from the neighborhood barber-surgeon; even the murder of Ithocles, by comparison to the murder of Vindice's Duke, is a triumph of mechanical engineering and brisk efficiency. But for all these differences, in both plays the verse functions similarly in one important respect, and that is in its congruence with dramatic situation and characterization. In *The Broken Heart*, the containment of the action, its restraint simply as a sequence of physical gestures, matches the understatement of the verse; with the notable exception of Bassanes, the characters not only act with a semblance of self-control but also speak a measured language with deliberate variations on the iambic pentameter line. A similar congruence is at work in *The Revenger's Tragedy*, where the metrical extravagance of the verse reflects the events, relationships, and states of mind in the play, ranging from Vindice's hyperbolical disguises to Spurio's all-inclusive pedigree, to the imagery of brimming and surging, to the murders that finally move out of Vindice's control. In both plays the poetry thus has a clear metaphoric function: in *The Broken Heart* the well-tempered line becomes a felt expression of the tensions characteristic of Spartan life; in *The Revenger's*

Tragedy, the momentum of the verse and the marginal ability of Vindice to rein it in convey the sense of boundless appetite and wholesale gratification that is characteristic of Tourneur's Italy.

Such parallels between the movement of the poetry, the physical action onstage, and the mental activity of the characters seem to exist only intermittently in *Cymbeline* and the two plays by Webster. In *Cymbeline* the congruence breaks down repeatedly. The delicate poetic modulations of Iachimo, entering from his steamer trunk, are contradicted by his own crude purposes and vile behavior (his treacherous concealment, his kissing Imogen, and so forth). Imogen's pathetic lament over the body of "Posthumus" shows a similar incongruity between the poetic features of her speech and its dramatic function; the Imogenolators who swooned over her speeches could do so only by disregarding their deliberate lack of connection with the fuller context. Throughout the play, verse often distances the action, defining it not as process but as artifact, a tableau to be admired with an ironic awareness of its place in the larger design. This curious and self-reflexive quality is much less pronounced in Shakespeare's management of the verse in *The Winter's Tale* or *The Tempest*, which more resemble the rest of the canon in their deep continuity between verse, action, character, and theme. By contrast, *Cymbeline* approaches *Pericles, The Two Noble Kinsmen,* and the plays of Fletcher in their common suspension of verse style between the other elements of dramatic meaning. We assume that this incongruity is consciously intended in *Cymbeline* because the play appears to be preceded and followed by plays that have a thorough coherence, making all the more intriguing the internal logic of this particular play.[1]

In Webster's plays, forms of congruity are established momentarily, only to be withdrawn as Webster insinuates material from his workbooks. Webster has invested deeply in his sententiae and dark wit, of that there is no question; their dense rhetoric and general manners are not greatly different from those of his own prefaces. In sharp distinction from these, the verse of Webster's climactic scenes invariably shows a congruity between character and the immediate action; the nervous responsiveness of the blank verse in *The White Devil* and *The Duchess of Malfi* comes to mirror the mental state of the characters, as well as the sort of action they have to take in order to survive in the world. Moreover, in those crucial scenes the verse also functions metaphorically; the self-mockery, surrealism, and asymmetrical structures of Webster's two plays find correspondence in the impatient and jittery verse style. At the climax of both plays, Webster's verse lets us into the irregular yet powerful movements of the characters' minds.

In Webster the final and surprising conjunction of dramatic event, language, and character may be the source of what some critics used to call his "intensity" or "fire." It is a quality that later dramatists like

Fletcher seem incapable of achieving, or do not want to achieve, much as they may build toward scenes of impassioned rhetoric. Such lines as these in *Philaster* (1620), for example, are written out of a set of assumptions very different from those in the momentous speeches in Webster:

> Turne all your eyes on me, here stands a man
> The falsest and basest of this world:
> Set swords against this breast some honest man,
> For I have lived till I am pitied:
> My former deedes were hatefull, but this last
> Is pittifull, for I unwillingly
> Have given the deere preserver of my life
> Unto his torture: is it in the power
> Of flesh and bloud, to carry this and live?[2]

The full and anguished consciousness to which Philaster lays claim seems to mesh oddly with the gracious versification; a man who has traveled five acts to find out what he is might at least be breathing hard, and the absence of rhythmic animation—and, for that matter, imagery—belies Philaster's proclamation of strong feeling. Such disjunctions seem characteristic of the Fletcher style,[3] and their effectiveness depends upon the audience's withholding expectations of a bond (realized or impending) between poetic texture, action, and characterization. If those expectations are *not* withheld, then the experience of the play falls apart; it would take a man with a heart of stone not to laugh at the death of little Hengo in *Bonduca*.

Cymbeline presents a model for the study of this problem in Jacobean drama. The management of awareness on the part of the characters is linked in a quite systematic way with the poetic development of their speeches, although the level of a character's awareness does not always parallel the energy of his speech. To judge from the speeches in *Cymbeline* that are addressed to the audience, some of the excitement in watching a play of this kind should consist of our relishing a character's verbal outpourings while knowing more about the context of the action onstage than he does. Shakespeare's technique involves a deepening of Fletcher's usual practice, in which important bits of information are withheld from the audience until the last possible minute. The audience's greater awareness has certain corollaries that affect the poetry of a play, because with our larger knowledge we are more free to listen to *how* an event takes place and are less directed to the mere circumstance of *what* takes place. This wider knowledge in the audience is created chiefly by the management of the scenes, their succession and alternation, and thus one essential requirement for a drama that is to reflect upon its own poetry will be a solid (but not necessarily simple) dramatic structure. The typical Fletcher play is assembled with care and a sense of high design, and its structure will resemble that of *Cymbeline* in the way it insists upon perspectives by incongruity. Although in the case of a Fletcher play the structure will usually be designed to display the motion of word order rather than the rhythmic pattern, schemes rather than tropes,[4] the final destination, with its rifts between language and character, will have much in common with what we see in Shakespeare's play. Such disjunctions between character and verbal texture may not be to every playgoer's or reader's taste, but even today the genre still has imaginative resources and an audience, as the plays of Tom Stoppard amply show.

For audiences accustomed to the conventions of blank verse, the plays treated in the preceding chapters also offer four different approaches to listening and understanding. With its minute and subtle variations, *The Broken Heart* requires more scrupulous attention than *The Revenger's Tragedy*, whose rhythmic extravagance would be obvious to even the most casual listener. In *Cymbeline* the modulations are more subtle and the limits on the metric clearer; the rhythmic patterns range from understated to bold, and the dramatist's engagement with his characters is constant at every point. Webster's two tragedies are more problematic in their engagement, as they seem at times not to trust the audience or its attention span, and readily drop into prose lectures to underscore ideas; at other times event and character will take control directly in the verse. Webster's drama often shows a deliberate resisting of poetic occasion, an offhand dismissal of effects that could be secured easily, and a profound distrust of lyricism for its own sake. These habits are in marked contrast to those of Ford, who develops the poetic logic of every scene, including those that run against the Spartan grain.

Considering the ways that audiences might have heard the poetry of these plays, one could readily describe the differences in response as being the result of external factors, such as variations in the economic classes or social pretensions of their respective audiences and, connected with this, differences in the size and shape of the theaters and in the size and personnel of the respective acting companies. But this kind of description would presuppose one rather limited model for the relation of dramatic poetry to its audience. To suppose that a court audience would not appreciate a romp in huff-snuff rhetoric, or that a Bankside audience would not understand allegorical mime, would probably be to oversimplify the range of both audiences and their tastes. At even the most primitive theaters a wily dramatist could give his play some special interest by importing devices from his artful contemporaries. Edmund Gayton's memoir of crowds tearing the theater apart until they got the tear-throat recitations they wanted may have its amusing aspects, but one need not go from this to the conviction of the Victorians (amply rebutted on many sides) that the Elizabethan audience constitued some form of the missing link. To maintain, as Swinburne did in his spellbinding essay on Beaumont and Fletcher,[5] that Fletcher's tastes were too subtle for his time would be to ignore both his great contemporary popularity and the flattery that Shakespeare paid his drama by writing a play that would overgo it. Audiences may have been far more adaptable and catholic in their tastes than our special theses may require.

These five exemplary plays also suggest that much in the development of English drama as a medium for the creation of character and the representation of action may have been the result of changes within dramatic poetry itself. The increased facility of the poets, from about 1590 onward, in managing subtle variations from the dogtrot of steady iambics, in moving away from inflexible end-stopping, and in accommodating these variations to the syntax and rhythms of colloquial speech all made possible an expansion of the range and depth of feeling that would be presented on the stage. In time, physical action onstage could afford to become more restrained because the suggestive power of language had risen and the audiences were responsive to that power. In place of the overt violence of the earlier Elizabethan stage—"He brains himself against the cage," or *"Enter* Lavinia, *her hands cut off, and her tongue cut out, and ravish'd"*—it becomes possible to suggest enormous violence by presenting the smallest stage properties in tense and restrained verse:

> De Flores.   I've a token for you.
> Beatrice.   For me?
> De Flores.   But it was sent somewhat unwillingly,
>   I could not get the ring without the finger.[6]

By a kind of displacement, verse may have assumed some of the role of physical activity, and indeed it almost had to, if only because imaginative language has so many more resources and variations than physical mayhem. At this point we might note in passing that some modern dramatists such as Antonin Artaud, who have enthusiastically endorsed the violent and specifically sadistic elements in Elizabethan and Jacobean plays,[7] have tended to obscure the substantial differences between the plays and their action. Stage murders may occur in all sorts of ways, but the variety in the event itself is only circumstantial. In poetic drama, the significance that a murder may possess will be conferred upon it by the things the characters have to say about it, and the compelling pressure of their thoughts will appear in their verse. To regard the Jacobeans as forerunners of the Theater of Cruelty would be to overlook the way that they are interested in apprehending the effect of violence upon the mind. The experience of that understanding will be revealed in the unfolding motion of the characters' verse. That many of the plays of Fernando Arrabal, for instance, contain acts of surreal violence that resemble the violence in Webster, is in the end irrelevant; for Webster the violence is only a way of engaging other problems, and it functions this way in Jacobean comedy and farce as well. Murder presents in extremis such problems as those posed by conflicting definitions of the self: the act appears to offer the possibility of controlling utterly another person's being, and controlling it in one decisive gesture; and that is a theme to be found not only in *The Duchess of Malfi* but also in *Volpone* and *A New Way to Pay Old Debts*. In each case the verse allows the writer to present directly the emotional pressure of the main character as he confronts the experience of others. Violence onstage is not essential to that end and often need only be hinted at, as Massinger's play shows when Overreach's rage against others and his violent self-punishment can be heard in the tensions of his verse lines.

The development of this extraordinary capacity and flexibility would have been hard to predict, say, in 1590, but historical hindsight can show us how soon and how steadily that capacity began to develop. Although few early Elizabethan plays hold together as complete poetic structures, still the fundamental integration of poetry and drama was sought from the beginning, and it may be helpful to suggest here, in retrospect, how some of that searching took place. There are obvious illustrations in Kyd, Marlowe, and the Shakespeare of *Henry VI*, but there may be more point in turning to a specimen of drama that almost assuredly had no public impact, but which demonstrates, by its having been written at all, the readiness of the Elizabethan literary mind to think of dramatic action directly in terms of verse. The Countess of Pembroke's *Tragedie of Antonie,* written in 1590 and published in 1592, makes dramatic language itself the locus of the action in the play, and does so by the deliberate use of blank verse. In electing to translate Robert Garnier's *Marc-Antoine* out of rhymed alexandrines into unrhymed pentameter (while retaining the lyrical stanzas of the choruses), the Countess made a decision that finally enabled her to stress the heroic stance of the principal characters. The conflict in the play has both Antonie and Cleopatra threading their way through two kinds of temptation, those they feel within themselves and those they are offered by the choruses, who reiterate the shortness of human life and the impossibility of heroism. The changes that the Countess made in translating the verse of the play show that she found in Garnier's material—as Garnier himself did not—an opportunity to let the poetic form of the play follow the development of the main characters. As they move through the temptations of the choruses to meet their own personal temptations, their blank verse helps to suggest the range of choices ahead. By contrast, the metrical variations in the stanzas granted the Egyptian choruses make their arguments seem all the more like ingenious evasions; it is significant that while the chorus argues, in elaborate and interlocking forms, that man is a prisoner of fate, the principals are left to understand their own destinies in the freedom of blank verse:

day and night,
In watch, in sleepe, her Image follow'd thee:
Not dreaming but of her, repenting still
That thou for warre had such a Goddes left.[8]

The Countess uses the flexibility of the pentameter line to express, in its own movements, the tensions within the characters, and this is most apparent if we revisit an old comparison, that between *Antonie* and Thomas Kyd's *Cornelia* of 1594, another translation from Garnier that *Antonie* apparently inspired. Usually Kyd's play is held to have more vigorous and artistic poetry, but this view overlooks the way that Kyd's verse lacks a dramatic function as metaphor. In *Cornelia* the distribution of passages in rhymed and blank verse bears little relation to the development of the characters and their conflicts; the ideas and the poetic voice of the choruses are also little differentiated from those of the main characters. Unlike the choruses in *Antonie,* Kyd's set up no resonances between the forms of the speeches and their content; Kyd's production-line work seldom takes the liberties with Garnier's forms that might animate the play, liberties that in *Antonie* are functional and necessary. The give and take between form, character, and theme, which the Countess saw as a possibility in Garnier and went on to reinforce, is almost wholly missing from Kyd's play, where the verse seldom registers any change in temperature, although we are often assured that the characters' body heat is indeed on the rise.

The point is not that verse plays must contain a certain minimum quotient of formal variation, any more than they must have action or short-winded characters. The only matter at stake is how fully the poetry can penetrate the other elements of meaning, that is, how much the rhythms and movements of the verse are allowed to make their own discoveries and establish relationships within the play. Those relationships may be absent, and we may still have a brilliant or even a great play; but it will be a play in prose, not verse, even if that prose is adorned with rhymes or songs. One of the identifying marks of poetic drama is that in the hands of a craftsman, the formal range of the poetry, taken in its entirety, can become a master metaphor for the development of the characters, themes, and structure. Ideally this formal range will reflect the conflicts and resolution at the heart of the play, as they undergo their gradual definition and changes. It would be difficult to claim that the Countess has succeeded in making her poetic style such a complete and controlling metaphor. Her revisions in Garnier's *Antoine* show, however, that she knew this could be done, and that through this she could expand the range of meaning open to Garnier's situation and psychology. While there were other poets at her time who were able to write more moving dramatic poetry, there were few with a surer grasp of the essential nature and pleasures of poetic drama.

It might be salutary to regard the development of English blank verse drama as being informed from the beginning by this impulse to have dramatic action bodied forth directly in the movement of the language itself, rather than by the accumulation of certain technical tricks or turns by themselves. We often lose sight of this point, and it is extremely significant. When T. S. Eliot, for example, attributed *Arden of Feversham* to Kyd and remarked its poetic deficiencies in comparison to *Tamburlaine*, he stressed Marlowe's knack for running syntactic units across line-ends, and thus gave a kind of emphasis to technique isolated from subject that disregarded the truly functional properties of blank verse.[9] Yet in the same essay Eliot makes an ultimately more useful suggestion (which might have been noticed by those who ridiculed his scholarship), and that is the idea that Marlowe was on the way to writing a marvelous kind of caricature, in which the verse of his drama would have an implied comment to make on the stage action. The poetry of Marlowe's plays may contain a form of action, a form of *criticism,* that can comment on the events onstage and even be in tension with them. If we take Eliot's suggestion and turn back to *Antonie,* we may even hazard the guess that this advance in the expressiveness of dramatic language had its source in the opportunities and responsibilities that come with performance before an audience, and an audience that the dramatist knows can listen intelligently.

The most conspicuous demonstrations of this new range of expressiveness occur in contexts that are ironic or comic, as in *Volpone,* where Jonson has his lecherous magnifico, who is made up to resemble nothing so much as a corpse, leap out of bed and sing a delicate lyric adapted from Catullus. Use of the device involving a different verse form may be seen in Middleton's *A Mad World, My Masters* (1608), where the mother addresses her courtesan daughter in a series of wisely cynical saws. The counterpoint of poetic form (in this case, sententiously moralizing couplets) and dramatic situation (the mother as bawd) help establish the realistic tone of the scene. In both examples the effect of disjunction occurs on a small scale, but larger set speeches can often bring a play to a grinding halt, as the highly studied form of the speech may bear little relation to its content or its place in the total design of the play. As we have seen, Webster was a master at making a play out of this inner criticism, but one would have little trouble finding examples of plays in which set speeches fail to knit with the dramatic context. The tendency was evident at the time of our first great plays, and one relatively sophisticated early example would be Clarence's description of his dream in *Richard III* (1592?). Because this speech is a dream narrative it can enter the play with credentials that let us overlook its anomalous relation to Clarence's character and the dramatic moment. Somewhat similar, though of course much later, is Enobarbus's description of Cleopatra in her barge (act 2, scene 2). While it could be claimed that this seasoned veteran is laying on the lyricism for his companions who have had to remain stateside, this would give Enobarbus a ventriloquist's mind and gift that he does not have elsewhere. English drama as a whole does show some increasing sophistication in the way it grants credentials to set speeches, and one virtuoso example of the practice may be found in *The Atheist's Tragedy* (1611), where Borachio describes the drowned Charlemont. The lyricism of this speech is astonishing, as the syntax returns upon itself after each line-end, catching up the motion of the surf lapping the drowned man:

> Walking next day upon the fatall shore,
> Among the slaughter'd bodies of their men,
> Which the full-stomack'd Sea had cast upon
> The sands, it was m'unhappy chance to light
> Upon a face, whose favour when it liv'd
> My astonish'd minde inform'd me I had seene.
> Hee lay in's Armour; as if that had beene
> His Coffine, and the weeping Sea (like one
> Whose milder temper doth lament the death
> Of him whom in his rage he slew) runnes up
> The Shoare; embraces him; kisses his cheeke,
> Goes back againe and forces up the Sandes
> To burie him; and ev'rie time it parts,
> Sheds teares upon him. . . .[10]

The performance is both sustained (this is only half the speech) and totally out of character, as D'amville notes in an aside to Borachio, but it also serves the immediate purpose of rousing all present to a feverish state of grief, which the later action will require.

Just as there was more than one way to use dramatic poetry that would jar within its context, so there were many ways to knit the poetry and the context into one. The fit between the two did not always have to end in an exact correspondence; *Cymbeline* shows how far it was possible to go in exploiting the gap between a character's poetry and that character's self-awareness, or between this gap and our own sense of the relations between the characters. The result in *Cymbeline* is paradoxically satisfying, both in terms of the jewellike set speeches and the multiple ironies they create as they reflect off each other; and behind the audience's satisfaction is its awareness that the artist is trying to work a deliberate enchantment with artifice.

In most of Fletcher's work, and in many plays by Massinger, Ford, and Shirley, the effects are of this kind but simpler and more immediate. Fletcher might almost have set out to codify the human starting points of

Cymbeline, for that play offers an index of the feelings that dominate Fletcher's drama, such as selfless generosity, noble renunciation, reconciliation, deception, and the torments of what might be called the more strictly social emotions: lechery, ambition, jealousy, envy, the high pleasure of giving offense. All appear in *Cymbeline,* and our understanding of each is complicated splendidly by the patterns in the verse. In Fletcher, on the other hand, these emotions are simplified and flattened to a great extent by the deliberate limitations in poetic technique. Generally the prosody of Fletcher and those he influenced employs few extreme variations and admits of ready construction; there is little exploration of the use of cadences that could form a character's signature, and although there are some notable separations of verse and character, these are never transformed into the concern of the drama (the example of Webster) nor do they shed light on each other when considered in the aggregate (the example of *Cymbeline*). Earlier we looked at a brief speech from *Philaster* to remark the parting of style from immediate context; this same kind of stretching and thinning of the ties between dramatic poetry, character, and structure allowed Shakespeare to form networks of meaning in *Cymbeline,* but if *Philaster* is coming together in this way, Fletcher has managed to conceal it well.

On the whole it seems to have been the conjunction of the changes we have been discussing that gave the later Stuart drama its distinctive poetic character. At the same time that dramatic poets were becoming increasingly self-conscious about the blank verse line as a subject of controlled art in itself, fashion began to require both an increase in the use of implausible conflicts as the basis for plays and a decrease in the more extreme forms of bloodletting onstage. One interesting thing about the prefatory remarks to the Beaumont and Fletcher Folio is that the writers there see nothing incongruous in praising both the lapidary smoothness of Fletcher's meters and his emphasis upon the extremes of passion. We need not suppose that the English had developed, between 1600 and 1630, some marvelous new powers of self-containment; instead they simply wished to present upon the stage a different image of human action, and the poetry of drama is first an audible presentation of that action.

One dramatist who seems to have sensed what was happening was James Shirley, and no brief exhibit of this development could be more apt than *The Cardinal* (1641). Shirley himself regarded this play as "the best of my flock,"[11] and from our point of view the play is indeed a tour de force as a transformation of the high Jacobean mode of dramatic poetry. Commentators have shown in detail how much Shirley relies in this play upon *The Duchess of Malfi,* and one modern edition has laid out several pages of parallels, adding for good measure many echoes from *The White Devil.*[12] If we go to *The Cardinal* hoping for a replay of Webster, however, we are bound to be disappointed; in their regular outlines and orderly development the speeches lack Webster's surprising logic, and as rhythmic structures they contain nothing like Webster's nervous variations. Instead Shirley offers something satisfactory on its own terms, focusing the stage action in such a way as to have it mirror his language. He does this by following one basic principle: where he lifts Webster's memorable and climactic lines, he typically places them where the action does not involve the violence or horrific effect that is more typically their context in Webster. The practice is consistent throughout the play and is observed with detail; for example, at the end of some speeches containing several echoes from Webster, Shirley has his Duchess say "My heart is in a mist" (1.2.239), the line clearly echoing a line in *The White Devil,* "O I am in a mist" (5.6.260). But Webster's line is spoken by a character who is dying miserably, while Shirley's Duchess is only embarking on the love plot, holding death at a discreet distance:

> direct
> Two lovers in their chast embrace to meet;
> *Columbo's* bed contains my winding sheet.
>
> [1.2.240-42]

The same controlled diffusion occurs elsewhere in the play; Webster will bring a coffin onstage as part of the baffling of the Duchess of Malfi, while in similar circumstances Shirley will only use a coffin as a metaphor in a speech. Shirley consistently translates into his poetry much of what Webster presents as action.

On the surface the action of *The Cardinal* (like that of *Cymbeline*) may appear to be simply an assemblage of later Jacobean devices, such as touches of the pastoral and romantic or the vaguely exotic; the mandatory theme of honor; the motif of the lover's test; the Arcadian song; and, of course, the Machiavellian intrigue. Yet for all its familiar devices, *The Cardinal* shows a sure understanding of the use of dramatic speech, and takes its own tack through the conventions of the time. Unlike *Cymbeline, The Cardinal* seldom luxuriates in the poetic range of a speaking voice, much less explores the hiatus between a voice and its dramatic context. In several places Shirley explicitly rejects this possibility, as in Antonio's second-act description of the Duchess, who is

> Serene, as I
> Have seen the morning rise upon the spring,
> No trouble in her breath, but such a wind
> As came to kiss and fan the smiling flowers,
>
> [2.1.120-23]

to which the imperious Columbo replies "No poetry" (2.1.124). In this play lyricism seldom gets its wings. But when Shirley needs to have a character rise out of a stock situation, he can propel him rapidly by means of

the verse. When Hernando is preparing to kill the Cardinal, he meditates
on his duties as a member of a long and distinguished line of revengers;
and while the lines might seem at first to roll out in the standard Caroline
expostulation on honor, by the end we realize that little or none of this is
borrowed, and that the note is peculiarly Shirley's:

> I have a sword about me, and I left
> My own security to visit death.
> Yet I may pause a little, and consider
> Which way does lead me to't most honorably;
> Does not the Chamber that I walk in tremble?
> What will become of her, and me, and all
> The world in one small hour? I do not think
> Ever to see the day agen, the wings
> Of night spread o'r me like a sable Herse-cloath,
> The Stars are all close mourners too; but I
> Must not alone to the cold silent grave,
> I must not; If thou canst *Alvarez*, open
> That Ebon curtain, and behold the man,
> When the worlds justice fails shall right thy ashes,
> And feed their thirst with blood; thy Dutchess is
> Almost a Ghost already; and doth wear
> Her body like a useless upper garment,
> The trim and fashion of it lost.
>
> [5.3.65–82]

The surprise of yoking ecce homo with the vow of revenge; the biblical
allusions in the final metaphor; the composed tone, with the subtly varied
metrical substitutions and the frequent pauses coming near the ends of the
lines—all give the poetry a stamp of immediacy and let it avoid both the
predictable and the implausible. The speech transcends simple pathos, for
by extending and linking his metaphors, Shirley has endowed Hernando's
passion with the force of logic, and the result is a speech that is internally
coherent yet still makes an histrionic appeal to the audience with a favorite
Caroline theme.

Shirley seems to have been conscious of his mingled purposes, for his
Epilogue stresses an ideal of restraint and self-control in the audience's
reaction to the play:

> Blister not your hands in [the Poet's] applause,
> Your private smile, your nod, or hum, to tell
> My fellows, that you like the business well.
>
> [17–19]

Yet the immediate context is, of course, ironic—*The Cardinal* was one of
the first tragedies to use a comic epilogue—and the speaker turns around

to say that we may as well let the author know if we liked the play. In short, the Epilogue reminds us once more of Shirley's effort to merge forms and modes; as he had told the audience in the Prologue, "Keep your fancy active" (l. 5), adding that we should not be preoccupied with whether the play is a comedy, romance, or "direfull Tragedy" (l. 14); the only important matter is whether the play is any *good*, and all the cagey author will say about the genre is that the play "Might rivall with his best" (l. 24).

Shirley is working toward a dramatic unity that is peculiarly his own and resists critical efforts at disintegration. The reader convinced that English drama had undergone a general decline might say that Hernando's long speech was Caroline until it came to the midpoint, where the latent Jacobean took over for the chilling peroration; but the speech holds together too well as a fictive utterance to allow this kind of fracturing. Hernando's preoccupation with honor, for example, is not just Caroline window dressing; it is authentic because the whole dramatic context has prepared for it: Hernando is only alive now because Columbo, the honorable fighter, returned his sword during the duel. In the end, character and plot merge with verbal form; Shirley has managed to embrace both the grandiloquent rhetoric of honor and the subdued and somber close on revenge, making both, for the moment, completely authentic. As with his "translation" of Webster's action into language, or his control of the physical action onstage, it would be hard to say whether Shirley's poetry is a function of the dramatic structure or the other way around.

If Shirley's achievement in dramatic poetry seems, however, rather tepid—which is evidently the opinion of the last hundred and fifty years or so—that may be due in great part to his very success in assimilating other plays and his reluctance to take risks. Shirley's is a drama of compromise, and it would not be too far off the mark to say that *The Cardinal*, and Shirley's plays modeled more closely after the drama of Fletcher, represent some beautiful pieces of work by a master at orchestral transcription. Shirley's importance for the present study lies in his attempt to unite the old themes with the new tragicomic forms; the old passionate characters with smoothly lapped verse technique; the old violent situations with the fashionable new rhetoric of social obligation. It is appropriate that Shirley's plays were popular both in the 1630s and after the Restoration (although they were regarded as old-fashioned by then); his place is thus similar in some ways to that of the Countess of Pembroke, who sums up one set of dramatic conventions while pointing ahead to another.

In contemplating all that would soon change in English blank verse drama, many writers tend to adopt an elegiac tone, but any lament here would be misplaced. The achievement of blank verse drama seems in retrospect an unpredictable series of gifts and blessings, and it would be impossible to pinpoint one segment of the line between 1590 and 1642 as being the crest of the dramatic impulse. Any given year might see as much miracle as handiwork, and not infrequently both would come from the same pen. Hearing drama through poetry was not difficult, because a whole educational system, a whole way of grasping experience, had made that possible and natural; but creating it was another matter. Often a poet would succeed in finding a language that might convey by its very texture the movement of a character's mind, and a pattern of event in the structure as a whole; but demonstrated achievements in the writer's own past were no guarantee that he could do it again or do it as well. Finding poetic forms that could provide a master metaphor involved not simply the poet's ear but also his knowledge of the heart and his intellectual grasp of his themes; and it was not always necessary or advisable to engage these capacities every time he sat down to write. As always the writer's law of simultaneity assured that the same man could produce both *The Duchess of Malfi* and part of *Appius and Virginia*, or both *The Shoemaker's Holiday* and *Match Me in London*. The law works for the age as well as the individual: *Coriolanus* may well have been first performed the very year after *Mulleasses the Turk*, *Cynthia's Revels* the year after *Lust's Dominion*, *Antony and Cleopatra* the year after *The Miseries of Enforc'd Marriage*.[13] Yet the age does seem one in which a brilliant play might come from any hand; in which every writer had, if not an equal chance at producing a body of masterpieces, at least the possibility of writing a handful of scenes that might have come from even the greatest writer of the time.

These stubborn contraries may shed some light on the question, so often proposed, as to whether English poetic drama had not suffered some loss of vital spirit by the later 1630s. More irascible readers answer this question with positive gratitude that the Puritans finally stepped in and closed the theaters, a sentiment often accompanied by the thinly veiled desire that the authorities might foreclose more often on seemingly bankrupt art forms. What was more likely than the loss of some mystic spirit was that writers began to hear the drama of poetry in new ways. By the later 1630s, we may recall, the poetic statutes for balance, order, and control that had been observed in Fletcher were also accepted in other literary genres. 1642 saw not only the closing of the theaters but also the publication of "Cooper's Hill," and Sir John Denham's much-admired poem focuses an aesthetic that had begun to control most of the non-dramatic poetry of the time. In its emphasis upon the *concordia discors*, the new aesthetic departed in several important respects from the values that stood behind Jonson's oeuvre, with its conjunction of discipline and irrepressible—even madcap—imagination.[14]

The strategy of equilibrium was attempted for dramatic as well as lyric and narrative forms, and may explain both the strengths and the comparative limits of later Caroline dramatists such as Shirley. As we noted earlier, the growing restraint of the poetic line was analogous to changing concepts of dramatic action. This development is most apparent in the role of physical violence onstage. While there came to be fewer direct exhibitions of poisoned skulls and other ghoulish paraphernalia, along with less visual representation of sadistic torture and murder, there was a greater reliance upon only the suggestion of impending violence; much might be gained by keeping mayhem in the wings, and individual lines of a play might profit from being

> Though deep, yet clear, though gentle, yet not dull,
> Strong without rage, without ore-flowing full.[15]

The shift in stage decorum was in turn linked to the relocation of intellectual and emotional complexity in characterization. At their fullest, characters in post-Restoration drama possess intelligences tuned to social understanding of a kind seldom seen or required on the Jacobean stage; if these characters also seem to have fewer abstract ideas, seem to have read less and have more sparsely furnished minds than their Jacobean forebears, that is no more a deficiency with them than it is with the characters of Henry James, of whom the same criticisms might be made. One could scarcely imagine Flamineo turning up in *The Ambassadors,* or Volpone in *Washington Square.* The characters of post-Restoration drama—tragedy as well as comedy—are not necessarily simpler, they only make different demands upon themselves; and as depth in characterization moves to new ground, there is correspondingly less need for a language that has nerves and muscles the new movements do not require. When dramatic characters become instruments more finely tuned to social adaptation, the verse they speak can naturally become smoother and more equable, if not less complex.

Ultimately, the changes in dramatic verse technique are related to other changes more properly the concern of intellectual history. Evolving concepts of mind and language during the seventeenth century undoubtedly had some bearing upon dramatic characterization and the kind of speech that characters could be given. Here it might be more to the point, though, to note just briefly one turn in intellectual history that had an immediate connection with the writing of verse drama, and that is the changing concept of mind and historical continuity. One conclusion we can draw from our five exemplary plays is that blank verse proved particularly indispensable in its creation of time within the play-world. The cadences and rhythmic patterns of a play help establish both the time-sense of the characters and the imaginative density of their element; the texture of the verse gives an immediately felt indication of the difficulty or ease with which a character will move through time and accomplish his passage on the stage. The important changes in the idea of time and temporal connection that occupied Renaissance philosophy may have received intuitive definition in the drama of the earlier seventeenth century.[16] The bonds between time and perception received tangible shape in dramatic verse, and in its interplay of poetry and structured action the drama could offer, in effect, an ostensive definition of history.

In other words, dramatic poetry changed because the wider contexts of human action and possibility changed; these conceptions shifted in such a way as to encourage certain forms of poetic discovery in drama and to discourage certain others. The drama had not run out of energy in 1642 or 1660, much less (to continue the interval) in 1678; what had been transformed instead was the metamorphosis itself, of poetry into drama. The converging forces that had produced the drama of the Renaissance could not, by their nature, be repeated or prolonged: the cresting of an essentially feudal social order, which when it fell would take the king and his politics with it; the continued belief that fundamental religious truths still held, but with this the fear that in looking up to heaven, man confounds knowledge with knowledge; the steady advance of geographic exploration, which could open new imaginative and moral frontiers while bringing in a high return upon the dollar; the confidence that nothing intellectual lay beyond man's grasp, not even infinite waste and loss. These are the grand perspectives that carry the reader out over the artist and his art standing as linked historical phenomena. When we return from those heights, we shall find the dramatist at home in his poetry, discovering in its sounds and motion that solid joy of the interior.

NOTES

CHAPTER ONE

1. Lewis, "Hamlet: The Prince or the Poem," British Academy Lecture (1942), rpt. in *Hamlet*, ed. Cyrus Hoy (New York: Norton, 1963), p. 217.

2. Bacon, in Book 2 of *The Advancement of Learning* (1605), in *Critical Essays of the Seventeenth Century*, ed. J. E. Spingarn (Oxford: Clarendon Press, 1908), 1:5.

3. Selden, *Table Talk*, ed. Samuel Harvey Reynolds (Oxford: Clarendon Press, 1892), p. 134.

4. Every year the *Bowker Annual* publishes the statistics in the section titled "Book Prices and Sales"; beginning with the 1980 volume, I have worked back seven years, using their combined figure for poetry and drama (there is not a separate figure, although a librarian tells me that poetry comprises by far the greater part of the total). Statistics in trade paperbacks are the significant indicator, and they have gone from 330 titles in 1972 to 875 in 1979, the most recent year for final statistics.

5. See Bentley's Introduction to *The Profession of Dramatist in Shakespeare's Time* (Princeton: Princeton University Press, 1971), pp. 3-10. Bentley may have been overstating the matter; for one example of a study before 1971 that is both textually and dramatically oriented, see Nevil Coghill's *Shakespeare's Professional Skills* (Cambridge: At the University Press, 1964). Other studies that have the same focus would be too numerous to cite, although the work of Muriel Bradbrook remains always faithful to the facts of dramatic life, and no citation of this sort could fail to include mention of John Dover Wilson. An important study that would meet Bentley's requirement is Kenneth Muir's *Shakespeare the Professional* (Totowa, N.J.: Rowman and Littlefield, 1973).

6. Hughes, ed., *Shakespeare: A Choice of Verse* (London: Faber, 1971); see also Hughes's *Shakespeare's Poem* (London: Lexham Press, 1971).

7. Shakespeare has always been the prime subject of such studies, for which the presiding genii were Fleay and Furnivall. The establishment of the Globe text was the key to their operation, although they were following general principles laid down long before by Roderick (1758) and Malone (1778). Malone was of course one of the first to attempt to date Shakespeare's plays by means of metrical tests; their application allowed him to pinpoint *Twelfth Night* as the last play. Some still-useful statistics are gathered by E. K. Chambers in *William Shakespeare: A Study of Facts and Problems* (Oxford: Clarendon Press, 1930), 2:397-408.

8. Sipe, *Shakespeare's Metrics*, YSE no. 166 (New Haven: Yale University Press, 1968). Another, more recent study, less concerned with verse rhythms but very

important in its implications for any full account of Shakespeare's poetics, is Dolores M. Burton's *Shakespeare's Grammatical Syle* (Austin: University of Texas Press, 1973). Burton's notes on "Aspects of Word Order" are particularly interesting; see pp. 115–45. Generally these provide a detailed supplement to the groundwork laid by Josephine Miles. The difficulty of applying strictly statistical data may be illustrated by Georgia Dunbar's "The Verse Rhythms of *Antony and Cleopatra*" *(Style* 5 [1971]: 231–45; here the data are used to supply "objective" (232) confirmation of the characters' transcendence. One statistical analysis of style that does not flinch from the erratic data it generates is Ants Oras's *Pause Patterns in Elizabethan and Jacobean Drama* (Gainesville: University of Florida Press, 1960).

9. T. B. Tomlinson, *A Study of Elizabethan and Jacobean Drama* (Cambridge: At the University Press, 1964), pp. 123, 115-16, 276.

10. D. J. Enright, "Poetic Satire and Satire in Verse," in *The Apothecary's Shop* (London: Secker and Warburg, 1957), pp. 60, 67, et passim; John D. Jump, "Middleton's Tragedies," in *The Age of Shakespeare,* ed. Boris Ford (Baltimore: Penguin, 1964), pp. 355-56.

11. Collected in Eliot's *Essays on Elizabethan Drama* (New York: Harcourt Brace, 1960). Eliot's general essays on drama (n. 61 below) also contain many remarks on Elizabethan through Caroline drama.

12. John Wain, *The Living World of Shakespeare* (New York: St. Martin's Press, 1964), p. 213; F.E. Halliday, *The Poetry of Shakespeare's Plays* (London: Duckworth, 1954), p. 179. The play is *Cymbeline.*

13. James as quoted in the New Cambridge edition, ed. J. C. Maxwell (Cambridge: At the University Press, 1960), p. xl; James is describing the Henry Irving production of 1896.

14. G. R. Hibbard, "'The Forced Gait of a Shuffling Nag,'" in *Shakespeare 1971,* ed. Clifford Leech and J. M. R. Margeson (Toronto: University of Toronto Press, 1972), p. 78. Despite the apparent reference of Hibbard's title to poetic rhythms— and Hotspur himself is referring to the way meter sets his teeth on edge—Hibbard's comments are all confined to what is more properly termed rhetoric.

15. See ch. 11, "Various Modes of Poetry in Drama," in Peacock's *The Art of Drama* (London: Routledge and Kegan Paul, 1957), pp. 214-40; the quotation is from p. 218. Another study offering a broad definition of the term is Michael Black's *Poetic Drama as Mirror of the Will* (London: Vision Press, 1977), which ranges from Marlowe and Shakespeare through Racine and the nineteenth century, with many good remarks on figurative language as well as musical forms.

16. Donoghue, *The Third Voice: Modern British and American Verse Drama* (Princeton: Princeton University Press, 1959), p. 6.

17. Spanos, *The Christian Tradition in Modern British Verse Drama* (New Brunswick, N.J.: Rutgers University Press, 1967), pp. 64ff. Spanos implies that when distanced by its presence in drama, any event with metaphoric significance may be termed *poetic.* That may yield some valuable insights into modern poetic drama, but I do not think the premise would have been accepted by dramatists, actors, or audiences in the seventeenth century.

18. This is not to deny the great usefulness of the three books mentioned, along with several other studies of modern poetic drama; one that I have found helpful is Andrew K. Kennedy's *Six Dramatists in Search of a Language* (Cambridge: At the University Press, 1975).

19. Doran, *Shakespeare's Dramatic Language* (Madison: University of Wisconsin Press, 1976). See, e.g., p. 27, where I think Doran accepts a rather limited and peculiarly modern perception of verse in drama. Nonetheless, the book remains a brilliant study; it does superbly what it sets out to do.

20. Langer, *Feeling and Form* (New York: Scribners, 1953), p. 322.

21. Collected in Smith, *Shakespearean and Other Essays* (Cambridge: At the University Press, 1974).

22. See, e.g., Brown, *Shakespeare's Dramatic Style* (London: Heinemann, 1970); Coghill, *Shakespeare's Professional Skills;* and Flatter, *Shakespeare's Producing Hand* (New York: Norton, 1948).

23. Alpers, *The Poetry of "The Faerie Queene"* (Princeton: Princeton University Press, 1967), esp. ch. 2, "Narrative Materials and Stanzas of Poetry," and ch. 3, "Spenser's Poetic Language"; Alpers also shows convincingly *why* we need to read for every line.

24. The best to my mind is the one made indirectly by the first chapter of Robert B. Heilman's *Magic in the Web* (Lexington: University of Kentucky Press, 1956). A more specifically historical perspective is taken by T. J. B. Spencer in "Shakespeare: The Elizabethan Theater-Poet," in *The Elizabethan Theatre*, ed. David Galloway (London: Macmillan, 1969), pp. 1-20.

25. Cf. J. L. Styan's *Drama, Stage, and Audience* (Cambridge: At the University Press, 1975): "The impact of imagery studies on the understanding of Shakespeare has been out of all proportion to the function of imagery in the theater" (p. 56; see also pp. 57-58).

26. Many theoretical accounts are of little help in clarifying the role of poetry in dramatic structure; see, e.g., Jackson G. Barry, *Dramatic Structure: The Shaping of Experience* (Berkeley: University of California Press, 1970), esp. ch. 7, "The Structures of Narrative and Poetry," pp. 110-25. Here imagery and incident carry the day, and there is no suggestion that poetry, in its rhythmic or aural aspect, could much affect that structure. More instructive are practical studies such as J. L. Styan's *Shakespeare's Stagecraft* (Cambridge: At the University Press, 1971), which provides a good general introduction to the ways poetry can work in drama. At once more fragmentary and suggestive are Una Ellis-Fermor's remarks on "Some Functions of Verbal Music in Drama," *SJH* 90 (1954): 37-48.

27. Clive James in the *Observer Review*, 30 March 1975, p. 22.

28. Robertson, *The Parthenon Frieze*, with photographs by Alison Frantz (New York: Oxford University Press, 1975), unpaginated; see the captions for detail photographs 7 and 8, and the commentary on the last slab on the north (XLII). See also the remarks in the caption for detail photograph 5.

29. As in Panofsky, *Meaning in the Visual Arts* (Garden City, N.Y.: Anchor Books, 1955), pp. 30-31: "A really exhaustive interpretation of the meaning or content might even show that the technical procedures characteristic of a certain country, period, or artist ... are symptomatic of the same basic attitude that is discernible in all other specific qualities of his style." For an application of the idea to a modern painter, see Sam Hunter, "The Recent Work of Larry Rivers," *Arts* 39 (April 1965): 45-50.

30. Kozintsev, *Shakespeare: Time and Conscience*, trans. Joyce Vining (London: Dennis Dobson, 1966), p. 268.

31. These matters are discussed in more detail in the next chapter.

32. See, e.g., Alfred Harbage on "The Words," in *William Shakespeare: A Reader's Guide* (New York: Noonday Press, 1963), pp. 8-13; Inga-Stina Ewbank, "Shakespeare's Poetry," in *A New Companion to Shakespeare Studies*, ed. Kenneth Muir and S. Schoenbaum (Cambridge: At the University Press, 1971), pp. 99-115; William G. Leary, "Verse and Prose," in *Shakespeare Plain* (New York: McGraw-Hill, 1977), pp. 177-218. Maurice Charney, in the section on poetry in his *How to Read Shakespeare* (New York: McGraw-Hill, 1971), pp. 47-71, discusses mainly imagery. Cf. Harry Levin, on pp. 8-14 of the General Introduction to *The Riverside Shakespeare* (New York: Houghton Mifflin, 1974), and David Bevington, on pp. 39-42 of

Complete Works of Shakespeare (New York: Scott Foresman, 1973); in both there are intelligent summaries of the different periods of Shakespeare's verse, and of the dramatic function of verse in selected passages, but hardly a hint of how to treat the verse of a whole play. Even in such generally excellent surveys as the *Revels History of Drama in English*, vol. 3, ed. J. Leeds Barroll et al. (London : Methuen, 1975) or the *Sphere History of Literature in the English Language*, ed. Christopher Ricks (London: Barrie and Jenkins, 1971), the poetry of the drama receives only passing notice, and there is no discussion of Elizabethan attitudes toward it.

33. As an example of their attention, see the interview with Trevor Nunn in Ralph Berry's *On Directing Shakespeare* (New York: Barnes and Noble, 1977), in which Nunn explains how he has his actors begin by reading Shakespeare's sonnets, and then proceed to coping with tensions against the pentameter line, the uses of line-endings, and so forth (see pp. 69-70). On pp. 89-90 of the same volume, Michael Kahn acknowledges the difficulty American actors have integrating verse and feeling.

34. Donoghue, "Viewpoint," *TLS*, 21 December 1973, p. 1564.

35. Dionysius was a student of none other than Aristarchus; see John Edwin Sandys, *A History of Classical Scholarship*, 2d ed. (Cambridge: At the University Press, 1906), 1:138 ff., and J. W. H. Atkins, *Literary Criticism in Antiquity* (Cambridge: At the University Press, 1934), 1:182-83.

36. Structuralist readings tend to do the same, but their impact upon undergraduate education is still uncertain at the present.

37. Williams, "The English Language and the English Tripos," *TLS*, 15 November 1974, p. 1294.

38. Frye, *Anatomy of Criticism* (Princeton: Princeton University Press, 1957), pp. 270-81.

39. From an interview with Pinter in *Writers at Work*, 3d ser. (New York: Viking, 1967), p. 358. Cf. the similar comments by Lillian Hellman and Edward Albee in the same volume, pp. 122-23, 342.

40. See Henry Fitzgeffrey's description of Webster at work:

> Was ever man so mangl'd with a *Poem*?
> See how he draws his mouth awry of late,
> How he scrubs: wrings his wrests: scratches his Pate.
> A *Midwife*! helpe? By his *Braines coitus*,
> Some *Centaure* strange: some huge *Bucephalus*,
> Or Pallas (sure) ingendred in his Braine,—
> Strike *Vulcan* with thy hammer once again.

(Quoted by John Russell Brown in the Introduction to *The White Devil*, 2d ed. [London: Methuen, 1966], p. xxiv.) The reasons for this agony are clearer after reading R. W. Dent's detailed studies of the ways in which Webster assembled his plays; see esp. *John Webster's Borrowing* (Berkeley: University of California Press, 1960).

41. Styan, *Drama, Stage, and Audience*, pp. 147-49. Cf. Robert Weimann, in *Shakespeare and the Popular Tradition in the Theater* (Baltimore: Johns Hopkins University Press, 1978): "It is a new sense of the interdependence of character and society, and a fully responsive interplay between dramatic speech and dramatic action in the process of reproducing the cause and effect of human behavior that defines 'realism' in the Renaissance theater" (p. 197).

42. Brook uses the term in *The Empty Space* (1968), and Styan relates it to Renaissance drama: see *Drama, Stage, and Audience*, pp. 148-49, 157.

43. Mack, *King Lear in Our Time* (Berkeley: University of California Press, 1965).

44. Lucas, in his Introduction to *Any Thing for a Quiet Life*, in *Complete Works of John Webster* (London: Chatto and Windus, 1927), 4:70.

45. See Rabkin's *Shakespeare and the Common Understanding* (New York: Free Press 1967), esp. pp. 1-29; his Foreword to *Reinterpretations of Elizabethan Drama* ed. Rabkin (New York: Columbia University Press, 1969), pp. v-x; and his essay "Meaning and Shakespeare," in *Shakespeare 1971*, pp. 89-106. Cf. Richard Levin's remarks on concepts of dramatic unity, in ch. 1 of *The Multiple Plot in English Renaissance Drama* (Chicago: University of Chicago Press, 1971), pp. 1-20. Levin's *New Readings vs. Old Plays* (Chicago: University of Chicago Press, 1979) mounts a vigorous attack upon thematic criticism that isolates discursive patterns from character and action.

46. The idea occurs often in Eliot's poetry and prose and was picked up by a generation of critics; one fairly recent reference is in *Elizabethan and Early Stuart Drama* (London: Evans, 1965), where John E. Cunningham sees Donne in the Duchess of Malfi's last speech (see p. 99). Cf. also the remark by Jim Hunter in *The Metaphysical Poets* (London: Evans, 1965), on Richard the Second's soliloquy in act 5, scene 5: "This is something like a motto for Metaphysical poetry: 'I'll hammer it out.' . . . One is not fully appreciating a Metaphysical poem unless one sees both brain and soul at work" (pp. 30-31).

47. Baker, *Chronicle of the Kings of England*, 1st ed. (1643), quoted by R. C. Bald in *John Donne: A Life* (Oxford: Oxford University Press, 1970), p. 72.

48. In line 33 of "The Calme" Donne describes the becalmed boat as being "Like *Bajazet* encag'd, the shepheards scoffe." The "shepheard" in this case must have been Edward Alleyn, but of his mastery Donne makes no mention. In the verse letter to Sir Henry Wotton ("Heres no more newes,") l.20, Donne says that "To be like the Court, was a playes praise"; the syntactic obscurity seems symptomatic of the general vagueness of Donne's relation to the drama. (My text for these is *Satires, Epigrams, and Verse Letters*, ed. W. Milgate [Oxford: Clarendon Press, 1967].) There is a full discussion of Donne and the theater, with further references and citation of possible echoes, in Bald's *Life*, pp. 73-74; in Bald's words, "the drama seems to have left surprisingly few traces on Donne's work" (p. 73).

49. John Donne, *The Courtier's Library, or Catalogus librorum aulicorum . . .* , ed. Evelyn M. Simpson (London: Nonesuch Press, 1930), pp. 23-24.

50. *Pierce Pennilesse*, in Nashe, *Works*, ed. R. B. McKerrow, rev. F. P. Wilson (Oxford: Blackwell, 1958), 1:210. Cf. Brome's *Antipodes* (1640), in which the aptly named Letoy, whose house is "an amphitheater / Of exercise and pleasure," lists among his exercises fencing, dancing, and music, adding that "Stageplays and masques are nightly my pastimes" (1.5.52-56, in the text edited by Ann Haaker for the Regents Renaissance Drama series [Lincoln: University of Nebraska Press, 1966]).

51. The play was acted in 1602 but not printed until 1606; my text is that in English Reprints, ed. Edward Arber (London, 1879), act 4, scene 5, p. 58.

52. Fish, *Is There a Text in This Class* (Cambridge: Harvard University Press, 1980), p. 14.

53. In Shakespeare's case there was, however, a demonstrable interest in the readers of his nondramatic poems; see Bentley's essay "Shakespeare and the Readers of His Plays," in his *Shakespeare and His Theatre* (Lincoln: University of Nebraska Press, 1964), pp. 1-26.

54. Ibid., p. 26.

55. Berry, *Poetry and the Physical Voice* (London: Routledge and Kegan Paul, 1962), pp. 138-39. The enclosure of a poem, when placed in a dramatic structure, can itself act as an element of characterization or meaning; G. K. Hunter pursues the

implications of this in his essay "Poem and Context in *Loves Labours Lost*," which appears in *Shakespeare's Styles*, ed. Philip Edwards, Inga-Stina Ewbank, and G. K. Hunter (Cambridge: At the University Press, 1980), pp. 25-38.

56. For a gloss on Stanislavski's term, see Daniel Seltzer's essay "Shakespeare's Texts and Modern Productions," in *Reinterpretations of Elizabethan Drama*, ed. Rabkin, pp. 89-115.

57. The same is of course true of an Elizabethan lyric sung to a setting. The audience for "Weepe no more, you sad fountaines" would not have expected a sustained bardic performance in the manner of Henryson; in both cases the time schemes would be intimated early on, in a variety of ways. For some sensible comments on these and related matters, see Barbara H. Smith, *Poetic Closure* (Chicago: University of Chicago Press, 1968), especially the remarks on blank verse, pp. 78-84.

58. Stephen Booth suggests something like this in his essay "On the Value of *Hamlet*," in *Reinterpretations of Elizabethan Drama*, ed. Rabkin, pp. 137-76. By means of prosodic devices, Booth says, a dramatist may create "nonsignificant coherences" that correspond to "an alliteration of subjects—a sort of rhythm of ideas whose substance may or may not inform the situation dramatized" (pp. 172, 174). I would add that such repetitions need not have been set up consciously by the dramatist.

59. Thus the many studies of "prosody" in seventeenth-century poetry that discuss only stanza form.

60. The problem is common and not confined to plays of high seriousness. In, for example, Middleton's *A Mad World, My Masters*, when Penitent Brothel persuades Mistress Harebrain that for virtue's sake they should stop their liaison (act 4, scene 4), the poetry soars off quite out of character, with perhaps intentional comic effect. A study of Shakespeare that is extremely suggestive on the matter of poetry rising into drama is Richard David's *The Janus of Poets* (Cambridge: At the University Press, 1935).

61. Eliot, "Poetry and Drama," in *On Poetry and Poets* (New York: Farrar, Straus and Giroux, 1957), p. 92. See also "The Possibility of a Poetic Drama" and "'Rhetoric' and Poetic Drama," which appeared in *The Sacred Wood* (1920) at the start of Eliot's work as a dramatist.

62. The original version of *J.B.* was published by Houghton Mifflin in 1958; the Broadway version was published later that year by Samuel French. The differences between the two are discussed by Signi Lenea Falk in *Archibald MacLeish* (New York: Twayne, 1965), pp. 138-50. Also of interest is an exchange between MacLeish and Kazan, published in *Esquire* 51 (May 1959): 144-58. I owe to Madeline DeFrees the suggestion of looking into the stage history of *J.B.*

63. From the interview with Arthur Miller in *Writers at Work*, 3d ser., p. 214.

64. Eliot, "Poetry and Drama," p. 85. Cf. the similar statement by Allardyce Nicoll in *The Theory of Drama*, originally published as *An Introduction to Dramatic Theory* (1931; rpt. New York: Benjamin Blom, 1966), p. 143.

CHAPTER TWO

1. Hall, *Virgidemiarum* (London, 1597), p. 7.

2. Frye uses the terms in several places; for a relevant illustration, see "Agon and Logos," in *The Prison and the Pinnacle*, ed. B. Rajan (Toronto: University of Toronto Press, 1973; rpt. in Frye's *Spiritus Mundi* [Bloomington: Indiana University Press, 1976]), pp. 201-27; see especially pp. 210-13.

3. Gosson, *The Schoole of Abuse* (1579), in English Reprints, ed. Edward Arber, no. 3 (London, 1869), p. 32.

4. Ibid. Cf. Plato in Book 10 of *The Republic*: "People who are as ignorant as [the poet is], and judge only from his words, imagine that if he speaks of cobbling, or of military tactics, or of anything else, in metre and harmony and rhythm, he speaks very well—such is the sweet influence which melody and rhythm by nature have. And I think that you must have observed again and again what a poor appearance the tales of poets make when stripped of the colors which music puts upon them, and recited in simple prose" (trans. B. Jowett [New York: Dial Press, (1936)], pp. 386-87).

5. Gosson, *Schoole of Abuse*, pp. 24-25.

6. See J. W. Robinson, "Medieval English Acting," *TN* 13 (1959): 83-88; O.B. Hardison, *Christian Rite and Christian Drama in the Middle Ages* (Baltimore: Johns Hopkins University Press, 1965), pp. 276 ff; Glynne Wickham, *Early English Stages 1300-1660* (London: Routledge and Kegan Paul, 1966), 1:xxvii; and Richard J. Collier, "A Re-evaluation of the Poetry of the York Corpus Christi Plays," Ph.D. diss., Washington University, 1969.

7. Prologue to *Tamburlaine*, line 1, in Marlowe, *Complete Works*, ed. Fredson T. Bowers (Cambridge: At the University Press, 1973), 1:79.

8. Prior, *The Language of Tragedy* (New York: Columbia University Press, 1947), p. 31. Actually Prior's chapter on "The Elizabethan Tradition" is as a whole less concerned with verse form than with figurative language. His contention about the shift away from rhetoric would be disputed by more recent writers such as Richard Lanham (see *The Motives of Eloquence* [New Haven: Yale University Press, 1976]), who would maintain that formal rhetoric was itself continuously being adapted to new sensibilities. On the Jacobean stage the chief agent for the remodeling was probably Fletcher; but Lanham's finely studied examples all come from lyric forms and prose.

9. From *If This Be Not a Good Play, the Devil Is In It* (1612), in *The Dramatic Works of Thomas Dekker*, ed. Fredson T. Bowers, 4 vols. (Cambridge: At the University Press, 1958), 3:121-22. All subsequent references to Dekker's plays are from this edition; citations appear in the text.

10. Gosson, reprinted in W. C. Hazlitt, *English Drama and Stage under the Tudor and Stuart Princes* (1832; rpt. New York: Burt Franklin, 1969), p. 201.

11. My text for Webster is that in the Revels series, ed. John Russell Brown, 2d ed. (London: Methuen, 1966), p. 2.

12. In the Induction to *Every Man Out of His Humour*, Asper says the same of "attentive auditours" who come to "feed their understanding parts" by using their ears (ll. 201-8); and the Stage Prologue to *The Staple of Newes* asks "Would you were come to hear, not see, a play" (l. 2). The text for these and all subsequent references to the works of Jonson is (unless otherwise noted) *Ben Jonson*, ed. C. H. Hereford, Percy Simpson, and Evelyn Simpson, 11 vols. (Oxford: Clarendon Press, 1925-52). Citations for quotations are given in the text; later references in the notes cite this edition as *H & S*.

13. The whole Praeludium is reprinted in *The Seventeenth-Century Stage*, ed. Gerald Eades Bentley (Chicago: University of Chicago Press, 1968), pp. 28-37; these lines appear on p. 31. The author of the Praeludium was possibly Richard Brome, and Bentley surmises that the play was performed sometime between 1620 and 1630 (see Bentley, ed., *The Jacobean and Caroline Stage*, 7 vols. [Oxford: Clarendon Press, 1941-68], 4:501-5; this work is hereafter cited as *JCS*).

14. Heywood, *An Apology for Actors*, ed. Richard H. Perkinson (London, 1612; rpt. New York: Scholar's Facsimile Reprints, 1941), B3^r.

15. Fitzgeffrey, in *Certain Elegies done by Sundrie Excellent Wits* (London, 1618), A7^v.

16. Marston, *Plays*, ed. H. Harvey Wood (Edinburgh: Oliver and Boyd, 1938), 2:5.

17. From the epistle *To the Gentlemen Students of Both Universities* (1589), in

Nashe *Works*, ed. Ronald B. McKerrow, rev. F. P. Wilson, 5 vols. (Oxford: Blackwell, 1958), 3:311-12.

18. In Greene, *Life and Complete Works in Prose and Verse*, ed. Alexander B. Grosart, 15 vols. (London, 1881-86; rpt. New York: Russell and Russell, 1964), 12:144.

19. Hall, *Virgidemiarum*, p. 10.

20. Brome, Prologue to *The Northern Lasse* (London, [1632]), A4^v.

21. Jonson, prefatory poem, A3^r.

22. These lines from Brome's Praeludium appear in *Seventeenth-Century Stage*, ed. Bentley, p. 34.

23. Horace's speech in praise of Virgil (act 5, scene 1) also makes a nice distinction between the poet's learning or "matter" and his "poesie," which is

> so ramm'd with life,
> That it shall gather strength of life, with being,
> And live hereafter, more admir'd, then now.
>
> [ll. 136-38]

Considering Jonson's satiric intent in the play, the lines form a sharp comment on dramatists like Marston, who in disregarding the art of verse technique, ensure that their plays will not be read for their learning.

24. In an essay that makes this point, Alfred Harbage has also concluded that the acoustics of the Globe would have been well enough damped that the actors would not have had to be the "tear-throats" that they were in the northside theaters; see *Theatre for Shakespeare* (Toronto: University of Toronto Press, 1955), p. 116. Francis Berry, working from the text, has reached a similar conclusion in "Shakespeare's Voice and the Voices of His Instruments," in *Poetry and the Physical Voice* (London: Routledge and Kegan Paul, 1962), pp. 117-60. Cf. Martin Holmes, *Shakespeare and Burbage* (London: Phillimore, 1978), which argues—unconvincingly, I think—that Burbage's vocal manner influenced the shape of the plays; Holmes does have some useful remarks on rhyme, however.

25. Turner is quoted in E. K. Chambers, *The Elizabethan Stage*, 4 vols. (Oxford: Clarendon Press, 1923), 2:339 (this work is hereafter cited as *ES*); Digges's poem prefixed to Shakespeare's *Poems* (1640), is reprinted in *The Shakespeare Allusion Book*, ed. John Munro, which was reissued with a preface by E. K. Chambers (London: Oxford University Press, 1932), 1:456.

26. Catherine Ing, in *Elizabethan Lyrics* (London: Chatto and Windus, 1951), is quite sensitive to the Elizabethan poet's sense of the line, although there is some theoretical confusion in her approach to the definition of metrical feet. Many of these difficulties have been resolved by Sipe's later work (see n. 8, ch. 1).

27. Jonson's lines are quoted in the *Riverside Shakespeare*, ed. G. Blakemore Evans et al. (New York: Houghton Mifflin, 1974), p. 66; all quotations of Shakespeare are from this edition. The same phrase had been used earlier by Francis Meres in *Palladis Tamia* (1598), when he commended Shakespeare's "fine filed phrase" (see *Elizabethan Critical Essays*, ed. G. Gregory Smith, 2 vols. [Oxford: Clarendon Press, 1904], 2:318). The metaphor of lapping, or removing roughness, has an obvious reference to the Elizabethan—or at least pre-Donnean—prosodic ideal.

28. May, *The Heir*, quoted by Bertram Joseph in *Elizabethan Acting*, 2d ed. (Oxford: Oxford University Press, 1964), p. 2. Cf. Chapman in *The Widow's Tears* (1605): "He does it preciously for accent and action, as if he felt the part he played; he ravishes all the young wenches in the palace" (3.2.19-21, in *The Comedies*, ed. T. M. Parrott [1910; rpt. New York: Russell, 1961], 1:402).

29. Hall, *Virgidemiarum*, pp. 8, 13-14. Perhaps Hall, like other Renaissance critics,

is recognizing a distinction between dramatic and heroic blank verse, just as Milton appears to much later at the start of *Paradise Lost*; in any case, the second passage shows the characteristically Elizabethan use of terms from quantitative prosody to describe accentual meters.

30. Jonson, "Elegie: Let me be what I am," l. 27, in *H & S*, 8:200. The same poem sketches a sexual deviate who, "though he play'd in prose,/He would have done in verse" (ll. 61-62).

31. Here the most comprehensive single study for the present purposes remains T. W. Baldwin's *William Shakspere's small Latine and lesse Greeke*, 2 vols. (Urbana: University of Illinois Press, 1944). See also Donald Lemen Clark, *John Milton at St. Paul's School* (New York: Columbia University Press, 1948).

32. See Joan Simon, *Education and Society in Tudor England* (Cambridge: At the University Press, 1967), p. 378; see also p. 111. Some relevant examples are quoted by Nicholas Orme in *English Schools in the Middle Ages* (London: Methuen, 1973), pp. 102-3.

33. On Colet and Vives see Simon, *Education and Society*, pp. 77-79, and 111-14; in Ascham see Book 2 of *The Scholemaster* (1570), especially section 1. The general subject of how the Elizabethans read Latin verse and learned to construe classical meters has been thoroughly treated in Derek Attridge's *Well-Weighed Syllables* (Cambridge: At the University Press, 1974).

34. See chapters 5 and 10 of Sir Thomas Elyot, *The Boke named the Governour* (1531); see also William Harrison Woodward, *Studies in Education during the Age of the Renaissance* (Cambridge: At the University Press, 1906), pp. 268-94.

35. The Stanbridge and Whittinton *vulgaria* have been edited by Beatrice White for EETS, orig. ser., no. 187 (1932); the *vulgaria* in the Arundel collection of the British Library has been edited by William Nelson as *A Fifteenth-Century School Book* (Oxford: Clarendon Press, 1956). Lyly's tract was titled *Carmen de Moribus*; there are comments on its influence in Simon, *Education and Society*, p. 79. The little manual was known even to Faustus's servant Wagner; see line 353 of act 1, scene 4, in Marlowe's "Faustus", ed. W. W. Greg (Oxford: Clarendon Press, 1950), pp. 183, 316.

36. See White's edition of the *vulgaria*, p. liii, and on the subject in general see ch. 41, "Shakspere's Exercise of Versifying," in Baldwin, *Shakspere's small Latine*, 2:380-416. Also relevant is ch. 8, "Exercises for Praxis," in Clark, *Milton at St. Paul's*, pp. 185-249.

37. A sample sestet is quoted in Simon, *Education and Society*, p. 387. On the curriculum offered the petties see Kenneth Charlton, *Education in Renaissance England* (London: Routledge and Kegan Paul, 1965), pp. 98 ff. Baldwin also has much to say on verse in the curriculum.

38. The full title of Newbery's book tells it all: *The Booke in Engliysh Metre After the Great Marchaunt Man Called Dives Pragmaticus, very pretty for children to rede whereby they may the better and more readyer rede and wryte wares and implements in this world contayned*; see Charlton, *Education in Renaissance England*, p. 103.

39. Quoted in Charlton, *Education in Renaissance England*, p. 116; see also pp. 8-13 of the Stanbridge *vulgaria*, and p. xv of the Arundel *vulgaria*, both cited in n. 35 above.

40. Some examples are quoted in Simon, *Education and Society*, p. 380; other verses by schoolchildren clowning around appear in Orme, *English Schools in the Middle Ages*, pp. 139-41.

41. On the way these materials were assimilated, see Charlton, *Education in Renaissance England*, pp. 122 ff.; on the diffusion and influence of *Palladis Tamia*, see D. C. Allen's introduction to the little edition of Meres's work for Scholar's Facsimile Reprints (New York, 1938), pp. iii-xv.

42. See esp. ch. 15, "The Triumph of the Vernacular," in Simon, *Education and Society*, pp. 369–403.

43. Quoted in *The Vulgaria*, ed. White, p. xv. The Latin schoolmaster was to be distinguished from the second schoolmaster, who taught ciphering, the casting of accounts, and the secretary and Roman hands.

44. See the remarks on education in Joseph, *Elizabethan Acting*, pp. 7–12, 21, 26–27, 66–68, 71, et passim, and also Joseph's *The Tragic Actor* (London: Routledge and Kegan Paul, 1959), pp. 5–7, 12–13.

45. See Jonson, *H & S*, 10:208.

46. Puttenham, *The Arte of English Poesie* (1589), ed. Gladys Doidge Willcock and Alice Walker (Cambridge: At the University Press, 1936), p. 82.

47. Ford, prefatory poem to Brome's *The Northern Lasse*, A3^v.

48. Stephens, in Fitzgeffrey's *Certain Elegies*, F8^r.

49. Reprinted in Chambers, *ES*, 4:254.

50. Quoted in Arthur C. Kirsch, "A Caroline Commentary on the Drama," *MP* 66 (1968): 257–259.

51. *A Refutation of the Apology for Actors* (London, 1615), p. 40; the *Refutation* is reprinted with Heywood's *Apology* in the edition cited in note 14 above.

52. *The Guls Horn-Booke*, in Dekker, *Non-Dramatic Works*, ed. Alexander B. Grosart, 5 vols. (London, 1885; reprinted London: Russell and Russell, 1963), 2:204.

53. Randolph is quoted by Gerald Eades Bentley in *The Profession of Dramatist in Shakespeare's Time* (Princeton: Princeton University Press, 1971), p. 224. See also ch. 4, "Dramatists' Contractual Obligations," pp. 111–44.

54. See Kenneth Muir, "Shakespeare's Poets," in *Shakespeare the Professional* (Totowa, N.J.: Rowman and Littlefield, 1973), pp. 22–40.

55. Bradbrook, "The Triple Bond: Audience, Actors, Author in the Elizabethan Playhouse," in *The Triple Bond*, ed. Jospeh G. Price (University Park, Pa.: Pennsylvania State University Press, 1975), p. 61.

56. The stage direction introduces a passage of some forty lines that Marston (?) inserted at line 43 of act 1, scene 4, in the third edition (1604); see *The Malcontent*, ed. M. L. Wine, for the Regents Renaissance Drama series (Lincoln: University of Nebraska Press, 1964).

57. Davies's complete elegy—the longest version of it—is reprinted by Edwin Nungezer in *A Dictionary of Actors* (New Haven: Yale University Press, 1929); the lines quoted appear on p. 75.

58. Flecknoe's elegy is also reprinted ibid., p. 78.

59. *The Countess of Pembrokes Arcadia* (London, 1590), fol. 220^r. Sidney is describing Clinias, who "oft had used to be an actor in Tragedies."

60. John Downes, *Roscius Anglicanus*, ed. Montague Summers (1708; rpt. New York: Benjamin Blom, 1968), p. 17; see also Summers' note on p. 149.

61. Nungezer, *Dictionary*, p. 343. See also the use of pace in *The Merchant of Venice* (emphasis added):

> Where is that horse that doth untread again
> His tedious *measures* with the unbated fire,
> That he did *pace* them first?

> [2.6.10–12]

Cf. *Much Ado About Nothing*, 3.4.93. For another use of the term see Hall's first Satire, quoted above (see note 29 and accompanying text), which refers to "pacing" spondees. The *OED* does not record that *pace* had a distinctly metrical application at this time; but in general any term metaphorically related to *foot* seems to have been susceptible to appropriation. The Countess of Pembroke (in part 7 of her translation of Psalm 50) refers to a change in meter as "another pace." There is a cognate usage in *As You Like It* (3.2.113) which is also parallel to Jonson's use of *false pace* in *Volpone*, quoted below.

62. My text is the reprint of Gainsford's *The Rich Cabinet* (1616), in Hazlitt's *English Drama and Stage*, p. 228.

63. Gayton's *Pleasant Notes upon "Don Quixote"* (1654) are quoted by Gerald Eades Bentley in *Shakespeare and His Theatre* (Lincoln: University of Nebraska Press, 1964), pp. 111-12.

64. In Nashe, *To the Gentleman Students of Both Universities* (1589), in Nashe, *Works*, 3:323 ff.; cf. Greene's *Groats-worth of Wit* (1596), in Greene, *Works*, 12:130 ff., and *Francesco's Fortunes* (1590), in *Works*, 8:132 ff.

65. Stephens, *Certain Elegies*, F8^r.

66. Dekker, *The Guls Horn-Booke*, in Dekker, *Non-Dramatic Works*, 2:205.

67. Tarleton's knack is mentioned by Francis Meres in *Palladis Tamia*; see also Smith, *Elizabethan Critical Essays*, 2:308, and Nungezer, *Dictionary*, pp. 359, 395. Greene's *Groats-worth of Wit* pokes some fun at this; for a commentary, see Chambers, *ES*, 4:241.

68. Brome, Praeludium to *The Careless Shepherdess*, in *The Seventeenth-Century Stage*, ed. Bentley, p. 32.

69. Nungezer, *Dictionary*, p. 221; but as usual, the most concise reference to the problem is in Jonson, where the Preface to *The Alchemist* describes the takeover of the jigs. Baskerville's *The Elizabethan Jig* (Chicago: University of Chicago Press, 1929) remains a useful compendium.

70. This description appears in *The Magnificent Entertainment Given to King James* (1604), in Dekker, *Dramatic Works*, 2:260. On Alleyn's voice and delivery see Andrew Gurr, "Who Strutted and Bellowed?", *Shs* 16 (1963):95-102.

71. Puttenham, *The Arte of English Poesie*, pp. 160-61.

72. "Of the Accent," in *H & S*, 8:502.

73. Webster, *Works* ed. F. L. Lucas (London: Chatto and Windus, 1927), 4:43. Through a pun Webster goes on to connect the actor to the audience specifically by the poetic line: "sit in a full Theater, and you will thinke you see so many lines drawne from the circumference of so many eares whiles the *Actor* is the *Center*."

74. Quoted in Nungezer, *Dictionary*, p. 79. See also Chambers, *ES*, 3:306-10.

75. See Mulcaster's *Elementarie* (1582), ed. E. T. Campagnac (Oxford: Clarendon Press, 1925); the actors are discussed in Nungezer, *Dictionary*, pp. 390, 135 ff., and Bentley, *JCS*, 3:300. Field was a student and friend of Jonson and acted in several of his plays.

76. Nungezer, *Dictionary*, p. 261; Chambers, *ES*, 2:16, n.2.

77. For Alleyn, see Chambers, *ES*, 3:296; the rest are described under the appropriate entries in Nungezer, *Dictionary*.

78. Nungezer, *Dictionary*, pp. 93-94; the story is related at length in J. C. Adams, *Shakespearean Playhouses* (Boston: Houghton Mifflin, 1917), pp. 210-13. The father carried the case—or his revenge—as far as the Star Chamber. Ned Field also began his career with the Children of the Chapel at Blackfriars by being kidnapped; see Bentley, *JCS*, 3:300. The men at Blackfriars seemed fond of these recruiting methods, having also seized (among others) a boy named Stephen Hammerton (see Bentley, *JCS*, 2:371).

79. Lodge, *Defense of Poetry, Music, and Stage-Plays*, ed. David Laing, Shakespeare Soc. Pubs. no. 48 (London, 1853), pp. 19-20. A *dump* is a mournful tune; see, e.g., *Two Gentlemen of Verona* (3.2.84).

80. Brown, "The Theatrical Element of Shakespearean Criticism," in *Reinterpretations of Elizabethan Drama*, ed. Norman Rabkin, English Institute Essays for 1968 (New York: Columbia University Press, 1969), p. 193.

81. Brome, Epilogue to *The Court Beggar* (1634-39?), in Bentley, *JCS*, 2:373.

82. Greene, *Francesco's Fortunes* (1590), in *Works*, 8:131-33.

83. Johannes Rhenanus, in the Preface to *Speculum Aistheticum*, trans. David Klein in "Did Shakespeare Produce His Own Plays?" *MLR* 57 (1962): 556. Klein offers many allusions to the practice, noting that it continued into Restoration drama.

84. Heywood, *An Apology for Actors*, C4^v and E3^r. On university training see also Joseph, *Elizabethan Acting*, pp. 21-22.

85. From *Jests to Make You Merrie* (1607), in Dekker, *Non-Dramatic Works*, 2:303, 352-53.

86. Nashe dedicated *Strange News* to Beeston, and the Epistle Dedicatory consists of a learned and happy series of insults; see Nashe, *Works*, 1:255-58.

87. My text for Earle is that found in Beaumont and Fletcher, *Works*, ed. Arnold Glover, 10 vols. (Cambridge: At the University Press, 1905); page references in volume 1 are cited in the text.

88. Baker, *Theatrum Triumphans*, quoted in Joseph, *Elizabethan Acting*, p. 43. Beaumont's lines on *The Faithful Shepherdess* make the same point: Your censurers now must have the qualitie/Of reading" (in *Works*, 2:447).

89. Harbage, *Theatre for Shakespeare*, pp. 113-14. Gurr elaborates on the term in "Who strutted . . . ," cited above, n. 70.

90. Bulwer, *Chironomia* (1644), quoted by Bertram Joseph in *The Tragic Actor* (p. 9). Cf. Abraham Fraunce in *The Arcadian Rhetorike* (1588), ed. Ethel Seaton (Oxford: Blackwell, 1950): "Gesture must follow the change and variety of the voice, measuring thereunto in every respect" (p. 120).

91. Gainsford, *The Rich Cabinet*, reprinted in Hazlitt, *English Drama and Stage*, p. 230. Thus Chapman's lines on *Sejanus* stress that Jonson's listeners become spectators able to imagine the action. At several points in acts 1 and 2 of *The Gentleman Usher* (1601), Chapman also ridicules the excessive projection of action from a few dramatic lines.

92. Edward Sharpham, *Cupid's Whirligig* (London, 1607), K3^r.

93. To ignorant readers, "should a man present them with the most excellent Musicke, it would delight them no more, then *Auriculas Citherae collecta sorde dolentes*" (Webster, *Works*, 2:236).

94. E.g., Seymour Chatman, in *A Theory of Meter* (The Hague: Mouton, 1965), who offers metrical analyses and sound spectrograms of Shakespeare sonnets as read by professional actors; Chatman wants "to recognize the verse instance as a sum or common denominator of all meaningful delivery instances" (p. 96).

95. In *The Language of Renaissance Poetry* (London: Deutsch, 1971), p. 188, A. C. Partridge interprets these lines as meaning "'giving its value to each syllable of trisyllabic feet'; the movement implied is of the dactylic or anapestic kind." This seems rather fanciful, as the speech occurs in a prose paragraph; in the context of contemporary remarks on the handling of blank verse, Hamlet seems likelier to be warning the Player against the heavy-handed bombast of loud, even meters.

96. *Essay of Dramatick Poesy*, in Dryden, *Works*, ed. Edward Niles Hooker and H. T. Swedenberg, Jr., et al. (Berkeley: University of California Press, 1956-76), 17:57; Preface to *All for Love*, in Dryden, *Essays*, ed. W. P. Ker, 2 vols. (Oxford: Clarendon Press, 1900), 1:201; Epilogue to *The Conquest of Granada, Part 2*, in Dryden, *Essays*, 1:160.

97. The relations of this debate to other critical problems of the period are well traced by Robert D. Hume in *The Development of English Drama in the Late Seventeenth Century* (Oxford: Clarendon Press, 1976), especially pp. 149-85.

98. *Essay of Dramatick Poesy*, in Dryden, *Works*, 17:72.

99. Howard, Preface to *Four New Plays* (1665), in Spingarn, ed., *Critical Essays*, 2:101. It must be said, however, that when Howard came to *write* his own plays he

could let the Muses take over in the old style, as he says in the Preface to *The Great Favourite* (1968): "I will not therefore pretend to say why I writ this Play, some scenes in blank Verse, others in Rhime; since I have no better reason to give then Chance, which waited upon my present Fancy, and I expect no better a reason from any ingenious person then his Fancy for which he best relishes" (Spingarn, ed., *Critical Essays*, 2:107). It is relevant to our purposes to note that this play is probably a revision of a lost play by John Ford (see Alfred Harbage, "Elizabethan-Restoration Palimpsest," *MLR* 35 [1940], 287-319), and as James T. Boulton has suggested, Howard is probably "making a clumsy attempt to cover his tracks"; see Boulton's edition of Dryden, *Of Dramatick Poesie*, which also includes Howard's Preface (Oxford: Oxford University Press, 1964), p. 185. Much could still be done with the study of Restoration style imposed upon Elizabethan plays.

100. Dennis, Prologue to *The Comical Gallant: or the Amours of Sir John Falstaff* (1702; rpt. London: Cornmarket Press, 1969), p. 50.

101. From Rymer's *A Short View of Tragedy* (1963), in Spingarn, ed., *Critical Essays*, 2:212. Fifteen years before, in *The Tragedies of the Last Age*, Rymer had taken a very different tack, pointing out that an actor's physical gestures can so charm an audience "that *deformities* in the Poetry cannot be perceiv'd" (Spingarn, 2:184).

102. *Literary Criticism of Alexander Pope*, ed. Bertrand A. Goldgar (Lincoln: University of Nebraska Press, 1965), p. 173.

103. This was Charles Gildon, in *An Essay on the Art, Rise, and Progress of the Stage in Greece, Rome and England* (London, 1710). Generous excerpts are readily available in Vickers, *Shakespeare: The Critical Heritage*, 2:216-62. In his efforts Gildon anticipated those modern editors who introduce the student to Shakespeare's versification by scanning lines with the macron and breve.

104. Moseley, "To the Reader," in *Comedies, Tragi-comedies, with other Poems*, in *Plays and Poems of William Cartwright*, ed. G. Blakemore Evans (Madison: University of Wisconsin Press, 1951), p. 830; *Essay upon the Genius and Writing of Shakespeare*, in Dennis, *Critical Works*, ed. Edward Niles Hooker (Baltimore: Johns Hopkins University Press, 1943), 2:4-5. As D. Nichol Smith noted (see 2:426 in Hooker's edition), Dennis's last sentence forms two iambic pentameter lines. To see just how far criticism had traveled by this time, compare Dennis's statement with the following by Thomas Campion in *Observations in the Art of English Poesie* (1602): "Iambick verse . . . . being yet made a little more licentiate, that it may therby the neerer imitate our common talke, will excellently serve for Comedies" (in Smith, ed., *Elizabethan Critical Essays*, (2:338).

105. Preface to the *Works of Shakespeare* (1725), in *Literary Criticism of Alexander Pope*, ed. Goldgar, p. 172.

106. Wright, *Historia Histrionica*, (London, 1699), pp. 2, 3.

107. See *Pierce Pennilesse* in Nashe, *Works*, 1:215.

108. Wright, *Historia Histrionica*, p. 6. Wright is exaggerating here, for scenes had crept in during Caroline times (*JCS*, 6:51-53); on the general subject see Lily B. Campbell, *Scenes and Machines on the English Stage during the Renaissance*, 2 vols. (Cambridge: At the University Press, 1923).

109. Flecknoe, *Short Treatise of the English Stage*, in Spingarn, ed., *Critical Essays*, 2:95; J. Payne Collier, *History of English Dramatic Poetry and Annals of the Stage* (London, 1831), 3:366.

110. There are some good comments on this by Stanley Wells in *Literature and Drama* (London: Routledge and Kegan Paul, 1970), esp. ch. 2, "The Printing of Plays," pp. 25-55.

111. Ian Watt, *The Rise of the Novel* (Berkeley: University of California Press, 1957).

112. M. C. Bradbrook, *The Rise of the Common Player* (Cambridge: Harvard University Press, 1962), and Bentley, *The Profession of Dramatist*. Chambers's chapter on "The Actor's Economics" (*ES*, 1:348-88) remains a useful summary. Another standby,

Phoebe Sheavyn's *The Literary Profession in the Elizabethan Age*, has been revised by Wilbur Sanders, with new material specifically on the drama (Manchester: Manchester University Press, 1967); on the periphery of matters at hand but still of occasional interest is Edwin H. Miller's *The Professional Writer in Elizabethan England* (Cambridge: Harvard University Press, 1959).

113. See Bentley, *The Profession of Dramatist*, pp. 221ff.

114. Prologue to *Volpone*, in *H & S*, vol. 5., p. 24, ll. 16-18. Generally, though, Jonson was a slow worker.

115. Prologue to *If You Know Not Me You Know Nobody*, in Heywood, *Dramatic Works*, [ed. R. H. Shepherd], 6 vols. (London, 1874; rpt. New York: Russell and Russell, 1964), 1:191. Bentley (*The Profession of Dramatist*) compares to this the dedication to *The Four Prentices* (1615), in which Heywood emphasizes the new judiciousness of the reader. Bentley's whole ch. 10, "Publication," is an invaluable florilegium of material relevant to the discussion here.

116. For more information, as well as a list of the plays, see W. W. Greg, *A Bibliography of the English Printed Drama to the Restoration* (London: The Bibliographical Society, 1957), 3:1306-13.

117. Bentley, *The Profession of Dramatist*, pp. 51-53.

118. On this subject see D. J. Gordon's definitive essay "Poet and Architect: The Intellectual Setting of the Quarrel between Ben Jonson and Inigo Jones," (1949), reprinted in *The Renaissance Imagination*, ed. Stephen Orgel (Berkeley: University of California Press, 1975), pp. 77-101.

119. Heywood, *Dramatic Works*, 4:5.

120. For more on Jonson's Folio and its implications, see Bentley, *JCS*, 4:609ff.

121. See H. James Jensen, *John Dryden's Critical Terms* (Minneapolis: University of Minnesota Press, 1969), p. 81. The idea was not new with Dryden; Puttenham, for example, had used "numerositie" in *The Arte of English Poesie* (1589), pp. 77, 147, 160 et passim; his context is that of lyric, but the term does not seem to have been picked up by his contemporaries; the *OED* records the next usage as Cowley's in 1656. The ideal of smoothness in dramatic poetry was sought well before this; see, e.g., Thomas Carew's praise of Thomas May's *The Heir* (1622) for its "equall feet [that] slide into even numbers" (Carew, *Poems*, ed. Rhodes Dunlap [Oxford: Clarendon Press, 1949], p. 92, ll. 14-15).

122. Pope, Preface to Shakespeare, in *Literary Criticism of Pope*, ed. Goldgar, p. 163.

123. Dedication to *The Spanish Friar* (1681), in Dryden, *Essays*, 1:248; Aristotle, *Poetics*, trans. Ingram Bywater (Oxford: Clarendon Press, 1924), ch. 6 (1450b. 17-18), ch. 26 (1461b. 29-31); cf. ch. 7 (1451a. 6-8) and ch. 14 (1453b. 1-4).

124. On these and related matters see Elizabeth L. Eisenstein's important study *The Printing Press as an Agent of Change*, 2 vols. (Cambridge: At the University Press, 1979), especially part 1, which does some general mapping of what Lucien Febvre has called the shift from "the age of the ear" to "the age of the eye" (quoted by Eisenstein, 1:41). On the shift to visual representation I have found especially suggestive Peter Holland's *The Ornament of Action: Text and Performance in Restoration Comedy* (Cambridge: At the University Press, 1979); although Holland's first chapter, "The Text and the Audience," does not refer specifically to poetry, it helps define the context under discussion here.

CHAPTER THREE

1. As one estimate: in the first two-thirds of the play, 7 percent of Vindice's speech is in prose; in the last third, 2 percent. This count is only approximate and is based

upon the edition by R. A. Foakes for the Revels series (London: Methuen, 1966); Foakes recasts some of Tourneur's prose into verse. The count takes as verse any blank verse line that Vindice finished, but not the parts of lines he only started. His couplets appear to be evenly distributed throughout the play.

2. 4.2.15-21, 4.4.68-76. Line numbers and all subsequent quotations, unless otherwise noted, are from the edition by Allardyce Nicoll in Tourneur, *Works* (1929; rpt. New York: Russell, 1963). Unlike many editors, Nicoll preserved the lineation of the Quarto; the importance of this is discussed in the fourth section of this chapter. I also follow Nicoll's attempt to sort out the punctuation of the Quarto, but to keep the play from seeming anachronistic in the company of the modern-spelling editions used in later chapters, I have adopted modern spellings except where elision is indicated. For convenience's sake I refer to the author of the play as Tourneur; the best summary of the debate over the authorship remains that in Samuel Schoenbaum's *Internal Evidence and Elizabethan Authorship* (Evanston, Ill.: Northwestern University Press, 1966), pp. 200-217.

3. Paul Valéry, *Analects*, trans. Stuart Gilbert (Princeton: Princeton University Press, 1970), pp. 242-43.

4. To pick up some studies spaced more or less evenly through the years: C. V. Boyer, *The Hero as Villain in Elizabethan Tragedy* (London: Routledge, 1914); G. B. Harrison's Introduction to the Temple edition of the play (London: Dent, 1934); Una Ellis-Fermor, *The Jacobean Drama* (London: Methuen, 1947), pp. 153 ff.; Philip J. Ayres, "Parallel Action and Reductive Techniques in *RT*," *ELN* 8 (1970): 103-7.

5. See, e.g., Robert Ornstein's comment that Tourneur's characters are "'large' or 'small,' distinct or vague," but strictly two-dimensional, allowing Vindice to grow only from distortion to perversion (*The Moral Vision of Jacobean Tragedy* [Madison: University of Wisconsin Press, 1960], p. 108). Cf. Brian Gibbons's Introduction to the New Mermaid edition, in which he states flatly (p. xxix) that "[Vindice] does not develop or decrease in stature, he achieves no deep self-knowledge" (London: Benn, 1967).

6. Eliot, *Essays on Elizabethan Drama* (New York: Harcourt Brace, 1960), p. 120.

7. This may explain why Eliot's essay on Tourneur is basically ambivalent: it has valuable insights into the poetry, which in this play is developed most fully by a single character, but at the same time it is committed to seeing the play as a "document on humanity" (*Essays on Elizabethan Drama*, p. 120). A similar bias is present in L. G. Salingar's 1938 essay "*RT* and the Morality Tradition," reprinted in *Essays on Elizabethan Drama*, ed. Ralph J. Kaufmann (New York: Oxford University Press, 1961), pp. 208-24. Stating that "[Tourneur's] poetic material is ranged and ordered by reference to the experience of society as a whole" (p. 211), Salingar has to assert also Tourneur's "imperviousness to the psychological makeup of individuals" (p. 218). Cf. Salingar's later view in "Tourneur and the Tragedy of Revenge," in *The Age of Shakespeare*, ed. Boris Ford (London: Penguin, 1956), pp. 334-54. Generic studies regarding the play as fundamentally satiric—e.g., John Peter, *Complaint and Satire in Early English Literature* (Oxford: Oxford Univeristy Press, 1956), pp. 255-73, or Alvin B. Kernan, *The Cankered Muse* (New Haven: Yale University Press, 1959), pp. 221-32—have to disregard the development of Vindice's character, for as Kernan points out, the satiric character usually undergoes intensification rather than genuine change. (Kernan's reading of the play is more flexible than this formula might suggest, though; see his comments on the ending, p. 232). The persistence of Eliot's and Salingar's influence may be seen in Gibbons's remark that "Tourneur's dramatic method subordinates character and incident to his main concern, the presentation of a deeply ironic and disquieting view of human nature . . ." (New Mermaid edition, p. xvi). Doctrinal commitment to a view of the play as either satire or moral allegory seems to

preclude a priori any account of the demonstrable changes in Vindice's poetry. Cf. M. C. Bradbrook, who writes of "the purely arbitrary and dissociated nature of Vindice's different personalities"; she has to regard the character this way because she is committed to a view of the play as "a *drame à thèse* on the contrasts between earthly and heavenly vengeance, and earthly and heavenly justice" (*Themes and Conventions of Elizabethan Tragedy* [Cambridge: At the University Press, 1935], p. 166). This judgment, however, like the others cited above, seems to begin from the category and then proceed without close attention to the poetry. Finally, even if Tourneur did attempt to produce a *drame à thèse* with its obligatory set characters, that would not imply that the characters could not escape the planned pattern.

8. Kernan notes (*Cankered Muse*, p. 229) that Vindice cannot "separate [Gloriana's] beauty and virtue from the fleshly attraction it exerted in the sinful world," but this may glance past the way that Vindice's own passion requires the desires of others.

9. When Vindice finally sees Spurio with the Duchess, he says this is the second time they have met, although we never learn how he obtained this information; Hippolito does not tell him about their relationship until act 2, scene 3. Shakespeare could manage a situation like this with more tact, as in Hamlet's "O my prophetic soul!" (Many readers have claimed to notice verbal parallels with *Hamlet*, but it would be well to recall the substantial differences in theme and technique; see R. A. Foakes, "The Art of Cruelty: Hamlet and Vindice," *ShS* 26 [1973]:21-31). This lacuna in Tourneur's narrative is not unique in the play: at line 57 of act 1 scene 1, Vindice refers to Hippolito's wrongs, about which we never learn; Hippolito seems in fact to enjoy a privileged position at court. And in his last speech, Vindice says that "Piato brought forth a knavish sentence once," but the sentence in question was uttered at line 57 of act 5, scene 1, by the Third Noble. This is not likely to be a textual error, as Vindice has the punch line that follows the sentence. (Howard Pearce has capitalized upon this odd hiatus; see n. 44, below.)

10. John Peter has commented on Vindice's reference to sin and damnation in these passages; see "*The Revenger's Tragedy* Reconsidered," *EIC*, 6 (1956):131-43; cf. Peter B. Murray, *A Study of Cyril Tourneur* (Philadelphia: University of Pennsylvania Press, 1964), pp. 214-16.

11. Critics offended by Vindice's rhymes often fail to note that they differ greatly in their poetic styles and their effects in context. T. B. Tomlinson, in *A Study of Elizabethan and Jacobean Drama* (Cambridge: At the University Press, 1964), tries to account for their variety after deploring Tourneur's "couplet morality" (p. 118), saying that "the jingling sententious couplets almost always yield wit and energy which are in fact the reverse of the sententious moral maxims" (pp. 123-24). It is not clear how energy is the reverse of a maxim. See also Peter, "*The Revenger's Tragedy* Reconsidered." Foakes is good on the ironic relevance of many of the couplets (Revels edition, pp. xxvii-xxx).

12. The imagery of the play has been studied by Una Ellis-Fermor in "The Imagery of *The Revenger's Tragedy* and *The Atheist's Tragedy*," *MLR* 30 (1935):289-301; Marco K. Mincoff in "The Authorship of *The Revenger's Tragedy*," *Studia Historico-Philologica Serdicensia* 2 (1940):1-87; and by Inga-Stina Ewbank in "An Approach to Tourneur's Imagery," *MLR* 54 (1959):489-98. Peter B. Murray refers to imagery throughout *A Study*, especially pp. 173-257; and in "Tourneur's Imagery and *The Revenger's Tragedy*," *PLL* 6 (1970):192-97, Stanford Sternlicht notes the dominant image clusters, using them to argue that the author of *The Revenger's Tragedy* was not the author of *The Atheist's Tragedy*. Much broader than any of these is the study by Daniel J. Jacobson, *The Language of "The Revenger's Tragedy,"* JDS no. 38 (Salzburg: University of Salzburg, 1974). J. L. Simmons has an ingenious reading of one image and its intellectual context: "The Tongue and Its Office in *The Revenger's*

Tragedy," PMLA 92 (1977); 56-68. Louis Charles Stagg's *Index to the Figurative Language of Cyril Tourneur's Tragedies* (Charlottesville: Bibliographical Society of the University of Virginia, 1970), is useful.

13. In *"The Revenger's Tragedy:* A Study in Irony," *PQ* 38 (1959): 242-51, Peter Lisca (following the lead of John Peter) discusses a "sincere moral framework" behind the irony, but does not describe the way in which Vindice's comments surge up in spite of himself: Vindice *thinks* he has made the case for evil.

14. Brian Morris sees in the play "the complete absence of any positive moral standards, any norm of human behavior, any impulse toward altruism, to say nothing of Love" ("Elizabethan and Jacobean Drama," in *English Drama to 1710,* ed. Christopher Ricks [London: Barrie and Jenkins, 1971], p. 102); whatever a "norm of human behavior" may be, the rest of the statement disregards Castiza and Gratiana—to say nothing of John Peter and Robert Ornstein. The two women may be tedious and over-simplified in themselves, but still they play an important role in the growth of Vindice's imagination, which is more the subject of the play than is the definition of moral standards. There is a good reading of the temptation scenes by Ronald Huebert in *"The Revenger's Tragedy* and the Fallacy of the Excluded Middle," *UTQ* 48 (1978): 10-22.

15. On the theme of character transformation see Murray, *A Study,* pp. 190-97, 200-205, although much of this appears to be an elaboration of Bradbrook's earlier note that "the main structure of the play ... is an enlarged series of peripeteia" (*Themes and Conventions,* p. 165). Murray's account of Vindice's transformations seems overingenious in that it calls for Vindice to experience a disillusionment as Piato that changes his character; but as Foakes observes (Revels edition, p. xxxi, n. 3), Vindice has left the world of goodness long before act 1, scene 1. Being engaged by Lussurioso is hardly shattering; that destruction is a gradual process that Vindice does to himself as he goes along. More recently, the theme of alienation has been studied by François Camoin, who remarks enigmatically that Vindice is a character "we can endow with a subconscious without being overtly ridiculous. We will be irrelevant, however, for Vindice's psyche has not much to do with the play except to be there" (*The Revence* [sic] *Tradition in Tourneur, Webster, and Middleton,* JDS no. 20 [Salzburg: University of Salzburg, 1972], p. 35).

16. See lines 128-30 of act 1, scene 1. In act 3, scene 5, Vindice tells the Duke that his father "died in sadness" (171); "He had his tongue, yet grief made him die speechless" (173).

17. In *A Study,* p. 225, Murray states that throughout the play *discontent* suggests evil or ambition; if true, this should force Murray to revise his own opinion of Vindice's father.

18. The terms *usury* and *usuring* have been explained as referring in this play to a commercial class "destroying the remnants of a feudal society and its values" (Murray, *A Study,* p. 210; cf. Peter, *Complaint and Satire,* p. 128). These inheritors of Salingar's 1938 essay disregard the way that the lines refer to "a usuring *Father,"* and that the old Duke himself is the remnant of a feudal society. *Usury* may also have the sexual reference that it does in Shakespeare (e.g., sonnet 134) or Donne ("Loves Usury"). A fuller view of the social problems behind the play may be gained from Lawrence Stone, *The Crisis of the Aristocracy* (Oxford: Clarendon Press, 1965), esp. ch. 11, "Marriage and the Family," pp. 589-671, which suggests that at their worst, Elizabethan marriages and extramarital relations were not greatly different from those in *The Revenger's Tragedy.*

19. In *Themes and Conventions* (p. 166), Bradbrook objects that the speech is "frankly artificial," but it does seem consistent with Vindice's absorption in his role as Piato.

20. Further, having Vindice present when Lussurioso bursts in on the Duke would

look like Tourneur's joke on Vindice—at least if Vindice were not so indignant.

21. It may be too that Tourneur was working from accounts of historical incidents that did not depict such a scene.

22. The high pitch of Vindice's excitement is emphasized by Hippolito's perkily regular verse; its comparative lack of variety is one of Tourneur's chief means of establishing the character's naïveté.

23. John Hollander has some helpful comments on logical modifications and reversals in enjambed blank verse; see "'Sense Variously Drawn Out': Some Observations on English Enjambment," in *Literary Theory and Structure: Essays in Honor of William K. Wimsatt*, ed. Frank Brady et al. (New Haven: Yale University Press, 1973), pp. 201-25.

24. Bradbrook, Salingar, Peter, and Murray all have comments on this, as do Theodore Spencer, in *Death and Elizabethan Tragedy* (Cambridge: Harvard University Press, 1936), pp. 238-40, and F. R. Leavis, in "Imagery and Movement: Notes in the Analysis of Poetry," *Scrutiny* 13 (1945):120-22. Lawrence J. Ross annotates the passage in detail in his edition for the Regents Renaissance Drama series (Lincoln: University of Nebraska Press, 1966), and Clifford Leech has some comments in *The Dramatist's Experience* (London: Chatto and Windus, 1970), p. 158. After all this, one could step back from the speech and admire its fine control in contrast to Ben Jonson's silkworm speech in *The Devil is an Ass* (2.2).

25. Bradbrook, *Themes and Conventions*, p. 169.

26. See Lisca, "*The Revenger's Tragedy*: A Study in Irony," and Murray, *A Study*, pp. 218-24, for summaries and reinterpretations.

27. Ideal here would be large, stuffed hand puppets of the sort used in the recent Royal Shakespeare Company production of *Doctor Faustus*, which were frightening precisely because one saw that only a demented man could regard them as real.

28. But it is also true that Tourneur does not seem especially interested in the women of the play. If we never learn what Vindice did with Gloriana, we also fail to see the vile Duchess suffer in the end; she is merely banished (5.3.7).

29. Readers have noted a similarity between *The Revenger's Tragedy* and *The Jew of Malta*, pointing to a similar entertainment given the corpse, but the basic resemblance is more properly structural. Both Barrabas and Vindice degenerate into devising elaborate schemes simply to conceal an initial crime, and end finally pitted against mere buffoons and hypocrites.

30. As editors have been unable to distinguish more than one compositor at work, for convenience I use the singular throughout. See George R. Price, "The Authorship and the Bibliography of *The Revenger's Tragedy*," *The Library*, 5th ser., 15 (1960): 272-73. My remarks here use the typography and layout of the Quarto.

31. See Foakes, Introduction to Revels edition, p. lvii, n. 1.

32. Price, "Authorship and Bibliography of *The Revenger's Tragedy*," 262-77.

33. At H1^v, I2^v, and I3^v. On D2^r is a stage direction printed on two lines, although it could have gone on one line without crowding—and usually does in modern editions.

34. The twelve instances, with the equivalent line numbers in the Revels edition: E2^r (2.3.89), F3^r (3.5.186), F3^v (3.5.223), F4^v (3.6.68), G1^r (4.1.1; Foakes notes this one), G3^r (4.2.59), G3^v (4.2.111), I1^v (5.1.128), I2^v (5.2.26), I3^r (5.2.30), I4^r (5.3.84), and I4^v (5.3.91).

35. See, for example, B4^v and I3^r. Even on the last formes, where the compositor adds lines to each page in order to fit in the text, there are many passages that are not cramped together.

36. R. A. Foakes, "On the Authorship of *RT*," *MLR* 48 (1953):130, 132.

37. Needless to say, shifts from verse to prose may have different functions at different points within a play, and different dramatists will use the technique to suit their

own immediate purposes. In view of the many echoes of *Hamlet* in *The Revenger's Tragedy*, comparison of the shifts in the two plays might be useful. Harry Levin suggests that the shifts in *Hamlet* indicate a distinction between the inner and outer man, a metaphor that has an obvious function in *The Revenger's Tragedy* (see *The Question of "Hamlet"* [New York: Oxford University Press, 1959], pp. 117-18).

38. Leo Kirschbaum has some trenchant remarks on editing that cannot palate mixed prose and verse; see his textual notes to *1* and *2 Tamburlaine* in *Plays of Christopher Marlowe* (Cleveland: World, 1962), pp. 457-59. In *The Revenger's Tragedy*, the movements into and out of prose not only indicate the characters' development but provide a felt equivalent to the imagery, which frequently relies upon the associations of light flickering in darkness, and to the theme of condensed time and expanded time.

39. The Revels edition prints all of the passages above as prose, although in his apparatus Foakes incorrectly records the last line of Spurio's verse as ending at *signs*.

40. Allardyce Nicoll concedes that Tourneur's characters may be "grotesques" but captivating nontheless; "unquestionably, the paradox has to be explained largely by reference to the intensity of the verse" ("*The Revenger's Tragedy* and the Virtue of Anonymity," in *Essays on Shakespeare and Elizabethan Drama in Honor of Hardin Craig*, ed. Richard Hosley [Columbia: University of Missouri Press, 1962], p. 313). One problem with this is that, as most commentators agree, nearly all the "intense" verse is spoken by Vindice—and Spurio.

41. If we disregard the turns and shifts in Vindice's style we shall miss much of the care that Tourneur has put into this characterization. Thus it is hard to agree with Madeline Doran in *Endeavors of Art* (Madison: University of Wisconsin Press, 1954) that "Tourneur is not really interested in how a man may be drawn into doing wrong to right wrong" (p. 358). The very process by which a person can draw *himself* into doing all sorts of things seems of great interest to Tourneur.

42. Inga-Stina Ewbank has some comments on the masque in "'These Pretty Devices': A Study of Masques in Plays," in *A Book of Masques in Honor of Allardyce Nicoll* (Cambridge: At the University Press, 1970), pp. 443-45. See also Samuel Schoenbaum, "*The Revenger's Tragedy*: Jacobean Dance of Death," *MLQ* 15 (1954): 201-7.

43. For some time it seemed appropriate to speak of Antonio as the voice of Christian authority: see, e.g., Lacy Lockert "The Greatest of Elizabethan Melodramas," in *Essays in Dramatic Literature: The Parrott Presentation Volume*, ed. Hardin Craig (Princeton: Princeton University Press, 1935), p. 125, or Fredson Bowers, *Elizabethan Revenge Tragedy* (Princeton: Princeton University Press, 1940), p. 134; the tradition has been carried on by John Peter and Irving Ribner. Robert Ornstein sorts matters out evenly in *Moral Vision*, p. 112, while Murray goes to the other extreme and regards Antonio as a monster of cynical cunning (*A Study*, pp. 224-28).

44. Most studies describe Vindice's confession as an assertion of pride. Ornstein refers to "a final ironic twist of fate" (*Moral Vision*, p. 112), "a malicious Fate" (p. 113), but then adds that Vindice dies because of the "courtly impudence which he once mockingly assumed" (p. 115). For reasons that will be apparent, I cannot agree with Gibbons's suggestion that Vindice's fall may be "meant to be a joke" (New Mermaid edition, p. xv). More resourceful is Howard Pearce's reading in "*Virtù* and *Poesis* in *The Revenger's Tragedy*," (*ELH* 43 [1976]:19-37), which sees Vindice's last speech as an ironic and defiant act of artistic creation, the reference to Piato being a creative misattribution.

45. Eliot, *Essays on Elizabethan Drama*, p. 123.

46. The suggestion is attractive because of Middleton's having written *The Viper and Her Brood* (lost). Foakes has argued against identifying this play with *The Revenger's Tragedy*; see "On the Authorship of *The Revenger's Tragedy*," pp. 129-38. Further,

The Revenger's Tragedy does not account for either the death or the discomfiture of the Duchess, which would be a singular omission if she were the eponymous protagonist.

47. The subject of social and familial bonds in the play has been traced by Jonas Barish in his valuable study "The True and False Families in *The Revenger's Tragedy*," in *English Renaissance Drama: Essays in Honor of Madeline Doran and Mark Eccles*, ed. Standish Henning, Robert Kimbrough, and Richard Knowles (Carbondale: Southern Illinois University Press, 1976), pp. 142-54.

48. It may be significant that among the plays that Humphrey Moseley entered in the Stationers' Register were two (now lost) that were purported to be by Tourneur: *The Nobleman* and *The Great Man* (see W. W. Greg's *A Bibliography of the English Printed Drama to the Restoration* [London: Bibliographical Society, 1951], 2:972, 989). Tourneur's nondramatic writings also show an obvious fascination with the idea of the man who exists both in and above this world.

CHAPTER FOUR

1. Unless otherwise noted, all quotations are from the Arden edition, ed. J. M. Nosworthy (London: Methuen, 1969). Act, scene, and line numbers for quotations are cited hereafter in the text.

2. The passage has occasioned a clutch of emendations it would be tiresome to discuss; Nosworthy rightly rejects them all. None of the critics and editors in the Variorum seem to have realized that Iachimo's obscurity is intentional and functional.

3. In a brilliant note to line 36, Nosworthy remarks that Iachimo is seeing things "as it were through the eye of God." There may be a biblical parallel in this passage (Matt. 10:30), but like the many others in the play, it does not seem to fit into a coherent scheme. See Naseeb Shaheen, "The Use of Scripture in *Cymbeline*," *ShS* 4 (1968):294-315; cf. Hugh M. Richmond in "Shakespeare's Roman Trilogy: The Climax of *Cymbeline*," *SLitI* 5 (1972):130.

4. The metrical characteristics of Shakespeare's later verse have been set out by Percy Simpson in "Shakespeare's Versification: A Study in Development," in *Studies in Elizabethan Drama* (Oxford: Clarendon Press, 1955), pp. 64-88, and by Frank Kermode in his Introduction to the Arden edition of *The Tempest* (London: Methuen, 1958), pp. lxxvii-lxxxi.

5. Again I would refer the reader to Dorothy L. Sipe, *Shakespeare's Metrics*, YSE no. 166 (New Haven: Yale University Press, 1968).

6. Arthur C. Kirsch suggests in *Jacobean Dramatic Perspectives* (Charlottesville: University Press of Virginia, 1972), that "when he is attempting to seduce Imogen, Iachimo becomes so intoxicated with his own verbal extravagance that he subverts his own intentions" (p. 64). This seems to ignore the self-consciousness that permeates all of Iachimo's speeches; at the least, it makes him a rather dull fellow. Granville-Barker says that these speeches reduce Iachimo to a "slavering, lascivious fool" (*Prefaces to Shakespeare* [London: Batsford, 1946] 3:132, but this view is inconsistent with Granville-Barker's view of Iachimo's intelligence and vanity.

7. Iachimo (not Posthumus and not, certainly, Cymbeline) is the most complex character in the play and has attracted some splendid actors—Henry Irving, Laurence Olivier, Ian Richardson. Despite this obvious clue as to the center of the play, the character still has not attracted many critics.

8. Nosworthy's Arden edition is especially useful for the way it collates echoes of Shakespeare's other work, but when he says of one speech, for example, that "powerful images of *Macbeth* and *Antony and Cleopatra* have intruded here" (p. lxiii),

here should be understood as the critic's mind rather than Pisanio's; similar thinking governs terms like *revert* (p. lxix). Unfortunately, the citation of parallels does not tell us why Shakespeare wrote as he did in the play at hand. A more helpful approach might be to get back of the imagery, following Frank Kermode's suggestion that Shakespeare's state of mind in *Cymbeline*—"difficult, tortuous, ironical"—resembles that in the sonnets (*Shakespeare, Spenser, Donne* [New York: Viking, 1971], p. 232). William Barry Thorne has remarked some of the parallels between *Cymbeline* and the rest of the canon, but his concern is with situation rather than with verbal echoes; see *"Cymbeline*: 'Lopp'd Branches' and the Concept of Regeneration,"* ShQ* 20 (1969):143-59.

9. R. J. Schork has discussed some of the ironies of the allusion in "Allusion, Theme, and Characterization in *Cymbeline*," *SP* 59 (1972):210-16. However, Schork takes the ironies pretty much at face value, and does not comment on the way they are distanced by the action (e.g., Imogen's lack of interest) or by the self-conscious Elizabethanisms. An acceptance of Shakespeare's distance from his allusions is implicit in Jan Knott's study of "Lucian in *Cymbeline*,"* MLR* 67 (1972):742-44.

10. Quoted by Nosworthy in Arden edition, p. 196. John also steals three jewels from the heroine's chamber, but Iachimo is unconcerned about such rewards. By making Iachimo the brother of a great duke, Shakespeare effectively removed the old motivation. Besides Nosworthy's remarks in the Arden, there are discussions of the play's sources by Kenneth Muir in *Shakespeare's Sources* (London: Methuen, 1957), pp. 231-40, and F. P. Wilson, in *Shakespeare and Other Studies* (Oxford: Clarendon Press, 1969), pp. 130-42. The most thorough study (with all the documents) is that by Geoffrey Bullough in *Narrative and Dramatic Sources of Shakespeare* (London: Routledge and Kegan Paul, 1975), 8:3-111.

11. Karl F. Thompson, in *Modesty and Cunning: Shakespeare's Use of Literary Tradition* (Ann Arbor: University of Michigan Press, 1971), rightly says that Iachimo wants to "discredit and destroy faith in idealized love" (p. 150); but it seems doubtful that in his first encounter with Imogen he is "test[ing] her susceptibility to the frailties traditionally ascribed to those unworthy of love" (p. 152).

12. Iachimo's values have been mapped by Derek Traversi in *Shakespeare: The Last Phase* (London: Hollis and Carter, 1954), pp. 49-53, although Traversi does not account for Iachimo's odd fondness for the lyric mode.

13. See Nosworthy's Introduction to the Arden edition, p. 8.

14. Cf. Homer Swander's *"Cymbeline* and the 'Blameless Hero,'"* ELH* 21 (1964): 259-70. Swander has noted that this past quarrel, one of Shakespeare's first additions to his sources, helps establish the weakness of Posthumus's judgment. Swander is also specific on the way Shakespeare has elevated Posthumus above the conventional figure of the "virtuously boastful" husband.

15. As will be apparent, I cannot accept Bertrand Evans's view: "Highly circumspect, Posthumus fell victim because Iachimo's evidence was undeniable" (*Shakespeare's Comedies* [Oxford: Clarendon Press, 1960], p. 262). Iachimo's evidence is eminently deniable, as Philario points out. No rational man would doubt his wife on the basis of Iachimo's story, and further, Posthumus believes Imogen guilty before he has even heard it all.

16. *Cognizance* may be an image, however; see Nosworthy's note to this line in the Arden edition.

17. W. Gordon Zeeveld, *The Temper of Shakespeare's Thought* (New Haven: Yale University Press, 1974), p. 239.

18. See, e.g., E. M. W. Tillyard, *Shakespeare's Last Plays* (London: Chatto and Windus, 1938), p. 31, and Clifford Leech, *Shakespeare's Tragedies and Other Studies in Seventeenth-Century Drama* (London: Chatto and Windus, 1950), p. 134.

19. Hough-Lewis Dunn glosses the term in "Shakespeare's *Cymbeline*, 2.5.15-17," *Expl* 30 (1972), item 57.

20. The Folio hyphenates "Nice-longing" in line 178; this places the metrical stress upon the first word. I have used the Folio's lineation; most editors relineate at *knows* and *vice*, although it is suitable that at the end of his catalog Posthumus should be in a state of frenzy, which the length of the alexandrine mirrors; because of the choppy pauses it is hard to accept J. C. Maxwell's statement in his New Cambridge edition that the line is "very lumbering" (Cambridge: At the University Press, 1960), p. 167.

21. It has been suggested that the parts of Cloten and the First Gaoler were doubled (see Julia Engelen, *SJH* [1927], pp. 138-40, and W. M. Keck, *ShAssocBul* [1935], pp. 68-72), but in view of the close physical resemblance between Cloten and Posthumus the doubling of this pair seems more likely. There would be only one rapid costume change between scenes 3 and 4 of act 2, but given the parallels between the scenes—each ends with the character going out vowing to get vengeance upon Imogen—the change might be suggestive; and anyway, Posthumus has at least one other rapid change, the one into and out of his peasant garb. In *The Organization and Personnel of the Shakespearean Company* (Princeton: Princeton University Press, 1927), T. W. Baldwin proposed that Burbage played Posthumus to Armin's Cloten (pp. 238, 394); even if this guess is correct—and there are some problems with it—the imaginative connections between the two characters' minds are still established through their speech.

22. Granville-Barker feels that the disappearance and return of Posthumus was a botch on Shakespeare's part (*Prefaces*, 3:76), although he devotes little study to the character or his verse. Though an appreciative reader of individual scenes, Granville-Barker never asks in this essay if a character's accents change, or if they bear any relation to the structure of the whole; thus Iachimo's verse, for example, remains "merely decorative" (3:92) or "a new Euphuism" (3:112-16). Granville-Barker sees the verse as prompted by the dramatic needs of the moment rather than by the larger development of a character; his hit-or-miss attention seems designed to illustrate his claim that the plotting and emotional pressure do not support the tension of the verse (3:118). More recently, Roger Warren has viewed the style of *Cymbeline* as a sequence of charged passages, which comment upon the apparent simplicity of the scenic structures ("Virtuosity and Complexity in *Cymbeline*," *ShS* 29 [1976]:41-49; a fuller study along these lines, with many acute insights into the changing depths of the verse, is R. A. Foakes's chapter on *Cymbeline* in *Shakespeare's Last Plays* (Charlottesville: University of Virginia Press, 1971), pp. 98-118.

23. Because I am concerned chiefly with the central triangle of Imogen, Posthumus, and Iachimo, I have not discussed the pastoral themes of the play; these have been treated by Hallett Smith in *Shakespeare's Romances* (San Marino, Calif.: Huntington Library, 1972), Douglas Peterson in *Time, Tide, and Tempest* (San Marino, Calif.: Huntington Library, 1973), and Thomas MacFarland in *Shakespeare's Pastoral Comedies* (New Haven: Yale University Press, 1972). Especially valuable are the late Rosalie Colie's comments in *Shakespeare's Living Art* (Princeton: Princeton University Press, 1974), pp. 292-302.

24. Jackson Cope studies the relation of this scene to Posthumus's dream later, and to similar moments in *The Taming of the Shrew, A Midsummer Night's Dream, Pericles,* and *The Tempest*; see *The Theater and the Dream* (Baltimore: Johns Hopkins University Press, 1973), pp. 239ff.

25. From the neck down, Cloten must be as handsome as Posthumus, and not just on Imogen's testimony; Lucius describes the corpse as "a worthy building" now in ruins (4.2.355). For the relation of this disguise to others in the play, see John Scott Colley, "Disguise and New Guise in *Cymbeline*," *ShakS* 7 (1973):233-52. Colley re-

marks "how different is the reality of a Cloten from the reality of a Posthumus" (p. 249); but the reality here seems to be that the body before Imogen is in no sense different from Posthumus's (save for being dead). Cf. Robert Grams Hunter, *Shakespeare and the Comedy of Forgiveness* (New York: Columbia University Press, 1965), p. 158. An essay enlarging on the visual identification of Cloten and Posthumus is Joan Hartwig's "Cloten, Autolycus, and Caliban: Bearers of Parodic Burdens," in *Shakespeare's Romances Reconsidered,* ed. Carol McGinnis Kay and Henry E. Jacobs (Lincoln: University of Nebraska Press, 1978), pp. 91-103.

26. G. Wilson Knight has some wise comments on Imogen's endurance and self-awareness; see *The Crown of Life* (London: Methuen, 1965), pp. 154-156. With all his concern for values, Knight still never loses track of Imogen's function in the drama. The same cannot be said for another study of her endurance, Charles K. Hofling's "Notes on Shakespeare's *Cymbeline,*" *ShakS* 1 (1965): 118-36. Hofling sees Imogen as an illustration of Shakespeare's own mother-transference; she is a figure with whom Shakespeare personally identified, thus halting his own regression.

27. In "The Spoken Dirge in Kyd, Marston, and Shakespeare: A Background to *Cymbeline, (N & Q,* n.s. 11 [1964] : 146-47), G. K. Hunter notes that the speaking of the dirge represents the "unvarnished sincerity" of the youths; however, the context of the dirge also comments on the theatrical convention. D. R. C. Marsh makes an extended analysis of the dirge, showing its relation to the play's major themes; see *The Recurring Miracle: A Study of "Cymbeline" and the Last Plays* (Pietrmaritzburg: University of Natal Press, 1962), pp. 82-85.

28. The contrasts between these songs and their contexts have been discussed by Evans in *Shakespeare's Comedies,* pp. 258-59; see also Peter J. Seng, *The Vocal Songs in the Plays of Shakespeare* (Cambridge: Harvard University Press, 1967), pp. 214-18.

29. For the distance between what Imogen sees and what we see, Evans uses the term "discrepant awareness," although to stress its occurrence throughout the play he assumes that neither we nor Shakespeare's audience would be familiar with any versions of the calumniated wife story, or with any of the characters as representative types; see *Shakespeare's Comedies,* pp. 245-89. Barbara A. Mowat, in numerous remarks throughout *The Dramaturgy of Shakespeare's Romances* (Athens: University of Georgia Press, 1976), offers an analysis that builds upon the audience's different levels of awareness and their knowledge of the fables in the background.

30. Lurking behind *Cymbeline* is, of course, *Philaster;* one helpful note on the stylistic differences between the two plays is Kenneth Muir's "A Trick of Style and Some Implications," *ShakS* 6 (1970): 305-10.

31. The growth of a lyrical style is a private thing, and Shakespeare seldom shows it happening; in *King Lear,* e.g., Cordelia also learns a sweeter style offstage, but Shakespeare does not emphasize the arbitrariness of this by having her say that she will go to France and write satire.

32. In *The Poetry of Shakespeare's Plays* (London: Duckworth, 1954) F. E. Halliday says that "we neither know nor care much about" Posthumus, one of Shakespeare's "shadowy or scarcely credible creations, important only as they work out the story and speak the poetry, stock figures who do not really determine the action" (p. 173). On the contrary, Posthumus's poetry *is* "the action"; realizing this, one can see also the limitations of Tillyard's statement that the changes of style have "little apparent reason for their occurrence" (*Shakespeare's Last Plays,* p. 75). More plausible is Maynard Mack's analysis of the way the late Shakespearean hero reaches and passes through his own antithesis ("The Jacobean Shakespeare,"in *Jacobean Theatre,* ed. John Russell Brown and Bernard Harris, Stratford-upon-Avon Studies no. 1 [London: Arnold, 1960] , esp. pp. 33-41). The shifts in style that Posthumus undergoes are directly related to his moral growth.

33. The boys were three and two when Belarius took them; Belarius does not know that Cymbeline had a daughter, and Cymbeline is surprised that the three have met.

34. A point made also, from a quite different perspective, by Douglas Peterson in *Time, Tide, and Tempest*, p. 142.

35. The first reasoned argument in favor of the authenticity of the vision came from E. H. W. Meyerstein, "The Vision of *Cymbeline*," *TLS*, 15 June 1922, p. 396; other landmarks include Shaw's Foreword to *"Cymbeline" Refinished* (1945) and G. Wilson Knight's overwhelming demonstration in *The Crown of Life*, pp. 168–202. Hardin Craig has some brief remarks in "Shakespeare's Bad Poetry," *ShS* 1 (1948): 55; Nosworthy extends some of these in his Introduction to the Arden edition, pp. xxxv–xxxvi. J. C. Maxwell, editor of the New Cambridge edition, concurs that the vision is probably Shakespeare's, although Dover Wilson has a strongly dissenting Preface.

36. The ingenuity of the play's end has distracted many readers from the very real development of Posthumus, which has occurred prior to the divine intervention; thus it is hard to agree with Arthur Colby Sprague and J. C. Trewin, who say that "if the idea of a supernatural—providential—guidance is given to the happy ending, then we may be willing to accept what otherwise . . . seems over-plotted, or too pat" (*Shakespeare's Plays Today* [Columbia, S.C.: University of South Carolina Press, 1970], p. 44). As Peterson points out, we have seen more than either the Soothsayer or Cymbeline, and we know how Posthumus has transformed himself into an agent of renewal: "The heavens have intervened . . . but only after human agents have taken the initiative" (*Time, Tide, and Tempest*, p. 147).

37. Knight, Traversi, and Marsh, for example, finish off Iachimo with only a sentence or a clause, assuming that his exposure is the essential thing; but since the information in Iachimo's speech is all familiar, we can safely say that Shakespeare's interest lay in the manner in which it is presented. Similar difficulties occur in an approach to the play via the pastoral; neither Peterson nor Colie, for example, sets up a critical vocabulary that can deal with Iachimo. Whatever the merits of Shaw's ideas about the vision, he did realize that Iachimo has a deep relation to the ongoing concerns of the play's world, as is evident in his revision of the ending. Still believing that Imogen has slept with Iachimo, Posthumus nonetheless forgives her cheerfully, and asks—to her great disgust—if she would like to have Iachimo come live with them.

38. Northrop Frye has a tactful discussion of "arias" and operatic theatricality in the late plays; see *A Natural Perspective* (New York: Oxford University Press, 1965), pp. 23 ff.

39. Shakespeare's final concern with Iachimo perhaps should qualify F. D. Hoeniger's suggestion that at the end of the play "mockery yields to vision, the world of appearance to the world of reality" ("Irony and Romance in *Cymbeline*," *SEL* 2 [1962] : 220). A related group of readings of the play that seldom if ever acknowledge the existence of Iachimo, much less his role at the end, are those determined to see it as a Stuart allegory. The most challenging of these is that offered by Frances A. Yates, in *Shakespeare's Last Plays: A New Approach* (London: Routledge and Kegan Paul, 1975), pp. 41–61; Bernard Harris takes a similar yet more speculative line in "'What's past is prologue': *Cymbeline* and *Henry VIII*," in *The Later Shakespeare*, Stratford-upon-Avon Studies no. 8 (London: Arnold, 1966), pp. 202–33. Persuasive as these arguments are in themselves, they still ignore characterization and verbal texture, which have a great impact upon the audience and may supply levels of meaning that comment upon the historical themes.

40. Hugh M. Richmond, reading the play as a study in Christian history, feels that Posthumus reforms Iachimo at the end. See "Shakespeare's Roman Trilogy: The Climax in *Cymbeline*," p. 136.

41. As Frank Kermode said in his review of the RSC production at Stratford, "the

part of Iachimo is tense with oppositions between what he says and what he does"
(*Cymbeline* at Stratford," *TLS*, 5 July 1974, p. 710). Kermode objected, incidentally, to Richardson's edited Iachimo at Stratford; but it should be noted that by the
time the RSC brought the play to London, all of Iachimo's extravagant lines to
Imogen had been restored.

CHAPTER FIVE

1. I do not refer only to Webster's borrowing or his use of sources, matters that
have been thoroughly treated by Gunnar Boklund in *The Sources of "The White Devil"*
(Cambridge: Harvard University Press, 1957) and R. W. Dent in *John Webster's Borrowing* (Berkeley and Los Angeles: University of California Press, 1960); I am interested
rather in the way Webster holds back a character, letting the "sentences" come before
the requirements of his stage action or dialogue. Dent does establish pretty conclusively
the notebook methods by which Webster seems to have worked.

2. The Epilogue to *The White Devil* is reprinted on p. 187 of the Revels edition of
the play; all quotations come from this text, ed. John Russell Brown, 2d ed. (London:
Methuen, 1966). Act, scene, and line numbers are cited in the text. Brown discusses
the first performance on pp. xx–xxiii. Webster's interest in the character is also confirmed by his having added Flamineo to the source materials in the first place.

3. As Roma Gill has done in "'Quaintly Done': A Reading of *The White Devil*,"
E & S 19 (1966): 41–59.

4. At 5.2.70, Bracciano ordered the body to be taken to Cornelia's lodgings; but
judging from 5.4.31–47 and the presence of Giovanni, they are in Bracciano's house
when the curtain is drawn at line 65. Cf. the similarly adroit shift in act 1 of *The
Duchess*: Antonio meets the Duchess in the gallery, although the "scene" has not
changed from the antechamber where the act began.

5. As Boklund has pointed out (*Sources*, p. 173), Giovanni's platitudes are unconvincing, and besides, by the end the lad has begun to look suspiciously like Francisco
(see 5.4.30).

6. In his long Introduction to *John Webster's Borrowing*, Dent has some useful
comments on Webster's craftsmanship, and describes narrative lapses and inconsistencies similar to those I have mentioned. Dent attributes these to Webster's "imper-
fect fusion" of his sources (pp. 24–25), but it seems possible that Webster's larger
interests in situation and tone might explain the gaps better. The most direct treatment of Webster's difficulties in characterization, and their relation to his language,
is still to be found in M. C. Bradbrook's chapter on Webster in *Themes and Conventions of Elizabethan Tragedy* (Cambridge: At the University Press, 1935), especially
pp. 193–94, 209–210, 212. Clifford Leech has also discussed Webster's inconsistencies
in *John Webster: A Critical Study* (London: Hogarth Press, 1951), pp. 66–68. In his
brilliant essay "The Power of *The White Devil*," A. J. Smith has ranged widely over
Webster's theatrical expedients, relating them to Webster's moral sense; see the collection *John Webster*, ed. Brian Morris (London: Benn, 1970), pp. 69–91. In the same
volume J. R. Mulryne also discusses Webster's frank manipulation of illusion, in order to
define the play's genre; see "Webster and the Uses of Tragicomedy," pp. 133–45 in
particular.

7. *Voice* here denotes simply the movements of the mind, as conveyed in words.

8. In both passages G. K. Hunter has noted some additional classical borrowings,
besides those that Dent has remarked; see "Further Borrowings in Webster and Marston," *N & Q* 217 (1972): 452.

9. At the same time, the passage also is linked with numerous others in the play,

by virtue of its imagery; these connections are discussed by Hereward T. Price in "The Function of Imagery in Webster," *PMLA* 70 (1955): 717–39, and by Elizabeth Brennan in her Introduction to the New Mermaid edition of the play (London: Benn, 1966).

10. The ironies in Vittoria's rhetoric have been examined by H. Bruce Franklin in "The Trial Scene of Webster's *The White Devil* Examined in Terms of Renaissance Rhetoric," *SEL* 1 (1961), 35–51. However, referring to the scene as a "trial"—as I have done myself, to prevent a digression in the text—is inaccurate, for in the Quarto the scene is headed THE ARRAIGNMENT OF VITTORIA. Traditionally, arraignments proceed on somewhat different lines from trials; in English law, with which there is reason to believe that Webster may have been familiar, the procedure involves calling upon the prisoner by name, reading to him the indictment, demanding of him whether he is guilty or not, and then entering the plea. If he pleads guilty, the court then proceeds to judgment. (See Thomas Blount, Νομο-Λεξιχον [Nomo-Lexikon] : *a law dictionary* [London, 1670], s.v. "Arraine" and "Trial.") Much of Vittoria's rhetoric seems intended to outwit the judges on procedural points, although there is no doubt that Webster's Malfi has its own unique legal processes.

11. Cf. Ralph Berry's comment that "[Webster's] dramatic verse never maintains the same pace or accent for long. The fluidity is that of a rapid stream, always moving with a tension and unease, sometimes dropping suddenly and changing level or direction, negotiating with hectic suddenness a mass of rocks, then resuming its troubled flow" (*The Art of John Webster* [Oxford: Clarendon Press, 1972], p. 27). The trouble with this view is not merely that it relegates Webster's poetry to the role of movie background music, but that it also seems to undercut a connection between the poetry and the boundaries of the characters who speak it. As Inga-Stina Ekeblad remarked some time ago, in Webster's verse "movement of mind is directly projected in movement of language" ("Webster's Constructional Rhythm," *ELH* 24 [1957]: 174); as the rest of this landmark essay points out, those movements typically have a discernible pattern. Ekeblad's study would seem to owe its theoretical foundation to remarks in Francis Fergusson's *The Idea of a Theatre* (Princeton: Princeton University Press, 1949), esp. pp. 13–41.

12. In *The Seven Deadly Sinnes of London* (1606), as noted first by Sykes (see Revels edition p. 102). Dekker's work has another echo in Webster's play—actually in Webster's prologue, "To the Reader"—which may not have been pointed out before, and that is the description of the way candlelight creeps into London: "all the Citty lookt like a private Play-house, when the windowes are clapt downe, as if some *Nocturnall* or dismal *Tragedy* were presently to be acted before all the *Trades-men*" (Percy Reprints no. 4 [Oxford: Blackwell, 1922], p. 30).

13. Cf. Flamineo's very different lines at the end of the play, where as Ian Scott-Kilvert has noted, "he produces a *rallentando* through a sequence of heavily stressed monosyllables" (*John Webster*, Writers and Their Work no. 175 [London: Longmans, 1964], p. 32).

14. Using this speech of Flamineo's as a point of departure, J. F. Mulryne has some valuable comments on the moral tensions controlling the play; his caveats should be borne in mind by readers seeking a moral thesis. See Mulryne's Introduction to the play in the Regents Renaissance Drama series (Lincoln: University of Nebrasks Press, 1969), pp. xix-xxvii; see also Mulryne's essay "*The White Devil* and *The Duchess of Malfi*," in *Jacobean Theatre*, ed. John Russell Brown and Bernard Harris (London: Arnold, 1960), pp. 201–25. A recent study of the problem is Robert F. Whitman's "The Moral Paradox of Webster's Tragedy," *PMLA* 90 (1975): 894–903. Whitman projects the characters in almost Bradleyan terms, finding that "the ambiguity that lies at the heart of Webster's tragic vision lies not in the external world, but in the duality of human nature" (p. 902); but not all readers may assent to this or any one

set of dualisms, and by criteria such as these the characters may be induced to move out of the play altogether.

15. And how could Francisco have known that Flamineo would be going to Vittoria's in order to be murdered? We never learn, but tend to assume that Francisco found out somehow, and accept this as a sign of his "intelligence."

16. The text does not seem to support Norma Kroll's view that with Isabella's death Francisco "has become suddenly like Lodovico; his psyche is wholly permeated with disintegration" ("The Democritean Universe in Webster's *The White Devil*," *CompDrama* 7 [1973]: 17). However, this conclusion is related to Kroll's misreading of the last scene (p. 19), in which she claims that Francisco is ordered off to torture and death; apparently she confuses him with Gasparo. Franciso is still at large at the play's end.

17. Cf. Machiavelli: "If it should become necessary to seek the death of someone, [the prince] should find a proper justification and a public cause" (*The Prince*, trans. Thomas G. Bergin [New York: Appleton, 1947], p. 49; on the general subject of open proceedings see chs. 17 and 21).

18. Lodovico's hero-worship is evident in his catalog of the knights (4.3.6–17); he has studied their habits, institutions, and laws. Like most hero-worshippers he has a deep sense of propriety and is amazed that Francisco would take part in the murders (4.3.74–75).

19. This omission is important, for by reducing Lodovico's motivation to its lowest emotional level, Webster raises our sympathies for Flamineo.

20. Thomas B. Stroup has suggested that Flamineo "wants to appear as a self-sufficient humanist," but his earlier jest with the Comfortable Words of the liturgy (3.3.12–19) shows he cannot finally have "the comfort which follows them in the sacrifice of the Eucharist" ("Flamineo and the 'Comfortable Words,'" *RenP* [1964], pp. 12–16). A surer grasp of Flamineo's tone is evident in the young Rupert Brooke's comment on the "curious archaic effect" of Webster's "classical" couplets: "They went, these classicists, with a kind of glee; they liked to be in touch with the permanent vaguenesses" (*John Webster and the Elizabethan Drama* [New York: John Lane, 1916], pp. 95–96). The vagueness of reference in the thunder may be, as we shall see, a deliberate joke on Flamineo's part.

21. Francisco's control over Lodovico involves even Lodovico's reputation, as in the matter of his alleged piracy. Lodovico never mentions taking to the trade in act 1, scene 1, after he has been banished; the first we hear of piracy is from Francisco in lines 143–44 of act 2, scene 1. Later in that scene (l. 380) Monticelso mentions that the piracy was only a rumor; Lodovico was actually in Padua. The aplomb with which Francisco receives this news suggests that he knew it was only rumor; see lines 381–86 of act 2, scene 1. Not until line 62 of act 3, scene 3, does Flamineo get to show that he knew where Lodovico was.

22. In *The Moral Vision of Jacobean Tragedy* (Madison: University of Wisconsin Press, 1960), Robert Ornstein appears to accept at face value Flamineo's sarcastic description of Lodovico as a "glorious villain" (p. 140), although this seems to mistake the tone. Ornstein feels more generally that "Webster admired heroic villains" (p. 145; see also p. 149); and *glory* is also Madeline Doran's word for Lodovico's action (*Endeavors of Art* [Madison: University of Wisconsin Press, 1954], p. 139). Such readings ignore the way that Flamineo and Francisco regard Lodovico ironically. To some extent, Ornstein's thesis may require that all the characters, including figures like Lodovico, have a uniform depth of characterization; for example, Ornstein also talks about the "self-knowledge" of figures like Cornelia and Isabella (p. 137), who have few lines to speak and seem present only to go mad or die. On a more detailed level than Ornstein, Roma Gill (see n. 3 above) makes a case for Isabella's existence, while

James Smith sticks up for Cornelia in "The Tragedy of Blood," *Scrutiny* 8 (1939): 265-80; but neither essay ventures into claims of self-knowledge for the two characters. More systematic is George Holland's essay on "The Function of the Minor Characters in *The White Devil*," *PQ* 52 (1973): 43-54. Holland regards Isabella as "a fully individualized character" (p. 44) and makes a case for Cornelia's thematic importance. But the depths of literary characters are relative, not absolute; and although these two may be significant thematically, they—along with Lodovico and his cronies—still seem two-dimensional by comparison to Vittoria and Flamineo.

23. The care that has gone into the act structure of *The Duchess of Malfi* is evident in the clear divisions and detailed preparation that appear in the 1623 quarto. The text is described fully by John Russell Brown in the Introduction to his edition of the play for the Revels series (London: Methuen, 1964), pp. lix-lxix. All quotations from the play are taken from this edition; act, scene, and line numbers appear in the text. Cf. Gunnar Boklund's suggestion that the fault lay in Webster's sources; "No matter how he stretched his material . . . it was really not solid enough to cover his last two acts appropriately" (*"The Duchess of Malfi": Sources, Themes, Characters* [Cambridge: Harvard University Press, 1962], p. 58). But surely Webster, like so many other writers, could have found his sources in works that might have been as attractive for formal or structural reasons as much as for thematic reasons.

24. Having organized the play thematically, Boklund finds episodes such as these artistic blemishes, useful chiefly for establishing the mood of disgust (ibid., pp. 75-76, 80).

25. See 3.3.41-47. Incidentally, critics who seek a didactic moral design in the play usually overlook Delio, forgetting that if Julia deserves to die for her lust, then so should he, rather than becoming a figure in the restoration of order at the end.

26. By overlooking Bosola's early intuitions about his relation to the Duchess, some critics entangle the strands of his character pretty thoroughly. Ornstein, for example, finally sees Bosola as a divided figure, part Machiavellian, pathetically seeking good but not attaining it, "capable of true moral feeling" but in the end "appalled by Ferdinand's insane revenge upon the Duchess" (*Moral Vision*, p. 143). This will not work; it is not Ferdinand who supervises the murder of the Duchess; and it is hard to see how the conscious agent of a crime can be less guilty than the person who conceives it. Bosola sees things more clearly: he knows he is Ferdinand's instrument, and also knows at the end he "was an actor in the main of all" (5.5.85).

27. Rowley's commendatory lines are well known; Middleton seemed more impressed by her death. Both poems of tribute are reprinted in the Revels edition, pp. 4-5.

28. My text in this passage follows the lineation of the Quartos, although for convenience's sake the line references remain those of the Revels edition.

29. Readings that approach the play on a strictly thematic level usually require a zigzag development in Bosola: knowing that Ferdinand is overhearing them, Bosola plagues the Duchess with art; but his heart is not in it; although it *is* later when he kills her; but it is *not* immediately afterwards. Webster's technique causes problems if we wish to see Bosola existing in three dimensions at every point in the play.

30. Once again we may be touching bottom with Bosola's character. He has told Ferdinand he would not see the Duchess "in mine own shape,/That's forfeited by my intelligence" (4.1.134-35). But if she is going to die anyway, this makes no sense. It would be nice to think of Bosola as a kind of tragic Feste, who puts on a disguise to help his own imagination, but the text does not support this reading. This may be another place where it would be easy to be oversubtle in reading Bosola.

31. As before, the line numbers locate the passage in the Revels edition.

32. Roger Warren makes the nice point that while Bosola mocks the courtly world, the Duchess "uses the diamonds and pearls of that world to express her aristocratic

heroism" ("*The Duchess of Malfi* on the Stage," in *John Webster*, ed. Morris, p. 65).

33. The suggestion of sexual cannibalism in the last line is related to the play's incest motive, which has been treated by Clifford Leech in *Webster: "The Duchess of Malfi"* (Great Neck, N.Y.: Barron's, 1963), pp. 17, 57-60.

34. Larry S. Champion, in *Tragic Patterns in Jacobean and Caroline Drama* (Knoxville: University of Tennessee Press, 1977), says that this speech "[implies] a permanent and profound transformation of values" (p. 148), which holds through to the end; my own argument moves toward a different conclusion.

35. James Calderwood claims, however, that from this point on, Bosola becomes "a responsible individual capable of the independent action he performs in the last act of the play" ("*The Duchess of Malfi*: Styles of Ceremony," *EIC* 12 [1962]: 133-47). Certainly Bosola's verse in this scene contains a great deal of excitement; here it should be noted that when the play was presented publicly at the Globe by the King's Men, Bosola would have stabbed Antonio in the daylight: the suspense and power of the moment would have been conveyed by the poetry rather than by visual surprise. See Alan C. Dessen, "Night and Darkness on the Elizabethan Stage: Yesterday's Conventions and Today's Distortions," *RenP* (1978), pp. 23-30.

36. Graham Greene, *British Dramatists* (London: Collins, 1942), p. 24.

37. Cf. Stanley Fish on Milton: "The impact of the verbal texture resides not in the arrangement of the words on the page or in the moral commonplaces the words present, but in the reader who responds to them as he responds to old melodies which have become a part of him by having been a part of his experience" (*Surprised by Sin* [New York: St. Martin's Press, 1967], p. 303).

38. As Charles Forker notes of Webster's prose "characters," they "are founded on the principle of organized distortion, on a harmony of disproportions manifested in the wit of clashing imagery, syntactic restlessness, and rhythmic instability" ("'Wit's descant on any plain song': The Prose Characters of John Webster," *MLQ* 30 [1969]: 50).

CHAPTER SIX

1. There is a start toward a prosody in H. J. Oliver's *The Problem of John Ford* (Melbourne: Melbourne University Press, 1955), pp. 127-29.

2. Eliot's essay on Ford appeared in 1932 and is reprinted in *Essays on Elizabethan Drama* (New York: Harcourt Brace, 1960), pp. 125-40. Not long after this, and just as influential, were Muriel Bradbrook's remarks in *Themes and Conventions of Elizabethan Tragedy* (Cambridge: At the University Press, 1935, pp. 250-61), in which she stressed "the quietness of the statement," "the exhausted sound of Ford's dragging lines," and Ford's "getting into a rhythm and rocking himself to sleep in it." Bradbrook was also the first modern critic to bear down strongly on the alleged "split between dramatic and poetic method" (p. 260), a view that we shall encounter later. It would be repetitious to list the modern studies that make the statutory nod at Ford's quietness; here it might be better to suggest that older critics were less inclined than Eliot to value neurotic withdrawal above other effects. One might consider, for example, George Saintsbury's summing up: "[Ford's] verse is nervous, well proportioned, well delivered, and at its best a noble medium" (*A History of Elizabethan Literature*, 2d ed. [London: Macmillan, 1901], p. 408). A striking exception to the general modern rule is Brian Morris's commentary on Ford's language, in his New Mermaid edition of the play (London: Benn, 1965), pp. xxvi-xxx; Morris is unhappy with the emphasis upon Ford's quietness at the expense of his other tones, and offers a few illustrations of Ford's poetic variety.

3. Cf. the comment by Charles Osborne McDonald in *The Rhetoric of Tragedy* (Amherst: University of Massachusetts Press, 1966): "Orgilus and Ithocles, like all the other characters in this most polite play, take great pains to preserve a surface semblance of . . . rational behavior . . . no matter how far their minds have sunk in passion; hence the preternatural calm of the language" (p. 322). I shall be arguing that, viewed as a whole, much of the play's language is in fact not calm at all.

4. In Ralph J. Kaufmann's important essay "Ford's Tragic Perspective" (reprinted in his *Elizabethan Drama: Modern Essays in Criticism* [New York: Oxford University Press, 1961], pp. 356–72), there are many good notes on Ford's humor; Kaufmann also stresses Ford's interest (like Henry James's) in situations rather than problems. It may be relevant that McDonald, who is definitely interested in reading for problems, finds Ford "seeming to be totally devoid of the comic sense" (*Rhetoric*, p. 328).

5. Ford's Prologue to the play emphasizes that the humor is planned to be neither satiric nor overt:

> The title lends no expectation here
> Of apish laughter or of some lame jeer
> At place or persons; no pretended clause
> Of jests fit for a brothel courts applause
> From vulgar admiration.

                                                        [3–7]

6. With exceptions as noted, all quotations come from the text edited by Donald K. Anderson, Jr., for the Regents Renaissance Drama series (Lincoln: University of Nebraska Press, 1968). I have also relied extensively upon the annotation of Brian Morris's modern-spelling New Mermaid edition (London: Benn, 1965).

7. In *Tragic Patterns in Jacobean and Caroline Drama* (Knoxville: University of Tennessee Press, 1977), Larry Champion says that the "self-serving cowardice [of Groneas and Hemophil] underscores Ithocles' heroism" (p. 203), although their antics would actually seem to supply an ironic parallel to his own extreme selfishness. To come at this from another direction: Arthur C. Kirsch makes the very important point that the names of these and all the characters "really do describe the nature of Ford's characterizations precisely, for in what amounts to a baroque transformation of the morality play, personifications of moral states of mind (the traditional conception of humours) give way to personifications of states of emotion . . . ; [thus] the moral values of guilt or innocence and virtue or vice are manipulated almost entirely to create or sustain the dominant emotional traits of the central characters, and the plot is contrived to compose these traits into various designs and counterpoints" (*Jacobean Dramatic Perspectives* [Charlottesville: University Press of Virginia, 1972], p. 117). With such a little pin is pierced the castle wall of hard-line moral readings, e.g., Mark Stavig's *John Ford and the Traditional Moral Order* (Madison: University of Wisconsin Press, 1968).

8. The play's many structural ironies are described most fully by Glenn H. Blayney in "Convention, Plot and Structure in *The Broken Heart*," *MP* 56 (1958): 1–9, although he underplays the depth of the relationship between Penthea and Bassanes.

9. One might draw very different conclusions about the verse of Ford's other plays, particularly *'Tis Pity She's a Whore*, in which the poetry seems quite multifarious; but the large amounts of prose in that play would make unqualified comparison with *The Broken Heart* rather risky.

10. In *Tragedy and Melodrama* (Seattle: University of Washington Press, 1968), Robert B. Heilman has argued that all the principal characters of the play lack any division of impulses, which is hard to believe of Penthea and Bassanes. It does seem likely that Ford has tried to hear the other main characters with as much clarity

and consistency as possible, and to juxtapose them with these two characters who have divided minds.

11. As noted by Kaufmann in "Ford's Tragic Perspective," p. 362.

12. Orgilus later repeats the ominous image of kneeling in dust, first to Ithocles (4.3.136) and then at his own death (5.2.149).

13. See Anderson's edition for the Regents series, p. 75.

14. The frequent opacity of Ford's language here should be seen in contrast to the way that some characters are never given it.

15. See McDonald, *Rhetoric*, p. 322. One has reservations about Ornstein's judgment that Orgilus "achieves in the acceptance of death a dignity lacking in his struggle against the circumstances of his life" (*The Moral Vision of Jacobean Tragedy* [Madison: University of Wisconsin Press, 1960], p. 213).

16. Champion's reading of the play handles this theme; see *Tragic Patterns*, pp. 195-209.

17. Nearly every edition mentions it: see, e.g., Morris in the New Mermaid edition, p. xxix; and cf. Oliver, *Problem*, p. 65.

18. See 2.3.124-26.

19. Some aspects of the plot make one wonder if the play had a topical relevance. The play is dedicated to Lord Craven, who (like Ithocles) had fought in foreign wars and (like Orgilus) was rumored to have been secretly married. In any case, the play would still seem a peculiar way for Ford to ingratiate himself. Stuart P. Sherman proposed long ago that the play treated the relationship between Sir Philip Sidney and Penelope Devereux ("Stella and *The Broken Heart*," *PMLA* 24 [1909] : 274-85); there is a summary of the literature on this topic in Clifford Leech's *John Ford and the Drama of His Time* (London: Chatto and Windus, 1957). See also G. M. Carsaniga, "'The Truth' in John Ford's *The Broken Heart*," *CompLit* 10 (1958): 344-48.

20. In the Quarto, Ithocles' first line ends at *or*. Clearly something is missing, and most editors have agreed on *nearness*, which seems close to the sense of the passage and also has Ford's frequent light ending.

21. In one of Ford's typically meticulous details, Orgilus also calls Calantha "our kingdom's heir" (3.1.17); he is consistently obsessed with what he sees as Ithocles' ambition.

22. See the remarks by Oliver in *Problem*, p. 129; he regards her behavior as thoroughly consistent, though for reasons different from those advanced here (see *Problem*, pp. 69-70).

23. The most common view of Bassanes is that he is a thoroughly stock character; about the most warmly limited view of him is that taken by Saintsbury, who sees him as "a purely contemptible character, neither sublimed by the passion of jealousy nor kept whole by salt of comic exposition; a mischievous poisonous idiot who ought to have had his brains knocked out, and whose brains would assuredly have been knocked out, by any Orgilus of real life" (*Elizabethan Literature*, p. 407). This does get down to the problem. Clearly Ford drew heavily upon Burton's exposition of jealousy; see S. B. Ewing, *Burtonian Melancholy in the Plays of John Ford* (Princeton: Princeton University Press, 1940), and George F. Sensabaugh, *The Tragic Muse of John Ford* (Stanford: Stanford University Press, 1944), esp. ch. 2, "Scientific Determinism," pp. 13-93. However, it would be an oversimplification to say, as does Oliver, that Bassanes "is drawn from Burton rather than life" (*Problem*, pp. 62-63).

24. Gifford suggested that Ford often gave glides the metrical value of two syllables because he was a Devonshire man (see the New Mermaid edition, p. 91). However, only a few glides in the play take that value, and they all fall by design in crucial places. Consider, e.g., Ithocles' reply to Calantha, when she gives him the provincial wreath (1.2.68).

25. One is reluctant to join the critics who go into ecstasies over Penthea's nobly stoic suffering and "generous devotion," as Ornstein calls it (p. 216), or her "immutable virtues" (Ellis-Fermor, *The Jacobean Drama*, p. 246). She wants revenge for the wrongs done her; she encourages Orgilus to seek it; she protests to Calantha; and she insults her husband. Within the social forms of Ford's Spartan society there is not much else she could do to resist so openly. In *Elizabethan Love Tragedy 1587-1625* (New York: New York University Press, 1971) Leonora Leet Brodwin has some sympathetic remarks on Penthea, which one would like to see expanded beyond the note in which they appear (p. 394 n. 16). The fullest account of the stoic themes in the play, and their relation to the dramaturgy, is to be found in Eugene M. Waith's graceful essay "Struggle for Calm: The Dramatic Structure of *The Broken Heart*," in *English Renaissance Drama: Essays in Honor of Madeline Doran and Mark Eccles*, ed. Standish Henning, Robert Kimbrough, and Richard Knowles (Carbondale: Southern Illinois University Press, 1976), pp. 155-66.

26. The same half-glimpsed desire for revenge motivates Penthea when she makes her will and testament to Calantha in act 3, scene 5. Saving her best "gift" till last, she gives Ithocles to her in language that shows her trying to draw Calantha into the same psychological trap she is in herself; see especially lines 79-82, where she tries to purify Ithocles' motives and have Calantha pity him, while also stressing (ll. 105-6) how extremely cruel he has been.

27. Sensabaugh takes Bassanes' last sentence as an indication that he is impotent (*Tragic Muse*, p. 60). There is evidence, however, for Bassanes' virility: Orgilus says Penthea yielded up "her virgin freedom" (1.1.51); and Penthea's feeling of being a whore could make no sense if Bassanes were impotent. Evidently she has been reluctantly indulging her husband's appetite, for as mentioned earlier, she feels she is a whore "in art, [though] not in desires."

28. They cause discomfort wherever they go; more comically, Groneas goes to Calantha with the news that Nearchus has come to claim her, saying with prissy falling rhythms, "'Twas my fortune, madam / T'enjoy the honor of these happy tidings" (2.2. 106-7). Both get their reward at the end, when Calantha assigns them to wait on Bassanes (5.3.49-50); this is not the only comic leavening in the final scene.

29. However, Sensabaugh feels that "by intelligent self-treatment [Bassanes] achieves toward the end of the drama a partial if not a final cure" (*Tragic Muse*, p. 82).

30. Stavig, for example, says that after repenting, Bassanes "remains such a posturing sentimentalist that his change is more ludicrous than affecting" (*Traditional Moral Order*, pp. 157-58). Cf. Dorothy M. Farr, in *John Ford and the Caroline Theatre* (New York: Barnes and Noble, 1978), who sees in Bassanes a form of "tragic humour" (p. 99).

31. In her reading of the play, Anne Barton finds that Bassanes stops here in an "excruciating self-restraint" and is "restored to his rightful place" in Spartan society; see "Oxymoron and the Structure of Ford's *The Broken Heart*," in *E&S* (1980), p. 87.

32. See Ralph J. Kaufmann, "Ford's Wasteland: *The Broken Heart*," *RenD*, n.s. 3 (1970), pp. 167-87.

33. She could not be talking to Bassanes, because he is already old.

34. Morris argues that Bassanes undergoes an "expiatory agony" (New Mermaid edition, p. xiv) and is purified by his endurance, but this overlooks his manic excitement, his "roaring" (4.2.104), his bond to Orgilus, and his final outburst.

35. Sensabaugh says (*Tragic Muse*, p. 83) that Orgilus is taking Bassanes to the final masque, but this is a misreading; Orgilus is stone cold before the masque ever takes place.

36. Pompey offers the rationale in *Measure for Measure*, act 4, scene 2, lines 49-51.

37. In this regard I have found suggestive Jackson Cope's reading of the dramatic metaphors in *Perkin Warbeck*; see *The Theater and the Dream* (Baltimore: Johns

Hopkins University Press, 1973), pp. 122–23. In some ways Bassanes' misfortunes all have been the result of his inability to accept his role as an actor in the world. Indeed his remark to Penthea at 4.2.66–68 suggests that at the end he is entering a new and deeper dream.

EPILOGUE

1. One could always argue of *Cymbeline* that a great disorder is an order, and follow this with pages of illustrations; the disjunction between poetic style and character might be regarded as a congruity, because the characters are all alienated. It is difficult to imagine, however, what such an interpretation would do with the reality of a speaking voice onstage.

2. Quotations from Beaumont and Fletcher's plays come from *The Dramatic Works in the Beaumont and Fletcher Canon,* under the general editorship of Fredson T. Bowers (Cambridge: At the University Press, 1966), 1:479; *Philaster* was edited by Robert K. Turner, and these lines appear at 5.5.71–79.

3. On the different contributions of Beaumont and Fletcher to the canon see Cyrus Hoy, "The Shares of Fletcher and His Collaborators in the Beaumont and Fletcher Canon," *SB* 8 (1956): 129–46, 9 (1957): 143–62, 11 (1958): 85–106, and 12 (1958): 91–116. I am using "the Fletcher plays" in the sense employed by Clifford Leech in his study *The John Fletcher Plays* (London: Chatto and Windus, 1962), esp. ch. 1, "The Problem of Approach," pp. 1–23.

4. For insights into Fletcher's rhetoric I am indebted to Cyrus Hoy's paper "The Language of Fletcherian Tragicomedy," which Professor Hoy read at the annual meeting of the Modern Language Association in 1976.

5. To be found in the *Encyclopedia Britannica* as late as 1957; see 3:275–79, where it forms the introduction to the entry on Beaumont and Fletcher.

6. My text for *The Changeling* is that edited by N. W. Bawcutt for the Revels series (London: Methuen, 1958), 3.4.26–28.

7. The basic point of departure is Artaud's *The Theater and Its Double* (originally published in 1938); the pertinent comments are discussed by Jackson Cope in *The Theater and the Dream* (Baltimore: Johns Hopkins University Press, 1973), pp. 8–11.

8. The most readily available text of *Antonie* may be found in Geoffrey Bullough's *Narrative and Dramatic Sources of Shakespeare* (London: Routledge and Kegan Paul, 1964), 5:358–406; the quoted lines are 103–6.

9. See "Notes on the Blank Verse of Christopher Marlowe," in *The Sacred Wood* (London: Methuen, 1920), pp. 86–94. The problems with Eliot's scholarship in this essay are summarized by F. W. Bateson in his spirited introduction to literary study, *The Scholar-Critic* (London: Routledge and Kegan Paul, 1972), pp. 20–21.

10. My text is the 1611 Quarto, which has been reprinted in facsimile by the Scolar Press (Menston, 1969); the speech appears in act 2, scene 1.

11. From Shirley's Dedication, "To my worthily honored Friend *G. B.* Esq.," ll. 12–13, in *The Cardinal,* ed. Charles R. Forker (Bloomington: Indiana University Press, 1964), p. 3. All quotations are from this edition; act, scene, and line numbers are cited in the text.

12. See Forker's edition of *The Cardinal,* pp. xlviii–liii.

13. These dates—1608 and 1607, 1601 and 1600, 1607 and 1606—are those assigned in Harbage and Schoenbaum's *Annals of English Drama, 975–1700* (Philadelphia: University of Pennsylvania Press, 1964). While the individual dates are open to debate, other plays could readily be found to demonstrate the proposition.

14. The studies of Earl Miner are helpful here, especially *The Cavalier Mode From*

Jonson to Cotton (Princeton: Princeton University Press, 1971). Particularly suggestive also is Warren L. Chernaik's study of Waller, *The Poetry of Limitation* (New Haven: Yale University Press, 1968); chapter 5, "'Parent of English Verse'" bears upon the matters at hand. One might place alongside these Jonas Barish's *Ben Jonson and the Language of Prose Comedy* (Cambridge: Harvard University Press, 1960), which studies the evolving relationship between the logic of Jonson's verbal forms—in verse as well as prose—and the depth of his imaginative exploration.

15. This couplet that so epitomizes the theme of the whole poem first appeared in the 1655 edition of Denham's poem; for all the texts, see Brendan O Hehir, *Expans'd Hieroglyphics: A Critical Edition of Sir John Denham's "Cooper's Hill"* (Berkeley: University of California Press, 1969).

16. To select three studies very different in method and aim: Ernst Cassirer, *The Individual and the Cosmos in Renaissance Philosophy*, trans. Mario Domandi (New York: Harper, 1964); Georges Poulet, *Studies in Human Time*, trans. Elliott Coleman (Baltimore: Johns Hopkins University Press, 1956); and Ricardo J. Quinones, *The Renaissance Discovery of Time* (Cambridge: Harvard University Press, 1972).

INDEX